Movements and Ideas of the Extreme Right in Europe

Zivilisationen & Geschichte

Herausgegeben von
Ina Ulrike Paul und Uwe Puschner

Band 21

PETER LANG
EDITION

Nicola Kristin Karcher / Anders G. Kjøstvedt (eds.)

Movements and Ideas of the Extreme Right in Europe

Positions and Continuities

PETER LANG
EDITION

Bibliographic Information published by the Deutsche Nationalbibliothek
The Deutsche Nationalbibliothek lists this publication in the Deutsche Nationalbibliografie; detailed bibliographic data is available in the internet at http://dnb.d-nb.de.

Cover Design:
© Olaf Gloeckler, Atelier Platen, Friedberg

Ein Werbeoffizier fordert
auf den Straßen Berlins
zum Eintritt in die Grenzwehr
gegen den Feind im Osten auf,
Druck nach Fritz Grotemeyer (1919),
Sammlung Stefan Noack.

ISSN 1867-092X
ISBN 978-3-631-60136-5

www.peterlang.de

Norsk sammendrag

I denne antologien presenteres et bredt spekter av bevegelser, partier og personer. De ulike artiklene bidrar med ny kunnskap og utvidede perspektiver; samlet sett gir de et riss over forskningsfronten på en rekke felt. Bidragene spenner fra en refleksjon over relasjonene mellom ulike systemer for kroppsbevegelse og politiske ideologier, den tyske *völkisch*-bevegelsens forsøk på partipolitisk mobilisering til veteranforeningen *Stahlhelms* politiske strategier og dens relasjon til andre aktører på den antirepublikanske høyresiden. Dessuten analyseres det NSDAPs velgermobilisering før 1933, den britiske partilederen Oswald Mosleys vei mot fascismen og forsøket til det norske kollaborasjonsregimets utenriksorganisajons på å ensrette ulike norske foreninger i Tyskland under krigen. Med Julius Evola og Johann von Leers diskuteres to sentrale ideologiske premissleverandørers selvforståelse og evne til påvirkningskraft i årene etter 1945. I et mer samtidshistorisk perspektiv drøftes graden av kontinuitet og brudd blant høyreekstreme partier i etterkrigstidens Tyskland. Ideologiske kontinuiteter belyses på tvers av ulike historiske kontekster gjennom en analyse av New Age-inspirerte rasister og deres fortolkning av hekseprosessene. Avslutningsvis drøftes den rollen de fordrevne fra Sentral- og Øst-Europa etter 1945 har spilt i den tyske *Vergangenheitsbewältigung*.

Deutsche Zusammenfassung

In der vorliegenden Antologie wird ein breites Spektrum an Bewegungen, Parteien und Personen präsentiert. Die verschiedenen Artikel bieten neue Erkenntnisse und eine erweiterte Perspektive. Gesammelt geben sie eine Übersicht über die derzeitige Forschungsfront in einer Reihe von Feldern. Die Beiträge reichen von einer Reflexion über die Beziehungen zwischen verschiedenartigen Systemen von Körperbewegung und politischen Ideologien über die parteipolitischen Mobilisierungsversuche der völkischen Bewegung in Deutschland bis hin zu den politischen Strategien der Veteranenvereinigung Stahlhelm und deren Verhältnis zu anderen Akteuren der antirepublikanischen Rechten. Darüber hinaus wird die Wählermobilisierung der NSDAP vor 1933, die Hinwendung des britischen Parteipolitikers Oswald Mosley zum Faschismus und der Versuch der Auslandsorganisation des norwegischen Kollaborationsregimes, norwegische Einrichtungen in Deutschland während des Zweiten Weltkrieges gleichzuschalten, analysiert. Mit Julius Evola und Johann von Leers wird das Selbstverständnis und der Einfluss zweier zentraler Ideologen nach 1945 diskutiert. In einer mehr zeitgeschichtlichen Perspektive wird der Grad an Kontinuität und Zersplitterung zwischen den rechtsextremen Parteien im Nachkriegsdeutschland untersucht. Ideologische Kontinuitäten werden vor dem Hintergrund unterschiedlicher historischer Kontexte anhand einer Analyse von New Age inspirierten Rassisten und deren Bewertung der Hexenprozesse beleuchtet. Abschließend wird die Rolle der nach dem Zweiten Weltkrieg Vertriebenen aus Zentral- und Osteuropa innerhalb der deutschen Vergangenheitsbewältigung diskutiert.

Contents

Acknowledgements

The starting point of this anthology was the conference "Movements and Ideas of the Extreme Right in Europe: Positions and Continuities", which took place at the Humboldt University Berlin in December 2009. It was initiated and organised by Nicola Kristin Karcher and Anders G. Kjøstvedt at the Department for Archaeology, Conservation and History at the University of Oslo, and supported and funded by the then Henrik-Steffens-Professor at the Department for Northern European Studies at the Humboldt University, Jorunn Sem Fure.

The idea behind the conference was to bring together scholars from different European countries who all do research in the field of fascism, Nazism, right-wing extremism or the völkisch movement, discussing different positions, continuities and discontinuities within the broader framework of the extreme right before and after the Second World War. In the time since the conference took place, we have been fortunate to include further contributions and thereby broaden our perspectives.

A number of colleagues have commented upon the contributions or in other ways supported the publication of this volume. We would like to thank Hans Fredrik Dahl, University of Oslo; Conan Fischer, University of St. Andrews; Jorunn Sem Fure, Telemark Museum; Einhart Lorenz, University of Oslo; Uwe Puschner, Free University Berlin; Stefanie von Schnurbein, Humboldt University Berlin; Kjetil Simonsen, Centre for Studies of Holocaust and Religious Minorites in Oslo; and Ulrich Wyrwa, University of Potsdam and Centre for Research on anti-Semitism/Technical University Berlin.

The publication of this volume has been supported by the Freedom of Expression Foundation (Fritt Ord), Oslo, and the Faculty of Humanities, University of Oslo.

Oslo, October 2012

Nicola Kristin Karcher and Anders G. Kjøstvedt

Introduction

Nicola Karcher and Anders G. Kjøstvedt

The term "extreme right" continues to be in common usage, and is frequently employed in political discourse, in the media, and in academic debates. Although it lacks a generally agreed upon definition, the term seems to be more popular than ever. There are many reasons for this. The recession currently crippling several European countries has led to a heightened awareness of the possibility of a political crisis, and of the implications of increased support for extreme right-wing parties. Additionally, in the past couple of years Europe has been plagued by severe acts of terror, with perpetrators expressing extreme right world views. In November 2011 German police uncovered the National Socialist Underground (*Nationalsozialistischer Untergrund,* NSU), a terrorist group responsible for the murder of nine immigrants and one policewoman as well as several other violent attacks between September 2000 and April 2006. The xenophobic murders, and the extended period of time it took for German authorities to uncover the terrorist cell, have sent shock waves through German society, and the group's possible connections are now under investigation. Anders Behring Breivik's terrorist act on 22 July 2011 was not only the greatest crime committed in postwar Norwegian history; his bomb attack and murderous killing spree in a political youth camp on an isolated island were carried out in order to draw attention to his political "manifesto". The judicial process against Breivik earlier this year received worldwide attention and sparked renewed debate in Norway on the processes of radicalisation.

When using the term extreme right as a common denominator for the organisations and actors discussed in this anthology, we are well aware of the scientific and public controversies regarding its meaning and definition. Nevertheless, we believe that it is the most useful and precise collective term for all the subjects analysed here.

In the social sciences, most notably political science, there has been a number of attempts at supplying a scientific explanation, many of which partly contradict each other or exist in parallel. In this context Richard Stöss, the German political scientist and expert on right-wing extremism, has concluded that "[t]here is no generally accepted definition and in particular not just one theory of right-wing extremism".[1]

In Germany during the decades after 1945 the phenomenon of right-wing extremism was understood as an aftermath of National Socialism, and therefore it was not perceived as an object for academic research in its own right. From the 1980s onwards this attitude began to change, particularly in the face of a new wave of extreme right-wing violence at the beginning of the 1990s that escalated into the

1 Richard Stöss, *Rechtsextremismus im Wandel* (Berlin: Friedrich Ebert Foundation, 2007), 14.

xenophobic and murderous attacks in Hoyerswerda, Rostock-Lichtenhagen, Mölln, and Solingen.[2]

In contrast, Anglo-American researchers initiated academic studies much earlier, particular in terms of research on fascism. During the 1940s Theodor Adorno, the sociologist and leading representative of the so-called *Frankfurter Schule* who had himself escaped to the US from National Socialist persecution, was already developing the theory of authoritarianism with his research group. Their work, which was heavily influenced by the National Socialist experience, resulted in the publication of *The Authoritarian Personality* in 1950, which gained worldwide attention.[3]

Since the 1970s the idea of extremism – from both left and right – has become a permanent part of the public discourse, increasingly replacing the older concept of radicalism.[4] However, there is no consensus among scholars on the use of these concepts, and the terms right-wing extremism and right-wing radicalism are still used interchangeably with terms such as neo-Fascism and neo-Nazism.[5] The academic discourse about extremism is still very much influenced by the controversy surrounding its classification, an ambiguity which also applies to the use of the words left and right.

In 1994 Norberto Bobbio, the renowned Italian philosopher and historian, made a contribution to this debate with his internationally-recognised study *Destra e Sinistra* (Right and Left).[6] Instead of the words right and left, he makes use of the terms extreme egalitarian and extreme anti-egalitarian on one axis. On a second axis he places the words authoritarian and liberal at opposite ends of the scale. Using this conceptualisation, the extreme right is characterised by Bobbio as anti-egalitarian authoritarianism and the extreme left as anti-liberal egalitarianism, highlighting the struggle against liberty as a common feature.

Since right-wing extremism is perceived first and foremost as a collective term, superordinate definitions within political science describe this phenomenon by emphasising a vast number of overlapping and contradicting characteristics, such as

---

2 In the early 1990s several pogrom-like attacks on immigrants and asylum seekers shook German society. In Hoyerswerda and Rostock-Lichtenhagen, both in the former East German Republic, attacks on immigrants and asylum seekers took place in September 1991 and August 1992. In November 1992 three Turkish immigrants, including two children, were killed in arson attacks in the northern German town of Mölln. In May 1993 a similar event took place in the north-western town of Solingen, where arson attacks on Turkish immigrants killed five people, including three children. These incidents received worldwide attention and became a synonym for right-wing extremism.

3 Theodor W. Adorno et al., *The Authoritarian Personality* (New York: Harper, 1950).

4 Researchers such as the German political scientist Armin Pfahl-Traughber have even argued for the removal of the word radicalism as an alternative to the word extremism. See Armin Pfahl-Traughber, "Extremismus und Terrorismus. Eine Definition aus politikwissenschaftlicher Sicht", *Jahrbuch für Extremismus- und Terrorismusforschung* 2008, 18.

5 See e.g. Wolfgang Benz, ed., *Rechtsradikalismus: Randerscheinung oder Renaissance?* (Frankfurt a.M.: Fischer, 1980).

6 Norberto Bobbio, *Destra e sinistra. Ragioni e significati di una distinzione politica* (Rome: Donzelli editore, 1994).

excessive nationalism combined with imperialism; the rejection of the right to freedom and the rights of equality; the struggle against democratic-pluralistic systems based on the sovereignty of the people; the wish to establish an authoritarian or totalitarian state; a racist, xenophobic and anti-Semite ideology; the belief that indigenous society and culture is under threat from foreign elements; and the conviction that people are principally unequal.[7] The latter point, the rejection of the principle of equality among all human beings, proposes a hierarchy in which one's own race or nation is placed highest. In addition, Islam's alleged threat against the Western world is playing an increasingly important role within the extreme right – especially since 11 September 2001 and the increase in Islamist terrorism.[8]

The concept which defines both left- and right-wing extremism, alongside the minimal definition of a constitutional democracy, has played an important role within research on extremism. Nevertheless, this theoretical approach is still heavily debated.[9] While it locates the extreme right outside the democratic order, defining it first and foremost by the wish to abolish the existing democratic system, right-wing radicalism is perceived as a more moderate version of the same philosophy, sharing a number of the same goals but supporting the idea of democracy. However, right-wing radicals claim that democracy is flawed and does not work for the true benefit of the people; rather, it functions to support and maintain a secluded political elite.[10] This approach has also been adopted in recent Norwegian research in the post-Breivik era, using the term right-wing extremism primarily in relation to the established political democracy. Those who want to replace the political system in Norway, whatever methods they wish to use, are classified as extremists.[11] In

---

7 See Stöss, *Rechtsextremismus im Wandel*, 24ff; Hans-Gerd Jaschke, "Rechtsextremismus", Bundeszentrale für politische Bildung, September 19, 2006, http://bpb.de/politik/extremismus/rechtsextremismus/41889/rechtsextremismus (accessed September 25, 2012).

8 Cf., among others, Bernt Hagtvet, "Høyreektremismens forvandlinger", in *Høyreektremisme. Ideer og bevegelser i Europa*, eds. Øystein Sørensen, Bernt Hagtvet and Bjørn Arne Steine (Oslo: Dreyers Forlag, 2012), 320-342.

9 This is especially the case concerning the use of the terms right-wing and left-wing extremism. Cf. e.g. Christoph Butterwegge, "Extremismus-, Totalitarismus- und Populismustheorien: Ideologien zur Diskreditierung der Linken. Eine Grundsatzkritik an ihren analytischen Defiziten, verborgenen Interessen und politischen Implikationen", *Jahrbuch für Extremismus- und Terrorismusforschung* 2009/2010, 33-60; Wolfgang Wippermann, "Politologenbetrug. Ideologiekritik der Extremismus-Legende", *Standpunkte* 10 (2010), 1-7. See also Wolfgang Wippermann, *Totalitarismustheorien. Die Entwicklung der Diskussion von den Anfängen bis heute* (Darmstadt: Primus, 1997); Uwe Backes and Eckhart Jesse, *Politischer Extremismus in der Bundesrepublik Deutschland* (Bonn: Bundeszentrale für politische Bildung, 1996); Uwe Backes, *Politische Extreme. Eine Wort- und Begriffsgeschichte von der Antike bis zur Gegenwart* (Göttingen: Vanderhoeck & Ruprecht, 2006).

10 This definition is also the basis for the work of the German Federal Office for the Protection of the Constitution *(Bundesamt für Verfassungsschutz):* The radical is still acting within the democratic order. Cf. Pfahl-Traughber, "Extremismus und Terrorismus", 18.

11 See Øystein Sørensen, Bernt Hagtvet and Bjørn Arne Steine, "Forord", in *Høyreektremisme. Ideer og bevegelser i Europa*, 7-13.

contrast to this, researchers such as the political scientist Roger Eatwell do not limit the term right-wing extremism to an attitude towards constitutional democracy.[12] This makes it possible to define parties such as the Austrian FPÖ or the French Front National as representatives of the extreme right.

As with the lack of consensus on what constitutes the extreme right, "fascism"[13] as a generic concept has proven to be equally elusive. The term fascism has been in scholarly use since the 1920s, but without an agreed-upon definition. There are many reasons why it has been difficult to arrive at a working definition of this ideology. Political convictions, especially the belief that fascism was nothing but a defence of capitalism against the inevitable victory of the working class, have muddied the waters considerably. The lack of acknowledgment that fascism contains more than negations (for example, anti-Marxism, anti-Liberalism, anti-Egalitarianism), or the belief that it was a mishmash of other political ideas without an ideological core of its own, have resulted in and continue to contribute to a considerable lack of interest in finding a working definition of fascism. In addition, many scholars labouring in the field have been convinced that the various fascist movements, such as Nazism in Germany and the Iron Guard in Romania, are too unique and too heavily integrated within their specific national histories to be considered as part of a generic fascism. Others argue that a collective term encompassing various fascist movements would necessarily be too broad to have any analytical meaning.

Conventionally, historical fascism has been regarded as a product of a unique historical period and as a result of the upheavals surrounding the cultural pessimism of the 1890s, the "nationalization of the masses", the First World War, and the Russian Revolution. Scholars are in agreement that this distinct historical period ended in 1945. However, the core ideological values and world views which were part of historical fascism were not erased, even though the fascist regimes were toppled and the currency of fascist policy and thought reached its nadir in the European post-war settlement.

With a growing consensus within research on fascism, there has been renewed effort towards trying to find the core values of the ideology – values that are independent of fascism's various manifestations in specific times and places. This process began in the 1960s, and an early attempt to arrive at a common definition of fascism – a "fascist minimum" – was attempted by Ernst Nolte. His definition, which centres on anti-Marxism and "resistance to transcendence", has been con-

12 See e.g. Roger Eatwell, "Ten Theories of the Extreme Right", in *Right-Wing Extremism in the Twenty-First Century*, eds. Peter H. Merkl and Leonard Weinberg (London/Portland: Frank Cass, 2003), 47-73. See also Cas Mudde, *The Ideology of the Extreme Right* (Manchester/New York: Manchester University Press, 2000).

13 As has become standard, we use lower-case for fascism in general and upper-case for the ideology, movement, and regime in Mussolini's Italy.

troversial, but it spurred debate and was therefore an important preliminary stage.[14] Further contributions that took fascism and fascist ideology seriously and analysed it on its own account were made by Eugen Weber, George L. Mosse, Walter Laqueur, Zeev Sternhell, A. James Gregor, and Juan Linz in the 1960s and 1970s.[15] Even in the absence of a working definition, comparative fascist studies flourished in the 1970s and 1980s.[16]

Since the early 1990s, Roger Griffin has made important contributions to the search for a working definition of fascism.[17] Griffin's approach has been to narrow fascism down to an ideal type which formed the basis for different manifestations in various ideological, organisational, and political terms. To Griffin, the core value, or *genus*, of fascism is its "palingenetic ultra-nationalism": The insistence on national rebirth and renewal in a time of perceived decadence and decline. This approach emphasises the revolutionary, organic, and modernising elements of fascism, as well as its insistence on the mobilisation of the population, setting it apart from authoritarian regimes. Similar or congruent definitions have been developed by other leading scholars, and this new consensus allows for the individual ideologies, movements, and regimes to be treated simultaneously as both unique and as permutations of a generic fascism.[18] However, this interpretation has not been immune to criticism.[19]

---

14 Ernst Nolte, *Der Faschismus in seiner Epoche. Action française, der italienische Faschismus, der Nationalsozialismus* (Munich: Piper, 1963). English edition: *Three Faces of Fascism. Action Française, Italian fascism, National Socialism* (London: Weidenfeld and Nicolson, 1965).

15 Eugen Weber, *Varieties of Fascism. Doctrines of Revolution in the Twentieth Century* (New York: Van Nostrand, 1964); George L. Mosse, *The Crisis of German Ideology. Intellectual Origins of the Third Reich* (London: Weidenfeld and Nicolson, 1964); idem., "The Genesis of Fascism", *Journal of Contemporary History* 1 (1966), 14-26; idem., *The Nationalization of the Masses. Political Symbolism and Mass Movements in Germany from the Napoleonic Wars through the Third Reich* (New York: New American Library, 1975); Walter Laqueur, ed., *Fascism. A Reader's Guide. Analyses, Interpretations, Bibliography* (Aldershot: Wildwood House, 1976); Zeev Sternhell, "Fascist Ideology", in *Fascism. A Reader's Guide*, 385-399; A. James Gregor, *The Ideology of Fascism: The Rationale of Totalitarianism* (New York: Free Press, 1969); idem., *Interpretations of Fascism* (Morristown: General Learning Press, 1974); Juan Linz, "Some Notes towards a Comparative Study of Fascism in Sociological Historical Perspective", in *Fascism. A Reader's Guide*, 13-78.

16 Cf. Stein Uglevik Larsen, Bernt Hagtvet and Jan Petter Myklebust, eds., *Who Were the Fascists? Social Roots of European Fascism* (Bergen: Universitetsforlaget, 1980).

17 Roger Griffin, *The Nature of Fascism* (London: Pinter, 1991); idem., ed., *International Fascism: Theories, Causes and the New Consensus* (London: Arnold, 1998); idem., "The Primacy of Culture: The Current Growth (or manufacture) of Consensus Within Fascist Studies", *Journal of Contemporary History* 37 (2002), 21-43.

18 Roger Eatwell, *Fascism. A History* (London: Chatto & Windus, 1995); Stanley G. Payne, *A History of Fascism, 1914-1945* (Madison: University of Nebraska Press, 1995); Robert O. Paxton, *The Anatomy of Fascism* (London: Allen Lane, 2004). Also in general agreement is Walter Laqueur, *Fascism. Past, Present, Future* (New York: Oxford University Press, 1996).

19 See Roger Eatwell, "The Nature of 'Generic Fascism': The 'Fascist Minimum' and the 'Fascist Matrix'", in *Rechtsextreme Ideologien in Geschichte und Gegenwart*, ed. Uwe Backes (Cologne: Böhlau, 2003), 93-137. Particularly severe in his criticism is A. James Gregor in "Roger Griffin, social science, 'fascism' and the 'extreme right', in *Fascism. Past and Present, West and East.*

Recent developments in the understanding of fascism make it easier to discuss its continuity into post-war Europe, especially as this new understanding is based on ideology rather than political style or institutions. Different permutations of generic fascism have moved into the metapolitical sphere, although they retain the core values of "palingenetic ultra-nationalism". Common across the post-1945 manifestations of fascism is that they are all a long way from demonstrating the political mass-mobilisation of the interwar years, since the political, social, and economic environment in post-war Europe is radically different. These fascist "groupuscules" work to destroy the liberal-democratic, globalising, and multicultural order. They belong to political and ideological subcultures, finding a niche in unconventional, "uncivic" political space, and they are decentralised and autonomous, although they often have informal transnational links.[20] Therefore, the broad definition of generic fascism has been used as an analytical tool to discuss a very broad and heterogeneous range of political activism in the post-war period, ranging from the "intellectual", anti-liberal, and ethnopluralist French Nouvelle Droite and the violent, anti-immigration sectarianism of the English Defence League to the counter-jihadists on internet sites such as "Gates of Vienna" and political terrorists such as NSU and Breivik.

This volume reflects positions and continuities which encompass the space of a century. Even with the development of generic fascism, we still believe that the term extreme right – when used carefully – still has utility as an analytical term. Especially when taking into account ideological positions and continuities over an extended period of time, from the end of the First World War to the first decades of the twenty-first century, we feel that the approach to generic fascism has become too narrow to be utilised as a common analytical description of the themes and problems discussed in this book.

Kerstin Bornholdt's opening contribution to the volume reflects on the relations between systems of body movements and political ideologies, asking the question whether specific exercise forms are "empty vessels" or more adequate for certain political systems than others. The following chapters analyse political movements and pressure groups that were important in shaping extremist opposition to the liberal-democratic order, but which did not belong to the fascist creed themselves. Stefanie Schrader discusses the German Völkisch People's Party, an attempt to give the heterogeneous *völkisch* movement a political representation in the new German Republic. The topic of Alessandro Salvador's contribution is the political and ideological development of the veterans' league *Stahlhelm*. Both of these movements vehemently opposed the Weimar Republic and envisaged some kind of national, or even racial, renewal and rebirth, but at the same time they lacked a

---

An International Debate on Concepts and Cases in the Comparative Study of the Extreme Right, eds. Roger Griffin, Werner Loh and Andreas Umland (Stuttgart: ibidem, 2006), 115-122.

20 Roger Griffin, "Fascism's New Faces and New Facelessness in the 'Post-fascist' Epoch", *Erwägen – Wissen – Ethik* 15/3 (2004). See also Ami Pedazhur and Leonard Weinberg, "Modern European Democracy and Its Enemies: The Threat of the Extreme Right", *Totalitarian Movements and Political Religions* 2 (2001), 52-72.

revolutionary impetus, making a generic application of the term fascism unfitting. However, they had an undeniable influence on other fascist permutations, including the Nazi movement, which is discussed in Anders G. Kjøstvedt's chapter. The NSDAP, together with other fascist movements, was convinced that it had found a modern solution to modern challenges, a theme that is further discussed in Matthew Worley's chapter on Oswald Mosley and his decision to launch a fascist movement in Britain. Moving forward to the Second World War, Nicola Karcher explores the difficulties connected with collaboration in Norway, and the attempts by a fascist regime in power to bring into line associations that were more or less affiliated with Nazism's ideological obsession with the Nordic countries.

Other contributions to this volume show us how the delimitations between the broad interpretation of generic fascism and the extreme right may become blurred. Elisabetta Cassina Wolff and Martin Finkenberger discuss two important figures, Julius Evola and Johann von Leers, who both retained the core values of their political convictions, but only one of whom was able to remain relevant in the changed political climate of post-1945 Europe.

Continuing into the contemporary period, additional contributions discuss political parties and associations that are linked to and have ideological touching points with generic fascism, but who still remain outside this paradigm themselves. Gideon Botsch argues that there is good reason to emphasise the levels of continuity within the extreme right scene in postwar Germany, despite frequent claims to the opposite in most work on the subject. Important issues within the aspect of continuity and points of contact within the extreme right outlook from a historical perspective are similarily raised in Felix Wiedemann's contribution, analysing New Age-inspired modern racists and their obsession with the witch trials of Early Modern Europe. Astrid Dypvik's chapter puts the contemporary German extreme right into perspective by analysing the role played by the Federation of Expellees and its participation in the German postwar debate on *Vergangenheitsbewältigung*, and by discussing its partially overlapping topoi of interpreting the suffering of German civilians in the aftermath of the Second World War in line with the interpretation of the extreme right party NPD.

Bibliography

Adorno, Theodor W. et al. *The Authoritarian Personality*. New York: Harper, 1950.

Backes, Uwe. *Politische Extreme. Eine Wort- und Begriffsgeschichte von der Antike bis zur Gegenwart.* Göttingen: Vanderhoeck & Ruprecht, 2006.

Backes, Uwe and Eckhart Jesse. *Politischer Extremismus in der Bundesrepublik Deutschland.* Bonn: Bundeszentrale für politische Bildung, 1996.

Benz, Wolfgang, ed. *Rechtsradikalismus: Randerscheinung oder Renaissance?* Frankfurt a.M.: Fischer, 1980.

Bobbio, Norberto. *Destra e sinistra. Ragioni e significati di una distinzione politica.* Rome: Donzelli editore, 1994.

Butterwegge, Christoph. "Extremismus-, Totalitarismus- und Populismustheorien: Ideologien zur Diskreditierung der Linken. Eine Grundsatzkritik an ihren analytischen Defiziten, verborgenen Interessen und politischen Implikationen", *Jahrbuch für Extremismus- und Terrorismusforschung* 2009/2010, 33-60.

Eatwell, Roger. "Ten Theories of the Extreme Right". In *Right-Wing Extremism in the Twenty-First Century*, edited by Peter H. Merkl and Leonard Weinberg, 47-73. London/Portland: Frank Cass, 2003.

Eatwell, Roger. "The Nature of 'Generic Fascism': The 'Fascist Minimum' and the 'Fascist Matrix'". In *Rechtsextreme Ideologien in Geschichte und Gegenwart*, edited by Uwe Backes, 93-137. Cologne: Böhlau, 2003.

Eatwell, Roger. *Fascism. A History*. London: Chatto & Windus, 1995.

Gregor, A. James. "Roger Griffin, social science, 'fascism' and the 'extreme right'. In *Fascism. Past and Present, West and East. An International Debate on Concepts and Cases in the Comparative Study of the Extreme Right*, edited by Roger Griffin, Werner Loh and Andreas Umland, 115-122. Stuttgart: ibidem, 2006.

Gregor, A. James. *Interpretations of Fascism*. Morristown: General Learning Press, 1974.

Gregor, A. James. *The Ideology of Fascism: The Rationale of Totalitarianism*. New York: Free Press, 1969.

Griffin, Roger. "Fascism's New Faces and New Facelessness in the 'Post-fascist' Epoch", *Erwägen – Wissen – Ethik* 15/3 (2004).

Griffin, Roger. "The Primacy of Culture: The Current Growth (or manufacture) of Consensus Within Fascist Studies", *Journal of Contemporary History* 37 (2002), 21-43.

Griffin, Roger, ed. *International Fascism: Theories, Causes and the New Consensus*. London: Arnold, 1998.

Griffin, Roger. *The Nature of Fascism*. London: Pinter, 1991.

Jaschke, Hans-Gerd. "Rechtsextremismus", Bundeszentrale für politische Bildung (September 2006), http://bpb.de/politik/extremismus/rechtsextremismus/41889/rechtsextremismus (accessed September 25, 2012).

Laqueur, Walter. *Fascism. Past, Present, Future*. New York: Oxford University Press, 1996.

Laqueur, Walter, ed., *Fascism. A Reader's Guide. Analyses, Interpretations, Bibliography*. Aldershot: Wildwood House, 1976.

Linz, Juan. "Some Notes towards a Comparative Study of Fascism in Sociological Historical Perspective". In *Fascism. A Reader's Guide*, edited by Walter Laqueur, 13-78. Aldershot: Wildwood House, 1976.

Mosse, George L. *The Nationalization of the Masses. Political Symbolism and Mass Movements in Germany from the Napoleonic Wars through the Third Reich*. New York: New American Library, 1975.

Mosse, George L. "The Genesis of Fascism", *Journal of Contemporary History* 1 (1966), 14-26.

Mosse, George L. *The Crisis of German Ideology. Intellectual Origins of the Third Reich*. London: Weidenfeld and Nicolson, 1964.

Mudde, Cas. *The Ideology of the Extreme Right*. Manchester/New York: Manchester University Press, 2000.

Nolte, Ernst. *Der Faschismus in seiner Epoche. Action française, der italienische Faschismus, der Nationalsozialismus*. Munich: Piper, 1963. English edition: *Three Faces of Fascism. Action Française, Italian fascism, National Socialism*. London: Weidenfeld and Nicolson, 1965.

Payne, Stanley G. *A History of Fascism, 1914-1945*. Madison: University of Nebraska Press, 1995.

Paxton, Robert O. *The Anatomy of Fascism.* London: Allen Lane, 2004.

Pedazhur, Ami and Leonard Weinberg. "Modern European Democracy and Its Enemies: The Threat of the Extreme Right", *Totalitarian Movements and Political Religions* 2 (2001), 52-72.

Pfahl-Traughber, Armin. "Extremismus und Terrorismus. Eine Definition aus politikwissenschaftlicher Sicht", *Jahrbuch für Extremismus- und Terrorismusforschung* 2008, 9-33.

Sternhell, Zeev. "Fascist Ideology". In *Fascism. A Reader's Guide*, edited by Walter Laqueur, 385-399. Aldershot: Wildwood House, 1976.

Stöss, Richard. *Rechtsextremismus im Wandel.* Berlin: Friedrich Ebert Foundation, 2007.

Sørensen, Øystein, Bernt Hagtvet and Bjørn Arne Steine, eds. *Høyreektremisme. Ideer og bevegelser i Europa.* Oslo: Dreyers Forlag, 2012.

Uglevik Larsen, Stein, Bernt Hagtvet and Jan Petter Myklebust, eds. *Who Were the Fascists? Social Roots of European Fascism.* Bergen: Universitetsforlaget, 1980.

Weber, Eugen. *Varieties of Fascism. Doctrines of Revolution in the Twentieth Century.* New York: Van Nostrand, 1964.

Wippermann, Wolfgang. "Politologenbetrug. Ideologiekritik der Extremismus-Legende", *Standpunkte* 10 (2010), 1-7.

Wippermann, Wolfgang. *Totalitarismustheorien. Die Entwicklung der Diskussion von den Anfängen bis heute.* Darmstadt: Primus, 1997.

Body Movements as Political Actors?

Kerstin Bornholdt

Where the soul of the German people acts entirely unreserved, it aspires more to rhythm than to symmetry.

The opening quotation is drawn from August Julius Langbehn's book *Rembrandt als Erzieher* from 1890. The book became a bestseller among the German *Bildungsbürgertum* and can be linked to the *völkisch* movement.[1] In 1923, gymnastic instructor Rudolf Bode chose to use Langbehn's statement on rhythm as the epigraph for his collection of essays on rhythm and physical education. Rhythm, such was the claim, created a sense of belonging to a greater community. Rhythm was the movement principle that was innate to the German *Volk*. Through Bode and his student Hinrich Medau, rhythmical gymnastics became "German gymnastics" after 1933 and as such an integral part of physical education in the Third Reich.[2]

---

1 For the reception of Langbehn's book, see: Bernd Behrendt, "August Julius Langbehn, der 'Rembrandtdeutsche'", in *Handbuch zur "Völkischen Bewegung" 1871-1918*, eds. Uwe Puschner and Walter Schmitz (Munich: Saur, 1999); Bernd Behrendt, *Zwischen Paradox und Paralogismus: Weltanschauliche Grundzüge einer Kulturkritik in den 90er Jahren des 19. Jahrhunderts am Beispiel August Julius Langbehn* (Frankfurt a.M.: Peter Lang, 1984). Mosse presents Langbehn as an important ideological precursor of National Socialism, see: George L. Mosse, "The Mystical Origins of National Socialism", *Journal of the History of Ideas* 22/1 (1961), 81-96. On Langbehn, see in addition George L. Mosse, *Die Völkische Revolution: Über die Geistigen Wurzeln des Nationalsozialismus* (Weinheim: Beltz Athenäum, 1991), 40-55; Fritz Richard Stern, *The Politics of Cultural Despair: A Study in the Rise of the Germanic Ideology* (New York: Doubleday, 1965), 131-177.

2 Rudolf Bode (1881-1971) studied natural sciences, psychology and music in Kiel and Leipzig and established his own gymnastics school in Munich in 1913. In 1922 he founded the federation *Bode-Bund*. Bode was a member of the National Socialist party from 1922 onwards. In 1929 he became a member of the Fighting League for German Culture (*Kampfbund für Deutsche Kultur*) and in 1933 he was appointed leader of the League's department for *Körperbildung* and dance, as well as for gymnastics and dance. In 1935 Bode was appointed leader of the Reich Food Estate's *Reichsschule für Leibesübungen*. On Bode's life, see Barbara Freckmann, "Wesen und Formen der Gymnastik", in *Leibesübungen und Sport in Deutschland vom Ersten Weltkrieg bis zur Gegenwart*, ed. Horst Ueberhorst (Berlin: Bartels & Wernitz, 1982), 1011-1013; Adolf Söhrmann, "Rudolf Bode, Ein Lebensbild", *Rhythmus. Monatsschrift für deutsche Kultur* 14/10 (1936), 258-263; Hans Frucht, "Zur Geschichte der Organischen Bewegungslehre", in *Der Rhythmus als Erzieher: Festschrift zum 60. Geb. von Rudolf Bode, 3. Febr. 1941*, ed. Hans Eggert Schröder (Berlin: Widukind, 1941), 35; Bernd Wedemeyer-Kolwe, *"Der Neue Mensch." Körperkultur im Kaiserreich und in der Weimarer Republik* (Würzburg: Königshausen & Neumann, 2004), 98-99. Bode's student Hinrich Medau formulated "German gymnastics" and was in charge of developing a gymnastics for the *BDM-Werk Glaube und Schönheit*. See Hinrich Medau and Hermann Baumann, *Deutsche Gymnastik: Lehrweise Medau* (Stuttgart: Union Deutsche Verlagsgesellschaft, 1940); Helmut Günther, "Geschichtlicher Ablauf der Deut-

Taking the title of this anthology literally, I will investigate the interactions between body movements and political movements, and ask if it is possible to establish a link between different political systems and different systems of physical exercises. Are specific exercise forms more adequate for certain political systems than others? Moreover, do specific exercise systems foster specific political ideologies and practices? In other words, do body movements produce meaning, do they "make" politics? Or is everything about context? Are body movements arbitrary and can they be associated and inscribed with any political purpose?

I will pursue these questions by focusing on four different systems of physical exercises that co-existed in Germany, Denmark and Norway in the interwar years: *Turnen* (apparatus gymnastics), Ling gymnastics, sports and rhythmical gymnastics. Each of these movement systems was created in specific national and historical situations. They were created with specific intentions in mind and different meanings have been ascribed to them over time and in different spatial contexts. After giving a brief overview of these four movement systems, I will primarily focus on the ideology and practice of rhythmical gymnastics and its possible entanglement with the ideology of National Socialism.

Turnen and Ling Gymnastics: Heritage and Origin

Two movement practices started to travel the world in the 19th century: German *Turnen* and Swedish Ling gymnastics. From 1811 onwards Friedrich Ludwig Jahn assembled young men in a public park in Berlin for exercises on apparatuses and play. Jahn called his physical practice *Turnen.* For Jahn himself, *Turnen* meant practicing both gymnastics and battle; the gymnast was a warrior. Jahn had created *Turnen* in order to train bodily and mental strength, as well as to generate a sense of national belonging and resistance against the Napoleonic occupation. Jahn and some of his *Turners* volunteered for the Free Corps *(Frei Korps) Lützower Jäger* and fought against Napoleon's army in the *Völkerschlacht* near Leipzig in October 1813. The battle became an important legend for German nationalists, and the *Turner* movement that was drawn upon until the 1930s.[3] However, throughout the years,

schen Rhythmusbewegung", in *Handbuch Bewegungserziehung: Ästhetische und Rhythmische Perspektiven*, eds. Eva Bannmüller and Peter Röthig (Butzbach: Afra-Verlag, 2005), 36-37.

3 Friedrich Ludwig Jahn published two influential books, *Deutsches Volkstum* in 1810 and *Deutsche Turnkunst* in 1817. For an overview of Jahn's exercise system, the history of *Turnen* and its interconnection with the German nationalist movement, see Michael Krüger, *Einführung in die Geschichte der Leibeserziehung und des Sports*, vol. 2: *Leibeserziehung im 19. Jahrhundert. Turnen fürs Vaterland* (Schorndorf: Hofmann, 2005), 42-46, 52-69; Christiane Eisenberg, *"English Sports" und Deutsche Bürger. Eine Gesellschaftsgeschichte 1800-1939* (Paderborn: Ferdinand Schöningh, 1999), 105-120; Christiane Eisenberg, "Friedrich Ludwig Jahn – der Erfinder des Deutschen Turnens", *Sportwissenschaft* 30/2 (2000), 125-140; Hajo Bernett, *Grundformen der Leibeserziehung* (Schorndorf: Hofmann, 1975), 33-39; Svenja Goltermann, *Körper der Nation: Habitusformierung und die Politik des Turnens 1860-1890* (Göttingen: Vandenhoeck & Ruprecht, 1998). On the role and importance of the *Völkerschlacht*, see Uwe Puschner, "18. Oktober 1813: 'Möchten die Deutschen Nur Alle und Immer Dieses Tages Gedenken!' – die Leipziger Völker-

the *Turner* movement was linked to different political goals: Initially to an upheaval against Napoleon; in the failed revolution of 1848-49, parts of the *Turner* movement were associated with a fight for democracy and even the beginning of a workers' sports movement;[4] by the end of the 19th Century the *Turner* movement was linked to a Bismarckian loyalist conservatism[5] and finally to the *völkisch* movement that supported National Socialism and Hitler's seizure of power. In April 1933, and in anticipatory obedience, the *Turner* movement chose to exclude Jewish and Marxist members and deliberately put itself under the command of the National Socialist regime before the enforced political conformity *(Gleichschaltung)* dissolved and re-organised the rest of the sports movement.[6] It is in particular its linkage to the National Socialist regime that later on overshadowed the political history of the *Turner* movement.

At about the same time Jahn founded *Turnen* in Berlin, the Swede Pehr Henrik Ling, and later his son Hjalmar Ling, created a gymnastics system in Stockholm that soon travelled the world as "Swedish gymnastics". Swedish Ling gymnastics and German *Turnen* were developed at the same time and under similar conditions, for instance as national reactions to the Napoleonic wars.[7] Moreover, both movement systems shared an opposition to competition, maximum performances and elitism, which were to become the basic principles of sports. Yet, despite all similarities, in many countries the two systems ended up in an almost dichotomous opposition. What were the differences between the systems?

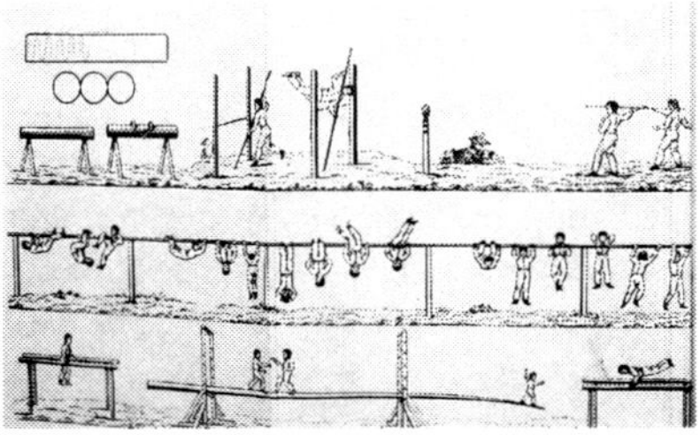

Figure 1 *Turnen: Apparatus gymnastics*[8]

schlacht", in *Erinnerungstage: Wendepunkte der Geschichte von der Antike bis zur Gegenwart*, eds. Etienne François and Uwe Puschner (Munich: C.H. Beck, 2010), 145-162.

4 On the role of the *Turner* movement in the failed revolution of 1848-49, see Arnd Krüger, "The German Way of Worker Sport", in *The Story of Worker Sport*, eds. Arnd Krüger and James Riordan (Champaign, IL: Human Kinetics, 1996), 3.

5 Eisenberg, "*English Sports" und Deutsche Bürger*, 128.

6 Hajo Bernett, *Der Weg des Sports in die Nationalsozialistische Diktatur* (Schorndorf: Karl Hofmann, 1983); Michael Krüger, *Einführung in die Geschichte der Leibeserziehung und des Sports*, vol. 3: *Leibesübungen im 20. Jahrhundert. Sport für alle* (Schorndorf: Hofmann, 2005), 135-138.

7 Jan Lindroth, *Ling – Från storhet till upplösning: Studier i svensk gymnastikhistoria 1800-1950* (Eslöv: Brutus Östling Symposion, 2004), 134.

8 The picture is taken from a reprint of Jahn's *Deutsche Turnkunst* and displays some of Jahn's gymnastic apparatuses. Friedrich Ludwig Jahn and Ernst Eiselen, *Die Deutsche Turnkunst zur Einrichtung der Turnplätze* (Frankfurt a.M.: Wilhelm Limpert-Verlag, 1961[1816]).

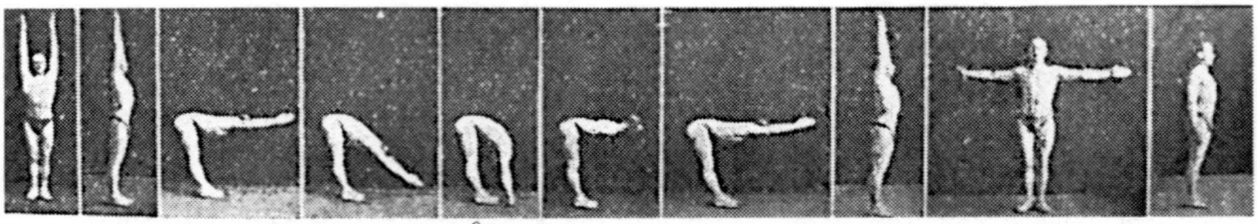

Figure 2 *Ling gymnastics: Free exercises*[9]

First of all, Ling gymnastics banned exercises on gymnastic apparatuses and favoured collective free exercises that were supposed to be based on physiological and anatomical laws. Every limb had to be moved separately, according to its own laws. The body had to be worked through symmetrically – first the left arm, then the right arm, then the left leg, then the right leg. Ling gymnastics was meant to build a harmonious body and an upraised posture that was regarded as a sign of health. The typical German gymnastic apparatuses, parallel bars and horizontal bars, were regarded as a threat to the goals of Ling gymnastics. *Turnen* overdeveloped muscles of the arms and shoulders and thus produced an asymmetrical and inharmonious body. The major goal of German *Turnen* was the performance of a skilful movement on gymnastic apparatuses. *Turnen* required its practitioners to overcome their fear; it was supposed to teach courage and bravery. The creation of a harmoniously developed body was not a primary objective.[10]

Looking more closely at the actual practice of the two systems and the spatial arrangements of the gymnasts, more differences become apparent. In Ling gymnastics a whole group of gymnasts performed the same movement simultaneously. A gymnastic squad was lined up geometrically in several rows and performed single geometrical movements following the commands of a gymnastics instructor, who was positioned in front of the squad. In *Turnen* one individual after the other performed exercises on the apparatuses. The gymnasts were not a homogenous whole but separated in different squads. There was not "one" instructor but several *Vorturner*. The gymnasts were grouped into squads and each group decided to choose their *Vorturner*, the one who showed the exercises to the others and who was responsible for his squad.[11]

Turnen and Ling Gymnastics: Ascribing and Inscribing Meaning

The characteristic movements of *Turnen* and Ling gymnastics have been interpreted in strikingly different ways. Ling gymnastics have been perceived as military gym-

9 The picture is taken from a Scandinavian journal for Ling gymnastics. J. Thulin, "Anmälan", *Fysisk Fostran och Vetenskapen* 1/1 (1932), 2.

10 On Ling gymnastics, see Lindroth, *Ling;* Jens Ljunggren, *Kroppens bildning: Linggymnastikkens manlighetsprojekt 1790-1914* (Eslöv: Brutus Östling Symposium, 1999).

11 Eisenberg links the relationship of squads and *Vorturner* both to progressive military reforms and to the English sports movement, where a team elected its captain. Eisenberg, *"English Sports" und Deutsche Bürger*, 114.

nastics where an omnipresent leader dictates a movement to de-individualised gymnasts, and it has been described as a collective and cooperative movement practice. The de-centralised organisation of the *Turner* squads could be interpreted as paving a way for a more liberal and democratic way of moving and organising individuals and groups of people. At the same time *Turnen* was linked to a de-individualising drill and discipline at the service of a powerful state.[12]

Until today, Danish literature presents Ling gymnastics as a tool for the emancipation of Danish farmers. Swedish Ling gymnastics literally strengthened the backs of the farmers, enabling the political emancipation of the rural population, thus fostering the democratisation process in Denmark. Ling gymnastics travelled to Denmark via the Grundtvigian high school movement from the 1880s onwards. In Ling gymnastics the rural population literally started to move together. They were perceived as an exercise system where everybody could participate as one individual among equals. It was a movement form that paralleled a cooperative way of production and as such fostered an agrarian modernism and supported the farmers in their fight for political participation.[13]

In German publications, however, Ling gymnastics were perceived as disciplining military gymnastics, as an instrument that drained the life force of the German *Volk*. Introduced by military representatives as a means to weaken the political influence of the *Turner* movement in the 1840s, Ling gymnastics never lost its military connotations in Germany. Introducing Ling gymnastics meant to ban the gymnastics apparatuses that had become a symbol for "Germanness". In particular the parallel bars were perceived as a symbol for a common German culture, "grown" inside the German *Volk* when Germany did not yet exist as a national state. Ling gymnastics were not only introduced by the military, its whole setup with one central instructor controlling rows of gymnasts reminded of military drill. Compared to this, *Turnen* was decentralised and allowed self-motivation and more independent organisation.[14]

---

12 Kai Reinhart and Michael Krüger, "Funktionen des Sports im Modernen Staat und in der Modernen Diktatur", *Historical Social Research* 32/1 (2007), 51.

13 Ove Korsgaard, *Kampen om kroppen: Dansk idræts historie gennem 200 år* (Copenhagen: Gyldendal, 1997), 80-82, 105-106, 175; Else Trangbæk et al., "Innledning", in *Dansk Idrætsliv*, eds. Else Trangbæk et al. (Brøndby: Danmarks Idræts-Forbund, 1996), 8-9; Jørn Hansen, "De første år og de første aktiviteter", in *Dansk Idrætsliv*, eds. Else Trangbæk et al. (Brøndby: Danmarks Idræts-Forbund, 1996), 52-55; Thomas Skovgaard, "Den gode, den smukke og den virkelig sunde. En historie om sundhed, idræt og skole fra det moderne Danmark", in *Folkets sundhed eller lykke? En antologi om humanistisk sundheds- og idrætsforskning*, ed. Jørn Hansen (Odense: Odense Universitetsforlag, 2001), 158-159.

14 For the reception of Ling gymnastics in Germany and the struggle between *Turnen* and Ling gymnastics, see: Carl Euler, "Jahn'sches Turnen", in *Encyklopädisches Handbuch des Gesamten Turnwesens und der Verwandten Gebiete*, ed. Carl Euler (Vienna: Pichler, 1894); Horst Ueberhorst, "Die Rezeption der Schwedischen Gymnastik in Preussen und der Barrenstreit", in *Congress Report*, 8th International Congress for the History of Sport and Physical Education, Uppsala, June 4-9, 1979; Michael Krüger, *Leibeserziehung im 19. Jahrhundert*, 130-132. For a Swedish perspective on the struggle between Ling gymnastics and German *Turnen* in Prussia, see Lindroth, *Ling*, 86-87.

Finally, in Norway the imported physical exercise systems of German *Turnen* and Swedish Ling gymnastics merged to a movement system called "Norwegian gymnastics". In Norway, neither *Turnen* nor Ling gymnastics received a similar political status as in Germany and Denmark. Norwegian gymnastics were a physical exercise system that trained the body; it was not perceived as a political tool.[15]

Physical exercises – such is my claim, which rests on my own cross-national analysis – emerges in specific national and historical contexts. Yet, the origin and heritage do not determine the meaning and the practice. Different intentions that were initially attached to physical exercise systems did not determine their later reception and practice. *Turnen* was not in itself a body practice that led to specific political stances. Ling gymnastics is neither necessarily militaristic, nor does its practice inevitably lead to a cooperative mindset that supports democratic processes. The same movements have been contextualised in different ways and have been inscribed with contradictory meanings.

Sports – A Movement System Fostering a Modern Society?

Turnen was created in Germany, Ling gymnastics in Sweden and sports in England. When sports such as rowing, cycling, football and track and field migrated to Germany, Norway and Denmark by the end of the 19th century they were linked to their British origin and welcomed as modern and international, or they were dismissed as an alien movement practice that threatened national systems such as *Turnen* and Ling gymnastics.[16] Sports were performed as competitions under standardised international rules. Sports performances became measurable in time, distance or points. Abstract goals such as bravery, a beautifully performed exercise, health and comradeship were of secondary importance. The local context of the sports performance was made similar and the specificity of time and place as irrelevant as possible. The conditions for sports performances had to become reproducible in order to ensure the comparability of records. A football field had one universally defined size, rowing boats had to have a specific shape, different national handball rules had to be internationalised. More than the two other exercise systems, *Turnen* and Ling gymnastics, sports became a universal physical exercise.

---

15 Per Hauge-Moe, *Norges Gymnastikk- og Turnforbund 100 År: 1890-1990. Ogsaa vi, naar det blir krevet* (Rud: Norges gymnastikk- og turnforbund, 1989), 76-77; Matti Goksøyr, *Idrettsliv i borgerskapets by: En historisk undersøkelse av idrettens utvikling og organisering i Bergen på 1800-tallet* (Oslo: Norges Idrettshøgskole, 1991), 174-184.

16 For an overview of sports in the interwar years as a universal international phenomenon and system with a British origin, see Barbara J. Keys, *Globalizing Sport: National Rivalry and International Community in the 1930s* (Cambridge, MA: Harvard University Press, 2006). On the implementation of British sports in Denmark, see Korsgaard, *Kampen om kroppen*, 132-133, 277; Jørn Hansen, "Idrætten og samfundets fremgang", in *Geschichte der Leibesübungen. Leibesübungen und Sport in Deutschland vom Ersten Weltkrieg bis zur Gegenwart*, eds. Else Trangbæk et al. (Berlin: Danmarks Idræts-Forbund, 1995), 16. For Norway, see Finn Olstad, *Norsk idretts historie*, vol. 1 (Oslo: Aschehoug, 1987), 75-78, 116. For Germany, see Eisenberg, *"English Sports" und Deutsche Bürger*, 152-156.

Contemporary observers linked, and the research literature continues to link, the process of sportification to the 20th century's modern, standardised, capitalist production. Sports were an urban phenomenon that spread rapidly by the end of the 19th century and became the dominant form of exercise in the course of the inter-war years. Sports superseded local forms of exercise systems and supplanted evaluations of style and values of community with individual maximum performance. The growth of sports and its characteristics made the linkage to processes of modernisation self-evident. Sports, such is a frequent claim, was closer to modern "society" than to a traditional organic "community".[17] Christine Eisenberg, for example, states that the National Socialist regime decided in favour of society, *Gesellschaft,* instead of community, *Gemeinschaft,* by privileging the sports movement vis-à-vis the *Turner* movement, which was dissolved in 1935.[18] Whether sports are an expression of, or a motor for, the modernisation of the respective societies, is debated in research literature.[19]

Sports have been embraced by manifold regimes and ideologies. Sports have been practiced as workers' sports, communist sports, by diverse religious sports organisations and they were promoted by the National Socialist regime. By the end of the 1930s, sports became the hegemonic movement practice both in National Socialist Germany and in the Scandinavian Social Democratic welfare states. Although the ideology connected to sports differed, the actual movement practices were similar.[20] In a comparative study of physical education under National Social-

---

17 This draws upon a famous distinction presented by the German sociologist Ferdinand Tönnies. To him, the transition from community to society marks the transition from a traditional society to a modern society. Ferdinand Tönnies, *Gemeinschaft und Gesellschaft: Grundbegriffe der Reinen Soziologie* (Berlin: Curtius, 1912).

18 Eisenberg, "*English Sports" und Deutsche Bürger*, 393. Alkemeyer interprets the decision for sports as a decision for using physical exercises most effectively. Sports were embraced by the masses. Thus, the National Socialist regime needed sports to efficiently control the population. Moreover, sports fostered solitary elites who were supposed to become elites in the service of the state. Thomas Alkemeyer, "Images and Politics of the Body in the National Socialist Era", *Sport Science Review* 4/1 (1995), 60-90.

19 For Germany, Eisenberg points out that sport was a motor for modernisation; it accelerated the reluctant mental adjustment to the modern economic status quo. Eisenberg, "Friedrich Ludwig Jahn", 231. Olstad links the emergence of sports in Norway to economic and social modernisation in Norway's bigger cities that were open to international impulses. Olstad, *Norsk idretts historie*, 173. Barbara Keys explains the growth of the sports movement in the interwar years with modernisation. Keys, *Globalizing Sport*, 17-21. Krüger too establishes a linkage between modern working conditions and sportification: Krüger, *Leibesübungen im 20. Jahrhundert*, 66-67. Alkemeyer characterises sports as "a child of industrial, capitalist society", whereas *Turnen* would be traditional, collectivistic, quasi-military drill. Alkemeyer, "Images and Politics of the Body", 62. Behringer, however, is a rare voice in literature that claims that the making of sports cannot be linked to industrialisation and modernisation. Sports had roots far back to the early modern times. Wolfgang Behringer, "Arena and Pall Mall. Sport in the Early Modern Period", *German History* 27/3 (2009), 331-357.

20 For workers' sports compared to bourgeois sports in Germany, see: James Riordan, "The Worker Sports Movement", in *The International Politics of Sport in the Twentieth Century*, eds. James Riordan and Arnd Krüger (London: E&FN Spon, 1999), 105-116; Arnd Krüger, "The

ism and Stalinism, Barbara Keys convincingly demonstrated that both regimes used sports as a political tool, but she claims that it is not possible to determine what sports as a body practice *did* and *does;* it is not possible to judge if distinct ways of exercising produce an inclination for a distinct political ideology. Does this suggest that body movements are an empty container that can be filled with any ideological content?[21]

When it comes to rhythmical gymnastics, the research literature has so far linked this movement form to one ideology only. Rhythmical gymnastics have been accused of collaborating in the production of a mindset compatible to National Socialism by promoting and inscribing a de-individualising sense of community in the bodies of its performers.

Rhythmical Gymnastics – A Total Movement for a Totalitarian State?

From the end of the 19th century onward, "rhythm" became a central movement concept that was translated into manifold exercises and dance systems after the First World War. Two important pioneers of rhythm were François Delsarte from France and Émile Jaques-Dalcroze from Switzerland. Some of their students became pioneers of modern dance, among them Isadora Duncan and Rudolf von Laban, who became Mary Wigman's teacher. Other students became founders of different gymnastic schools, among them the German gymnastics instructors Rudolf Bode and his student Hinrich Medau. The German gymnasts were most of all inspired by Jaques-Dalcroze.[22]

German Way of Worker Sport", 14. In Norway some attempts were made to make sports more accessible for everyone by, e.g., introducing different performance classes for their competitions. But as a whole, the workers' sports too focused on individual elites and maximum performance. Olstad, *Norsk idretts historie*, 213-217, 267. In Denmark, the differences between the two movements' sports practices were even less visible. Ebbe Hansen, "Arbejderidrætten i Danmark med særlig henblik på D.A.I. i perioden 1929-43", *Den jyske Historiker* 19-20 (1981), 153-167.

21 Barbara Keys, "The Body as a Political Space: Comparing Physical Education under Nazism and Stalinism", *German History* 27/3 (2009), 395-413. Sports historians Krüger and Reinhart reject the thesis that sports are "neutral" but claim its interrelation with different political regimes and interests. However, they state too that the specific historical context and individual practices determine whether sports practice is affirmative or resistant. Reinhart and Krüger, "Funktionen des Sports".

22 For a systematic overview of the different schools of gymnastics in Germany, see: Wedemeyer-Kolwe, *"Der Neue Mensch"*, 25-128; Gabriela Wesp, *Frisch. Fromm. Fröhlich. Frau. Frauen und Sport zur Zeit der Weimarer Republik* (Königsstein: Ulrike Helmer Verlag, 1998), 73-101; Helmut Günther, "Gymnastik- und Tanzbestrebungen vom Ende des 19. Jahrhunderts bis zum Ersten Weltkrieg", in *Leibesübungen und Sport in Deutschland von den Anfängen bis zum Ersten Weltkrieg*, ed. Horst Ueberhorst (Berlin: Bartels & Wernitz, 1980), 569-593; Freckmann, "Wesen und Formen". On Delsarte, see Günther, "Gymnastik- und Tanzbestrebungen", 571-575; Inge Baxmann, *Mythos Gemeinschaft: Körper- und Tanzkulturen in der Moderne* (Munich: Fink, 2000), 114-116. For a contextualisation of the rhythmical movement into the *Lebensreform* movement, see Gabriele Brandstetter, "Ausdruckstanz", in *Handbuch der Deutschen*

Jaques-Dalcroze aimed at translating music into body movements. He wanted to develop a sense for rhythm and music in the performers, what he called a rhythmic mentality. Jaques-Dalcroze taught his students to illustrate and express different aspects of a given piece of music; its meters, beats and note values, with different body parts. The arms would beat the time – for example the left arm a three-four time, the right a four-four time and even the head might have to beat yet another time while the feet reproduced note values. The appliance of polymetric music to body movements required to teach polycentric body movements: Different muscles and body parts/sides had to be moved independently from each other.[23]

Jaques-Dalcroze's student Rudolf Bode inverted important concepts from his teacher. He did not want to take the starting point in a given music with a given form and beats. Instead he wanted to take the starting point in the bodies' supposed inherent needs and movement forms.[24] Moreover, Bode switched the focus from time/meter – which he considered as an instrument for disciplining the body – to rhythm. For Bode time/meter was a quantitative principle of the mind; rhythm, however, was a qualitative principle of vitality and the unconscious "life force" *(Lebenskraft)*.[25] As a tool for freeing the body from a dictating beat and the ruling of a disciplining mind, Bode developed his signature movement: The total movement.

Figure 3 *A student of Hinrich Medau demonstrates the total movement*[26]

Reformbewegungen: 1880-1933, eds. Diethart Kerbs and Jürgen Reulecke (Wuppertal: Hammer, 1998). See in addition footnote 34.

23 On Dalcroze, see: Günther, "Gymnastik- und Tanzbestrebungen", 578-580; Wedemeyer-Kolwe, *"Der Neue Mensch"*, 35-36, 42-44, 76-76; Karl Eric Toepfer, *Empire of Ecstasy: Nudity and Movement in German Body Culture, 1910-1935* (Berkeley: University of California Press, 1997), 15-21.

24 Günther, "Geschichtlicher Ablauf", 30.

25 Bode, *Rhythmus*, 25-26.

26 Hinrich Medau, "Die Grundlagen der Ausdrucksgymnastik von Dr. Bode", *Gymnastik* 1/3-4 (1926), 40.

Rudolf Bode's basic movement was a rhythmical, swinging, "total movement"; a movement that had its starting point in the body's centre of gravity, located in the middle of the body. The movement started by a swinging movement in which the gymnasts went down, bending her/his knees and swinging the arms, which come from behind, down and then up in a fluid motion of the whole body. The primary movement force was initiated by the hip area and grew through the whole body. It propagated and flew from the centre of the body to all extremities, enforced by the bodies' own inertia. The swinging movement thus guaranteed a constant change of tension and relaxation; a wavelike movement evoking the "life wave" and the "cosmic wave". The terms "life force", "life wave" and "cosmic wave" already indicate that Bode was highly inspired by philosopher of life Ludwig Klages and the so-called "cosmic-circle" who longed for a lost connection with nature, a retrieved harmony of every individual with the greater whole of the community, that again was only a part of the greater cosmos. According to Klages, rhythm was one important tool for obtaining this goal. A rhythmical movement was like a wave that does not start or end, it floats continuously in an eternal periodicity of surging and flowing back, enabling the experience of the infinite that cannot be grasped with the capacities of the human mind – it can only be experienced by being oblivious to oneself.[27]

Rudolf Bode and his student Hinrich Medau presented rhythmical gymnastics as a means to re-discover a lost natural rhythm in order to fight modernity's "tensions", which were not least explained with an exaggerated stress on willpower and discipline. Tension was interpreted both as a sign of individual and national decline. The modern person had to be taught to loosen up, to relax in rhythmic movements. Rhythm was not a product of willpower, but of the unconscious. Students should not be taught to move rhythmically, they should abandon themselves to the rhythm. To move rhythmically was considered the ideal way of freeing the body's and the person's inherent capacities and to establish a linkage to primordial forces *(Ur-Kräfte)* that connect every individual with the "cosmic pulse". Rhythmical gymnastics were considered as a means for individual transcendence and as a means for rebuilding the sense of a community that was lost. Gymnasts performed rhythmical movements together with others. Every single body was meant to express its own individual and natural rhythm, while all the bodies were connected through the rhythm and thus responding to other moving, sounding bodies that belonged to the (gymnastic) collective.[28]

---

27 On Klages and the cosmic circle, see Thomas Rohkrämer, *Eine Andere Moderne? Zivilisationskritik, Natur und Technik in Deutschland 1880-1933* (Paderborn: Ferdinand Schöningh, 1999), 162-211; Walter Schmitz and Uwe Schneider, "Völkische Semantik bei den 'Münchner Kosmikern' und im George-Kreis", in *Handbuch zur "Völkischen Bewegung" 1871-1918,* 711-746. On Klages' concept of rhythm, see his own publication "Vom Wesen des Rhythmus", in *Sämtliche Werke,* eds. Hans Eggert Schröder and Ernst Frauchiger (Bonn: Bouvier-Verlag, 1974), 499-551.

28 Günther, "Geschichtlicher Ablauf"; Medau, "Die Grundlagen", 12-13; Bode, *Rhythmus,* 12-13. Bode and Medau shared their goals with the German Gymnastic Federation *(Deutscher*

Although it is impossible to state that the creators and performers intended a linkage to National Socialist ideology, it is striking to observe how well the total movement and the concept of rhythm fitted with the rhetoric and ideology of the Third Reich. After 1933, rhythmical gymnastics were renamed into German Gymnastics and the total movement became a useful symbol for the totalitarian state. Rhythmical gymnastics could be used and was used by the National Socialist regime. At least single actors inside the rhythmical movement supported the Third Reich. A manifesto on how National Socialist gymnastics were supposed to look like, among others formulated by Rudolf Bode, associated the totality of the state to the organic totality of every single individual. The tree served as an analogy: Every single leaf on a tree would both be an individual form in itself while simultaneously serving the totality of the tree. Thus, teaching total movements meant teaching an organic wholeness that produced a sense of coherence and connection with the entire *Volk:*

> A German gymnastics is based on the understanding of factually apprehensible undisputable laws of the human movement and has the task 1.) to subsume all physical exercises under the law of performance with minimal effort. It is of fundamental importance for a) the education of a citizen; in the same way each leaf serves the whole of the tree while having an individual shape, the organic totality of each individual is the precondition for the totality of the state. One tool for achieving this education is to develop a sense for uniform life utterances in the movements of the human body.[29]

Movements in rhythmical gymnastics were not the result of willpower and deliberate individual decisions, but the result of sounding and responding bodies in an organic collective. The movement principle of rhythm made it possible for individuals to connect with each other on a subconscious level. The mystical and anti-intellectual concept of rhythm seemed to be attractive to propagators of National Socialist ideology. A stress on rhythm can for example be found in Alfred Rosenberg's *Der Mythos des 20. Jahrhunderts.* Here, Rosenberg presented an opposition between rhythm and individualism. According to Rosenberg, isolated individuals, individualism and universalism were like straight lines. They would lead into the emptiness of eternity. Individuals that acted in the service of the race, however, were like rhythmical forces that were able to create.[30] This sounds very similar to

---

Gymnastikbund), founded in 1925. The head of the gymnastic federation, Franz Hilker, stressed that gymnastics focus on internal functioning; the goal was to develop a personality by reactivating the unconscious. Gymnastics should re-establish a balance between instinctive nature and culture which was lost by an exaggerated focus on will power. Franz Hilker, "Chronik des Deutschen Gymnastik-Bundes", *Gymnastik* 8/11-12 (1933), 165-178.

29 Quoted in Hans Hinkel et al., "Die Geistigen Grundlagen für Körperbildung und Tanz im Nationalsozialistischen Staat", *Deutsche Turnzeitung* 78/41 (1933), 853-854.

30 Alfred Rosenberg, *Der Mythus des 20. Jahrhunderts: Eine Wertung der Seelisch-Geistigen Gestaltenkämpfe Unserer Zeit* (Munich: Hoheneichen-Verlag, 1933), 106. Rosenberg's biographer Ernst Piper does not discuss this line of argumentation, but it can be connected to the concept of *Rassenseele.* Ernst Piper, *Alfred Rosenberg: Hitlers Chefideologe* (Munich: Blessing, 2005).

Langbehn's opposition of symmetry and rhythm, an opposition that can be read in light of the long-time opposition between Ling gymnastics and German movement forms as well.

A stress on rhythm can also be found in Hans F.K. Günther's popular book on racial science. Günther linked specific movement forms to specific races. The Nordic race was characterised by rhythmical movements, for instance a continuous movement that flows through the whole body. In particular Nordic women were supposed to show this innate movement principle of the Nordic race:

> Most of all for the unburdened walk of the Nordic women, it is striking that a lowering of the head, a downward gaze, is indicated by a preliminary wave through the upper body, in a sense a wave through the whole body: the body expresses itself as a whole and one would like to say, the movement, each movement passes as a flow before or concurrently through the whole body. [...] In the arm-swing of the Nordic race, the freedom of expression attracts attention, which reveals itself in every movement of the hand. Each part of the arm, each muscle, each finger maintains its special individual value; while the movement flows in its interplay with the whole body.[31]

In his description of the natural movement of the Nordic women, Günther describes the "Bode-wave" perfectly. It is not possible to tell whether it is by accident or intentional that his characterisation resembles the description of the total movement inside rhythmical gymnastics. In the interwar years, rhythmical gymnastics had developed into the most acceptable exercise form for women in Germany,[32] thus it is very likely that Günther had encountered a display of this exercise form.

Figure 4 *The total movement inside the collective*[33]

31 Quoted in Hans F.K. Günther, *Rassenkunde des Deutschen Volkes* (Munich: J.F. Lehmann, 1928), 170-171.

32 Kerstin Bornholdt, "Between Exhausting Sports and Swinging Rhythm. An Inquiry into Medical Knowledge Production about Women's Sports and Women's Gymnastics in Norway, Denmark and Germany in the Interwar Years" (PhD diss., University of Oslo, 2011), 298-304.

33 "Gymnastikschule Medau [Photo]", *Deutsche Turnzeitung* 76/2 (1931).

The scene presented in figure 4 illustrates the idea of rhythmical gymnastics. Rhythmical gymnastics aimed at re-discovering and expressing an almost lost connection to a true inner nature that simultaneously connected the performer to the surrounding powers of nature and of his and her community. Although rhythmical gymnastics were performed by women in cities, in this picture and in the ideology, modern urban life was as absent as it could be.

The desire for a shelter against modern life was not unique to the rhythmical movement. In this regard, the rhythmical movement was in the tradition of the Life Reform *(Lebensreform)* movement, which aspired to a lost balance of body and mind.[34] A longing for a lost connection to "nature" was not enough to necessarily link rhythmical gymnastics to National Socialist ideology. It is the concept of rhythm and the total movement that provoke suspicion in the literature on the topic.

In her study on the pioneers of modern dance, Sabine Huschka exempts modern dance, which shared movement origins with gymnastics, from any suspicion of being a National Socialist movement form. Rhythmical gymnastics, however, was well adapted to the ideology of the Third Reich. She criticises the ban of isolated movements and the doctrine that a movement always has to start in the body's centre. Starting a movement from the body mass' centre would capture the whole body; one movement law dictates every movement from the inside out to every external limb and every single muscle fibre. Huschka interprets the total movement as a strict movement system that subjects the body to one single will, making it functional. Thus, the body becomes a functional and disciplined apparatus, well-adjusted to National Socialist ideology.[35] This interpretation suggests that rhythmical gymnastics inscribed the *Führerprinzip* into the body of the gymnasts, preparing and pre-disposing the gymnast to become a follower and instrument for political purposes.

In an article on rhythmical gymnastics from 1978, sports historian Hajo Bernett accuses rhythmical gymnastics for its historical and still prevalent mystical focus on bodies and its supposedly inherent capacities. Bode and other propagators of

---

34 For a contextualization of the gymnastic movement in the Lebensreform movement, see e.g. Maren Möhring, *Marmorleiber: Körperbildung in der Deutschen Nacktkultur (1890-1930)* (Cologne: Böhlau, 2004); Kai Buchholz, *Die Lebensreform: Entwürfe zur Neugestaltung von Leben und Kunst um 1900* (Darmstadt: Häusser, 2001); Diethart Kerbs and Jürgen Reulecke, eds. *Handbuch der Deutschen Reformbewegungen: 1880-1933* (Wuppertal: Hammer, 1998); Rohkrämer, *Eine Andere Moderne?;* Wolfgang R. Krabbe, *Gesellschaftsveränderung durch Lebensreform: Strukturmerkmale einer Sozialreformerischen Bewegung im Deutschland der Industrialisierungsperiode* (Göttingen: Vandenhoeck & Ruprecht, 1974).

35 Sabine Huschka, *Merce Cunningham und der Moderne Tanz: Körperkonzepte, Choreographie und Tanzästhetik* (Würzburg: Königshausen & Neumann, 2000), 50-51. In their study on modern dance in the Third Reich, Karina and Kant link modern dance to National Socialist ideology. The German expressive dance would fit the ideology very well "because it emerged from the same reactionary, cultish, racist, mystical circles that spawned many Nazis and Nazi ideas". Lilian Karina and Marion Kant, *Hitler's Dancers. German Modern Dance and the Third Reich* (New York: Berghahn Books, 2003), xi.

rhythmical gymnastics had ascribed bodies an inherent need, a form-power, and a kind of "body knowledge" that was opposed to rational knowledge. They had propagated physical exercises as an effective tool for the National Socialist state. More than the thinking intellect, the body/soul was more deeply connected to the origin of its heritage – as the leader of the gymnastics movement Hans Hinkel put it: "[T]he circulating bloodstream of the 'German womb' *[Mutterschoß]*"[36]

Bodies in rhythmical movement, such is the claim, activate and generate levels of knowledge and dispositions that cannot be reached by words and discussions. Body movements are a silent knowledge, a tacit knowledge.[37] Embodied knowledge was, and is, inaccessible for public discussions, it is only accessible for the practicing insider and it remains inaccessible in a Habermasian setting of negotiating meaning in discourse governed by commensurable, rational rules.[38] It is the fear of an anti-enlightenment process that turns the concept of body knowledge into a suspicious "body romanticism" that is still closely linked to Hitler's Germany.[39]

This difficulty of grasping the indescribable is what makes embodied knowledge a fascinating research topic in postmodern times.

Body Movements as Political Actors?

30 years after Hajo Bernett expressed his discomfort with the concept of "body knowledge", research on this topic thrives as a trendy interdisciplinary research agenda.[40] Not unlike the claims of the proponents of the rhythmical movement, the

---

36 Hinkel et al., "Die Geistigen Grundlagen", 853-854; Hajo Bernett, "Die Ideologie der Deutschen Gymnastik", *Sportwissenschaft* 8/1 (1978), 22.

37 On the difference between corporeal knowledge production and reflective as well as scientific knowledge production, see Volker Schürmann, "Reflexion und Wiederholung. Mit einem Ausblick auf 'Rhythmus'", in *Körperliche Erkenntnis: Formen Reflexiver Erfahrung*, eds. Franz Bockrath et al. (Bielefeld: Transcript, 2008), 53-54. On tacit knowledge, see in addition Henry M. Collins, "What is Tacit Knowledge?", in *The Practice Turn in Contemporary Theory*, eds. Theodore R. Schatzki et al. (London: Routledge, 2001), 107-119.

38 E.g., Kasper Maase encourages analysing the body as a medium for aesthetic experiences, but warns of the danger of body romanticism. Kasper Maase, "Bewegte Körper, Populäre Kultur – Ästhetische Erfahrungen. Kulturwissenschaftliche Überlegungen", in *Bewegungsraum und Stadtkultur. Sozial- und Kulturwissenschaftliche Perspektiven*, eds. Jürgen Funke-Wieneke and Gabriele Klein (Bielefeld: Transcript, 2008), 42-43.

39 Volker Schürmann argued that it is not the question whether people were forced together into an organic community, or whether they felt an organic togetherness or not, but the belief in an authentic experience that could not be verbalised, that could not be shared if one was not part of it, which is the problematic non-democratic aspect. The public did not have any access to the circle of the inaugurated. Volker Schürmann, "Logik des Ausdrucks", in *Wissenskultur Tanz: Historische und zeitgenössische Vermittlungsakte zwischen Praktiken und Diskursen*, eds. Gernot Böhme and Sabine Huschka (Bielefeld: Transcript, 2009), 111.

40 Franz Bockrath et al., eds., *Körperliche Erkenntnis;* Sabine Gehm et al., eds., *Knowledge in Motion: Perspectives of Artistic and Scientific Research in Dance* (Bielefeld: Transcript, 2007); Thomas Alkemeyer et al., eds., *Ordnung in Bewegung: Choreographien des Sozialen. Körper in Sport, Tanz, Arbeit und Bildung* (Bielefeld: Transcript, 2009).

claim of today's researchers on embodied knowledge is that bodily movements provide a new kind of knowledge that contests established academic knowledge.[41]

Are body practices "doing" anything? Is it possible to discern whether specific body movements themselves have produced distinct bodily experiences that are predisposed for, or even produced distinct ideologies?

Drawing on the example of popular music and recent developments in dance music, Kasper Maase claims that rhythm and sound have overshadowed melody. Thus, an immediate expression of bodily emotions, a bodily transcendence, has replaced conscious processes of cognitive, intellectual understanding. Sound and rhythm produces meanings that cannot be formulated by language.[42] The body is not a blank material for the inscription of meaning; the body produces meaning. And again rhythm is a crucial actor.

Most of the researchers who investigate embodied knowledge draw on Bourdieu's concept of disposition. Human bodies have natural predispositions that can be actualised and acquire abilities and competences. Bourdieu offers a line of reasoning between mechanical materialism and constructivist idealism. The term disposition enables Bourdieu to argue that actors have the power to act and to construct reality, whilst they have at the same time already been socially constructed. Knowledge and power are not only inscribed or put into bodies. Bodies produce knowledge through repeated practices.[43]

Sports historian and sociologist Thomas Alkemeyer draws upon Bourdieu when he claims that physical exercises are a pre-reflexive mastering of the social world. The body bears meaning, it is inscribed with meaning and it produces meaning. Yet again, which meaning the body and body movements produce is difficult to grasp from a theoretical perspective. According to Alkemeyer, physical exercises have polysemantic qualities – embedded in distinct social, cultural and political contexts, they gain their specific meanings.[44] The same bodily practice can obtain opposing meanings in different contexts.

---

41 Hortensia Völckers, "Preface", in *Knowledge in Motion: Perspectives of Artistic and Scientific Research in Dance*, eds. Sabine Gehm et al. (Bielefeld: Transcript, 2007); Gabriele Brandstetter, "Dance as Culture of Knowledge. Body Memory and the Challenge of Theoretical Knowledge", in *Knowledge in Motion*, eds. Sabine Gehm et al., (Bielefeld: Transcript, 2007); Alkemeyer et al., *Ordnung in Bewegung*.

42 Kasper Maase, "Die Erforschung des Schönen im Alltag. Sechs Thesen", in *Die Schönheiten des Populären*, ed. Kasper Maase (Frankfurt a.M.: Campus Verlag, 2008), 56-57.

43 In his book *Pascalian Meditations* Bourdieu delineated the embodiment of societal structures in a sub-chapter on body knowledge. Pierre Bourdieu, *Pascalian Meditations*, trans. Richard Nice (Stanford: Stanford University Press, 2000). Sports historians Kai Reinhart and Michael Krüger use Foucault's concept of the *dispositif* for arguing that sports disciplines its performers and is a technology of power. Reinhart and Krüger, "Funktionen des Sports im modernen Staat", 43-77.

44 Thomas Alkemeyer, "Das Populäre und das Nicht-Populäre. Über den Geist des Sports und die Körperlichkeit der Hochkultur", in *Die Erforschung des Schönen im Alltag. Sechs Thesen*, ed. Kasper Maase, 232-235.

The Disturbing Comparative Perspective: Rhythmical Gymnastics as a Facilitator for Modernity?

As shown above, theoreticians of body knowledge claim that distinct body movements produce a distinct knowledge. At the same time, body movements are filled with meaning in a specific context only. I have shown how *Turnen* and Ling gymnastics changed their meanings in different spatial and historical contexts. Ling gymnastics was perceived as an important tool for liberating Danish farmers and it was perceived as a disciplining project of the ruling authorities in Norway and Germany. Sports could be integrated in diverse political systems and ideologies too; both into the Scandinavian welfare state, into Stalinism and the Third Reich. A transnational approach is able to show that context matters. This is the case with rhythmical gymnastics as well. When German rhythmical gymnastics travelled to Denmark, it was no longer a facilitator for National Socialist ideology. In Denmark, German rhythmical gymnastics were neither German nor an expression of a National Socialist ideology – they were perceived as modern.[45] Confronted with the new German body practices in gymnastic displays and international gymnastic festivals, Scandinavian proponents for Ling gymnastics did not witness a total movement that connected every individual to a collective whole, they saw a lack of discipline and a threat for the kind of gymnastic community they had created and envisioned. To the Ling gymnasts, the total movement was not an expression of anti-modernism and a retreat into a lost community, but an expression of urban modernity that threatened Ling gymnastics' stress on collectively performed movements.[46] As described above, the total movement took its starting point in the point of gravity that differed from body to body. Each body had its own acceleration and leverage according to the length of the limbs. Accordingly, each body's individuality was a dominant factor that determined a movement's pace. Modern rhythmical gymnastics literally opened the synchronism of the gymnastic squad that was a characteristic of Ling gymnastics. It soon became apparent that the movement principle of rhythm challenged central orders of the gymnastic instructor. It was no longer possible to dictate one movement for everybody – every individual body had an individual rhythm of its own. Uniformity inside the gymnastic squad was only achievable by concordance of all actors involved. One had either to let every person perform an exercise in her own pace, or one had to agree on a compromise. Rhythmical gymnastics was more in line with a modern society comprised of individual actors than the collectivism of Ling gymnastics. It was a movement form that young and urban Copenhagen girls embraced in their craze for new un-

---

45 For an overview on the reception of German rhythmical gymnastics in Denmark, see Birgit Brink Lund, "Medaugymnastikkens modtagelse i det danske kvindegymnastikmiljø 1936-1941", in *Kvinder, køn og krop. Kulturelle fortællinger*, eds. Anne Lykke Poulsen and Else Trangbæk (Odense: Odense Universitetsforlag, 2006); Bornholdt, "Between Exhausting Sports and Swinging Rhythm", 328-352.

46 For Danish reactions from the interwar period, see e.g. Ellen Paul-Petersen, "Betragtninger over tysk gymnastikk", *D.K.G. Medlemsblad for Dansk Kvinde-Gymnastikforening* 3/2 (1936), 1-4; Gudrun Abrahamsen, "Medaugymnastik", *Nordisk Kvinnogymnastik* 26/2 (1943), 32-33.

practised movement possibilities. The gymnastic instructors, who wanted to save their "Nordic way" of moving, had to give in to the demands of young girls, who saw new individual movement possibilities, who experienced liberation in the movements of rhythmical gymnastics. Apparently, rhythmical gymnastics was something else in Denmark than in Hitler's Germany.[47]

Again, which effect did rhythmical gymnastics have, which meaning did it produce and is it possible to associate rhythmical gymnastics with a distinct political ideology? The answer is as follows: It was a totalitarian movement for a totalitarian state and a modern movement for a democratic society.

Bibliography

Abrahamsen, Gudrun. "Medaugymnastik". *Nordisk Kvinnogymnastik* 26/2 (1943), 32-33.

Alkemeyer, Thomas. "Images and Politics of the Body in the National Socialist Era". *Sport Science Review* 4/1 (1995), 60-90.

Alkemeyer, Thomas. "Das Populäre und das Nicht-Populäre. Über den Geist des Sports und die Körperlichkeit der Hochkultur". In *Die Erforschung des Schönen im Alltag. Sechs Thesen*, edited by Kasper Maase, 232-235. Frankfurt a.M.: Campus Verlag, 2008.

Alkemeyer, Thomas, Kristina Brümmer, Rea Kodalle and Thomas Pille, eds. *Ordnung in Bewegung: Choreographien des Sozialen. Körper in Sport, Tanz, Arbeit und Bildung*. Bielefeld: Transcript, 2009.

Baxmann, Inge. *Mythos Gemeinschaft: Körper- und Tanzkulturen in der Moderne*. Munich: Fink, 2000.

Behrendt, Bernd. "August Julius Langbehn, der 'Rembrandtdeutsche'". In *Handbuch zur "Völkischen Bewegung" 1871-1918*, edited by Uwe Puschner and Walter Schmitz, 94-113. Munich: Saur, 1999.

Behrendt, Bernd. *Zwischen Paradox und Paralogismus: Weltanschauliche Grundzüge einer Kulturkritik in den 90er Jahren des 19. Jahrhunderts am Beispiel August Julius Langbehn*. Frankfurt a.M.: Peter Lang, 1984.

Behringer, Wolfgang. "Arena and Pall Mall. Sport in the Early Modern Period". *German History* 27/3 (2009), 331-357.

Bernett, Hajo. *Grundformen der Leibeserziehung*. Schorndorf: Hofmann, 1975.

Bernett, Hajo. "Die Ideologie der Deutschen Gymnastik". *Sportwissenschaft* 8/1 (1978), 7-23.

Bernett, Hajo. *Der Weg des Sports in die Nationalsozialistische Diktatur*. Schorndorf: Hofmann, 1983.

Bockrath, Franz, Bernhard Boschert and Elk Franke, eds. *Körperliche Erkenntnis: Formen Reflexiver Erfahrung. Körperkulturen*. Bielefeld: Transcript, 2008.

Bode, Rudolf. *Rhythmus und Körpererziehung. Fünf Abhandlungen*. Jena: Diederichs, 1923.

Bornholdt, Kerstin. "Between Exhausting Sports and Swinging Rhythm. An Inquiry into Medical Knowledge Production about Women's Sports and Women's Gymnastics in Norway, Denmark and Germany in the Interwar Years". PhD diss., University of Oslo, 2011.

Bourdieu, Pierre. *Pascalian Meditations*. Translated by Richard Nice. Stanford: Stanford University Press, 2000.

Brandstetter, Gabriele. "Dance as Culture of Knowledge. Body Memory and the Challenge of Theoretical Knowledge". In *Knowledge in Motion: Perspectives of Artistic and Scientific Research in Dance*,

47 Signe Fog, "Kan man bevare formen i moderne gymnastik?", *Nordisk Kvinnogymnastik* 23/1 (1940), 27-31; Martha Christensen, "Kvindegymnastik", *Gymnastisk Tidsskrift* 15/1 (1929),1-9.

edited by Sabine Gehm, Pirkko Husemann and Katharina von Wilcke, 37-48. Bielefeld: Transcript, 2007.

Brandstetter, Gabriele. "Ausdruckstanz". In *Handbuch der Deutschen Reformbewegungen: 1880-1933*, edited by Diethart Kerbs and Jürgen Reulecke, 451-463. Wuppertal: Hammer, 1998.

Brink Lund, Birgit. "Medaugymnastikkens modtagelse i det danske kvindegymnastikmiljø 1936-1941". In *Kvinder, køn og krop. Kulturelle fortællinger*, edited by Anne Lykke Poulsen and Else Trangbæk, 55-64. Odense: Odense Universitetsforlag, 2006.

Buchholz, Kai. *Die Lebensreform: Entwürfe zur Neugestaltung von Leben und Kunst um 1900*. Darmstadt: Häusser, 2001.

Christensen, Martha. "Kvindegymnastik". *Gymnastisk Tidsskrift* 15/1 (1929), 1-9.

Collins, Henry M. "What is Tacit Knowledge?". In *The Practice Turn in Contemporary Theory*, edited by Theodore R. Schatzki, Karin Knorr-Cetina and Eike von Savigny, London: Routledge, 2001.

Eisenberg, Christiane. *"English Sports" und Deutsche Bürger. Eine Gesellschaftsgeschichte 1800-1939*. Paderborn: Ferdinand Schöningh, 1999.

Eisenberg, Christiane. "Friedrich Ludwig Jahn – der 'Erfinder des Deutschen Turnens'". *Sportwissenschaft* 30/2 (2000), 125-140.

Euler, Carl. "Jahn'sches Turnen". In *Encyklopädisches Handbuch des Gesamten Turnwesens und der Verwandten Gebiete*, edited by Carl Euler, 574-585. Vienna: Pichler, 1894.

Fog, Signe. "Kan man bevare formen i moderne gymnastik?". *Nordisk Kvinnogymnastik* 23/1 (1940), 27-31.

Freckmann, Barbara. "Wesen und Formen der Gymnastik". In *Leibesübungen und Sport in Deutschland vom Ersten Weltkrieg bis zur Gegenwart*, edited by Horst Ueberhorst, 1008-1025. Berlin: Bartels & Wernitz, 1982.

Frucht, Hans. "Zur Geschichte der Organischen Bewegungslehre". In *Der Rhythmus als Erzieher: Festschrift zum 60. Geb. von Rudolf Bode, 3. Febr. 1941*, edited by Hans Eggert Schröder, 16-24. Berlin: Widukind, 1941.

Gehm, Sabine, Pirkko Husemann and Katharina von Wilcke, eds. *Knowledge in Motion: Perspectives of Artistic and Scientific Research in Dance*. Bielefeld: Transcript, 2007.

Goksøyr, Matti. *Idrettsliv i borgerskapets by: En historisk undersøkelse av idrettens utvikling og organisering i Bergen på 1800-tallet*. Oslo: Norges Idrettshøgskole, 1991.

Goltermann, Svenja. *Körper der Nation: Habitusformierung und die Politik des Turnens 1860 - 1890*. Göttingen: Vandenhoeck & Ruprecht, 1998.

Günther, Hans F.K. *Rassenkunde des Deutschen Volkes*. Munich: J.F. Lehmann, 1928.

Günther, Helmut. "Gymnastik- und Tanzbestrebungen vom Ende des 19. Jahrhunderts bis zum Ersten Weltkrieg". In *Leibesübungen und Sport in Deutschland von den Anfängen bis zum Ersten Weltkrieg*, edited by Horst Ueberhorst, 569-593. Berlin: Bartels & Wernitz, 1980.

Günther, Helmut. "Geschichtlicher Ablauf der Deutschen Rhythmusbewegung". In *Handbuch Bewegungserziehung: Ästhetische und Rhythmische Perspektiven*, edited by Eva Bannmüller and Peter Röthig, 13-49. Butzbach: Afra-Verlag, 2005.

Hansen, Ebbe. "Arbejderidrætten i Danmark med særlig henblik på D.A.I. i ierioden 1929-43". *Den jyske Historiker* 19-20 (1981), 139-203.

Hansen, Jørn. "De Første År og de Første Aktiviteter". In *Dansk Idrætsliv*, edited by Else Trangbæk, Jørn Hansen and Nils Kayser Nielsen, Brøndby: Danmarks Idræts-Forbund, 1995.

Hansen, Jørn. "Idrætten og Samfundets Fremgang". In *Geschichte der Leibesübungen. Leibesübungen und Sport in Deutschland vom Ersten Weltkrieg bis zur Gegenwart*, edited by Else Trangbæk, Jørn Hansen and Nils Kayser Nielsen, Berlin: Danmarks Idræts-Forbund, 1995.

Hauge-Moe, Per. *Norges Gymnastikk- og Turnforbund 100 År: 1890-1990. Ogsaa vi, naar det blir krevet.* Rud: Norges gymnastikk- og turnforbund, 1989.

Hilker, Franz. "Chronik des Deutschen Gymnastik-Bundes". *Gymnastik* 8/11-12 (1933), 165-178.

Hinkel, Hans, Rudolf Bode and Gustav Schäfer. "Die Geistigen Grundlagen Für Körperbildung und Tanz Im Nationalsozialistischen Staat". *Deutsche Turnzeitung* 78/41 (1933), 853-854.

Huschka, Sabine. *Merce Cunningham und der Moderne Tanz: Körperkonzepte, Choreographie und Tanzästhetik.* Würzburg: Königshausen & Neumann, 2000.

Jahn, Friedrich Ludwig and Ernst Eiselen. *Die Deutsche Turnkunst zur Einrichtung der Turnplätze.* Frankfurt a.M.: Wilhelm Limpert-Verlag, 1961[1816].

Karina, Lilian and Marion Kant. *Hitler's Dancers. German Modern Dance and the Third Reich.* New York: Berghahn Books, 2003.

Kerbs, Diethart and Jürgen Reulecke, eds. *Handbuch der Deutschen Reformbewegungen: 1880-1933.* Wuppertal: Hammer, 1998.

Keys, Barbara J. *Globalizing Sport: National Rivalry and International Community in the 1930s.* Cambridge, MA: Harvard University Press, 2006.

Keys, Barbara. "The Body as a Political Space: Comparing Physical Education under Nazism and Stalinism". *German History* 27/3 (2009), 395-413.

Klages, Ludwig. "Vom Wesen des Rhythmus". In *Sämtliche Werke*, edited by Hans Eggert Schröder and Ernst Frauchiger, 499-551. Bonn: Bouvier-Verlag, 1974.

Korsgaard, Ove. *Kampen om Kroppen: Dansk idræts historie gennem 200 år.* Copenhagen: Gyldendal, 1997.

Krabbe, Wolfgang R. *Gesellschaftsveränderung durch Lebensreform: Strukturmerkmale einer Sozialreformerischen Bewegung im Deutschland der Industrialisierungsperiode.* Göttingen: Vandenhoeck & Ruprecht, 1974.

Krüger, Arnd. "The German Way of Worker Sport". In *The Story of Worker Sport*, edited by Arnd Krüger and James Riordan, 1-25. Champaign, IL: Human Kinetics, 1996.

Krüger, Michael. *Einführung in die Geschichte der Leibeserziehung und des Sports*, vol. 2: *Leibeserziehung im 19. Jahrhundert. Turnen fürs Vaterland.* Schorndorf: Hofmann, 2005.

Krüger, Michael. *Einführung in die Geschichte der Leibeserziehung und des Sports*, vol. 3: *Leibesübungen im 20. Jahrhundert. Sport für alle.* Schorndorf: Hofmann, 2005.

Lindroth, Jan. *Ling – Från storhet till upplösning: Studier i svensk gymnastikhistoria 1800-1950.* Eslöv: Brutus Östlings Symposion, 2004.

Ljunggren, Jens. *Kroppens Bildning: Linggymnastikkens Manlighetsprojekt 1790-1914.* Eslöv: Brutus Östling Symposium, 1999.

Maase, Kasper. "Bewegte Körper, Populäre Kultur – Ästhetische Erfahrungen. Kulturwissenschaftliche Überlegungen". In *Bewegungsraum und Stadtkultur. Sozial- und Kulturwissenschaftliche Perspektiven*, edited by Funke-Wieneke and Gabriele Klein, 31-49. Bielefeld: Transcript, 2008.

Maase, Kasper. "Die Erforschung des Schönen im Alltag. Sechs Thesen". In *Die Schönheiten des Populären*, edited by Kasper Maase, 42-57. Frankfurt a.M.: Campus Verlag, 2008.

Medau, Hinrich. "Die Grundlagen der Ausdrucksgymnastik von Dr. Bode". *Gymnastik* 1/3-4 (1926), 38-41.

Medau, Hinrich and Hermann Baumann. *Deutsche Gymnastik: Lehrweise Medau.* Stuttgart: Union Deutsche Verlagsgesellschaft, 1940.

Möhring, Maren. *Marmorleiber: Körperbildung in der Deutschen Nacktkultur (1890-1930).* Cologne: Böhlau, 2004.

Mosse, George L. *Die Völkische Revolution: Über die Geistigen Wurzeln des Nationalsozialismus.* Weinheim: Beltz Athenäum, 1991.

Mosse, George L. "The Mystical Origins of National Socialism". *Journal of the History of Ideas* 22/1 (1961), 81-96.

Olstad, Finn. *Norsk idretts historie.* vol. 1, Oslo: Aschehoug, 1987.

Paul-Petersen, Ellen. "Betragtninger over Tysk Gymnastikk". *D.K.G. Medlemsblad for Dansk Kvinde-Gymnastikforening* 3/2 (1936), 1-4.

Piper, Ernst. *Alfred Rosenberg: Hitlers Chefideologe.* Munich: Blessing, 2005.

Puschner, Uwe. "18. Oktober 1813: 'Möchten die Deutschen nur Alle und Immer Dieses Tages Gedenken!' – die Leipziger Völkerschlacht". In *Erinnerungstage: Wendepunkte der Geschichte von der Antike bis zur Gegenwart*, edited by Etienne François and Uwe Puschner, 145-162. Munich: C.H. Beck, 2010.

Reinhart, Kai and Michael Krüger. "Funktionen des Sports im modernen Staat und in der modernen Diktatur". *Historical Social Research* 32/1 (2007), 43-77.

Riordan, James. "The Worker Sports Movement". In *The International Politics of Sport in the Twentieth Century*, edited by James Riordan and Arnd Krüger, 105-116. London: E&FN Spon, 1999.

Rohkrämer, Thomas. *Eine Andere Moderne? Zivilisationskritik, Natur und Technik in Deutschland 1880-1933.* Paderborn: Ferdinand Schöningh, 1999.

Rosenberg, Alfred. *Der Mythus des 20. Jahrhunderts: Eine Wertung der Seelisch-Geistigen Gestaltenkämpfe Unserer Zeit.* Munich: Hoheneichen-Verlag, 1933.

Schmitz, Walter and Uwe Schneider. "Völkische Semantik bei den 'Münchner Kosmikern' und im George-Kreis". In *Handbuch zur "Völkischen Bewegung" 1871-1918*, edited by Uwe Puschner and Walter Schmitz, 711-746. Munich: Saur, 1999.

Schürmann, Volker. "Reflexion und Wiederholung. Mit einem Ausblick auf 'Rhythmus'". In *Körperliche Erkenntnis: Formen Reflexiver Erfahrung*, edited by Franz Bockrath, Bernhard Boschert and Elk Franke, 53-72. Bielefeld: Transcript, 2008.

Schürmann, Volker. "Logik des Ausdrucks". In *Wissenskultur Tanz: Historische und Zeitgenössische Vermittlungsakte zwischen Praktiken und Diskursen*, edited by Gernot Böhme and Sabine Huschka, 107-116. Bielefeld: Transcript, 2009.

Skovgaard, Thomas. "Den gode, den smukke og den virkelig sunde. En historie om sundhed, idræt og skole fra det moderne Danmark". In *Folkets sundhed eller lykke? En Antologi om humanistisk Sundheds- og Idrætsforskning*, edited by Jørn Hansen, 32-61. Odense: Odense Universitetsforlag, 2001.

Söhrmann, Adolf. "Rudolf Bode, Ein Lebensbild". *Rhythmus. Monatsschrift für deutsche Kultur* 14/10 (1936), 258-263.

Stern, Fritz Richard. *The Politics of Cultural Despair: A Study in the Rise of the Germanic Ideology.* New York: Doubleday, 1965.

Thulin, J. "Anmälan". *Fysisk Fostran och Vetenskapen* 1/1 (1932), 2.

Tönnies, Ferdinand. *Gemeinschaft und Gesellschaft: Grundbegriffe der Reinen Soziologie.* Berlin: Curtius, 1912.

Toepfer, Karl Eric. *Empire of Ecstasy: Nudity and Movement in German Body Culture, 1910-1935.* Berkeley: University of California Press, 1997.

Trangbæk, Else, Jørn Hansen and Nils Kayser Nielsen. "Innledning". In *Dansk Idrætsliv*, edited by Else Trangbæk, Jørn Hansen and Nils Kayser Nielsen, Brøndby: Danmarks Idræts-Forbund, 1996.

Ueberhorst, Horst. "Die Rezeption der Schwedischen Gymnastik in Preußen und der Barrenstreit". *Congress Report*, 8th International Congress for the History of Sport and Physical Education, 57-63. Uppsala: 1979.

Völckers, Hortensia. "Preface". In *Knowledge in Motion: Perspectives of Artistic and Scientific Research in Dance*, edited by Sabine Gehm, Pirkko Husemann and Katharina von Wilcke, 9-13. Bielefeld: Transcript, 2007.

Wedemeyer-Kolwe, Bernd. *"Der Neue Mensch." Körperkultur im Kaiserreich und in der Weimarer Republik.* Würzburg: Königshausen & Neumann, 2004.

Wesp, Gabriela. *Frisch. Fromm. Fröhlich. Frau. Frauen und Sport zur Zeit der Weimarer Republik.* Königsstein: Ulrike Helmer Verlag, 1998.

Völkische Weltanschauung on the Back Benches – The Deutschvölkische Freiheitspartei and the Reichstag of the Weimar Republic[*]

Stefanie Schrader

During the years of the Weimar Republic, the German public witnessed the coming and going of a hardly countable number of small political parties, in particular right-wing political parties, which aspired to enter the Reichstag and other influential positions. Nevertheless, when it comes to accounts of Weimar Germany's political parties the focus is often rather quickly, probably even too rashly, diverted to the NSDAP, the National Socialist German Workers' Party, as the only radical party on the far right that succeeded in becoming a mass movement with a substantial faction in the Reichstag by 1930. Evidently, there are obvious reasons for reviewing the rise of the National Socialists as a political party, which tried to play the parliamentary game during the late 1920s and succeeded in doing so with fatal consequences for parliamentarian culture even before 1933. But there are also good reasons for an inquiry into the ideological background and political agenda of neighbouring, if not rivalling groups such as the German *Völkisch* Freedom Party (*Deutschvölkische Freiheitspartei*, DVFP).[1]

---

* This paper was originally given at the *International Conference on English and German Nationalist and Anti-Semitic Discourse (1871-1945)* at Queen Mary, University of London, November 10-11, 2010.

1 Little in-depth research has been done on the DVFP itself, although the party figures in a number of accounts on the *völkisch* movement or the rising National Socialist Party, most recently Stefan Breuer, *Die Völkischen in Deutschland. Kaiserreich und Weimarer Republik* (Darmstadt: Wissenschaftliche Buchgesellschaft, 2008); Uwe Puschner, "Strukturmerkmale der völkischen Bewegung (1900-1945)", in *Das konservative Intellektuellenmilieu in Deutschland, seine Presse und seine Netzwerke (1890-1960)*, eds. Michel Grunewald and Uwe Puschner (Bern et al.: Peter Lang, 2003), 445-468. See furthermore Uwe Puschner, *Die völkische Bewegung im wilhelminischen Kaiserreich. Sprache – Rasse – Religion* (Darmstadt: Wissenschaftliche Buchgesellschaft, 2001); Uwe Lohalm, *Völkischer Radikalismus. Die Geschichte des Deutschvölkischen Schutz- und Trutzbundes 1919-1923* (Hamburg: Leibniz, 1970); George L. Mosse, *The Crisis of German Ideology. Intellectual Origins of the Third Reich* (New York: Grosset & Dunlap, 1964); Martin Döring, *Parlamentarischer Arm der Bewegung. Die Nationalsozialisten im Reichstag der Weimarer Republik* (Düsseldorf: Droste, 2001); Jan Striesow, *Die Deutschnationale Volkspartei und die Völkisch-Radikalen 1918-1922*, 2 vols. (Frankfurt a.M.: Haag & Herchen, 1981); Reinhard Figge, *Die Opposition der NSDAP im Reichstag* (Cologne: Wasmund, 1963); Bernd Kruppa, *Rechtsradikalismus in Berlin 1918-1928* (Berlin: Overall, 1988). The only book on the party's history, Reimer Wulff, *Die Deutschvölkische Freiheitspartei 1922-1928* (Marburg: author's private publishing, 1968), suffers severely from the author's restricted access to source material held by the Central Archive of the German Democratic Republic at Potsdam. An article in an East German handbook on political parties, Manfred Weißbecker, "Deutschvölkische Freiheitspartei 1922-1933", in *Lexikon der Parteiengeschichte. Die bürgerlichen und kleinbürgerlichen Parteien und Verbände*

The author of a highly critical three-volume handbook on the *völkisch* movement, published between 1929 and 1931, remembered the DVFP in direct comparison with the National Socialists as having been the more influential party in parliament only a couple of years ago.[2] Already the name, *Deutschvölkische Freiheitspartei,* is difficult to grasp. It is almost impossible to translate without inaccurately reducing the meaning of the adjective *völkisch* to national or nationalistic, racial or racist, ethnic, folkish or anti-Semitic. Where the party is mentioned in a small number of anglophone publications for instance of the 1960s, it usually figures as "German Racist Freedom Party"[3] or "German Volkish Freedom Party".[4] More recent authors prefer to leave the term *völkisch* untranslated.[5] But the lack of conceptual clarity is far more that just a problem of translation into other languages.[6] First and foremost, the inflationary contemporary use of the adjective and the absence of a precise definition of what the concept *völkisch* actually was supposed to mean are characteristic features of the German discourse about the term in the 1920s. The distinctly heterogeneous character of the *völkisch* movement on the threshold between the German Empire and the Weimar Republic and its ideological complexity are a confusing, if not elusive phenomenon. The DVFP was thus just one of many groups, which labelled themselves *völkisch*. The unique aspect of this particular *völkisch* organisation was its being the first *völkisch* political party in the Reichstag of the Weimar Republic.[7]

The DVFP was established in December 1922 by three former members of the Reichstag group of the German National People's Party (*Deutschnationale Volkspartei,* DNVP), who split after months of internal conflict regarding the assassination of

---

in Deutschland (1789-1945), vol. 2, ed. Dieter Fricke (Leipzig: Bibliogr. Institut, 1984), 550-558, is laden with communist phraseology. Merely the party's struggle with the authorities of the Weimar Republic is discussed thoroughly by Bernhard Sauer, "Die Deutschvölkische Freiheitspartei und der Fall Grütte", *Geschichte und Gegenwart. Jahrbuch des Landesarchivs Berlin* (1994), 179-203.

2 Anonymous, *Deutschvölkischer Katechismus*, vol. 2: *Völkische Organisationen, Parteien, Vereine, Verbände, Orden* (Leipzig: Oldenburg, 1931), 9, 16.

3 Lewis Hertzman, *DNVP. Right-wing Opposition in the Weimar Republic, 1918-1924* (Lincoln: University of Nebraska Press, 1963).

4 Mosse, *Crisis of German Ideology*.

5 Uwe Puschner, "'One People, One Reich, One God'. The Völkische Weltanschauung and Movement", *Bulletin of the German Historical Institute*, 24/1 (2002), 5-28.

6 For a discussion of the concept in current historical research, see Uwe Puschner, "Völkisch. Plädoyer für einen engen Begriff", in *"Die Erziehung zum deutschen Menschen" – Völkische und nationalkonservative Erwachsenenbildung in der Weimarer Republik*, eds. Paul Ciupke et al. (Essen: Klartext, 2007), 53-66.

7 The German Empire saw several anti-Semitic, though not essentially *völkisch* parties from the late 1870s. The German *Völkisch* Party *(Deutschvölkische Partei)*, founded in 1914, was a merger of two of these, the German Social Party (*Deutschsoziale Partei)* and the German Reform Party *(Deutsche Reformpartei)*. It constituted a first attempt at *völkisch* party politics but was already dissolved in 1918 and had no lasting impact. See Dieter Fricke, "Deutschvölkische Partei 1914-1918", in *Lexikon der Parteiengeschichte*, vol. 2, 59ff.; Puschner, *Die völkische Bewegung im wilhelminischen Kaiserreich*, 53.

the Minister for Foreign Affairs, Walther Rathenau, who as a political liberal with a Jewish family background had been the target of anti-Semitic propaganda for a long time.[8] The formative party meeting was joined by roughly 150 supporters most of which had been or still were members of radical nationalist or *völkisch* organisations such as the Pan-German League *(Alldeutscher Verband)* or the banned German-*Völkisch* Protection and Defence League *(Deutschvölkischer Schutz- und Trutzbund)*. The DVFP actually profited from the ban and was able to attract a substantial number of the league's members.[9] The federal state of Mecklenburg, where the newly proclaimed party leader Albrecht von Graefe (1868-1933)[10] held his constituency, and Prussia, particularly the Berlin-Brandenburg area, where the constituency of the party's second in charge Reinhold Wulle (1882-1950)[11] was situated, became the centres of propaganda activity and election campaigning. Nevertheless, branches were established relatively quickly in other North German states, for in-

8 On the withdrawal of *völkisch* party members and MPs from the DNVP in 1922, see Striesow, *Die Deutschnationale Volkspartei*, vol. 1, 341ff.

9 See Uwe Lohalm, *Völkischer Radikalismus*. The founding members of the DVFP were named on the party's initial pamphlet, see "Gründungsaufruf der Deutschvölkischen Freiheitspartei", Bundesarchiv Berlin (BA Berlin), R 1507/285, fol. 44.

10 Albrecht von Graefe, a retired cavalry major and son of a renowned ophthalmologist, owned an estate in Goldebee, Mecklenburg, were he also maintained a Reichstag constituency since 1912. Having volunteered for military service once again during the First World War, he returned to his political career immediately afterwards. In December 1922 Graefe was one of the co-founders of the DVFP. He successfully led the party through the national elections of 1924, negotiated the temporary strategic alliance with the National Socialists and chaired the *völkisch* faction in the Reichstag until the election in May 1928, when the party lost all electoral mandates. Graefe, who formerly had been a close ally of Erich Ludendorff, consequently withdrew from politics and was succeeded by Reinhold Wulle as chairman of the DVFP. A contemporary "Who is Who" of the *völkisch* movement described him in 1925 as one of the most influential men within the *völkisch* movement. See Heinz Eisgruber, *Völkische und Deutschnationale Führer. 100 Heldenbilder* (Leipzig: Oldenburg, 1925), 27. For further biographical details, see Stefanie Schrader, "Albrecht von Graefe", in *Handbuch des Antisemitismus. Judenfeindschaft in Geschichte und Gegenwart*, vol. 2/1: *Personen*, ed. Wolfgang Benz (Berlin: de Gruyter, 2009), 304-306.

11 Reinhold Wulle was the DVFP's most prolific publicist. The son of a Lutheran Parson, he had briefly studied theology, literature and history before he sought a career in journalism. He had already worked as an editor of several major right-wing newspapers, including the *Deutsche Zeitung*, which was financed by the Pan-German League, when he was elected into the Reichstag in 1920. Together with Graefe, he left the nationalist faction of the DNVP in December 1922 and founded the DVFP. Until 1928 Wulle remained second in charge and was responsible for the party's daily newspaper *Das Deutsche Tageblatt* and numerous other official publications. In the December 1924 election he succeeded to keep his seat in the Reichstag and also gained a seat in the Prussian Landtag. In accordance with Graefe and the party's board, he opted for the Prussian state parliament where he led the *völkisch* group until 1928. After the DVFP's defeat in 1928 and Graefe's resignation, Wulle took up the party's leadership and held this post while the DVFP dwindled into insignificance and was finally banned by the National Socialists in 1933. For further biographical details, see Stefanie Schrader, "Reinhold Wulle", in *Handbuch des Antisemitismus. Judenfeindschaft in Geschichte und Gegenwart*, vol. 2/2: *Personen*, ed. Wolfgang Benz (Berlin: de Gruyter, 2009), 892-893.

stance in Saxony, were the DVFP had a prominent supporter in the veteran anti-Semitic writer and publisher Theodor Fritsch, as well as in Thuringia, where the anti-Semitic novelist Artur Dinter was temporarily working for the party.

But establishing a political party and intending to run for elections posed a notable problem for older *völkisch* circles, since the various branches of the pre-World War One *völkisch* movement did not consider themselves as party politicians in the first place.[12] The self-perception was more that of a cultural, educational or religious movement. Even in the early 1920s many adherents of the *völkisch* movement still rejected a political party as a form of organisation and were unwilling to accept that the only way to change things in a parliamentary democracy was to participate in parliament. Hence, it is hardly surprising that the DVFP, when venturing to one of their first election campaigns for the state parliament of Mecklenburg in February 1924, used the catch phrase: "Into parliament in order to fight the parliamentary system!"[13]

Making sure that broader *völkisch* circles were going to accept and consequently vote for a *völkisch* party was crucial. Reinhold Wulle emphasised that the foundation of a party was a sheer necessity, a kind of last resort for the *völkisch* movement,[14] since a number of other organisations which were not appearing as political parties had witnessed restrictions or even complete bans by the authorities. Even Theodor Fritsch who, in earlier years, had denounced democratic parliaments as the "most disgusting inheritance of the French Revolution", and who still had reservations concerning the question whether adherents of the *völkisch* movement should run a political party, admitted that under the given circumstances "one has to bow to necessity and get on with a party".[15] The times of Adolf Stoecker were recalled, when the Protestant Reverend to the Prussian court established an anti-Semitic party, which gained seats in the imperial Reichstag in the 1880s and 1890s. So, in the end, pragmatic justifications outweighed ideological scruples within the DVFP.[16]

---

12 For the rejection of party politics in the pre-war *völkisch* movement, see Puschner, *Die völkische Bewegung im wilhelminischen Kaiserreich*, 52, 271. Compare also Theodor Fritsch, who in later years ran for Reichstag elections, but who was regularly uttering harsh criticism concerning parliamentarianism and political parties. Theodor Fritsch, "Die Zukunft des Reichstages und die politischen Parteien", in *Deutschlands Wiedergeburt durch Blut und Eisen*, ed. Richard Ungewitter (Stuttgart: Ungewitter, 1918), 180-186.

13 Rallying cry for the state elections in Mecklenburg-Schwerin in February 1924, published in the local *völkisch* newspaper, which was supported by Albrecht von Graefe, the *Mecklenburger Warte*, January 10, 1924, BA Berlin, R 1507/288, fol. 190.

14 *Kampfschriften der Deutschvölkischen Freiheitspartei* 2 (1923), 3.

15 R. S. [Rodrich Stoltheim, pseud. of Theodor Fritsch], "Die neue Partei", *Hammer* 493-494/22 (1923), 8.

16 One of the major arguments in this context was the advantage of jurisdictional immunity which any member of parliament would benefit from. Public statements that were targeting the democratic-republican political order of Germany could be reported to the police and affect surveillance and legal proceedings, finally even the ban of an organisation. *Völkisch* MP and activist Jürgen von Ramin, a distant relative of Otto von Bismarck, in later years even admitted during a speech in parliament that immunity had initially been his principal motive

In the run-up to the national elections in May 1924, the DVFP's officials realised that the party needed a strategic partner in the south of the country, where it hardly had any local branches. As early as in 1923, Albrecht von Graefe had travelled to Munich in order to discuss the possibility of an alliance with representatives of the NSDAP, including Hitler. Hitler's reaction was apparently reluctant, and there are passages in *Mein Kampf* which explain this reluctance as the result of a deep mistrust with regard to adherents of the pre-World War One *völkisch* movement. To him they appeared as a rather passive and unsuccessful bunch of distinguished gentlemen, who, in spite of years or in some cases even decades of promoting *völkisch* ideas, had had no effect.[17] But other leading National Socialists were rather in favour of the idea of registering a joint list for the next national elections, especially since the NSDAP was still banned and had to rely on replacement organisations. Besides, in February 1924 the DVFP proved anything but unsuccessful: In the state elections in Mecklenburg the party gained 19.3 per cent of the votes cast and became the second largest faction in the Mecklenburg Landtag. In the end, Albrecht von Graefe seemed to have convinced at least parts of the struggling National Socialists to temporarily join forces. The list, which was registered by the DVFP with National Socialist candidates as the junior partners for the national elections on 4 May 1924, received 6.5 per cent. This may seem little, but considering the circumstances, it was indeed a success, since these votes resulted in 32 seats, most of which went to the DVFP and only about a third to their National Socialist allies.[18] Party leaders Albrecht von Graefe and Reinhold Wulle were able to keep their constituencies and Graefe, as the longest serving MP of the group, was immediately appointed parliamentary chairman. Newcomers in included the above-mentioned Theodor Fritsch, the well known publicist and journal editor Ernst Graf zu Reventlow and Wilhelm Kube, a successful organiser of youth groups on the part of the DVFP, as well as Wilhelm Frick, Gottfried Feder and Ernst Röhm on the part of the NSDAP and Erich Ludendorff as an independent candidate.

The reluctance towards creating a new organisation in the shape of a political party was followed by an unwillingness to publish a party programme. Although the DVFP existed formally for a full decade, it never issued a written programme. To deliberately avoid drafting a party programme was again almost a programmatic feature. This party appeared as heterogeneous as the *völkisch* movement in general. Written programmes were considered as a feature of parliamentary democratic parties, which they put down as conventional. Graefe, while campaigning in Mecklenburg in January 1924, wrote in one of the newspapers associated with the party, that the DVFP decided to issue "guidelines and aims" instead of a programme, since any programme could be nothing but a cage to the *völkisch* movement. He in-

to run in the Reichstag election. See *Verhandlungen des Reichstags. III. Wahlperiode. Stenographische Berichte*, vol. 391 (Berlin: Verlag der Reichsdruckerei, 1927), 8609.

17 He contemptuously called long-standing *völkisch* activists "pseudo-*völkisch*" *(Scheinvölkische)*. Adolf Hitler, *Mein Kampf*, vol. 2: *Die nationalsozialistische Bewegung* (Munich: Eher, 1927), 102.

18 For an overview of Reichstag elections 1919-1933, see Ursula Büttner, *Weimar. Die überforderte Republik 1918-1933* (Stuttgart: Klett-Cotta, 2008), 802-803.

sisted that, concerning political and economic issues, nothing but "flexible guidelines" would serve the purpose of a *völkisch* party.[19] Reventlow went in the same direction when he wrote that an "organised freedom movement" such as the DVFP should always have "fixed aims" but would be well advised to avoid a "firm position". He feared that otherwise its character might no longer be any different from the other parties in parliament, and to be different from what Wulle labelled as the "Jewish-democratic system" was what they wanted.[20] But in the end, this avoidance of a central programmatic text could hardly conceal that an evident lack of unity and conclusiveness was one of the party's weakest points. They were anxious to become a political representation of all branches of the *völkisch* movement and thus were inevitably unable to reach a feasible consensus. They defined politics as a permanent fight which they wanted to encounter with both parliamentary and propaganda means. That they knew much more precisely what they were targeting instead of supporting, transpired already in one of the party's first publications in 1923:

> Free from the dictate of Versailles!
> Free from fruitless parliamentarianism!
> Free from the domination of the Jews and from stock-market capitalism!
> Free from the exploitation of labour!
> Free from Marxism and bolshevism, from class struggle and caste spirit![21]

It seems rather symptomatic that, when given the chance to enter a government coalition in Mecklenburg or Thuringia in spring 1924, the party leaders prevented it. Wulle wrote that *völkisch* members of any parliament would never become the junior partners in a national-conservative coalition for the price of watering down *völkisch* aims. Taking up the role of a persevering opposition in the parliaments of the Weimar Republic was apparently not the second best thing; it was the actual aim of the DVFP. Wulle commented that those "who think it to be awkward, are thinking in parliamentary and not in *völkisch* terms".[22]

The party leaders and MPs were certainly no political beginners when the DVFP was founded. It seems all the more striking that their political thought can be characterised as contradictory, partly naïve and far from being a self-contained system.

---

19 *Mecklenburger Warte*, January 19 and 30, 1924, as cited by *Deutschvölkischer Katechismus*, vol. 2, 17.

20 E. R. [Reventlow], "Der Weg zum völkischen Zukunftsstaat", *Mecklenburger Warte*, January 30, 1924, BA Berlin, R 1507/288, fol. 6; Reinhold Wulle, "Freiheitspartei und Reichstagswahlen! Programmatische Antworten", *Das Deutsche Tageblatt*, March 19, 1924, BA Berlin, R 8048/228, fol. 152.

21 "Gründungsaufruf der Deutschvölkischen Freiheitspartei", BA Berlin, R 1507/285, fol. 44r. The slogan remained the DVFP's political mantra and was published again e.g. in *Kampfschriften der Deutschvölkischen Freiheitspartei* 1 (1923), 3, or during the election campaign in spring 1924 in *Deutsches Tageblatt*, April 3, 1924, BA Berlin, R 8048/228, fol. 159.

22 Wulle, "Freiheitspartei und Reichstagswahlen!", BA Berlin, R 8048/228, fol. 152.

A small number of examples concerning the possible constitutional, economic and geographical shape of a future Germany may suffice to point this out.

The DVFP unanimously demanded the abolishment of the parliamentary republic which they denounced as "Jewish" and the creation of a *völkisch* German state instead. But the opinion leaders within the party offered different answers concerning the question of a prospective constitution for a *völkisch* Germany. Reventlow avoided the question during the election campaigns in 1924, stating that it was not yet the right time to discuss the structure of a new state and that all *völkisch* followers should focus on what he called the "liberation of the people from the dominance of the Jews and stock-market capital, Marxist class-struggle [...] and the deception of present-day parliamentarianism".[23] He did not go into any further details than stating that a "*völkisch* dictatorship" or even "*völkisch*-social dictatorship" might possibly be an appropriate temporary solution. First of all, he explained, there was a need for a "*völkisch* renewal" on all political, economic and cultural levels, thus again postponing the desired state to later discussion.[24] On the other, more conservative wing, party leader Graefe and even more so Wulle appeared to have been in favour of the restitution of a monarchy. Graefe carefully addressed the subject as early as in 1923 but conceded that any future German monarchy could be nothing but an entirely new one with a new *völkisch* monarch.[25]

After the social-revolutionary wing represented by Reventlow had left the party and the Reichstag parliamentary group in February 1927, claims for a *völkisch* monarchy surfaced less reluctantly than before. The "idea of a Germanic Empire or Kingdom" was taken up again by Wulle, who was an outspoken admirer of the former Prussian royal family and who referred quite often to Frederick the Great and also to Bismarck, both of whom he thought to have been on the right path to unite all Germans.[26] In spring 1927, at the first party congregation after the three defenders of a more national-social approach, Reventlow, Kube and Franz Stöhr, a spokesman of a *völkisch* trade union, had left the dwindling *völkisch* group in the Reichstag in order to join the now independent National Socialist group, Graefe gave a speech which was an open plea for what he described as the "social German monarchic idea of the constructive era of Frederick and Bismarck" compared to the "unsocial republic of the current decadent era". His notion of monarchy was that of a "people's empire" *(Volkskaisertum)*.[27] However, not even the remaining

23 E. R., "Der Weg zum völkischen Zukunftsstaat", BA Berlin, R 1507/288, fol. 6.

24 *Das Deutsche Tageblatt*, April 3, 1924, BA Berlin, R 8048/228, fol. 159.

25 *Der Reichswart*, January 27, 1923.

26 Report on the 1928 annual party congress, *Mecklenburger Warte*, September 18, 1928, BA Berlin, R 8048/229, fol. 76. The apotheosis of Prussian political and cultural heritage appears more frequently in later years, i.e. in *Deutsche Nachrichten*, a weekly paper edited by Wulle, March 9 and 30, 1930, BA Berlin, R 1501/126148, fol. 6 and 8.

27 Albrecht von Graefe, "Monarchie oder Republik?", *Das Deutsche Tageblatt*, February 20, 1927, BA Berlin, R 8048/229, fol. 51. Wulle gave a slightly more detailed account of *völkisch* monarchy, outlining the Prussian state as a German success story in his contribution to a party congregation which he published as *Der Weg zum völkischen Staat. Das Dritte Reich* (Berlin: Puhlmann, 1928). However, the idea of a "Germanic people's empire" had been discussed by

conservative wing conclusively tackled the issue of the origin and qualities of a potential *völkisch* monarchy.

Concerning the inner order of a future *völkisch* state, the DVFP favoured a decentralised administration of supposed "German tribes". The concept of tribes was far from marginal to the thought of the *völkisch* party members. They emphasised the existence of tribes prior to modern states and territories. Kube for example discussed the case of Bavaria at a party congregation in 1925. To him the Kingdom of Bavaria was an unnatural construction enforced by Napoleon and a prime example for the violation of ancient tribal rights, since Franconians and Swabians were incorporated into the Bavarian monarchy without having a say in this matter. Kube marked Prussia as the positive counterpart, since Prussia was structured by provinces with provincial representations and cultural autonomy, which, in his opinion, were a tribute to "the historic necessities of the tribes".[28] This hints at the fact that in *völkisch* thought, representative bodies were not entirely rejected as long as they were organised not democratically but according to profession, reputation and racial categories. Every German was thought to have a natural place in what the party named the "*völkisch* organism" with a "healthy officialdom" at the top.[29] It is an organic, if not biological understanding of state and society. Concerning the legal system, the DVFP rejected influences of Roman Law which was denounced as allegedly "Jewish" and demanded a reversion to Germanic legal traditions.[30] A true *völkisch* legal system was to be purged of all elements marked as ostensibly foreign or unnatural. Again, the thoughts did not go much further than this. Apart from the law of inheritance, the party did not elaborate on individual branches of the legal system.

The *völkisch* politicians offered even more vague and nebulous views concerning the economy. As much as they avoided elaborating on the question of a *völkisch*

---

the *völkisch* movement previously, i.e. by the genealogist Bernhard Koerner, who offered a racial interpretation of the concept. On Koerner, see Alexandra Gerstner, *Neuer Adel. Aristokratische Elitekonzeptionen zwischen Jahrhundertwende und Nationalsozialismus* (Darmstadt: Wissenschaftliche Buchgesellschaft, 2008), 302ff. Against the background of the *völkisch* aristocratic discourse outside the party, the absence of any mentioning of "racial aristocracy" *(Rassenadel)* in the DVFP's thought on monarchy seems odd.

28 *Deutsche Zeitung*, September 29, 1925, BA Berlin, R 1507/289, fol. 157. Reinhold Wulle considered a "union of German tribes" as a means for "overcoming the nation state". See Wulle, *Der Weg zum völkischen Staat*, 8ff. For an account of the *völkisch* idea of tribes as a modern continuation of ancient tribes, see Willi Oberkrome, "Stamm und Landschaft. Heimatlicher Tribalismus und die Projektion einer völkischen Neuordnung Deutschlands 1920-1950", in *Ordnungen in der Krise. Zur politischen Kulturgeschichte Deutschlands 1900-1933*, ed. Wolfgang Hardtwig (Munich: Oldenbourg, 2007), 69ff.

29 "Gründungsaufruf der Deutschvölkischen Freiheitspartei", BA Berlin, R 1507/285, fol. 44; similarly in the Supplement of the *Mecklenburger Warte*, January 30, 1924, BA Berlin, R 1507/288, fol. 6.

30 "Was heißt 'Deutschvölkisch'?", *Das Deutsche Tageblatt*, July 28, 1923, BA Berlin, R 43 I/2679, fol. 24; "Gründungsaufruf der Deutschvölkischen Freiheitspartei", BA Berlin, R 1507/285, fol. 44; Supplement of the *Mecklenburger Warte*, January 30, 1924, BA Berlin, R 1507/288, fol. 6.

constitution, they avoided precise ideas about an economic order for a future *völkisch* state. Bitter criticism of "mammonist and materialist thinking" was common, and quite often anti-capitalist statements were amended by hopes for a full recovery of the old economic middle classes and a romantic perception of the agrarian sector, which the DVFP once more wanted to see as the leading sector of the German economy.[31] In the highly industrialised 1920s this was of course entirely naïve and eclipsed even national-romantic visions of a future Germany.

Weimar's early *völkisch* political party neither acknowledged the German borders of 1919, nor the borders of the former German Empire, hence their aggressive and expansionist approach to foreign politics, which was accompanied by an infinite overestimation of Germany's own military capabilities. Reichstag MP Wilhelm Henning reflected in an address given in 1923 at one of the party's "patriotic evenings" on the French occupation of the Ruhr region and parts of the Rhineland. He considered the possibility of new wars of liberation such as the Napoleonic Wars, or even a modern Battle of the Teutoburg Forest, as a means not just to strip Germany of the French occupation but of all "Roman" influences.[32] That is where the notion of tribes comes back in. "Great Germany", sometimes even described by the *Völkisch* as "Great Germanic Country" *(Großgermanenland)*, was outlined as a huge European territory which was supposed to comprise all regions where people lived whose linguistic and cultural background was German, including Austria, Switzerland, parts of Northern Italy and France, of Belgium and the Netherlands, of Poland, Lithuania and various other Eastern European countries. The claims for a "Greater Germany" with European dimensions were accompanied by the idea of what the party's main newspaper called a "healthy settlement policy [...] according to social, racial and professional aspects".[33]

---

31 "Gründungsaufruf der Deutschvölkischen Freiheitspartei", BA Berlin, R 1507/285, fol. 44v; "Kampfschriften der Deutschvölkischen Freiheitspartei" 2 (1923), 2; similar wording in personal publications by the party leaders, e.g. Theodor Fritsch, "Völkisch-soziale Welt-Anschauung", *Hammer* 525/23 (1924), 165-169.

32 The Social Democratic newspaper *Vorwärts* paraphrased Henning's address, and commented sneeringly that little would be left of Germany if there should ever be a battle as Henning envisioned. *Vorwärts*, March 9, 1923, BA Berlin, R 1507/285, fol. 169. The Battle of the Teutoburg Forest in 9 AD was a substantial defeat of the Roman army against an alliance of Germanic tribes under the command of Arminius, chieftain of the Cherusci. Arminius, dubbed in German as "Hermann der Cherusker", became a popular myth as well as the battle itself. In the 1920s right-wing circles often paralleled the occupation of the Ruhr industrial area by French troops with the Roman invasion of Germanic tribal territories. By that time the *völkisch* movement had adopted the adjective "Roman" as a synonym for undesired international influence in Germany.

33 E. R. [Reventlow], "Der Weg zum völkischen Zukunftsstaat", BA Berlin, R 1507/288, fol. 6; *Das Deutsche Tageblatt*, September 13, 1927, Geheimes Staatsarchiv Preußischer Kulturbesitz (GStA), I. HA Rep. 84a, no. 55214, fol. 4. Concerning the geographic dimension of a "Greater Germany", the DVFP did not elaborate on assumed cultural and racial affinities with Scandinavia, although the idea of a joint Nordic heritage occasionally figured in *völkisch* racial thought.

If there was one ultimate ideological feature which embraced all others and which all leading representatives of the DVFP agreed on, than it was radical anti-Semitism in connection with ludicrous conspiracy theories such as the assumption of a dictatorial "Jewish high finance".[34] Drawing heavily on concepts such as tribe and race, "people's community" *(Volksgemeinschaft)* or even "community of blood" *(Blutsgemeinschaft)*[35] implied the dissociation from, and discrimination of, all parts of society that were perceived as non-German. This applied primarily to German Jews. In a programmatic article written shortly before the national elections in May 1924, Wulle drew on the old idea of an allegedly natural antagonism between Jews and Germans. He proclaimed the *völkisch* project of drastic legal sanctions against Jews, who he labelled not just as foreigners but as "racial foreigners" (*Fremdstämmige* or *Fremdvölkische*). The so-called "Jewish question" and the "racial question", Wulle wrote on behalf of the party, are "the core of our entire life" and other leading *völkisch* representatives such as Fritsch or Reventlow concurred with him.[36] According to Wulle, the DVFP intended to introduce special legislation for Jews (or rather against Jews). Those Jews who migrated to Germany during or after the First World War were to be expelled. The remaining Jews would have been stripped of all civil rights, including particularly the right to own property. Adding to this, the *völkisch* plan would also have introduced wide-ranging professional restrictions in order to prevent Jews from working as civil servants, members of parliament, judges, teachers, professors, theatre managers, publishers or journalists.[37] Fritsch even went a step further than Wulle by claiming the "complete elimination *[Ausscheidung]* of Jews from the life of the German people".[38] All of this, of course, is vocabulary which could have been taken from a National Socialist publication as well, and the anti-Semitic and racist consensus was no doubt crucial for the parliamentary mar-

34 This combined anti-Semitic and anti-capitalist thinking is omnipresent in virtually all party papers, e.g. Reinhold Wulle, "Freiheitspartei und Reichstagswahlen!", BA Berlin, R 8048/228, fol. 152; *Das Deutsche Tageblatt*, September 13, 1927, GStA, I. HA Rep. 84a, no. 55214, fol. 4; "Ziele der deutschvölkischen Freiheitsbewegung", in *Membership book of the Deutschvölkische Freiheitsbewegung of 1928*, Deutsches Historisches Museum (DHM)/ Hausarchiv, Do 65/2366, 17.

35 *Das Deutsche Tageblatt*, February 20, 1927, BA Berlin, 8048/229, fol. 51.

36 Reinhold Wulle's article "Freiheitspartei und Reichstagswahlen! Programmatische Antworten", *Deutsches Tageblatt*, March 19, 1924, BA Berlin, R 8048/228, fol. 152; correspondingly already in "Gründungsaufruf der Deutschvölkischen Freiheitspartei", BA Berlin, R 1507/285, fol. 44. See furthermore Fritsch's programmatic contribution "Was wollen die Völkischen?", *Hammer* 538/23 (1924), 425ff., and Reventlow's article "Der Weg zum völkischen Zukunftsstaat", in Supplement of *Mecklenburger Warte*, January 30, 1924, BA Berlin, R 1507/288, fol. 6.

37 *Das Deutsche Tageblatt*, March 19, 1924, BA Berlin, R 8048/228, fol. 152; also "Gründungsaufruf der Deutschvölkischen Freiheitspartei", BA Berlin, R 1507/285, fol. 44.

38 "Was wollen die Völkischen?", *Hammer* 538/23 (1924), 425-429. Fritsch's precautious wording and the use of "Ausscheidung", which has different meanings, was thus open to interpretation. Since the various branches of the *völkisch* movement did not necessarily share the same views on what should become of German Jews, Fritsch left it to his readers to decide whether he understood "Ausscheidung" as geographical expulsion or physical extermination.

riage of convenience of the *Völkisch* and the National Socialists between 1924 and 1927.

A marriage of convenience it certainly was, since neither the *völkisch* representatives nor the National Socialists thought highly of the other. A joint party congress which took place in Weimar in August 1924 on the fifth anniversary of the constitution, unanimously loathed by all branches of the *völkisch* movement, did not result in any improvement concerning the alliance between the *völkisch* DVFP and the National Socialist NSDAP apart from symbolic gestures. An attempt to found an entirely new party with a *völkisch* as well as National Socialist background, initiated with some delay in October 1924, was short-lived and without substantial results.[39] It did not escape the voters' attention that NSDAP and DVFP had very little to say to each other. The bill arrived only a couple of weeks later, when the Reichstag was prematurely dissolved and new elections were scheduled for December 1924. Both parties once more registered a joint list of candidates, but they received a mere 3 per cent of the vote which meant the loss of more than half of the seats in parliament.[40] While the outcome of the elections led the National Socialists to question the alliance and especially to question the dominance of the DVFP in general, the lifting of the ban on the NSDAP and its official reestablishment in February 1925 virtually marked the beginning of the end of the joint Reichstag faction. Fourteen seats were too few to be granted full parliamentary rights, hence there was from now on very little room for manoeuvre until the end of their second and final term in the Reichstag in May 1928. Besides, the reestablishment of the Munich-based NSDAP caused the Berlin-based DVFP to adjust their organisational structure, which led above all to it being renamed *Deutschvölkische Freiheits*bewegung, thus having the favoured concept of "movement" replace "party", although it in practice remained a party, which it was also still referred to as among the public.[41]

Eventually, the DVFP may have aimed at entering the Reichstag and the state parliaments, but the party rejected the formation of governmental coalitions when the chance came to do so. It strove to create a *völkisch* state but failed to explain what constitution this state was supposed to have. Its adherents rejected the abolition of private property but were at the same time suspicious of modern business

39 Döring, *Parlamentarischer Arm der Bewegung*, 71-73; Wolfgang Horn, *Führerideologie und Parteiorganisation der NSDAP (1919-1933)* (Düsseldorf: Droste, 1972), 163f., on growing National Socialist objections against a union of both parties, 189, 195. For a *völkisch* view on the prospect of a joint organisation, see "Einigt Euch", *Der Reichswart*, November 1, 1924. This edition of Reventlow's weekly journal comprised official appeals to followers of the DVFP as well as of the NSDAP.

40 Büttner, *Weimar*, 802-803. In her statistic of election results Büttner only mentions the list's name and does not distinguish the participating parties. Hence her figures for May and December 1924 include the joint list of DVFP and NSDAP, entitled *Nationalsozialistische Freiheitsbewegung*, whereas the figures from May 1928 onwards depict the individual list of the NSDAP.

41 The change of name was barely registered in public, and only the party's own publications consequently, though not consistently, used Deutschvölkische Freiheits*bewegung* instead of Deutschvölkische Freiheits*partei* from spring 1925 onward.

establishments such as corporations or stock-market companies. They desired a consolidation of the German economy but thought the appropriate way to achieve this would be to rely entirely on the agrarian sector. A prospering cultural and religious sphere was an important issue to them, but the definition of German culture excluded any cultural expression outside the assumed "people's community", or rather "racial community", and furthermore nearly any religious denomination apart from Lutheran Protestantism. Pan-Germanism, agrarian romanticism, the faint idea of a *völkisch* state of the future and the firm belief in the nebulous concept of a "*völkisch* renewal" might have been temporarily attractive, but in the long-term the DVFP was unable to find feasible answers to the questions and problems of the German electorate in the 1920s.

Ultimately they also failed to translate their syncretistic and fragmentary ideology into practical politics. The quantity of their contributions in the Reichstag stood in sharp contrast to the quality.[42] The overwhelming majority of *völkisch* addresses and motions in parliament had no other objective but the rejection of motions made by the government or by other parties. *Völkisch* parliamentary speeches were anti-speeches: Anti-democratic, anti-republican, anti-parliamentary, anti-liberal, anti-socialist, anti-Semitic, anti-American, anti-French, anti-Slav, anti-Roman, anti-pacifist, anti-capitalist, anti-urban, anti-international, anti-masonic, anti-Catholic and so on. Representatives of other political parties, in particular the Liberals and Social Democrats, were mostly scoffing at their *völkisch* colleagues in and outside parliament. Harry Graf Kessler for instance, who was campaigning for the liberal German Democratic Party (*Deutsche Demokratische Partei*) in 1924, saw his rallies more than once disturbed by the *Völkisch,* but he refused to enter any discussion since he expected personal insults. Instead, he sardonically requested the *völkisch* agitators to come forward with substantial thoughts on the subject matter he was just talking about. He wrote in his diary each time with unconcealed satisfaction that they were arguing a lot without actually saying much.[43] A tiny compendium on radical parties published by Gustav Stresemann's centre-right German People's Party (*Deutsche Volkspartei*) summed up the political contribution of the DVFP in the mid-1920s right to the point: The "lack of responsibility" and of any "real political understanding" in the *völkisch* party proved to be so blatant that in direct comparison the National Socialists appeared almost sophisticated.[44] If the predominantly Prussian DVFP had not lost the propaganda rat race to its rival and erstwhile strategic partner from Bavaria, it would have failed as a result of disa-

42 For an analysis of *völkisch* motions and addresses in parliament, see Stefanie Schrader, *Völkische Opposition. Die parteipolitische und parlamentarische Partizipation der Deutschvölkischen Freiheitspartei/Deutschvölkischen Freiheitsbewegung in der Weimarer Republik* (Frankfurt a.M.: Peter Lang, forthcoming 2013).

43 Harry Graf Kessler, *Das Tagebuch 1880-1937*, eds. Roland S. Kamzelak and Ulrich Ott, vol. 8: *1923-1926* (Stuttgart: Klett-Cotta, 2009), 534.

44 *Die rechtsradikalen Parteien, Flugschriften der Deutschen Volkspartei*, vol. 45 (Berlin: Staatspolitischer Verlag, 1924), 14f.

greement between its different wings with regard to the substance and the practice of *völkisch* politics.

Having said this, the *völkisch* party mirrored the *völkisch* movement of previous decades in many ways and was far from being the kind of modern political power-oriented mass movement which the NSDAP was very soon about to represent. The DVFP and its adherents may not have offered major contributions to political thought in general or to anti-Semitic thinking, which dominated their *Weltanschauung*. Nevertheless, this particular party and its MPs and opinion leaders were an important ideological and institutional link between the antecedent pre-World War One *völkisch* and anti-Semitic movements and the National Socialists, who, while struggling themselves until the mid-1920s, jumped at the chance to use the DVFP's resources and network in Northern Germany with the intention to obtain and hold seats in the Reichstag, thus successfully establishing themselves in Berlin for the first time.

Bibliography

Anonymous. *Deutschvölkischer Katechismus*, vol. 2: *Völkische Organisationen, Parteien, Vereine, Verbände, Orden*. Leipzig: Oldenburg, 1931.

Breuer, Stefan. *Die Völkischen in Deutschland. Kaiserreich und Weimarer Republik*. Darmstadt: Wissenschaftliche Buchgesellschaft, 2008.

Büttner, Ursula. *Weimar. Die überforderte Republik 1918-1933*. Stuttgart: Klett-Cotta, 2008.

Döring, Martin. *Parlamentarischer Arm der Bewegung. Die Nationalsozialisten im Reichstag der Weimarer Republik*. Düsseldorf: Droste, 2001.

Eisgruber, Heinz. *Völkische und Deutschnationale Führer. 100 Heldenbilder*. Leipzig: Oldenburg, 1925.

Figge, Reinhard. *Die Opposition der NSDAP im Reichstag*. Cologne: Wasmund, 1963.

Fricke, Dieter. "Deutschvölkische Partei 1914-1918". In *Lexikon der Parteiengeschichte. Die bürgerlichen und kleinbürgerlichen Parteien und Verbände in Deutschland (1789-1945)*, vol. 2, edited by Dieter Fricke, 559-561. Leipzig: Bibliogr. Institut, 1984.

Fritsch, Theodor. "Die Zukunft des Reichstages und die politischen Parteien". In *Deutschlands Wiedergeburt durch Blut und Eisen*, edited by Richard Ungewitter, 180-186. Stuttgart: Ungewitter, 1918.

Gerstner, Alexandra. *Neuer Adel. Aristokratische Elitekonzeptionen zwischen Jahrhundertwende und Nationalsozialismus*. Darmstadt: Wissenschaftliche Buchgesellschaft, 2008.

Hertzman, Lewis. *DNVP. Right-Wing Opposition in the Weimar Republic, 1918-1924*. Lincoln: University of Nebraska Press, 1963.

Hitler, Adolf. *Mein Kampf*, vol. 2: *Die nationalsozialistische Bewegung*. Munich: Eher, 1927.

Horn, Wolfgang. *Führerideologie und Parteiorganisation der NSDAP (1919-1933)*. Düsseldorf: Droste, 1972.

Kessler, Harry Graf. *Das Tagebuch 1880-1937*, vol. 8: *1923-1926*, edited by Roland S. Kamzelak and Ulrich Ott. Stuttgart: Klett-Cotta, 2009.

Kruppa, Bernd: *Rechtsradikalismus in Berlin 1918-1928*. Berlin: Overall, 1988.

Lohalm, Uwe. *Völkischer Radikalismus. Die Geschichte des Deutschvölkischen Schutz- und Trutzbundes 1919-1923*. Hamburg: Leibniz, 1970.

Mosse, George L. *The Crisis of German Ideology. Intellectual Origins of the Third Reich.* New York: Grosset & Dunlap, 1964.

Oberkrome, Willi. "Stamm und Landschaft. Heimatlicher Tribalismus und die Projektion einer völkischen Neuordnung Deutschlands 1920-1950". In *Ordnungen in der Krise. Zur politischen Kulturgeschichte Deutschlands 1900-1933*, edited by Wolfgang Hardtwig, 69-94. Munich: Oldenbourg, 2007.

Puschner, Uwe. *Die völkische Bewegung im wilhelminischen Kaiserreich. Sprache – Rasse –Religion.* Darmstadt: Wissenschaftliche Buchgesellschaft, 2001.

Puschner, Uwe. "'One People, One Reich, One God.' The Völkische Weltanschauung and Movement". *Bulletin of the German Historical Institute* 24/1 (2002), 5-28.

Puschner, Uwe. "Strukturmerkmale der völkischen Bewegung (1900-1945)". In *Das konservative Intellektuellenmilieu in Deutschland, seine Presse und seine Netzwerke (1890-1960)*, edited by Michel Grunewald and Uwe Puschner, 445-468. Bern et. al: Peter Lang, 2003.

Puschner, Uwe. "Völkisch. Plädoyer für einen engen Begriff". In *"Die Erziehung zum deutschen Menschen" – Völkische und nationalkonservative Erwachsenenbildung in der Weimarer Republik*, edited by Paul Ciupke, Klaus Heuer, Franz-Josef Jelich and Justus H. Ulbricht, 53-66. Essen: Klartext, 2007.

Sauer, Bernhard. "Die Deutschvölkische Freiheitspartei und der Fall Grütte". *Geschichte und Gegenwart. Jahrbuch des Landesarchivs Berlin* (1994), 179-203.

Schrader, Stefanie. "Albrecht von Graefe". In *Handbuch des Antisemitismus. Judenfeindschaft in Geschichte und Gegenwart*, vol. 2/1: *Personen*, edited by Wolfgang Benz, 304-306. Berlin: de Gruyter Saur, 2009.

Schrader, Stefanie. "Reinhold Wulle". In *Handbuch des Antisemitismus. Judenfeindschaft in Geschichte und Gegenwart*, vol. 2/2: *Personen*, edited by Wolfgang Benz, 892-893. Berlin: de Gruyter Saur, 2009.

Schrader, Stefanie. *Völkische Opposition. Die parteipolitische und parlamentarische Partizipation der Deutschvölkischen Freiheitspartei/Deutschvölkischen Freiheitsbewegung in der Weimarer Republik.* Frankfurt a.M.: Peter Lang, forthcoming 2013.

Striesow, Jan. *Die Deutschnationale Volkspartei und die Völkisch-Radikalen 1918-1922.* 2 vols. Frankfurt a.M.: Haag & Herchen, 1981.

Verhandlungen des Reichstags. III. Wahlperiode. Stenographische Berichte, vol. 391. Berlin: Verlag der Reichsdruckerei, 1927.

Weißbecker, Manfred. "Deutschvölkische Freiheitspartei 1922-1933". In *Lexikon der Parteiengeschichte. Die bürgerlichen und kleinbürgerlichen Parteien und Verbände in Deutschland (1789-1945)*, vol. 2, edited by Dieter Fricke, 550-558. Leipzig: Bibliogr. Institut, 1984.

Wulff, Reimer. *Die Deutschvölkische Freiheitspartei 1922-1928.* Marburg [author's private publishing], 1968.

Wulle, Reinhold. *Der Weg zum völkischen Staat. Das Dritte Reich.* Berlin: Puhlmann, 1928.

The Political Strategies of the Stahlhelm Veterans' League and the National Socialist German Workers' Party, 1918-1933

Alessandro Salvador

Introduction

During the Weimar Republic many political forces from the left and right tried to fight against the state in order to overthrow the republican and democratic order. The rapid and dramatic changes that led to the birth of democracy in Germany left many anti-democratic tendencies sufficient possibilities to develop and menace the existence of the new state. Among these forces, the National Socialist German Worker's Party (NSDAP), occupies a dominant role in historical literature, mainly because of the later establishment of the Third Reich. Other radical nationalist movements of the interwar period are less considered in the historical literature.[1] One of them, *Stahlhelm Bund der Frontsoldaten,* is from 1929 onward generally regarded as having been one of the supporters and protagonists of Hitler's rise to power. Moreover, as Stahlhelm is mostly considered as a veterans' movement, its role as a political organisation has so far been less studied. Alois Klotzbücher's dissertation from the mid-1960s is still the best, although unpublished, work on this topic.[2]

This contribution will provide an overview of the political and ideological development of Stahlhelm during the Weimar Republic. At the same time, the parallel and sometimes intersected development of the NSDAP will be shown in order to provide a comparative perspective. In this sense, when possible, interactions that took place between them will be considered, as well as their mutual influence on each other. Furthermore, the role of a third actor, the German National People's Party (*Deutschnationale Volkspartei,* DNVP), will be considered in order to give a complete overview of the general context within the "national opposition" against the republic. We will return to this historical and political concept later in the chapter. My goal is to draw attention to some underestimated aspects of the history of national opposition to the Weimar Republic. First, I intend to demonstrate that Stahlhelm was an important political factor in the different processes leading to the dissolution of the Weimar Republic and, in addition, that it developed political programmes based on a *Weltanschauung* that originated from the "front experience" *(Fronterlebnis).* Second, I will stress the fact that the development of the different

1 For an overview, see e.g. Uwe Puschner and Clemens Vollnhals, eds., *Die völkisch-religiöse Bewegung im Nationalsozialismus. Eine Beziehungs- und Konfliktgeschichte* (Göttingen: Vandenhoeck & Ruprecht, 2012); Stefan Breuer, *Die Völkischen in Deutschland. Kaiserreich und Weimarer Republik* (Darmstadt: Wissenschaftliche Buchgesellschaft, 2008).

2 Alois Klotzbücher, "Der politische Weg des Stahlhelm, Bund der Frontsoldaten" (PhD diss., University of Nuremberg, 1964).

movements of the national opposition was strongly influenced by the interactions between them. In my dissertation, of which this chapter represents a partial overview, I tried to overcome some shortcomings in existing literature concerning this argument. Summarising, there are two main shortcomings that should be addressed. First, Stahlhelm is clearly underrepresented in the literature. The only book entirely devoted to the veterans' league was written by Volker Berghahn about 40 years ago.[3] Although it remains a main reference on this issue, it is limited due to a lack of consideration of the interactions between Stahlhelm and other right-wing movements and the minor importance given to the political role of the veterans' league, especially the underestimation of the ideological creativity and originality.

The second limitation refers to the literature about the NSDAP and the DNVP. Although extensive literature about these two movements exists, it mostly concentrates on their individual development, and the interactions between them are mostly treated incompletely. An interesting exception is the recent work of Hermann Beck which, however, only devotes a minor part to the period preceding 1933.[4]

In this chapter, I will try to prove that significant interactions between various movements of the national opposition existed and that they played a considerable role in its development. Without claiming to be exhaustive, I will conclude with some suggestions on the possibilities to reconsider the study of the national opposition in the Weimar Republic, stressing the relational character of its actors.

The Origins of the NSDAP and Stahlhelm after World War One

Stahlhelm was established in Magdeburg on November 13, 1918, by a small group of former soldiers. Among them were an entrepreneur, Franz Seldte, and two of his brothers, Georg and Eugen. Initially, Stahlhelm was nothing more than one of the many small self-defence organisations that emerged after World War I in an attempt to counter the revolution and help the new state preserve law and order. These small organisations mainly represented the middle class, whose members felt menaced by the revolutionary events. The group around Seldte took its definitive form on December 25, 1918, and first appeared in public on January 6, 1919, with Franz Seldte speaking in Magdeburg. On that occasion, Seldte affirmed that the role of Stahlhelm was to aid the state in preserving the order against any revolutionary attempt from both the left and right.[5]

With regard to the social and political composition of the early Stahlhelm, we can consider it as a not well-defined organisation. Although the middle class was well represented and its interests were principally defended, the militants came from various social classes and political milieus. The most represented political component was to the right of liberal and conservative perspectives. However, so-

3 Volker Berghahn, *Der Stahlhelm Bund der Frontsoldaten* (Düsseldorf: Droste, 1966), 13-15.

4 Hermann Beck, *The Fateful Alliance. German Conservatives and Nazis in 1933. The* Machtergreifung *in a New Light* (New York/Oxford: Berghahn Books, 2010).

5 Berghahn, *Der Stahlhelm*, 13-15.

cial democrats were present, too. It is important to stress that most of the first militants had prewar political experience and continued their political activities within newly established parties, mostly in the German People's Party (*Deutsche Volkspartei*, DVP) or the DNVP. Stahlhelm, then, was rooted in the political life of the Empire, and it is not surprising that it maintained the old imperial flag (black-white-red), although it was not intended as a sign of hostility against the republic, at least not in the beginning. Some of the militants even proposed to adopt the new flag, but every discussion of this kind was suspended as any political issue was considered of secondary importance. Stahlhelm cooperated on many occasions with the new state and it enlisted volunteers for the Free Corps *(Frei Korps)* von Maercker.[6]

Stahlhelm acted as a cooperating force in the service of the Weimar Republic, and the good relationship with the state only started to deteriorate after the signing of the Treaty of Versailles. However, Stahlhelm did not use that occasion to become an open opponent to the republic as many other paramilitary organisations did. Only a small part of its members participated in subversive attempts, such as the Kapp-Putsch in 1920 or the Hitler-Putsch in 1923.[7] In this period, Seldte, who finally affirmed himself as leader of the Stahlhelm, did not directly attack the republic. He rather raised doubts about the abilities of the republican leadership. Another important aspect that should be stressed about the attitude of Stahlhelm towards Weimar is that we cannot find a clear and unanimous political idea among the veterans. Rather, the members were split into two main political directions. The first one considered the republic as a partner, although it criticised its revolutionary origins and its social democratic government. The second, and opposing view, considered the existing state as an enemy and hoped to return to the pre-war order. Magdeburg's local section of Stahlhelm was the stronghold of the moderate tendency and found its political collocation in a close relationship with the DVP to which Seldte belonged. The radicals had their stronghold in Halle with Theodor Duesterberg as their leader. He was a member of the DNVP and its followers also belonged to this political field. Halle's difficult situation in the interwar period, where the Spartakists were strong and provoked bloody clashes with Stahlhelm, is probably the main reason for the radical development in the region. The state intervened later in Halle than in other cities and was regarded with suspicion by the paramilitaries there. In addition, Stahlhelm was not a strongly centralised organisa-

6 Klotzbücher, *Der politische Weg des Stahlhelm*, 24-30.

7 Between 1920 and 1923 there were two major attempts to overthrow the republic. The first one happened in the spring of 1920 as the Free Corps led by Wolfgang Kapp tried to occupy Berlin, mainly in order to prevent the dissolution of the Free Corps itself. The second, and most famous attempt, was led by Adolf Hitler and Erich Ludendorff and occurred in November 1923 in Munich. For further information, see: Johannes Erger, *Der Kapp-Lüttwitz-Putsch. Ein Beitrag zur deutschen Innenpolitik 1919/20* (Düsseldorf: Droste, 1967); Ernst Deuerlein, ed., *Der Hitler-Putsch. Bayerische Dokumente zum 8./9. November 1923* (Stuttgart: DVA, 1962); Harold J. Gordon, *Hitlerputsch 1923* (Frankfurt a.M.: Bernhard & Gräfe, 1971).

tion until 1923 and every local situation produced different answers to the interwar crisis and different attitudes toward the state and its authority.[8]

If the origins of the Stahlhelm reflect some connections with the pre-war political experience and an ambivalent attitude towards the republic, in which the politics of compromise seemed to prevail, the case for the NSDAP was very different.

First we should consider that, although presenting itself as a political party, the NSDAP was a movement with a strong paramilitary character that gained major relevance mostly due to its subversive activities rather than because of its political role, at least in its first years. However, it was from the beginning, and quite different from Stahlhelm, an organisation that was strongly committed to politics. The NSDAP developed from the German Worker's Party (*Deutsche Arbeiterpartei*, DAP), a very radical nationalist party which was dominated by anti-Semitism and the demand for radical social reform. In some ways we can see it as a bridge between pre- and post-World War One political ideas. In this case, however, we should take as predecessors the nationalist opposition and pressure groups in the Empire. They were characterised by a strong anti-state feeling and they aimed towards subverting the state and refused any political compromise or debate.[9]

The DAP was, then, a subversive party which was organised as a small sectarian group according to the volition of Karl Harrer. Hitler's presence contributed to the development of the DAP and later of the NSDAP as a more open and developed party with connections to other political actors in Bavaria. However, the party always maintained its radicalism. Within a short period of time, Hitler established himself as a rather well-known politician among right-wing radicals in Munich, and the presence of his party as an enemy of the republic was clearly defined. Furthermore, it should be remembered that the situation in Bavaria was very different from other regions in Germany. The revolution in Bavaria started shortly before the events that led to Germany leaving the war. However, the situation remained unstable for a longer time because of clashes and rivalries between revolutionary forces, the establishment of the short-lived Soviet Republic and the powerful and violent reaction from governmental and non-governmental counter-revolutionary

---

8 Berghahn, *Der Stahlhelm*, 18-22.

9 These national pressure groups were political and economic organisations that tried to gather the middle and higher bourgeoisie and attempted to exercise political pressure in order to make the imperial government pursue certain policies. A few radical *völkisch* organisations emerged from these movements that at a certain point proposed the change of regime from the Empire to a nationalist dictatorship. See Geoff Eley, *Reshaping the German Right. Radical Nationalism and Political Change after Bismarck* (New Haven/London: Yale University Press, 1980). On the origins of the NSDAP, see, among others, Georg Franz-Willing, *Die Hitlerbewegung, der Ursprung 1919-1922* (Hamburg: Schenck, 1962); Werner Maser, *Frühgeschichte der NSDAP. Hitlers Weg bis 1924* (Frankfurt a.M./Bonn: Athenäum, 1965); Dietrich Orlow, *The History of the Nazi Party: 1919-1933* (Pittsburgh: University of Pittsburgh Press, 1969), 11-75; Albrecht Tyrell, *Vom 'Trommler' zum 'Führer'. Der Wandel von Hitlers Selbstverständnis zwischen 1919 und 1924 und die Entwicklung der NSDAP* (Munich: Wilhelm Fink, 1975).

forces.[10] This resulted in Bavaria becoming the stronghold of anti-state sentiments and movements. This was also fuelled by strong separatist feelings that considered Munich as an alternative to Berlin. Additionally, movements and parties that had normal relationships with the republic in the rest of Germany preserved a strong anti-republican feeling in their Bavarian sections.[11]

The 1923 Crisis and the Development of the National Opposition

Despite their different origins and aims, which gave them different attitudes toward the Weimar Republic, both Stahlhelm and the NSDAP changed significantly from 1923 onward. The French occupation of the Ruhr contributed to a further radicalisation among German nationalists. Thousands of militants belonging to many different nationalist and paramilitary organisations actively sabotaged French military operations and conducted guerrilla operations against the occupants in the Ruhr. Among them there were also militants from Stahlhelm, which in some cases collaborated with forces secretly developed by the official army, such as the Black Reichswehr.[12]

The German government appeared to be too weak to contain the French. This gave the radicals the chance and the arguments to increase their opposition against the republic. In this climate of political uncertainty, the NSDAP attempted a coup. In November 1923, Hitler, allied with former general Erich Ludendorff, gathered paramilitary and political forces in order to subvert the state, starting from Bavaria. Members of the Bavarian Stahlhelm did indeed participate in the putsch, but their national organisation did not take part, maintaining instead some sort of neutrality, similar to other nationalist movements.[13] Following that episode, the radical right entered a period of crisis in which many groups were disbanded and prosecuted by the state. The remaining organisations discussed among themselves strategies that had to be adopted after the violent assaults against democracy proved to be ineffective.[14]

The NSDAP was disbanded and was only able to restart its political activity effectively in 1925 after Hitler was released from prison. Stahlhelm was one of the few organisations that survived the crisis of radical nationalism, mostly because of its moderate attitude toward the state and its characterisation as a non-political vet-

10 For a wider overview of the events in Bavaria, see: Wolfgang Zorn, *Bayerns Geschichte im 20. Jahrhundert* (Munich: C.H. Beck, 1986), 206-209; Chris Harman, *The lost revolution: Germany 1918-23* (London et al.: Bookmarks, 1997), 125-126.

11 Orlow, *The History of the Nazi Party*, 11-24.

12 Berghahn, *Der Stahlhelm*, 32-33. On the Black Reichswehr, see Bernhard Sauer, *Schwarze Reichswehr und Fememorde. Eine Milieustudie zum Rechtsradikalismus in der Weimarer Republik* (Berlin: Metropol Verlag, 2004).

13 Reference to the participation of Stahlhelm members in the 1923 putsch are made in an article which appeared some years later in a National Socialist newspaper. See Jörg Jenatsch [pseud.], "Stahlhelmparolen", *Der Nationale Sozialist*, October 3, 1926.

14 James M. Diehl, *Paramilitary politics in Weimar Germany* (Bloomington: Indiana University Press, 1997), 135-136.

erans' league. In addition, the political connections with, and support from the DVP and the DNVP, contributed to its survival. Furthermore, the dissolution of many paramilitary organisations, including the Civic Militia *(Einwohnerwehr)*[15] and the Organisation Escherich, provided Stahlhelm with new militants and leaders, and the organisational framework of the veterans' league evolved between 1923 and 1924. This motivated Stahlhelm to redefine its organisation and its political role. Two new structures, the *Jungstahlhelm* for militants younger than 21 years of age and the *Landsturm* for older people without the military experience necessary for membership in Stahlhelm, were created in order to recruit new members. The core of Stahlhelm, into which only real veterans were admitted, was renamed into *Kernstahlhelm.*[16]

Following the reorganisation, Franz Seldte decided to rearrange the movement's political outlook in order to enable it to play a decisive role in future political struggles. The main aim was not only to make Stahlhelm become the centre for the political pressures of the veterans, but also to develop it into a national pressure group. Moreover, the veterans promoted constitutional reforms in order to turn the republic into a nationalist, authoritarian state. In addition, between 1925 and 1926 a radical nationalist-revolutionary tendency emerged within Stahlhelm. It was called the *Standartenkreis,* taking its name from the periodical it published, first as an attachment to Stahlhelm's official periodical and then independently of it. This faction was inspired by Ernst Jünger and Franz Schauwecker. The members opposed Seldte's leadership and the closeness of Stahlhelm to Gustav Stresemann's DVP. The Standartenkreis proposed a revolutionary way to overthrow the German government and build a fascist regime inspired by the Italian model. This faction was tolerated by Seldte until the end of 1926 when Jünger's excessive criticism of Seldte made it difficult for Stahlhelm to pursue its main political goal, for instance a merger with a radical right-wing organisation, the *Wiking Bund* led by Hermann Ehrhardt.[17]

Seldte was able to exclude all the main leaders of the Standartenkreis, but he did not manage to halt the opposition to his political leadership. A small circle of opponents gathered around Theodor Duesterberg and conspired to remove Seldte from his position. However, Duesterberg feared that such a solution might divide the movement, and in March 1927 the national leadership of Stahlhelm announced

---

15 The Civic Militia was one of many self-defence organisations established in Germany in the immediate postwar period. Due to its connections within the Bavarian government, it was able to outlive the Free Corps movement, and functioned as a meeting point for former Free Corps members. The Organisation Escherich was named after the Militia's leader Georg Escherich and was a nationwide semi-clandestine paramilitary organisation. See Hans Fenske, *Konservatismus und Rechtsradikalismus in Bayern nach 1918* (Bad Homburg/Berlin/Zurich: Gehlen, 1969), 78-80; Diehl, *Paramilitary politics*, 55-59.

16 Dirk Schumann, *Politische Gewalt in der Weimarer Republik. 1918-1933* (Essen: Klartext, 2001), 220-221.

17 Berghahn, *Der Stahlhelm*, 92-95.

both Seldte and Duesterberg as leaders. With the creation of the two-man leadership, the dualistic nature of the movement was officialised.[18]

Another factor influencing Stahlhelm's political course was the short-lived alliance with Hermann Ehrhardt and his organisation, the Wiking Bund, which was the successor of the Free Corps Ehrhardt and the *Organisation Consul.*[19] After a period of redefining his political strategy, Ehrhardt joined Stahlhelm, proposing a new political line with the slogan: "Hinein in den Staat" (Into the State). This strategy was centred on the possibility to achieve control of the state by working within it and by following legal methods only. Hence, the idea was to understand the mechanism that made the democratic order possible and, once understood, to use them to create an authoritarian state without crossing the boundaries of legality.[20]

But Ehrhardt's strategy and its relation to Stahlhelm were unclear. During the leadership crisis he in vain tried to propose himself as a leader able to overcome the differences within the movement. Moreover, the exact role of the members of the Wiking Bund within Stahlhelm remained unclear, and the leadership of the veterans exercised some pressure to merge the whole Wiking Bund into the Stahlhelm by imposing an ultimatum in November 1927. The result of this situation was the end of the cooperation between the two movements. However, the slogan and the subsequent strategy were not completely abandoned.[21]

Before considering the political contents included in the development of the Stahlhelm, we should keep in mind that even if its affirmed intention was to follow a legal way in the political struggle, political violence never disappeared as a method of asserting political pressure. As noted by Schumann, in this period Stahlhelm lived two different lives. On the one hand, the national policy-makers of the movement tried to corroborate a new strategy for the political struggle and to affirm themselves as reliable interlocutors. On the other hand, there were battles on the streets against socialist and republican paramilitary organisations, such as the Reichsbanner.[22]

The main steps of Stahlhelm's progressive involvement in politics were marked by the publication of the Stahlhelm Messages *(Stahlhelm-Botschaften)*. These were political manifestos that were usually announced during the league's national meetings *(Reichsfrontsoldatentage)*. The first one, stating the veterans' definitive entering of the

18 Klotzbücher, *Der politische Weg des Stahlhelm*, 105-110.

19 The Ehrhardt Brigade was a Free Corps led by Hermann Ehrhardt, a former Navy Captain. It was a major actor in counter-revolutionary activities in 1919 and 1920. After its dissolution it continued to operate underground, organising terrorist actions under the name of Organisation Consul. After the amnesty of 1925, Ehrhardt was able to return to open political action and established the Wiking Bund. See Gabriele Krueger, *Die Brigade Ehrhardt* (Hamburg: Leibniz, 1971); James H. MacGee, "The Political Police in Bavaria 1919-1936" (PhD diss., University of Florida, 1980).

20 Diehl, *Paramilitary Politics*, 219-222.

21 Klotzbücher, *Der Politische Weg des Stahlhelm*, 110-111.

22 Schumann, *Politische Gewalt*, 222. The author also stresses the increasing involvement of the Stahlhelm in the so-called "Kleinkaliber Schießvereine" that were a common cover for illegal paramilitary training at the time.

political arena, was spread during the meeting in Berlin on May 8, 1927, in the presence of 132,000 militants.[23] It was a moment of great relief for Stahlhelm, mainly thanks to the presence of a big counter-demonstration of leftists, which gave a great resonance to this meeting. The mass participation appeared to the public as though the movement was characterised by strength and unity. It should also be noted that the meeting received the official greetings of President Hindenburg, who publicly showed that representatives of the state relied on the Stahlhelm and supported it. But strength and unity were only a façade that concealed a period of great difficulties. The meeting took place amidst emerging tensions between Stahlhelm and the Wiking Bund and also during the above-mentioned leadership crisis.[24]

Internal difficulties were never resolved and lasted until the end of Stahlhelm as an independent organisation. However, the political programme was announced and received initial feedback from other political nationalist forces. The contents of the first political programme did not differ from general nationalist assertions to refuse the conditions of the Treaty of Versailles and denials of German responsibility for provoking the war. Peace treaties were considered as responsible for excessive territorial mutilations suffered by Germany. According to the nationalists, this unfair situation led to the economic and social crisis and produced the risk of a socialist revolution. The way out of the crisis should have led, according to their proposals, to conquer more vital and working space for the German people and to overcome differences between the social classes. According to Stahlhelm, future German society was to be based on class cooperation instead of class struggle. Furthermore, a general agrarian reform programme had to be introduced with the aim of creating rural colonies on German territory and abroad, especially in Eastern Europe.[25]

Stahlhelm did not completely disapprove of the present state as many other nationalists did, but it proposed some reforms in order to make it more "German". The two steps for a rebirth of the state according to Stahlhelm were first to empower the President of the Reich and, second, to implement an electoral act which allowed an embodiment of the real will of the German people. However, this last point was not explained, and it is unclear how Stahlhelm wanted to realise this reform. Connecting these assertions to previous declarations of the Stahlhelm leadership, we can argue that they wanted to give more electoral power to veterans because, in their opinion, they were entitled to first-class citizenship.[26]

As far as political strategy was concerned, Stahlhelm declared its intention to struggle for the reform of the state through legal methods and a strong adherence

---

23 Peter H. Merkl, *The making of a Stormtrooper* (Princeton: Princeton University Press, 1980), 47.

24 Berghahn, *Der Stahlhelm*, 103-105; Klotzbücher, *Der politische Weg des Stahlhelm*, 103. There are different opinions about when the double leadership began to be effective. Berghahn suggests from October 1926 and Klotzbücher from March 1927, a little more than one month prior to the national meeting.

25 The text of the Botschaft is published in Ernst H. Posse, *Die politischen Kampfbünde Deutschlands* (Berlin: Junker & Donnhaupt, 1930), 33-35.

26 Ibid.

to the constitution. Moreover, it declared that they would pursue their goals together with other political forces that shared some general issues, such as the acknowledgement of the veterans as "better" citizens and the denial of the Treaty of Versailles. Affirming the intention to conduct their struggle using legal methods only, the veterans clearly broke with their revolutionary tradition and officially started a new era for radical nationalism after the failure of Hitler's putsch in 1923.

The national meeting in Hamburg in 1928 represented another important step in the development of the Stahlhelm, since social issues were brought to the fore on that occasion. The *Hamburger Botschaft*, or *Sozialbotschaft*, declared that Germany had to become independent of foreign capital and imports. Partially recalling the fascist concept of autarchy, the social programme of the Stahlhelm had important implications for its political strategy, too. It tells us a lot about the relations between the veterans and the republic. In fact, the *Hamburger Botschaft* foresaw the possibility of actively intervening in the daily life of citizens and the state through social actions.[27]

The direct consequence was the establishment of the Stahlhelm Self-help (*Selbsthilfe*, Stas) in Halle in 1928 as a parallel organisation created with the aim of developing and applying the concept of Social Work *(Sozialarbeit)*.[28] This organisation was extended to the national organisation of the Stahlhelm by 1930, and it became a central aspect of the veterans' political activities. Although it did not manage to establish Stahlhelm among workers, except in central Germany, the Stas represented a centre for propaganda and ideological development within the veterans' movement.[29]

The Political Strategy of Stahlhelm and the Attempt to Unite the National Opposition

The Hamburg rally also confirmed that the main goal of Stahlhelm was to create a wide national front and to include as far as possible every important nationalist organisation. In Hamburg, however, the nationalist parties failed to unify the German nationalist opposition, and for this reason the veterans proposed themselves as the spearhead of this process. It was not the first attempt to unify the German national opposition, but this time Stahlhelm tried a different strategy. Stahlhelm thought that working within the society and the state would be useful to reach some preliminary results such as, for example, the approval of laws to help veterans and citizens in need.[30] This way, they could propose some immediate goals nationalists in general agreed upon. The Stahlhelm, then, used its relationships with political parties to propose two laws that aimed at the improvement of the veterans' social conditions.

---

27 Ibid.

28 The Stas was created as a workers' organisation in the state association of Middle Germany of the Stahlhelm. It was acknowledged two years later by the national organisation and officially became the workers' organisation of the Stahlhelm.

29 Schumann, *Politische Gewalt*, 221.

30 *Stahlhelm Handbuch* (Berlin: Stahlhelm, 1927), 31-34.

These laws were only partially supported by the nationalist parties and mainly considered minor improvements on everyday questions. Major topics such as the denial of Germany's responsibility for provoking the war and the revision of the peace treaty could not be pursued by following the parliamentary route exclusively.[31]

The leadership of Stahlhelm, then, tried to find a way to achieve mass mobilisation, the unity of the nationalists and political significance at the same time. Such a goal was partially reached by proposing a constitutional modification through a national referendum, or *Volksbegehren*. The basic idea of Stahlhelm was to propose a law to strengthen the powers of the president and, consequently, transform Germany into an authoritarian state. The parliament and the parties were, by contrast, supposed to occupy a minor role. A referendum was chosen in order to obtain another important result, for instance, the degree of consent that the Stahlhelm would be able to achieve with a concrete and strong political proposal. Since the veterans' league was not a party, it was according to the leaders the best way to show how Stahlhelm could realise mass mobilisation.[32]

The National Socialists were the main opponents of the constitutional modifications proposed by the veterans. Hitler, for instance, said that the state had to be radically changed at once and not through partial reforms. Furthermore, he considered the empowerment of the president a dangerous situation as it could eventually be an advantage to the leftists.[33]

Other nationalist forces had some doubts about the Stahlhelm project as well, including the major partner of the veterans' league, the DNVP led by Alfred Hugenberg. From 1928 onward, the German Nationalists changed their leadership and their political course by steering to the right and radicalising their opposition to the republic. Hugenberg, as the new leader of the party, radically reconsidered the previous policy of his party and turned to a new direction that included strengthening the relationships between German Nationalists and other political organisations, with a special attention to the Stahlhelm. Hugenberg, inspired by the aim of a referendum, became the main partner of the veterans. He argued diplomatically to convince Seldte and Duesterberg to change the wording and aim of the proposal. It ended up being a proposal against the Young Plan for war reparations and a denial of German responsibility for causing the war. This new aim, called Freedom Act *(Freiheitsgesetz)*, was considered a better way to reach a major consensus in the na-

31 Ibid., 47-49.

32 Report of the Reichskommissar für Überwachung der Öffentlichen Ordnung (RKO), October 31, 1928, Bayerisches Hauptstaatsarchiv (BHStA), MA 101249. The Stahlhelm also announced its new project one month before the report, see: "Stahlhelm-Volksbegehren", *Der Stahlhelm*, September 1928.

33 Letter from Hitler to the Stahlhelm leadership, undated [1929], Bundesarchiv Berlin (BA Berlin), NS 26/863.

tionalist field, and indeed, Stahlhelm's strategy under Hugenberg resulted in a great nationalist coalition in the summer of 1929.[34]

The campaign for the *Volksbegehren* showed how weak the nationalist front was. Although the German Nationalists and Stahlhelm seemed to collaborate well at this point, the National Socialists mainly worked on their own behalf which produced some worries among the allies. Hugenberg, however, did everything to render Hitler a partner of this initiative, and he eventually risked destroying the nationalist front in order to defend the National Socialists' radical requests on some aspects of the referendum.[35]

Stahlhelm remained neutral during the controversy between the DNVP and the NSDAP, although there were worries about Hitler's attitude. After the failure of the campaign for the Freedom Act, the veterans started to recognise that the collaboration with the parties could have been one possible obstacle to their political aims. Particularly the leadership of the Stahlhelm agreed that leaving the leadership of a united nationalist front to Hugenberg, who practically achieved major visibility during the whole campaign, meant to convey the idea that not all German nationalists were proponents of the idea but one specific political party only. This led to some discussions within the Stahlhelm about the necessity of re-acquiring a prominent role in the proposal and the pursuit of political targets as an "above-party-lines" movement.[36]

This change of strategy was first realised with the proposal of a new *Volksbegehren* in 1931 with the aim to dissolve the Prussian Landtag. The announcement of this new political campaign took place during the *Reichsfrontsoldatentag* in Koblenz at the beginning of 1931, and came as a surprise for both Hugenberg and Hitler. Stahlhelm was able to maintain the leadership of this new campaign while accepting the nationalist parties as partners. However, the failure of this referendum was, once more, attributed to the DNVP and the NSDAP.[37]

---

34 Memorandum by Otto Schmidt-Hannover concerning the relationships between the DNVP and the Stahlhelm, June 1932, Bundesarchiv Koblenz (BA Koblenz), Nachlass Schmidt-Hannover, N 1211/72.

35 Report of the National committee for the German *Volksbegehren*, July 11, 1929, BA Berlin, R 8048/262. For a complete overview of the NSDAP's attitude in the whole Reich, see transcript of the Stahlhelm national leadership, October 1, 1929, BA Berlin, R 72/11. Other details about the tensions existing within the front against the Young Plan can be found in the correspondence of the National Committee, BA Berlin, R 8048/263.

36 Some worries about the role of Hugenberg and how it could damage Stahlhelm were already present before Hugenberg's appointment was confirmed. See letter by Heinz Brauweiler to Seldte (with an attachment), October 8, 1928, Stadtarchiv Mönchengladbach (StAM), Nachlass Brauweiler, 15/13/112. The tendency of the Stahlhelm to stay away from the dialectic between the two parties can be seen in a letter by Wagner to Seldte, April 4, 1930, BA Berlin, R 72/25. See in addition memorandum by Otto Schmidt-Hannover concerning the relationships between the DNVP and the Stahlhelm, June 1932, BA Koblenz, Nachlass Schmidt-Hannover, N 1211/72.

37 Hildegard Pleyer, "Politische Werbung in der Weimarer Republik" (PhD diss., Westfälische Wilhelms-Universität, 1959), 40. See also transcript of the Stahlhelm national leadership, January 31/February 1, 1931, BA Berlin, R 72/15.

In the following, Stahlhelm more consistently pursued its strategy of maintaining itself equidistant from the parties. A meeting in Harzburg in October 1931 which was intended to build a definitive national opposition consisting of mainly the DNVP, the NSDAP, Stahlhelm and the Pan-German League (*Alldeutscher Verband)*, was more an attempt to demonstrate an illusionary unity than a real alliance between similar political forces. During the meeting the National Socialists already showed that their concept of unity was quite different from that of the DNVP, since the former constantly emphasised their originality and independence. Stahlhelm was so concerned about the attitude of the National Socialists that it became increasingly clear that "unity" was a word with no real content, despite the fact that the Harzburger Front was frequently recalled by the veterans' leader. Moreover, the NSDAP increased its influence among local sections of the Stahlhelm. At the same time, the veterans' league grew increasingly dissatisfied with the DNVP.[38]

In 1932 the nationalist front finally broke up, mostly because of the presidential elections. Hitler's decision to run for the presidency sparked the dissolution of the Harzburger Front. However, Duesterberg's candidacy and the decision of the Stahlhelm not to support any possible candidate of the DNVP suggest that the Harzburg alliance was a stillbirth experience. Furthermore, Stahlhelm decided to let its second leader, Theodor Duesterberg, run for office instead of supporting Hindenburg. The latter was an honorary member of the league and was idolised by the front-generation. This decision was a response to the fact that the old president was now supported by the Social Democrats, the democratic centre and right-wing parties which were considered as incarnations of the hated Weimar Republic. Duesterberg's catastrophic defeat and Hitler's surprising success, although not strong enough to defeat Hindenburg, had terrible consequences on Stahlhelm and its relationship with the German Nationalists.[39]

As usual, the veterans considered their alliance with Hugenberg the main cause of the defeat and tried to disengage from the agreement stipulated before the presidential elections. According to that agreement, Stahlhelm was now expected to support the DNVP during the Reichstag elections.[40] However, the leadership tried to delegate the communication of the agreement to the local sections, since they knew that local leaders would not support a single party. The latter was in their

38 The attempt to overcome the tensions can be seen in "Einigkeit und Recht und Freiheit!" and "Bei uns steht Deutschland", *Der Tag*, November 13, 1931. About the tensions that appeared in Harzburg, see Theodor Duesterberg, *Der Stahlhelm und Hitler* (Wolfenbüttel/Hanover: Wolfenbütteler Verlagsanstalt, 1949), 20-24. See also: Memoirs of Otto Wagener, vol. 36, 1-4, Institut für Zeitgeschichte (IfZ), Munich.

39 Larry E. Jones, "Hindenburg and the conservative dilemma in the 1932 presidential elections", *German Studies Review* 2 (1997), 235-259. On the position of the Stahlhelm, see also transcript of the Stahlhelm leadership, January 31/February 1, 1931, BA Berlin, R 72/15. On the attitude of the DNVP see: "Duesterberg als Kandidat der DNVP und Stahlhelm", *Der Tag*, February 23, 1932; "Parole: Duesterberg", *Der Tag*, February 24, 1932.

40 Agreement between DNVP and Stahlhelm for the presidential elections, February 18, 1932, BA Koblenz, Nachlass Schmidt-Hannover, N 1211/29.

opinion considered a betrayal of the "above-party-lines" spirit of the movement.[41] Furthermore, the behaviour of many local sections of the Stahlhelm showed not only that the general mistrust against the DNVP was so strong that many local leaders simply refused to obey the national leadership, but also that National Socialist influences were strongly present among the veterans' league.[42]

The final phase of the Weimar Republic witnessed Stahlhelms attempts to preserve its integrity against the hostility of the German Nationalists and the growing influence of the NSDAP among its ranks. The only chance that Seldte and Duesterberg had to avoid falling under the control of the National Socialists and at the same time to maintain a distance to the German Nationalists would have been a presidential government according to Article 48 of the Weimar Constitution. This solution would have simply bypassed the parliament and overcome party differences. For this reason, Stahlhelm supported the authoritarian government of Franz von Papen, hoping that this experience could avoid any further involvement of the parties in the political life of the republic and spare the veterans' league any further tension related to its difficult relationships with the parties.[43]

Moreover, the authoritarian government of a "veteran", such as von Papen, represented the right way for Stahlhelm to lead to a radical reform of the state in the sense of realizing the veterans' state. However, the failure of von Papen and the new governmental crisis brought Stahlhelm to other radical decisions and, for the first time since 1926, there was a decisive rupture between the two leaders. Therefore, Seldte accepted a cabinet position when Hitler was appointed Chancellor, against Duesterberg's strong opposition.[44]

The Political Strategy of the NSDAP: An Overview

Apparently, the path that Hitler followed to finally come to power was very different from that of Stahlhelm. The NSDAP was from the beginning a clear and strong opponent of the Weimar Republic and refused any cooperation with state institutions or any participation in activities that only had partial and moderate aims. Dur-

41 Letter from the Stahlhelm national leadership to the local section of West-Westfalen, March 9, 1932, BA Koblenz, Nachlass Schmidt-Hannover, N 1211/28. On the opposition from local sections to further cooperation with the DNVP, see memorandum by Otto Schmidt-Hannover concerning the relationship between the DNVP and the Stahlhelm, June 1932, BA Koblenz, Nachlass Schmidt-Hannover, N 1211/72. The attribution to the DNVP of the failure can be seen in a report on propaganda activities for Duesterberg, BA Koblenz, Nachlass Schmidt-Hannover N 1211/28; Newsletter of the Stahlhelm-Gau Saale-Thüringen to all local sections, March 16, 1932, BA Koblenz, Nachlass Schmidt-Hannover, N 1211/28.

42 On the influence exerted by National Socialists on the Stahlhelm, see the letters by Schmidt-Hannover to various local sections and to the Stahlhelm national leadership in BA Koblenz, Nachlass Schmidt-Hannover, N 1211/28.

43 *Deutscher Schnelldienst*, May 7, 1932, BA Koblenz, Nachlass Schmidt-Hannover, N 1211/28. See also confidential information on the political situation by Anton Scheibe, December 8, 1932, BA Koblenz, Nachlass Schmidt-Hannover, N 1211/72.

44 Duesterberg, *Der Stahlhelm und Hitler*, 13-14.

ing Hitler's imprisonment, the NSDAP split into many groups. Among them we can identify two main factions: Pioneers and revolutionaries. The first one was the prototype of the early National Socialist: Anti-Semitic, involved in pre-war nationalist movements and members of the middle to high bourgeoisie. The revolutionaries were rather the product of the war experience: Young veterans filled with ideals such as the exaltation of war, comradeship and the "socialism of the front" *(Frontsozialismus)*. Many of them were unable to find a place in the new German society.

Hitler's return to politics in February 1925 had lesser resonance in the northern National Socialist fractions. The organiser of the latter was Gregor Strasser, a man with great administrational abilities. He recognised that socialist and revolutionary matters could be more successful in Northern Germany, where the Munich party elite was mostly seen as reactionary and bourgeois. Furthermore, he fought against any attempt to centralise the leadership of Hitler's party in Bavaria and thus represented a branch within the National Socialist movement that wanted to give the Party a different orientation.[45]

At a leadership meeting in Bamberg in February 1926 Hitler held a long monologue during which he affirmed that no new programmatic contents would be introduced and that his leadership was undisputed. Strasser and the other northern leaders were taken by surprise and therefore could not answer appropriately. The latter had come to Bamberg to have a discussion. Upon arrival, however, they realised that Hitler was not in the least interested in a debate. At the same time he did not impose any sanctions against the "rebels" (although they never questioned Hitler's authority over the movement). On the contrary, they were all promoted to better positions within the party. Goebbels was assigned to direct the NSDAP in Berlin, and Strasser was confirmed in his position as the second most important person within the movement, after Hitler, with his appointment as Reich Propaganda Leader in September 1926 and as Reich Organisation Leader in January 1928.[46]

After re-establishing absolute control over the party, Hitler started a period of reorganisation based on the refusal of collaboration with other subjects. This isolation lasted until 1929. Hitler was convinced that trusting other partners was one of the main causes of the defeat in 1923. Any future agreement with any political or

45 Joesph L. Nyomarkay, "Factionalism in the National Socialist Workers' Party, 1925-26: The Myth and Reality of the 'Northern Faction'", *Political Science Quarterly* 1 (1965), 22-47, in particular 28 and 34. See also Orlow, *History of the Nazi Party*, chap. 3. On Strasser and the "Nazi Left", see Reinhard Kühnl, *Die nationalsozialistische Linke 1925-1930* (Meisenheim: Anton Hain, 1966); Reinhard Kühnl, "Zur Programmatik der nationalsozialistischen Linken: Das Strasser-Programm von 1925/26", *Vierteljahrshefte für Zeitgeschichte* 14 (1966), 317-333; Udo Kissenkoetter, *Gregor Stra□ er und die NSDAP* (Stuttgart: DVA, 1978); Peter D. Stachura, *Gregor Strasser and the Rise of Nazism* (London: Harper Collins, 1983).

46 Nyomarkay, "Factionalism", 36-40.

paramilitary movement was to be established on the basis of the absolute submission of the partner to the NSDAP.[47]

This radical attitude led to the failure of the first attempt to create a nationalist front, including parties and paramilitaries in Thuringia, the so-called *Völkischer Führerring Thüringen*. After the failure of this local experiment, the National Socialists decided to proceed alone. Their main goal was the seizure of power. During the second half of the 1920s, they concentrated their efforts on strengthening the inner structure of the party and trying to expand their ranks and to improve internal consensus. The first task was mainly solved by centralising the leadership and submitting important decisions to the leadership in Munich, hence avoiding too much autonomy to the local sections. This brought about a more disciplined party even if they had to pay the cost of a slower increase in terms of membership.[48]

The second task was pursued by both acquiring capable leaders from other movements, especially from Stahlhelm, and developing propaganda strategies. Propaganda aimed first to appeal to the urban workers and, second, to the rural population.[49] However, this strategy should not be confused with the idea that the National Socialists accepted the democratic rules when trying to achieve a parliamentary majority. The parliamentary representatives were clearly defined as tactical means to acquire visibility and not least to take advantage of representatives' benefits to improve sources of propaganda by, for example, using free train journeys to improve the mobility of speakers throughout Germany.

The clearest result of this approach was a hostile attitude against other nationalist protagonists, such as the DNVP and, especially, Stahlhelm. The latter was increasingly attacked by the National Socialist press during the second half of the 1920s, mainly with the aim of weakening the leadership of the movement and critisizing the political course of the veterans. In this sense, the concept of working within the state in order to produce changes in its structure was refused.[50]

---

47 Detlef Mühlberger, *Hitler's Voice. The Völkischer Beobachter, 1920-33*, vol. I: *Organisation and Development of the Nazi Party* (Oxford/Bern/New York: Peter Lang, 2004), 230. See also: Orlow, *History of the Nazi Party*, 88-90.

48 Orlow, *History of the Nazi Party*, 98-99.

49 For the role of labour-oriented strategies, see: Orlow, *History of the Nazi Party*, 76-127; a more extensive view is given by Conan Fischer, *The Rise of National Socialism and the Working Classes in Weimar Germany* (New York/Oxford: Berghahn Books, 1996). With regard to rural propaganda, see Gustavo Corni, *La politica agraria del nazionalsocialismo, 1930-1939* (Milan: Franco Angeli, 1989) or the English edition, *Hitler and the Peasants. Agrarian Policy of the Third Reich, 1930-39* (New York: Berg, 1990).

50 The National Socialist propaganda against the Stahlhelm and the DNVP can be seen especially in publications such as *Der Nationale Sozialist* and *Der Angriff*, with most of the examples in the period between 1927 and 1929. Reactions from the Stahlhelm are visible in the correspondence between local sections and national leadership referring to the hostility from the National Socialists, BA Berlin, R 72/10. Debates within the Stahlhelm about hostility from the NSDAP are also to be found in various transcriptions of the national leadership, BA Berlin, R 72/9; and letters and transcriptions concerning recruitment of Stahlhelm members by National Socialists, BA Berlin, R 72/11; and BA Berlin, R 72/12.

Despite the big efforts made by the National Socialists from 1925 to 1929, they did not seem to achieve any important results. The electoral results of the party were poor and the numerical increment of the membership was slow. In 1929, after the heavy critique Hitler launched against Stahlhelm about the project of constitutional reform via national referendum, he still accepted to pursue a partial result, and to use a democratic instrument, the referendum, and to adhere to an alliance of many political forces.[51]

This decision proved to be effective and the NSDAP gained great visibility for participating in the fight against the Young Plan. Its visibility was mainly due to the attention that the German press gave to the partnership between NSDAP and DNVP. The National Socialist press and the leaders of the party had, however, to struggle hard to convince the membership and sympathisers that this decision was only a question of political calculation and tactics. It meant in no way that the NSDAP accepted the rules and methods of parliamentary democracy. At the same time, any attribution of importance to the alliance with the German Nationalists and Stahlhelm was denied.[52]

Still, the final result of the *Volksbegehren* was a success for the NSDAP. The effects of the economic crisis also contributed to a decisive increase in ballots in some local elections in 1929. The National Socialists took advantage of the general mood of the electorate. In 1930, the two most radical anti-republican parties (National Socialists and Communists) gained significantly at the polls. Moreover, the increment was particularly visible in the rural areas. This convinced Hitler that more efforts had to be undertaken in that direction. As a result, he developed a new strategy for political agitation in the countryside. This effort contributed to the major electoral success of the NSDAP in 1930 and provoked some worries among the other nationalist movements and parties. The consideration that a stronger alliance with Hitler might be necessary brought about a crisis among the German Nationalists, too. The consequence was a split of the more moderate factions headed by Kuno von Westarp.[53]

After the results in 1930, Hitler more or less lost interest in any major involvement with his allies on the right. However, the NSDAP maintained an ambiguous strategy during 1931 and at the beginning of 1932. According to National Socialist propaganda, the party considered itself not to be involved in a united front of national opposition and continuously went on to stress its independence and auton-

51 "Der Aufmarsch zum Volksbegehren", *Der Tag*, July 10, 1929; report of the working committee for the referendum, July 11, 1929, BA Berlin, R 8048/262.

52 See e.g. letter from Gregor Strasser to Heinrich Himmler, August 12, 1929, BA Berlin, NS 26/2340. See also several articles in *Der Angriff* and *Der Nationale Sozialist*.

53 About the crisis in the DNVP, see Larry E. Jones, "The Dying Middle: Weimar Germany and the Fragmentation of Bourgeois Politics", *Central European History* 1 (1972), 41; Attila Chanady, "The disintegration of the German National People's Party 1924-1930", *The Journal of Modern History* 1 (1967), 85-87. An example of the debate within the party that contributed to the last crisis is found in a transcription of the meeting of the parliamentary group, July 2, 1930, BA Koblenz, Nachlass Schmidt-Hannover, N 1211/71.

omy and to criticise other nationalist parties and movements. Despite this critical attitude, the NSDAP participated in the referendum for the dissolution of the Prussian Landtag, and on many occasions worked together with the DNVP in the Reichstag. This probably led Stahlhelm and the DNVP to think that the national opposition as a whole existed. However, the NSDAP also seemed to seek interlocutors in the centre and moderate right parties which produced some worries among the German Nationalists and the Stahlhelm. In 1931, the NSDAP did not pursue a specific strategy but tried to find its way to power regardless of any previous alliance or any former hatred against other parties.

The conference in Harzburg in 1931 was principally intended to force Hitler into taking a final decision on his allies. The development of the conference day and the period immediately thereafter quite clearly revealed that this goal could not be achieved and that the National Socialists could not afford to involve themselves exclusively with one partner. Furthermore, their partners did not understand Hitler's strategy or, alternatively, were confident that their political and social position was so strong that Hitler could not attain power alone. Hugenberg was the first to understand these dynamics. It was only during the presidential elections, mainly on the part of the Stahlhelm, that it became clear that Hitler's strategy did not take into account the role of his allies. Finally, any hope of Hitler's allies to take control over the potential of the National Socialist movement revealed themselves as pure illusion. Unfortunately these hopes seemed to be the reason for Hindenburg's decision to appoint Hitler Chancellor with Hugenberg and Seldte, too, supporting this procedure.[54]

The Veterans' State: Outlining the Ideological Perspective of the Stahlhelm

As we have seen, Stahlhelm and the NSDAP developed different strategies in order to achieve power. It seems quite clear that Stahlhelm tried to act consistently and preserve its role and independence. By contrast, the approach of the NSDAP was incoherent, since it was more focused on achieving a goal than willing to observe a particular route. In a certain sense the perspective on the state of both movements were more similar than their political strategy. However a comparison may offer some new perspectives, in particular with regard to the Stahlhelm. Both movements refused the democratic and parliamentary order as unnatural for the German people and shared the same critical view of the parties as representatives of individual or partial interests. Both movements rejected political parties as an appropriate means to pursue national interests.

The perspective on the state in National Socialist propaganda was not very clear. Instead, it mainly focused on discussions about the role of socialism. However, as early as in 1927 and in the years to follow, Hitler used all his efforts to contain the anti-capitalist enthusiasm among his followers and tried to render the socialist as-

54 Larry E. Jones, "The greatest stupidity of my life. Alfred Hugenberg and the formation of the Hitler Cabinet, January 1933", *Journal of Contemporary History* 27 (1992), 63-87.

pects of his political programme compatible with the defence of private property and the liberty of enterprise in order to obtain the support of the rural and industrial elites in Germany.[55]

The NSDAP's view of the state was that of a corporative state based on the model of Italian Fascism and *völkisch* ideals of the organic state. It seems, however, that National Socialist propaganda was more a negative vision of contemporary times than a clear and organic view for future policies. In the propaganda the concept of dictatorship was sometimes presented as a solution that would suit the German state better than democracy, but these notions did not appear in any official programme, nor were they a major topic in the political programme. The National Socialist state was supposed to be composed of two parliaments, of which one represented the economic forces and was expected to deliberate on economic and financial questions only. The other one was expected to deal with the political decisions the chancellor, who was to be appointed for life, had made with the aid of a senate. In this sense, the reference to a dictatorship was generally made as a compromise between the old governmental form and the future National Socialist state. However, any reference to the form of the state and institutional reforms National Socialists made during the Weimar Republic must not be seen as unequivocal, because most of those assertions were made for political and tactical purposes only.[56]

Maybe a more precise, but as always ambiguous, idea of the state can be found in Hitler's *Mein Kampf*, where he described the state as a step leading to the realisation of the *Volksgemeinschaft* as an organic state. As pointed out by Klepsch, an interesting aspect of the concept of the state in *Mein Kampf* is the difference which existed between the 1925 edition and that of 1937 with regard to the way to choose the leader. In the first edition the leader was supposed to be elected by the people in order to be legitimated as a dictator, while in the second edition he was to be elected by a restricted circle of party-leaders only.[57] The last point to stress is that according to the National Socialist idea of the state, it was clear that the leadership of a future state was to be selected from members of the NSDAP. In terms of political strategy and ideology, then, the party was placed in a central position.

By contrast, Stahlhelm had as starting point the enhancement of the veterans' position within the institutions of the state. Organisation and leadership of the league did not seem to look for a central or leading role in the new state. Except for the candidateship of Duesterberg for president in 1932, Stahlhelm did not try to place its leaders into any major political role. Rather, it tried to support alternative or independent persons that could be considered a symbol for the nation, as it did

55 See above all Henry Ashby Turner jr., "Hitler's secret pamphlet for industrialists, 1927", *The Journal of Modern History* 3 (1968), 348-374; Dirk Stegmann, "Zum Verhältnis von Großindustrie und Nationalsozialismus", *Archiv für Sozialgeschichte* 13 (1973), 399-482.

56 Karl Dietrich Bracher, *Die Deutsche Diktatur: Entstehung, Struktur, Folgen des Nationalsozialismus* (Frankfurt a.M.: Ullstein, 1979), 157-160.

57 Thomas Klepsch, *Nationalsozialistische Ideologie* (Münster: Lit, 1990), 118-122.

for Hindenburg in 1925. The increasing role of personality and leadership in the Stahlhelm started after the difficult relationship with the NSDAP.

According to the Stahlhelm perspective of the state, the veterans did not represent an attempt towards monarchical restoration, despite their use of symbols from the Second Reich. On the contrary, they rejected the pre-war society as dominated by materialistic interests and superficial patriotism, which was based on empty rituals and national festivities without any real and deep patriotic feeling. The war, they thought, created the conditions to develop real patriotism, and only the revolution and the defeat prevented the realisation of a real German state. It was the war, according to Stahlhelm, which finally gave the Germans an aim for the future and paved the way to realise a new Reich.[58]

Stahlhelm propaganda was dominated, as the National Socialist one, by the presence of negative and critical assertions about contemporary society and unclear perspectives for the future. They also rejected the parliamentary system but, unlike the National Socialists, they considered parliamentary representation as a way to modify the state and produce the reforms needed to lead the country to its destiny. This was, quite clearly, the realisation of the *Volksgemeinschaft* as a society which was able to overcome the egotism of the capitalist world and the materialism of socialism. Their rejection of the Weimar "system" was foremost based on the idea that it relied more on the international forces of capitalism and socialism than on German autonomy and independence. In this sense, the campaign against the approval of the Young Plan was not only a tactical means but a major political goal, since it was one of the first tasks to reduce German dependence on international forces. Unlike the National Socialists, they thought that the new state could be realised through constitutional modifications and also through active work in society in order to produce a change of mentality that could prepare the success of any major political reform.[59]

Conclusion

After this overview of the political strategies by the NSDAP and the Stahlhelm, we can propose some general conclusions.

The origins and the organisation of the two movements had a significant impact on their respective political developments. Stahlhelm was initially a non-political organisation that was, however, established by politically involved persons who had experienced the system of the Wilhelmine Empire. First, this led to the fact that they did not fully consider that things had changed after World War One and, second, that they were able to understand the importance of compromise in politics. It is also noteworthy that they initially helped to defend the state because they regarded themselves as soldiers and servants of the state. In addition, when the situa-

58 Wilhelm Kleinau, *Stahlhelm und Staat. Eine Erläuterung der Stahlhelm-Botschaften* (Berlin: Stahlhelm, 1929), 10-12.

59 *Stahlhelm Handbuch*, 18-21.

tion changed and the relationships with the Weimar Republic became difficult, Stahlhelm, at least publicly, refused to revolt against the state. Stahlhelm preserved its role of political pressure group and maintained its ability to operate in public instead of risking going underground, as happened to many other paramilitary organisations that finally disappeared from the political and social scene.

Furthermore, the whole political strategy of the Stahlhelm seemed to be directed towards compromise and wide-ranging alliances and agreements more than to the achievement of power. This strategy was not only related to other organisations and parties of the nationalist right, but also to the political institutions of the republic and its constitutional structure. It can be affirmed that this collaboration with the state was pursued only in a tactical and not in a truly practical sense but, in the end, it seems that the Stahlhelm leadership was only trying to produce the conditions for a more authoritarian state. This state was supposed to be able to re-establish German autonomy and self-sufficiency, because the veterans thought that the Weimar Constitution was Germany's main problem. They were convinced that the republican state was incapable of strong policy-making.

The different strategy of the National Socialists is also attributable to the origins of the movement. It was a party composed mostly by people who did not have previous political experience. Moreover, for Hitler politics was a new experience and his basic ideas were formed during his experiences with the socialist revolution in Munich and the conditions of interwar Germany. According to Hitler, the Weimar Republic was the cause of all German problems and had to be fundamentally destroyed. After the failure of the 1923 coup, Hitler did not withdraw from his original plans and his change of strategy was not a sign of change of goals. What he learned from the experience in 1923 was not that a revolutionary strategy was fruitless, as many other radical nationalists did. Rather, he concluded from this experience that particular conditions for a revolution had to be realised and that his party had to wait until these conditions were met. He also realised that achieving political power in a legal way may very well be a condition for a revolution. Moreover, he learned that wide-ranging political alliances and agreements rendered his party dependent on the failures and errors of others. The whole strategy of the NSDAP after its reconstitution in 1925 then seemed to follow two directions. The first one was to strengthen the movement internally. The second one was to weaken the opponents in order to make them disappear or become dependent on the NSDAP. In this sense, the ambiguous positions of the NSDAP from 1929 until 1932 seems to have achieved the goal of wearing out the allies as well as the opponents thanks also to the skilful use of propaganda. The apparent will of reaching compromises helped the National Socialists to show the political inconsistence of their partners in the nationalist opposition. We surely cannot speak about a totalitarian aspect or tendency in the NSDAP during the interwar period but, unlike its allies, its ability to avoid compromises helped the party to remain strong and organized during the mid-1920s, when the radical nationalists encountered their worst period of crisis.

Finally, there are some remarks that has to be made about the mass character of the Stahlhelm and the NSDAP. Stahlhelm was, long before the NSDAP, a real mass organisation with collective rituals (national rallies), a strong identity (trench experience) and a significant role attributed to leadership, rooted in the pre-war Prussian militarist culture. However, it seems that Stahlhelm did not really understand the social and political significance of democracy and mass mobilisation. Since they usually despised parties and party politics, the veterans did not really understand that the support Hitler was gaining at the elections was not merely an increase in parliamentary representation but a source of legitimacy, too, that he could, and did use to achieve power.

During the second half of the 1920s, Stahlhelm tried to understand the institutional functions of the state in order to gain power in it but, apparently, it did not understand that the peoples' legitimacy was a major factor to achieve the power in a mass democracy. Moreover, the experience made by many Stahlhelm leaders could later be used by the National Socialists as they efficiently recruited among the ranks of the veterans' league.

Bibliography

Anonymous. *Stahlhelm Handbuch*. Berlin: Stahlhelm, 1927.

Beck, Hermann. *The Fateful Alliance. German Conservatives and Nazis in 1933. The* Machtergreifung *in a New Light*. New York/Oxford: Berghahn Books, 2010.

Berghahn, Volker. *Der Stahlhelm Bund der Frontsoldaten*. Düsseldorf: Droste, 1966.

Bracher, Karl Dietrich. *Die Deutsche Diktatur: Entstehung, Struktur, Folgen des Nationalsozialismus*. Frankfurt a.M.: Ullstein, 1979.

Chanady, Attila. "The disintegration of the German National People's Party, 1924-1930". *The Journal of Modern History* 1 (1967), 65-91.

Corni, Gustavo. *La politica agraria del nazionalsocialismo, 1930-1939*. Milan: Franco Angeli, 1989 (English edition: *Hitler and the Peasants. Agrarian Policy of the Third Reich, 1930-1939*. New York: Berg, 1990).

Diehl, James. *Paramilitary politics in Weimar Germany*. Bloomington: Indiana University Press, 1997.

Duesterberg, Theodor. *Der Stahlhelm und Hitler*. Wolfenbüttel/Hanover: Wolfenbütteler Verlagsanstalt, 1949.

Eley, Geoff. *Reshaping the German Right. Radical Nationalism and Political Change after Bismarck*. New Haven/London: Yale University Press, 1980.

Erger, Johannes. *Der Kapp-Lüttwitz-Putsch. Ein Beitrag zur deutschen Innenpolitik 1919/20*. Düsseldorf: Droste, 1967.

Fenske, Hans. *Konservatismus und Rechtsradikalismus in Bayern nach 1918*. Bad Homburg/Berlin/Zurich: Gehlen, 1969.

Fischer, Conan. *The Rise of National Socialism and the Working Classes in Weimar Germany*. New York/Oxford: Berghahn Books, 1996.

Franz-Willing, Georg. *Die Hitlerbewegung, der Ursprung 1919-1922*. Hamburg et al.: Schenck, 1962.

Gordon, Harold J. *Hitlerputsch 1923*. Frankfurt a.M.: Bernhard & Gräfe, 1971.

Harman, Chris. *The Lost Revolution: Germany 1918-23*. London et al.: Bookmarks, 1997.

Jones, Larry E. "Hindenburg and the Conservative Dilemma in the 1932 Presidential Elections". *German Studies Review* 2 (1997), 235-259.

Jones, Larry E. "The greatest stupidity of my life. Alfred Hugenberg and the formation of the Hitler Cabinet, January 1933". *Journal of Contemporary History* 27 (1992), 63-87.

Jones, Larry E. "The Dying Middle: Weimar Germany and the Fragmentation of Bourgeois Politics". *Central European History* 1 (1972), 23-54.

Kleinau, Wilhelm. *Stahlhelm und Staat. Eine Erläuterung der Stahlhelm-Botschaften.* Berlin: Stahlhelm, 1929.

Klepsch, Thomas. *Nationalsozialistische Ideologie.* Münster: Lit, 1990.

Klotzbücher, Alois. "Der politische Weg des Stahlhelm, Bund der Frontsoldaten". PhD diss., University of Nuremberg, 1964.

Krueger, Gabriele. *Die Brigade Ehrhardt.* Hamburg: Leibniz, 1971.

MacGee, James H. "The political police in Bavaria 1919-1936". PhD diss., University of Florida, 1980.

Merkl, Peter H. *The Making of a Stormtrooper.* Princeton: Princeton University Press, 1980.

Mühlberger, Detlef. *Hitler's Voice. The Völkischer Beobachter, 1920-33*, vol. 1: *Organisation and Development of the Nazi Party.* Oxford/Bern/New York: Peter Lang, 2004.

Noakes, Jeremy. "Conflict and Development in the NSDAP, 1924-1927". *Journal of Contemporary History* 1 (1966), 3-36.

Nyomarkay, Joesph L. "Factionalism in the National Socialist Workers' Party, 1925-26: The Myth and Reality of the 'Northern Faction'". *Political Science Quarterly* 1 (1965), 22-47.

Orlow, Dietrich. *The History of the Nazi Party: 1919-1933.* Pittsburgh: University of Pittsburgh Press, 1969.

Pleyer, Hildegard. "Politische Werbung in der Weimarer Republik". PhD diss., Westfälische Wilhelms-Universität, 1959.

Posse, Ernst H. *Die politischen Kampfbünde Deutschlands.* Berlin: Junker & Donnhaupt, 1930.

Sauer, Bernhard. *Schwarze Reichswehr und Fememorde. Eine Milieustudie zum Rechtsradikalismus in der Weimarer Republik.* Berlin: Metropol Verlag, 2004.

Schumann, Dirk. *Politische Gewalt in der Weimarer Republik. 1918-1933.* Essen: Klartext, 2001.

Stegmann, Dirk. "Zum Verhältnis von Großindustrie und Nationalsozialismus". *Archiv für Sozialgeschichte* 13 (1973), 399-482.

Turner, Henry Ashby jr. "Hitler's secret pamphlet for industrialists, 1927". *The Journal of Modern History* 3 (1968), 348-374.

Zorn, Wolfgang. *Bayerns Geschichte im 20. Jahrhundert.* Munich: C.H. Beck, 1986.

A National Alternative?
National Socialist Appeals to Labour in Berlin, 1925-1933

Anders G. Kjøstvedt

Introduction

In mid-February 1925, one and a half week prior to the official re-establishment of the National Socialist German Workers' Party (NSDAP) in Munich, a local branch was established in Berlin. The following month, on his first visit to the German capital after his release from Landsberg prison, Adolf Hitler confirmed the formation of *Gau* Groß-Berlin of the NSDAP. At the municipal elections in late October, the NSDAP was able to put up a list in the city district of Spandau only where it polled a meagre 137 votes, making it by far the smallest political party in the city. However, with the appointment of Joseph Goebbels as *Gauleiter* in November 1926, the NSDAP began to make progress and in the final stage of the Weimar Republic it was the leading political force in the German capital.[1]

Throughout its existence as an opposition party, the Berlin NSDAP put a lot of effort into attracting voters, members and activists from among the working class. This was partly self-evident, since Berlin was one of Germany's industrial centres

---

1 The literature on the development of National Socialism in Weimar Berlin is not extensive, although it has been growing in recent years. For general studies, see Martin Broszat, "Die Anfänge der Berliner NSDAP 1926/27", *Vierteljahrshefte für Zeitgeschichte* 8 (1960), 85-118; Gerhard Neuber, "Faschismus in Berlin. Entwicklung und Wirken der NSDAP und ihrer Organisationen in der Reichshauptstadt 1920-1934" (PhD diss., Humboldt University Berlin, 1976); Bernd Kruppa, *Rechtsradikalismus in Berlin 1918-1928* (Berlin: Overall, 1988); Jeremy R. S. Brown, "The Berlin NSDAP in the Kampfzeit", *German History* 7 (1989), 241-247; Detlef Schmiechen-Ackermann, *Nationalsozialismus und Arbeitermilieus. Der nationalsozialistische Angriff auf die proletarischen Wohnquartiere und die Reaktion in den sozialistischen Vereinen* (Bonn: Dietz, 1998), 166-212; Andreas Wirsching, *Vom Weltkrieg zum Bürgerkrieg? Politischer Extremismus in Deutschland und Frankreich 1918-1933/39* (Munich: Oldenbourg, 1999); Martin Schuster, "Die SA in der nationalsozialistischen 'Machtergreifung' in Berlin und Brandenburg 1926-1934" (PhD diss., Technical University Berlin, 2004); Sven Felix Kellerhoff, *Hitlers Berlin. Geschichte einer Hassliebe* (Berlin: be.bra verlag, 2005); Bernhard Sauer, "Goebbels 'Rabauken': Zur Geschichte der SA in Berlin-Brandenburg", *Berlin in Geschichte und Gegenwart. Jahrbuch des Landesarchivs Berlin* (2006), 107-164; Thomas Friedrich, *Die missbrauchte Hauptstadt. Hitler und Berlin* (Berlin: Propyläen, 2007); Anders G. Kjøstvedt, "Hitler's Metropolis? The National Socialist Movement in Berlin, 1925-1933" (PhD diss., University of Oslo, 2010). The locally oriented studies include Oliver C. Gliech, "Die Spandauer SA 1926 bis 1933. Eine Studie zur nationalsozialistischen Gewalt in einem Berliner Bezirk", in *Berlin-Forschungen III*, ed. Wolfgang Ribbe (Berlin: Colloquium Verlag, 1988), 107-205; André König, *Köpenick unter dem Hakenkreuz. Die Geschichte des Nationalsozialismus in Berlin-Köpenick* (Mahlow: Mein Verlag, 2004); Oliver Reschke, *Der Kampf der Nationalsozialisten um den roten Friedrichshain (1925-1933)* (Berlin: Trafo Verlag, 2004); Oliver Reschke, *Der Kampf um die Macht in einem Berliner Arbeiterbezirk. Nationalsozialisten am Prenzlauer Berg 1925-1933* (Berlin: Trafo Verlag, 2008).

and had a large working-class population. Additionally, Berlin was home to a vociferous and well-organised labour movement, chiefly represented by the Social Democratic Party (SPD), the Communist Party (KPD) and the major trade union *Allgemeine Deutsche Gewerkschaftsbund* (ADGB). For a political party that claimed to represent the well-being of the entire nation, appealing to the workers of Berlin was only natural. However, we should ask ourselves whether it was more than a simple opportunistic exercise of adapting to the radical and proletarian milieu in Berlin. The National Socialist attempt to appeal to the working-class vote in Weimar Berlin may have been more deep-seated than the basic understanding that it was necessary to win support from all social strata in order to achieve a majority at elections. This chapter seeks to explore the relationship between appealing to the workers and the political project of the NSDAP in general. How was the attempt to attract the workers integrated into the ideological outlook of the National Socialist movement, and in what ways and to what extent did it influence its political activism in the Weimar years? What policies were pursued in an attempt to appear to blue-collar workers as a real alternative to the parties of the Left?

By drawing on empirical evidence from the two main National Socialist newspapers in Weimar Berlin, *Berliner Arbeiter Zeitung* (BAZ)[2] and *Der Angriff*[3], we can analyse the centrality of the appeal to the workers in two major ways. Firstly, through its concordance with the fundamental ideological concept put forth by the Berlin National Socialists throughout the Weimar period: The necessity of a radical, even revolutionary, renewal of the German nation in order to combat the decadence of contemporary society and the inevitable – from a National Socialist viewpoint – political, social and moral collapse that would be the result of the rootlessness and individualisation of modern society. The overcoming of class consciousness was seen as a prerequisite for this renewal.

Secondly, I will discuss the drive to attract blue-collar workers as one of the main driving forces behind the organisational refinement of the National Socialist

2 The weekly BAZ was published by the *Kampfverlag*, a publishing house set up by Gregor and Otto Strasser and the Gauleiter of Pomerania, Theodor Vahlen, in March 1926. Hitler approved and allowed its weekly newspapers, included the BAZ, to carry the party emblem on the front page. BAZ was the official party organ in Berlin from 1926 to the summer of 1930. On June 30, 1930, Gregor Strasser broke off all links to the publishing house due to the conflict between Hitler and his brother Otto. Although the BAZ continued to run until December 20, 1930, it dismissed all ties to the NSDAP when Otto Strasser left the party on July 4, 1930. On this, see Max H. Kele, *Nazis and Workers. National Socialist Appeals to German Labor. 1919-1933* (Chapel Hill: University of North Carolina Press, 1972), 101-103, 134-136, 160; Udo Kissenkoetter, *Gregor Straßer und die NSDAP* (Stuttgart: DTA, 1978), 44-45; Peter D. Stachura, *Gregor Strasser and the Rise of Nazism* (London: Harper Collins, 1983), 4, 18, 56-81.

3 *Der Angriff* was established as a weekly on July 4, 1927, with Goebbels as editor-in-chief. It became a daily in November 1930 with a circulation of 60,000, reaching 110,000 in the election campaign on July 1932, making it one of the most influential National Socialist publications after the *Völkischer Beobachter*. On this, see Ernest Kohn Bramsted, "Goebbels and his Newspaper *Der Angriff*", in *On the Tracks of Tyranny. Essays presented by the Wiener Library to Leonard G. Montefiore*, ed. Max Beloff (London: Ayer Publishing, 1960), 45-65; Russel Lemmons, *Goebbels and der Angriff* (Lexington: University Press of Kentucky, 1994).

movement in Berlin. Although Gau Groß-Berlin always remained below the national average in terms of electoral support for the NSDAP, it displayed a remarkable ability for organisational development and laid down the basic foundation for a party structure that was later adopted on a national scale.[4] Although my approach is limited to Berlin as I draw my empirical data from this locality, this is a discussion that is relevant for other regions as well and for Germany as a whole.[5]

In the conclusion, I will briefly discuss how we can relate my findings from the National Socialist movement in Weimar Berlin with recent historiographical trends on National Socialism, specifically the interpretation of the Third Reich as a process of simultaneous practices of inclusion and exclusion.

A Revolutionary Rebirth of the National Community

In the Weimar period, the National Socialist movement in Berlin presented itself as a genuine revolutionary movement whose political project constituted a clean break with contemporary society. The outspoken aim of its political project was the destruction of the democratic Weimar Republic, placing in its stead an organic national community based on racial principles – a *Volksgemeinschaft*. This transformation was supposed to come about through a revolutionary renewal of the German nation. It had the specific purpose of saving the nation from certain destruction and economic, political, social and moral collapse. German society was seen as on the threshold of a new age, and the NSDAP regarded itself as a political party with a historic mission to usher in a new beginning following a period of national humiliation, foreign influence and internal decadence.[6]

The ideal of a homogenous national community was of course not a National Socialist invention. Already from the mid-19th century conservative reformers, witnessing the process of industrialisation, sought to reintegrate the workers into the nation and the state. For several political groups in late Imperial Germany the

4 In the May 1928 Reichstag election the average poll for the NSDAP was 2.6 per cent, in Berlin it achieved 1.5 per cent. As the turnout for the NSDAP rose, so did the differences between Berlin and the national average: In the September 1930 Reichstag election, the NSDAP polled 14.6 per cent in Berlin compared to a national average of 18.3 per cent; in the July 1932 Reichstag election, the vote for the NSDAP was 28.6 per cent in Berlin with a national average of 37.4 per cent; in November 1932, the figures were 33.1 per cent nationally and 26 per cent in Berlin. The figures are from Richard Hamilton, *Who Voted for Hitler?* (Princeton: Princeton University Press, 1982), table 4.2, 74.

5 In his study of the development of National Socialism in Saxony, Claus-Christian Szejnmann had a similar approach, focusing on the ideological and political struggle with the SPD and the attempt to establish the National Socialist movement in the workplace. See Claus-Christian Szejnmann, "The Rise of the Nazi Party in the Working-Class Milieu of Saxony", in *The Rise of National Socialism and the Working Classes in Weimar Germany*, ed. Conan Fischer (Providence/Oxford: Berghahn Books, 1996), 189-215; Claus-Christian Szejnmann, *Nazism in Central Germany. The Brownshirts in "Red" Saxony* (New York/Oxford: Berghahn Books, 1999). See also Wilfried Böhnke, *Die NSDAP im Ruhrgebiet 1920-1933* (Bonn: Verlag Neue Gesellschaft, 1974).

6 Kjøstvedt, "Hitler's Metropolis?", especially 62-70.

Volksgemeinschaft was regarded as a healthy opposite to modern society with its social contrasts and conflicts. It was also an important part of the youth movement *Wandervogel*, which saw it as an ideal future community. During the First World War, all the political parties adhered to it in principle, eschewing class war in favour of a common defence of the nation. It was also a very important political concept during the Weimar Republic, and was not only heralded by the conservative or nationalistic Right, but also by Liberal and Social Democratic politicians, such as Hugo Preuss and Friedrich Ebert. The concept of the *Volksgemeinschaft* was therefore deeply rooted in modern German political culture, which helps to explain why it was such a successful political concept in the years of the Third Reich, although the National Socialists gave it an unmistakeable racial interpretation.[7]

Gregor Strasser, the leading National Socialist in northern Germany and only next to Hitler in terms of importance for the NSDAP until he left the Party in December 1932, was a strong advocate of the revolutionary aspect of National Socialism. He claimed in an editorial in BAZ in June 1929 that the realisation of the NSDAP's political project would take form as an "earth-shattering upheaval" on the scale of the French Revolution. The reference to the French Revolution is important, as Strasser regarded the revolutionary project of the NSDAP as redemption from the liberal-bourgeois revolution of 1789: Its rational, capitalist and democratic dispositions were to be replaced by *völkisch* thought, nationalism and "German socialism".[8] Heavily influenced by his war service, Strasser regarded the sacrifices of the soldiers at the front as some sort of revelation of the unified nation, giving birth to a new and nationally conscious Germany. Strasser condemned the events of November 1918, with the abdication of the Kaiser and the proclamation of the republic, as a false revolution and a betrayal of Germany's national unity. According to him, it had brought destructive foreign influence to bear on Germany, most notably through the "un-German" republic, the Treaty of Versailles and the war reparations.[9]

Joseph Goebbels, Gauleiter of Gau Groß-Berlin from November 1926 to May 1945, also subscribed to the idea that the "false" revolution of 1918 had to be

---

7 Gunther Mai, "National Socialist Factory Cell Organisation and the German Labour Front: National Socialist Labour Policy and Organisations", in *The Rise of National Socialism and the Working Classes*, ed. Fischer, especially 123-126; Gunther Mai, "'Verteidigungskrieg' und 'Volksgemeinschaft'. Staatliche Selbstbehauptung, nationale Solidarität und soziale Befreiung in Deutschland in der Zeit des Ersten Weltkrieges (1900-1925)", in *Der Erste Weltkrieg. Wirkung, Wahrnehmung, Analyse*, ed. Wolfgang Michalka (Munich: Piper, 1994), 583-602, especially 590-596; Michael Wildt, "Die Ungleichheit des Volkes. 'Volksgemeinschaft' in der politischen Kommunikation der Weimarer Republik", in *Volksgemeinschaft. Neue Forschungen zur Gesellschaft des Nationalsozialismus*, eds. Frank Bajohr and Michael Wildt (Frankfurt a.M.: Fischer, 2009), 24-40. See also Bernd Stöver, *Volksgemeinschaft im Dritten Reich. Die Konsensbereitschaft der Deutschen aus der Sicht sozialistischer Exilberichte* (Düsseldorf: Droste, 1993).

8 Gregor Strasser, "Katastrophenpolitik", editorial in BAZ, June 9, 1929.

9 See Gregor Strasser, "Macht Platz, ihr Alten!", BAZ, May 8, 1927; Gregor Strasser, "Von der Revolte zur Revolution!", BAZ, November 6, 1927.

overcome so that a "true" National Socialist revolution could commence.[10] He described the political project of the NSDAP as a "restoration of a German Germany".[11] On more than one occasion Goebbels proclaimed the idealism of the National Socialist movement which was supposed to restore the German nation from its current misery through a stage of sacrifice and renewal, and lead it to redemption in a future Third Reich.[12]

It is important to clarify that the National Socialist idea of the *Volksgemeinschaft* was not presented as an actual political union meant to bridge a political, economic, social and religious divide in Germany. It was regarded as a continuous process that was supposed to be realised in a utopian ideal community of the future, where Germans would enjoy a deeper sense of recognition and belonging, social mobility and security. The national community was thus a promise to be realised in the future. The revolution pointed to in National Socialist propaganda should not necessarily be interpreted as a violent overthrow of established society, although it was envisaged as a clean, sharp break with the contemporary political regime. Indeed, Goebbels wrote and spoke disdainfully about democratic parlia-mentarianism and more than once distanced the NSDAP from democratic participation, but he also made it clear that destruction of the democratic system was to come from within and after the NSDAP had assumed political power.[13] The National Socialists always claimed that the revolution they represented was only a means to an end: It was carried out to achieve something specific, the restoration of an organic racial community. Thus the revolutionary concept of National Socialism was in essence an awakening, or rebirth, of German national unity. The NSDAP's political project was to revitalise what they regarded as an ethnic and holistic community; indeed, the National Socialist movement itself was heralded as a manifestation of the future society and Hitler as the prophet of unity.[14]

The fundamental principle of the need for national rebirth was manifest in many different ways. It was an important part of the National Socialists' virulent and paranoid anti-Semitism, in which the Jews were portrayed as leading a world conspiracy against the German nation. It can also be witnessed in the oft-repeated claim that the parties of the Left, the Social Democratic SPD and the Communist KPD, were actively seeking to obstruct the realisation of the *Volksgemeinschaft* by insisting

---

10 E.g., see Joseph Goebbels, "Aufbruch gegen die Revolte" and "Verrat am jungen Deutschland", both in *Der Angriff*, November 7, 1931.

11 Joseph Goebbels, "An alle Mitglieder und Anhänger unserer Bewegung!", *Der Angriff*, November 24, 1929.

12 See i.e. Joseph Goebbels, "Wir wählen Adolf Hitler!", editorial in *Der Angriff*, March 5, 1932.

13 Goebbels wrote very sharply against parliamentarism and democracy in the run-up to the Reichstag elections in May 1928 and September 1930. See his editorials before and after the May 1928 Reichstag election: "Verantwortlichkeit", *Der Angriff*, April 16, 1928; "Was wollen wir im Reichstag?", *Der Angriff*, April 30, 1928; "I.d.I.", *Der Angriff*, May 28, 1928. Perhaps the best example of Goebbels' criticism of the democratic system during the autumn of 1930, was his editorial "An das schaffende deutsche Volk!", *Der Angriff*, August 31, 1930.

14 For enlightening examples, see Herbert Blank, "Agitation und Propaganda", BAZ, August 4, 1929; Joseph Goebbels, "Die Revolution als Ding an Sich", *Der Angriff*, April 27, 1930.

on class struggle and international solidarity. Denunciations of the conservative Right may be interpreted in similar style.

An important prerequisite for the belief in the racial community was the conviction that people were essentially unequal, and that the true force in the history of mankind was struggle between nations and races. Realising an ethnic national community would necessarily come at the expense of those who were defined as outsiders. The NSDAP attributed this role above all to the Jews, who could never belong to the national community, and who were also regarded as string pullers behind the forces obstructing the realisation of national unity. The road to realising the German *Volksgemeinschaft* was thus blocked by the mere presence of Jews in the country, and in late August 1930 the anti-Semitic journalist Johann von Leers claimed in an article in *Der Angriff* that the "removal of the alien Jews" was an essential precondition for German national unity.[15]

This idea closely resembles what Roger Griffin has termed the palingenetic myth of rebirth in fascism. Griffin uses his definition mainly to better understand and analyse the fascist regimes established in Italy and Germany in the interwar period and the various fascist movements surfacing throughout Europe after the end of the First World War. In my opinion, Griffin's emphasis on the revolutionary break with decadent contemporary society and the quest to usher in an "organic" national community fits very well with the core ideological concept put forth by National Socialism in Berlin.[16]

From Class Struggle to the Volksgemeinschaft

The National Socialist discourse in Berlin was dominated by its protests against established society, various institutions of the democratic republic and other political parties and individuals, with the National Socialists being almost obsessed by creating hostile images of representatives of what they attacked. Through the use of enemy images, the National Socialists tried to delegitimize other political parties and their representatives, but they also used denunciations as a vehicle to bring across a message of change, although the real ramifications of the radical changes the NSDAP said it wanted to bring about were never formulated in great detail. The NSDAP's attempt to present itself as the only true workers' party was therefore partly a message of what the NSDAP wanted to do and what changes they would make, and partly accusations against the parties of the Left and the trade unions.

In an era when political affiliation was very much decided by socio-economic status, religious affiliations or region, and political parties rarely were able to draw significant electoral support across these cleavages, National Socialism stressed its dismissal of class and confessional consciousness. The National Socialists claimed

15 M. Thomas [pseud. Johann von Leers], "Auf dem Weg zum Dritten Reich", *Der Angriff*, August 31, 1930. On von Leers, see Martin Finkenberger's contribution to this anthology.

16 Griffin defines fascism as "a genus of political ideology whose mythic core in its various permutations is a palingenetic form of populist ultra-nationalism". Roger Griffin, *The Nature of Fascism* (London: Routlegde, 1994), 26.

to be the only true revolutionary force in Weimar Germany because they were the only ones to realise the necessity of national unity and of bridging the social gaps in society. The other parties, it was claimed, drew their very strength from these conflicts. To the National Socialists, the German workers had to be convinced into substituting class consciousness for a realisation that they were part of an ethnic "destiny of community" *(Schicksalsgemeinschaft)*[17] and Goebbels identified the inclusion of the working masses as a precondition for realising the national community.[18] The National Socialists were quite clear on how the workers were to be included in the nation as a whole. In political terms it would take the form of an exodus from the parties of the Left in favour of the NSDAP. In this process the internationalism of Marxism was to be discarded and replaced with the classless utopia of National Socialism, and National Socialist propaganda time and again returned to the image of the "workers of the brain and the fist" that was portrayed as having overcome the "un-German" cleavage between socio-economic groups. Hence, class struggle and international solidarity was dismissed as lies, deceit and "Jewish-Marxist swindle".[19] In February 1930, the publicist Ernst zu Reventlow, one of the founders of the German *Völkisch* Freedom Party (*Deutschvölkische Freiheitspartei*, DVFP)[20] who had joined the NSDAP in 1927, dismissed international solidarity as "a big lie and a delusion".[21] Marxism was dismissed as an intellectual construction based on reason and a materialist world view – both outlooks despised by the National Socialists – and totally bereft of revolutionary zeal. It was claimed that the Social Democratic Party was becoming increasingly bourgeois, filled to the brim with "philistines and cowards",[22] whilst the Communists had maintained some of their revolutionary spirit, but rather than directing it towards a renewal of Germany, they allegedly fought for "Jewish world domination" through the creation of an "uprooted, soulless proletariat".[23]

The imminent national community was interpreted as "socialism", and National Socialist commentators frequently returned to this term to describe the future. It

---

17 For an enlightening example, see Ernst Pfister, "Hinein in die Betriebe – damit der Arbeiter Deutschland befreit!", *Der Angriff*, November 10, 1931.

18 Joseph Goebbels, "Betriebszellen", editorial in *Der Angriff*, June 1, 1930.

19 As examples, see Joseph Goebbels, "Internationale", editorial in *Der Angriff*, March 26, 1928; Walter Schuhmann, "Die Internationale", *Der Angriff*, May 22, 1930; "Sozialismus!", *Der Angriff*, June 8, 1930; "Deutsche Arbeiter herhören!", *Der Angriff*, March 11, 1931; B.H., "Internationale Sozialpolitik oder Nationalsozialismus?", *Der Angriff*, April 9, 1932.

20 On the DVFP, see Stefanie Schrader's contribution to this anthology.

21 Ernst zu Reventlow, "Internationalismus: Arbeiterfreiheit?", BAZ, February 16, 1930.

22 Julius Lippert, "Was passiert am 1. Mai?", *Der Angriff*, April 29, 1929; "Betrachtungen über die Berliner Maienluft", BAZ, May 26, 1929; "Der Kettenhund des Bürgerblocks", *Der Angriff*, October 26, 1930; "Marxismus oder Bürgerlichkeit?", *Der Angriff*, February 25, 1931; "Revolte in der SPD", *Der Angriff*, October 5, 1932; "SPD. und Herrenklub", *Der Angriff*, October 6, 1932; "SPD. toleriert Herrn von Papen!", *Der Angriff*, October 27, 1932; "SPD.! Herunter mit der Maske!", *Der Angriff*, October 27, 1932; "Um ihre Pfründe verrät die Sozialdemokratie das Volk", *Der Angriff*, October 27, 1932.

23 Gregor Strasser, "Wir und die Wahlen", BAZ, March 11, 1928. See also "Zerfall der K.P.D.", BAZ, August 14, 1927.

was an ill-defined term, but it should not be regarded as some form of pseudo-socialism.[24] It was essentially synonymous to *Volksgemeinschaft,* in which the well-being of the ethnic community and the state was raised above the welfare of individuals: "Socialism is truly nothing else than community, national community. [...] The common good before the private good! That is socialism!"[25]

To the National Socialists, a necessary condition for radical improvement for the workers was for Germany to withdraw from her international obligations set after the end of the First World War, in particular the war reparations schemes. The National Socialists regarded the ratification of the Dawes Plan in 1926, dubbed as Germany's "second Versailles", and the Young Plan in 1929-30, not only a betrayal of the German nation, but of German workers in particular. Even though both the Dawes and Young plans secured a massive influx of cheap American capital to Germany which significantly aided the partial economic recovery of the mid-to-late 1920s, the National Socialists regarded them as delivering Germany into the hands of international capital. The National Socialists frequently referred to contemporary Germany as a "colony" and a "slave of international capital" due to its obligations to the reparations. Throwing off this foreign yoke was seen as absolutely essential for immediate national unity and improved living and working conditions for German workers.[26]

The Betrayal of the Social Democratic Party

The National Socialist discourse on workers in Berlin was exclusively directed against the parties of the Left. With an insignificant, at least in political terms, Catholic sub-culture in Berlin the National Socialists only directed negligible attention to workers who supported the Catholic Centre Party and Catholic trade unions. According to the National Socialists, both the Social Democrats and the Communists were political forces that separated the German nation, thereby obstructing national salvation. In the National Socialists' simplified rhetoric, both were accused of tearing the nation apart because of their insistence on class struggle and the primacy of socio-economic forces as the prime mover of history and societal change. In National Socialist propaganda it was claimed that German workers would forever be enslaved as long as the Marxist hegemony over them persisted as the parties of the Left failed to realise the importance of the nation and the *Volk*. The "purification" of the labour movement envisaged by the National Socialists can therefore be seen as a parallel to the general idea of a revolutionary awakening of the nation. However, the Social Democrats and the Communists

24 Thus my interpretation goes against those who mainly attribute the National Socialists' attempt to attract the workers to a minority within the movement usually referred to as a "Nazi Left". See above all Reinhard Kühnl, *Die nationalsozialistische Linke 1925-1930* (Meisenheim: Anton Hain, 1966); Kele, *Nazis and Workers*.

25 "Sozialismus!", *Der Angriff*, June 8, 1930.

26 Among the best examples are Joseph Goebbels, "Der Youngplan", editorial in *Der Angriff*, July 1, 1929; Joseph Goebbels, "Was dann?", editorial in *Der Angriff*, March 16, 1930.

were treated very differently in National Socialist propaganda. The Communists were very much considered as a one-dimensional physical threat and were presented as a foreign-led terror organisation. The SPD was regarded as much more important as it was closely associated with the democratic republic and stood between National Socialism and political power. The time and effort spent on degrading the Communists was dwarfed by the campaigns against the Social Democratic Party, thus it is National Socialist attacks on the Social Democrats that will be the main focus here.

To the NSDAP, the Social Democratic Party, more than any other political force in Weimar Germany, represented the ills that had befallen Germany since the First World War, making the faults of the Weimar Republic mainly the faults of the SPD. As a dominant Weimar party and by virtue of the Social Democratic leadership of the free trade unions, the SPD was seen as a guarantor of the hated republic and the main obstacle between the NSDAP and political power. The SPD was thus portrayed as the main obstruction to realising national unity and improving the economic and social conditions in Germany. The NSDAP promised to make a clean break with Social Democratic mismanagement and by that usher in a new dawn for Germany. In National Socialist dealings with the SPD, "betrayal" was the key term, both as a betrayal of the nation at large and a more specific betrayal of German workers. It was alleged that the SPD had betrayed the nation by selling out to international finance capital through the war reparations schemes and betrayed the German worker by not living up to the promises made in 1918-19. The National Socialists continuously attacked the SPD and the trade unions for failing to realise their social promises. Through the pages of *Der Angriff* the SPD was blamed for the decline in real wages, the failure to properly introduce the eight-hour day and the rising unemployment.[27] In an attempt to distance SPD members and voters from their leaders, the leadership of the SPD and the free trade unions were portrayed as corrupt "bigwigs" *(Bonzen)* that put money in their own pockets rather than fight for improved working conditions for German workers.[28] Reinhold Muchow claimed that it was the task of the NSDAP to remove the "incompetent and

---

27 On this, see "Maifeier – Götzendämmerung", BAZ, April 25, 1926; "Der stete Verrat der Sozialdemokratie", BAZ, July 25, 1926; Gregor Strasser, "Zum 29. August", BAZ, August 29, 1926; Gregor Strasser, "Marxismus – 8-Stundentag – Erwerbslosenfürsorge", BAZ, November 21, 1926; Gregor Strasser, "Die Lüge des 1. Mai!", BAZ, April 28, 1929; "Warme Suppen für Arme – Sekt für die Bonzen", BAZ, February 24, 1929; "Die SPD-Regierung gegen den 8-Stundentag. Eine kennzeichnende Debatte in Genf", BAZ, March 17, 1929; Reinhold Muchow, "Wir wollen den Achtstundentag!", *Der Angriff*, June 22, 1930; "Vierzehn Jahre Lohnraub. Ein Schuldkonto der SPD.", *Der Angriff*, July 13, 1932.

28 See i.e. "Scheidemanns Kaiser-Möbel", BAZ, June 24, 1928; "Hungerlöhne und Bonzengehälter", *Der Angriff*, July 8, 1929; "Gewerkschaftspaläste", *Der Angriff*, July 29, 1929; "Neuer Arbeiterverrat der S.P.D.", *Der Angriff*, August 26, 1929; "Riesengehälter von Arbeitergroschen", *Der Angriff*, December 9, 1930; "Die Gewerkschaftsbonzen gegen die Arbeiter", *Der Angriff*, January 12, 1931; "Maske herunter, SPD!", *Der Angriff*, July 23, 1932; Gerhard Starcke, "Ein SPD.-Genosse beschimpt Erwerbslose: Not und Elend auf der 'Wohle'", *Der Angriff*, November 1, 1932.

corrupt Marxist [trade union] leaders" for the benefit of the nation and the state.[29] Allegedly, the "corrupt"[30] and "Jewish-financed"[31] SPD had been selling out on the welfare of the German workers by agreeing to the war reparations. By accepting the Dawes Plan in 1924, the SPD had therefore made itself into an agent of international finance capital.[32] Further evidence of the capitalist-friendly politics of the SPD was found in the acceptance of the Young Plan in 1929-30. The SPD had chosen to be the arbiter of the policy of compliance, rather than to fight against it for the benefit of the working masses, and therefore the SPD had betrayed the workers and embraced capitalism.[33]

The View of Organised Labour

The National Socialists frequently claimed that they were not hostile to the idea of trade unions, for instance an organised representation of the workforce, but they did argue against what they regarded as the politicisation of the trade unions, especially by the SPD.[34] In March 1932, as part of the Presidential Election campaign, a rather comprehensive view of trade unions was presented in *Der Angriff*. The article demanded that the trade unions be purged of the "political entrepreneurs" of Social Democracy, and claimed that the SPD-led unions had contributed to the introduction of the Dawes and Young plans, thereby playing an instrumental role in worsening the living conditions of German workers. The National Socialist view of trade unions presented in this article was that the movement should not represent those employed within a specific branch of industry, or submit itself to internationalism; rather, it should be an integrated part of the *Volksgemeinschaft:* "The worker must recognise that his destiny is bound to that of his people."[35]

---

29 Reinhold Muchow, *Nationalsozialismus und 'freie' Gewerkschaften* (Munich: Eher, 1932), 112.

30 On the corruption of the SPD, see i.e. Joseph Goebbels, "Eine Mücke hat gehustet", editorial in *Der Angriff*, February 27, 1928; "Wer SPD. wählt – wählt Sklarek", BAZ, November 17, 1929; Joseph Goebbels, "Wo bleibt der zweite Mann?", editorial in *Der Angriff*, February 27, 1931; "Korruption in der SPD.", *Der Angriff*, January 19, 1932; "Korruptionsskandal um einen Sozialdemokraten", *Der Angriff*, February 15, 1932; "SPD. ist Korruption!", *Der Angriff*, April 23, 1932.

31 On this, see e.g. "S.P.D. schützt jüdische Hehler", *Der Angriff*, July 15, 1929; Hans Hinkel, "Jenseits von Jud' und Böß!", BAZ, October 20, 1929; "Herunter mit der Maske!", *Der Angriff*, August 28, 1930; "Der Proletarierführer", *Der Angriff*, March 22, 1932.

32 Joseph Goebbels, "Internationale", editorial in *Der Angriff*, March 26, 1928. See also "Dawes, der Arbeiter-Würger", BAZ, August 26, 1928.

33 Cited in "Herunter mit der Maske", *Der Angriff*, August 28, 1930. See also "Sozialdemokratie und Hochfinanz", BAZ, February 3, 1929; "Dirne Reichsbanner", BAZ, March 17, 1929; "Menschenjagd", *Der Angriff*, June 24, 1929; Paul Meier, "Der Reaktionäre Marxismus", BAZ, April 27, 1930; "Die marxistischen Gewerkschaften im Dienste des Bankkapitals", *Der Angriff*, November 25, 1930; "SPD. und KPD. für das Großkapital", *Der Angriff*, March 26, 1931.

34 See "Sind wir gewerkschaftsfeindlich?", *Der Angriff*, May 1, 1930; Ernst Pfister, "Erkennt die Gewerkschaften!", *Der Angriff*, September 15, 1931.

35 "NSDAP. und Gewerkschaften", *Der Angriff*, March 10, 1932.

The NSDAP claimed not to oppose the idea of organised labour *per se;* rather, it saw in the political and ideological project of National Socialism the preservation and restoration of what it regarded as an authentic German labour movement going back to the middle of the 19th century. According to the National Socialists, the German labour movement was originally embedded in the nation and persisted in its struggle to improve the living and working conditions of German workers, in a strictly German context. Ferdinand Lassalle's establishment of the first German labour party, *Allgemeiner Deutscher Arbeiterverein,* in 1863, was regarded as a natural development in the wake of industrialisation and increasing democratisation of society. Interestingly, Lassalle, despite the fact that he was Jewish, was given a positive review. According to the National Socialists, the German labour movement was derailed by Wilhelm Liebknecht and August Bebel, who were seen as importing Marxist ideas into the movement after the death of Lassalle in 1864. The National Socialists claimed that through Marxist influence, the German workers were removed from their cultural heritage, traditions and belief in the authoritarian state and forced into an uprooted proletariat.[36] The negative influence over the labour movement was seen as distinctly Jewish and the National Socialists regarded the foreign and alien control of the German labour movement as a step towards Jewish world domination. To remedy this allegedly Jewish-influenced disintegration of the labour movement, German workers had to be helped into developing a national or racial consciousness to fight off the "Jewish-Marxist" influence.[37]

Johannes Engel, leader of the first factory cell organisation in Berlin, lamented in January 1931 on the loss of the patriarchal bond between employer and employee, leading to an impersonal representation of labour and capital. Engel argued that the organisations representing labour and capital, for instance the trade unions and the employer's associations, were not working towards a common goal: The welfare of the nation; instead, they found the reason for their very existence in the struggle against each other. Although Engel realised that this was in part a natural development in a modern industrial economy, he claimed that this development was to the detriment above all of the employee, especially following the economic Depression, when the power of strikes had been hollowed out by rapidly increasing unemployment. To alleviate this, Engel claimed that the representatives of labour and capital had to stop bickering about wages and working hours and instead lift the debate to a higher level and to discuss the welfare of the nation as a whole, thereby eschewing class conflict for national unity. According to Engel, without each other the employer and employee were nothing, but together they were every-

36 See as examples Wilhelm Dreher, "Der Leidensweg des deutschen Arbeiters", *Arbeitertum. Blätter für Theorie und Praxis der nationalsozialistischen Betriebszellen-Organisation*, October 15, 1931; Franz Winkler, "Wofür kämpften die Arbeiter im alten Reich? Die Entwicklung der deutschen Arbeiterbewegung", *Arbeitertum*, February 15, 1932.

37 See Ernst Pfister, "Die Bedeutung der Rassenfrage für die Arbeiterschaft", *Arbeitertum*, January 1, 1932; Karl J. Weygold, "November", *Arbeitertum*, November 1, 1932; Bernhard Köhler, "Klassenkampf oder Arbeitsbeschaffung", *Arbeitertum*, November 1, 1932.

thing: A *Volk*.[38] Engel's argumentation in this article is typical for the Berlin National Socialists' view on the relationship between labour and capital.

Anti-Capitalism and Criticism of Imperial Germany

The National Socialists clad their appeals to labour in anti-capitalist rhetoric. In September 1927, the BAZ called for the nationalisation of all banks, in October 1929, Julius Lippert, chief editor of *Der Angriff* and from 1937 Lord Mayor of Berlin, repeated this demand.[39] A so-called "Stock exchange special edition" *(Börsen-Sondernummer)* of *Der Angriff* in March 1928 carried an article claiming that German workers would never be free as long as German industry was in ruins and indebted to the "Bank-Jews of Berlin and New York".[40] Jews were identified as the string-pullers behind international capital that was destroying the German economy: Capitalism was denounced as racially alien to Germany and Jews as capitalist exploiters.[41] According to the National Socialists, the major fault of the liberal-capitalist system was its insistence on individual profit and not the welfare of the nation as a whole, describing the profit-seeking of big business as "cancerous to the people".[42]

The often radical denunciations of capitalism, however, should not lead us to believe that National Socialism, in Berlin or elsewhere, dismissed capitalism as such. For one thing, they defended private property. They operated with two forms of capital: "Productive" and "parasitic". Finance capital, the stock exchange and banks were seen as "parasitic" and equated with international Jewish capital, making it "un-German", alien and damaging to the welfare of the nation. This idea allowed the National Socialist movement to maintain a radical anti-capitalist stance while at the same time looking for support from industry and big business.[43]

The National Socialists demanded state control of economic life and stressed the primacy of politics in guiding and controlling the economic development of Germany. They feared that in an uncontrolled world market the German worker

38 Johannes Engel, "Arbeiter und Unternehmer in der Volksgemeinschaft", *Der Angriff*, January 22, 1931.

39 "Banken unter Staatsaufsicht!", *Der Angriff*, September 12, 1927; Julius Lippert, "Sozialisiert die Banken!", *Der Angriff*, October 3, 1929.

40 "Von der Börse erwürgt!", *Der Angriff*, March 19, 1928.

41 "Kapitalismus und Judentum", BAZ, June 30, 1928; "Sklaverei von heute", BAZ, July 29, 1928; "Unseren Glückwunsch!", *Der Angriff*, April 29, 1929; "Jüdische Ausbeuter in Reinkultur", *Der Angriff*, October 31, 1929; Hans Hinkel, "Unser Deutschland in Moabit", BAZ, February 22, 1930; M. Thomas [pseud. Johan von Leers], "Wirtschaft und Nationalsozialismus", editorial in *Der Angriff*, July 10, 1930.

42 Cited in "Konzern!", *Arbeitertum*, December 1, 1931.

43 See as examples "Der Siegeszug des Leihkapitals", *Der Angriff*, September 5, 1927; Knipperdolling [pseud. Julius Lippert], "Wie an der Börse 'gearbeitet' wird", *Der Angriff*, March 19, 1928; "Ford als Börsenbazillus", *Der Angriff*, August 19, 1929; "Ein Teufelsplan der Großbanken", *Der Angriff*, December 8, 1929; "Diktatur des Bankkapitals", *Der Angriff*, December 22, 1929; "Ein Plan der Bankjuden: Zwangsarbeit für den deutschen Arbeiter?", *Der Angriff*, November 29, 1930.

would be replaced by those who were willing to work for less because they were racially inferior. The National Socialist ideal of an autarkic and self-sufficient nation, where the economy was the servant of the nation and the state, could only be achieved in an authoritarian, corporate state.[44]

Significantly, the Berlin National Socialists were very critical towards the social policy of Imperial Germany. As previously discussed, the defeat of Germany in the First World War, the fall of the Empire and the proclamation of the Republic in November 1918 are of fundamental importance to an understanding of National Socialism, and we have seen how the National Socialists interpreted a change of regime as a betrayal of the nation and the workers. This makes the events of autumn 1918 decisive in our understanding of National Socialism's relationship to the working class both before and after 1933. Not only was the political outlook of almost all of the leaders of the National Socialist movement, and subsequently the Third Reich, very much formed by the event as they took part in it, many of them criticised the lack of preparing society for war. Imperial Germany, although it was quick to defend its people and territory with the army and navy, failed to realise the importance of integrating society at large with the greater national cause. By allowing the growing industrial working class in Germany to live in pitiful conditions with inadequate housing, poor working conditions and low wages, the ruling elites had undermined the nationalisation of the working masses. Furthermore, the imperialist dreams of the German national elites had prevented them from seeing the misery and suffering in their midst, and thus opened the stage for Jewish intellectuals and their allegedly perverted view of socialism. For all their talk of a Jewish world conspiracy, the unpatriotic pacifism of the Left and the "stab-in-the-back", the National Socialist leadership understood very well that Germany had lost the war not only because of the combined military strength of the Entente, but also because civilian society had collapsed under the strain of total war. The leaders of Germany at the time were thus at fault for not recognising the importance of civil society in total war. This was a failure the National Socialists were determined not to repeat.[45]

Into the Factories

After focusing on major ideological aspects, we now turn to the National Socialists' attempt to appear as a viable alternative to the working class vote as a driving force behind the organisational refinement of the NSDAP. As mentioned in the introduction, one of the main aspects of the National Socialist movement in Weimar Berlin was its insistence on organisational development and improvement, and from the late 1920s onwards we can track the development of a conscious strategy

---

44 As examples, see Franz Stöhr, "Die Sozialpolitik und wir", BAZ, March 18, 1928; Walter Schuhmann, "Befreiung der deutschen Arbeit", *Der Angriff*, February 8, 1931.

45 One enlightening example is Paul Hofmann, "Der kommende Volksstaat", *Arbeitertum*, September 15, 1931. On this, see also Tim Mason, *Social Policy in the Third Reich. The Working Class and the "National Community"* (Providence/Oxford: Berg Publishers, 1993), particularly 19-21.

of projecting National Socialist ideas, interpretations of contemporary events as well as representatives of the National Socialist movement into spaces and areas usually closed off to it.

National Socialist propaganda, both before and after 1933, is usually identified as mass propaganda in the form of large public assemblies, street marches and outdoor rallies.[46] In addition there was the printed mass media in form of newspapers, posters, leaflets and other printed material. Print media was without doubt the most important method of political propaganda for all parties of the Weimar republic. What I would like to draw attention to is the realisation by some leading National Socialist officials how limited or confined the ordinary mass propaganda was in order to attract the segments of German society that regarded the National Socialist movement with varying levels of hostility. The two main groups that were underrepresented as supporters or members of the National Socialist movement were those affiliated with organised labour (SPD, KPD and the trade unions) and Catholicism. Both represented hegemonies that the National Socialists had great difficulties in breaking.

With no strong Catholic subculture in Protestant Berlin, it was the Social Democratic Party, the Communist Party and the trade unions that represented the political and social segment of the population National Socialists found themselves more or less unable to break into. National Socialist leaders would often speak of the marches and public assemblies they held in the proletarian quarters of the city, typically in Wedding, Neukölln, Friedrichshain and Lichtenberg, and they would present them as raids or conquests, as a symbolic occupation of the strongholds of "Red Berlin". They fought for terrain, with the brown-shirted Stormtroopers and the Communist equivalent, the Red Front Fighters League *(Rote Frontkämpferbund)*, playing the main roles. These actions often led to violent clashes and with the deepening of the political and economic crisis of the Weimar Republic, the number of casualties from such encounters increased.[47]

In the literature on the development of National Socialism in Weimar Berlin, these aggressive public propaganda campaigns initiated by Goebbels on his arrival

---

46 On National Socialist propaganda in the Weimar period, see above all Gerhard Paul, *Aufstand der Bilder. Die NS-Propaganda vor 1933* (Bonn: Dietz, 1990).

47 There is an extensive body of literature on this subject. See in particular Eve Rosenhaft, *Beating the Fascists? The German Communists and Political Violence 1929-1933* (Cambridge: Cambrigde University Press, 1983); Hans-Gerd Jaschke and Martin Loiperdinger, "Gewalt und NSDAP vor 1933. Ästhetische Okkupation und physischer Terror", in *Faszination der Gewalt*, ed. Rainer Steinweg (Frankfurt a.M.: Suhrkamp, 1983), 123-155; Richard Bessel: *Political Violence and the Rise of Nazism. The Storm Troopers in Eastern Germany 1925-1934* (New Haven/London: Yale University Press, 1984); Thomas Balistier: *Gewalt und Ordnung. Kalkül und Faszination der SA* (Münster: Verlag Westf. Dampfboot, 1989); Peter Longerich: *Die braunen Bataillone. Geschichte der SA* (Munich: C.H. Beck, 1989), especially 116-126; Paul, *Aufstand der Bilder*, especially 133-142; Marie-Luise Ehls, *Protest und Propaganda. Demonstrationen in Berlin zur Zeit der Weimarer Republik* (Berlin/New York: Walter de Gruyter, 1997); Wirsching, *Vom Weltkrieg zum Bürgerkrieg?*; Dirk Schumann, *Politische Gewalt in der Weimarer Republik 1918-1933. Kampf um die Straße und Furcht vor dem Bürgerkrieg* (Essen: Klartext, 2001).

in the city are considered to be the most important explanation for the rise of the National Socialist movement in the capital.[48] Although such clashes achieved legendary status and were an important part of myth-making in both National Socialist and Communist propaganda, some of the leaders realised the limits of such actions. It was an important realisation that despite the considerable gains of the NSDAP in the 1929 and 1930 elections, there were significant parts of the German electorate that felt almost completely alien to the National Socialist movement.

Unsurprisingly, the NSDAP's propaganda department regarded the September 1930 Reichstag election, at which the party polled 18.3 per cent, as a great success. Still, it acknowledged that a lot of work remained to be done and that most of the gain came from votes previously cast for the liberal and bourgeois parties, although there was a small gain of former SPD votes.[49] From now on, preparing for winning substantial numbers of votes formerly cast for the KPD and especially the SPD was the main task of National Socialist propaganda, and in the following year preparations were made to ensure that the NSDAP would triumph over the parties of the Left, too. The reasoning was simple: Goebbels believed that the parties of the Left consisted of large numbers of good-natured Germans who had been cheated and misled by their Marxist leaders. According to Goebbels, it was important to realise that the workers themselves were not to be targeted, but they had to be alienated from their leaders and their ideology. To the National Socialists, the increased effort to project the National Socialist movement into the workplace was an attempt to herd the misled German labourers back to their fold, for instance the future national community, or in more concrete political terms, the NSDAP. In a huge collective effort, ranging from NSDAP representatives in governments and parliaments to the public assemblies, newspapers and individual activists, the aim was to win the working masses for National Socialism.[50]

In order to achieve this, new methods were called for and this had already been expressed most pointedly by Goebbels and Gregor Strasser at the Weimar party rally in July 1926. In internal party discussions Goebbels in particular stressed the need to develop new methods of propaganda in order to reach out to the groups

---

48 This is the main argument in Carin Kessemeier, *Der Leitartikler Goebbels in den NS-Organen "Der Angriff" und "Das Reich"* (Münster: Fahle, 1967); Schmiechen-Ackermann, *Nationalsozialismus und Arbeitermilieus*, 168-175; Arne von Röpenack, *KPD und NSDAP im Propagandakampf der Weimarer Republik. Eine inhaltsanalytische Untersuchung in Leitartikeln von "Rote Fahne" und "Angriff"* (Stuttgart: Ibidem Verlag, 2002); Reschke, *Friedrichshain 1925-1933*, 30-37; Kellerhoff, *Hitlers Berlin*, 17-84; Friedrich, *Die missbrauchte Hauptstadt*, 113-226.

49 On the new voters for the NSDAP in this election, see Hamilton, *Who voted for Hitler?*, 516-517.

50 On this, see the monthly circulations by the Propaganda Department of the NSDAP (RPL), February 27 and March 18, 1931, in Bundesarchiv Berlin (BA Berlin), NS 18/916; Joseph Goebbels, "Richtlinien der Propaganda-Leitung", in *Wille und Weg. Monatsblätter der Reichspropagandaleitung der NSDAP*, April 1931.

that were unimpressed by the party's mass propaganda.[51] Johannes Engel argued in June 1929 that the workers of Berlin, especially those based in organised labour, could not be successfully appealed to through ordinary mass propaganda centring on public assemblies, demonstrations and printed mass media such as flyers and posters.[52]

The most important development that emerged from this was the increased insistence on *Kleinarbeit,* which basically referred to personal persuasion through individual members of the various parts of the National Socialist movement. Attention turned towards the personal persuasion of individuals, stressing the personal initiative of the rank-and-file membership. The idea was to turn every social arena on which a National Socialist appeared into a propaganda opportunity for the NSDAP. Each individual National Socialist was to become a propaganda tool for the movement in his residential area, at the workplace or in any social setting the individual National Socialist appeared.

In September 1931 Heinz Franke, Goebbels's deputy as leader of the NSDAP's propaganda department and editor of the internal propaganda organ *Wille und Weg,* stressed the need for an increased focus on systematic and persistent *Kleinarbeit.* In a highly significant article in the influential party organ, Goebbels' right-hand man at the propaganda department discussed the possibilities of individually processing small groups of people. To Franke, the most important strategy was to organise public events so that new people would come to the meetings. The goal of individual processing prior to public assemblies was to attract as many workers as possible. Previously, this had been sought by inviting members of the SPD and KPD to National Socialist assemblies and allowing them to bring their own speakers. According to Franke, this had had dubious results: Experience had shown that the workers who were affiliated with organised labour very rarely cared about attending National Socialist meetings. If they did, they did so in very large numbers and thereby either threatened to break up the event or attempted to turn it into a propaganda opportunity of their own by bringing with them skilled orators. Thus, by inviting the parties of the Left, the NSDAP risked losing control of its own event to the physical threat and skilled oratory of representatives of the SPD and KPD. Franke acknowledged that the SA units in Berlin were often not able to protect the growing number of meetings, and that only a handful of National Socialist speakers in the city were sufficiently well-versed in public oratory and National Socialist ideology. As an alternative, Franke wanted the local party organisation to look for workers who gave the impression of not being so deeply rooted in the Social Dem-

51 Strasser's and Goebbels' speeches can be found in BA Berlin, NS 26/389. For a contemporary and similar argument, see "Mehr Kleinarbeit! Konzentration der Kräfte!", BAZ, September 12, 1926.

52 Johannes Engel, "Pionier, du namenloser Kämpfer…", *Der Angriff,* July 22, 1929.

ocratic or Communist subculture, with the aim of inviting them, as individuals, to National Socialist meetings.[53]

A necessary condition for implementing this in the movement's political activism was to introduce a new organisational model for the NSDAP. Beginning in the summer of 1928, the local NSDAP in Berlin went through substantial organisational changes. This took place shortly after an eleven-month ban on the NSDAP in Berlin and the dismal showing at the May 1928 Reichstag election, in which the NSDAP polled 2.6 per cent, and only 1.5 per cent in Berlin. What they did was to create more organisational levels within the party, with the smallest, the street cell, consisting of no more than five people. Street cells were supposed to canvass their neighbourhood area, sometimes limited to a street, a particular part of a street or a tenement house. This system was first applied in Berlin and later exported to the rest of Germany.[54]

At the same time the NSDAP began to establish cells of National Socialist employees in various companies scattered around Berlin. It began at the latest as an informal coming together of National Socialist-minded employees at the Knorr-bremse AG in Berlin-Lichtenberg in June 1927, a factory producing brakes for locomotives.[55] These loosely organised cells were formally integrated into the NSDAP on July 30, 1928.[56] A similar development took place elsewhere, but it was Berlin that proved to be the nucleus of factory cell development within the National Socialist movement, serving as a model project for other regions.[57] In Berlin, forming factory cells resulted from a more conscious and purposeful development than elsewhere, and it received enthusiastic support from Gauleiter Goebbels. He recognised the propaganda value of the factory cells and believed that it would be a

53 Heinz Franke, "Mobilmachung", *Wille und Weg*, September 1931. Szejnmann notes similar difficulties in the working-class areas of urban Saxony. See Szejnmann, "The Rise of the Nazi Party", 205.

54 On this, see the document "Organisationssystem des Gaues Groß-Berlin" written by Reinhold Muchow in October 1929, in which Muchow detailed the reasoning behind the system and how it was supposed to work. No known copy of this document exists today, but an extensive report by Berlin's political police is exclusively based upon this document and quotes extensively from the original. See police report on the NSDAP's street cell system, Berlin, July 15, 1930, BA Berlin, R 1501/126129.

55 "Erklärung", BAZ, June 12, 1927.

56 "Bekanntmachung", BAZ, July 29, 1928.

57 According to Szejnmann, such cells were established for the first time in Gau Saxony in July 1929. Overall, attempts to establish National Socialist cells in the industrial towns of Saxony seem to have been a more isolated and limited effort. See Szejnmann, "The Rise of the Nazi Party", 201-205; Szejnmann, *Nazism in Central Germany*, 111-114. Böhnke describes a considerable propaganda effort by the NSBO in the Ruhr district in preparation for the factory council elections in 1931. See Böhnke, *Ruhrgebiet*, 174. On the importance of Berlin, see also Martin Broszat, *Der Staat Hitlers* (Munich: dtv, 1983), 63; Volker Kratzenberg, *Arbeiter auf dem Weg zu Hitler?* (Frankfurt a.M.: Peter Lang, 1989), 84-85; Mai, "National Socialist Factory Cell Organisation", 119; Joachim Bons, *Nationalsozialismus und Arbeiterfrage. Zu den Motiven, Inhalten und Wirkungsgründen nationalsozialistischer Arbeiterpolitik vor 1933* (Pfaffenweiler: Centaurus-Verlagsgesellschaft, 1995), 290-292.

successful undertaking given the proletarian nature of a large part of the city's population. Goebbels was undoubtedly important, but substantial and necessary contributions also came from Engel and Muchow.[58] By 1930 the factory cell system originating in Berlin had been exported to other areas of Germany and merged together as the National Socialist Factory Cell Organisation *(Nationalsozialistische Betriebszellen-Organisation,* NSBO).[59] The NSBO existed until 1935, but it lost its influence after the establishment of the German Labour Front *(Deutsche Arbeitsfront,* DAF) in May 1933.[60]

How did this system work? In theory, the structure of the factory cell organisation was very hierarchical and guided by the *Führerprinzip:* The cell leaders were supposed to report to higher functionaries and await instructions. In reality, however, the cell leaders were left very much to themselves to decide how they were to complete their tasks. The main task of the factory cell leader was to monitor political activity at the workplace and initiate propaganda he deemed appropriate in order to win new members. He was also tasked with educating the other cell members in all kinds of questions related to social policy. The main purpose of the propaganda of the cells was to reach those who did not visit National Socialist meetings nor read their newspapers. Guidelines stressed the need for flexibility, an indication of the freedom granted to cell leaders and the lack of guiding principles. Moreover, the type of activity much depended on the specific company in question.[61] However, there was one unmistakable command: Political activity at the workplace was not mass propaganda; it was to be *Kleinarbeit,* likening it to the activities of the street cells which worked from house to house, apartment to apartment. Indeed, mass propaganda was considered at larger companies, and in such cases flyers were a preferred method, usually distributed by unemployed party members.[62]

---

58 In his study Bons somewhat overstates the importance of Goebbels at the expense of the indispensable work being done by local activists such as Muchow and Engel. See Bons, *Nationalsozialismus und Arbeiterfrage*, 290-292; Kjøstvedt, "Hitler's Metropolis?", 105-109.

59 By 1930 the factory cell organisation in Berlin was being exported to the Reich. This is apparent in Muchow's organisational plan for the factory cells which came into force on May 1, 1930. See Reinhold Muchow, "Ziel und Systematik der Arbeit der Nationalsozialistischen Betriebszellen", Geheimes Staatsarchiv Preußischer Kulturbesitz (GStA), Rep. 77, Tit. 4043, No. 322, fol. 76-82. See also correspondence between Muchow and party headquarters in Munich (Org. Abt. I) in November 1930, BA Berlin, NS 22/1049.

60 On the strained relationship between the NSBO and the DAF in the early months of the Third Reich, see Hans-Gerd Schumann, *Nationalsozialismus und Gewerkschaftsbewegung. Die Vernichtung der deutschen Gewerkschaften und der Aufbau der 'Deutschen Arbeitsfront'* (Hanover/Frankfurt a.M.: Norddeutsche Verlagsanstalt, 1958); Mai, "National Socialist Factory Cell Organisation", especially 127-130; Ronald Smelser, *Robert Ley. Hitler's Labour Front Leader* (Oxford: Berg Publishers, 1988), 125-139.

61 Muchow, "Ziel und Systematik der Arbeit der Nationalsozialistischen Betriebszellen", GStA, A. Rep. 77, Tit. 4043, No. 322, fol. 80.

62 On this, see police report on the National Socialist factory cell organisation, Berlin, November 7, 1929, GStA, A. Rep. 77, Tit. 4043, No. 322, fol. 2-6; "Bericht über die Betriebszellen-Organisation des Gaues Gross-Berlin", Berlin, July 31, 1929, BA Berlin, NS 22/1049; Much-

The cell leader was also supposed to monitor members carefully and look for suitable people to be used as functionaries and weed out undesirable elements. This points to the cell structure as an instrument in grooming skilled party functionaries, and much time and effort was spent on educating NSDAP members. There was a distinct long-term perspective here, as the ultimate goal was to change German society from below. It also indicates an increasing bureaucratisation of the National Socialist movement. The Berlin branch of the NSDAP was far from the largest, but with 1,200 functionaries it had by far the highest amount of administrative personnel.[63]

As the source material is so scarce and non-National Socialist sources are virtually non-existent, it is almost impossible to get a firm grip of the development of the factory cells in Berlin. The lack of sources is simply astonishing. Apart from a few very rudimentary sources[64], we are left with searching through the columns of the National Socialist press in order to find some information about the development of the factory cells in Berlin. There are many risks connected with utilising what was essentially a propaganda newspaper as a source for the main developments of the factory cell organisation, it can, however, provide us with a cursory overview in some branches. Berlin was a nucleus of industry in Germany, especially for electro-technical and metal industry and some of the first factory cells were established at Berlin's industrial giants in this sector, such as Siemens, AEG, Borsig, Singer and Osram. Banks and insurance companies featured prominently in reports about National Socialist activity in the workplace, with cells being established at many of the major banks and insurance institutions represented in the capital. So did civic companies, such as the municipal electric and gas companies and the world's largest municipal company, the transport company *Berliner Verkehrs Aktiengesellschaft* (BVG). Other branches that dominated were commerce, publishing houses, hotels and restaurants and the post service.[65]

---

ow, "Ziel und Systematik der Arbeit der Nationalsozialistischen Betriebszellen", GStA, A. Rep. 77, Tit. 4043, No. 322, fol. 80.

63 According to the Prussian police, Gau Groß-Berlin had 52 sections with 12,000 members by October/November 1930, making it the seventh largest NSDAP Gau in Prussia. Gau Saxony was about three times larger in terms of membership. See the police report on the NSDAP, Berlin, November 27, 1930, GStA, Rep. 77, Tit. 4043, No. 302, fol. 147-149; police report on the NSDAP, Berlin, December 21, 1930, GStA, Rep. 77, Tit. 4043, No. 293. fol. 2-4.

64 The first of these documents is Johannes Engel's undated list (most likely from spring 1929) of 64 factory cells in Berlin, of which 13 consisted of one person only. The list is dominated by banks and insurance companies, newspapers and printers. The second document, "Übersichtskarte der Berliner Betriebsorganisation", also stems from Engel and lists 92 cells. Both documents are found in BA Berlin, NS 22/1049.

65 For a more detailed analysis of the factory cells' activity see Kjøstvedt, "Hitler's Metropolis?", 106-122.

Conclusion

In this chapter I have tried to argue that the National Socialist attempt to secure significant working-class support at the expense of the Social Democratic Party and the Communist Party played a pivotal role in the political project of the NSDAP and in its strategy of legality following the failed Munich putsch in November 1923. Even though the National Socialists in Berlin presented a social policy and demanded higher wages, better housing and improved working conditions, they did so only sporadically and with little conviction. However, their appeals to labour in Berlin were never about competing with the parties of the Left and the trade unions on social policy: What was important was the alternative posed by National Socialism and its insistence on exchanging class consciousness for a commitment to the national community. The importance thus lies in the National Socialist proposal of an alternative solution to the workers' question and the proclamation of alternative identities to social class. The National Socialists claimed not to oppose the idea of organised labour; rather, they regarded the political and ideological project of National Socialism as a means to preserve and restore an "authentic" labour movement which had been distorted and abused by Marxism. This is also why we should interpret the attempt to attract blue-collar workers to the NSDAP and its affiliated organisations as some sort of pseudo-Socialism instigated by a minority within the movement. Nor should we regard it as political activism more or less forced upon the National Socialists by the social composition of the city's population or its radical political milieu. All told, the National Socialists did not want to overcome social boundaries through progressive social policies. They regarded any cleavage within the nation as artificially constructed by the nation's enemies and sought to make them irrelevant by insisting on other categories: You were either a rightful and valuable member of the ethnic national community, or you were not.

It is important, I believe, to relate what has been discussed in this chapter to recent developments within the historiography of National Socialism. There is a quite distinctive trend towards exploring the efforts by the National Socialist regime in the period from 1933 to 1945 as a means to integrate a majority of the German population by insisting on the creation of a racial national community. Influential German and non-German scholars increasingly regard it as a regime that not only used coercion and terror in order to control and command its population, but also as a regime that consciously strove to promote an alternative society with which a large part of the population could feel attached to and be included into.[66] And, fur-

---

66 The most important are Robert Gellately, *Backing Hitler. Consent and Coercion in Nazi Germany* (Oxford: Oxford University Press, 2001); Hans-Ulrich Thamer, *Der Nationalsozialismus* (Ditzingen: Reclam, 2002); Hans-Ulrich Wehler, *Deutsche Gesellschaftsgeschichte*, vol. 4: *Vom Beginn des ersten Weltkrieges bis zur Gründung der beiden deutschen Staaten 1914-1949* (Munich: C.H. Beck, 2003); Götz Aly, *Rasse und Klasse: Nachforschungen zum deutschen Wesen* (Frankfurt a.M.: Fischer, 2003); Götz Aly, *Hitler's Volksstaat. Raub, Rassenkrieg und nationaler Sozialismus* (Frankfurt a.M.: Fischer, 2005); Eric A. Johnson and Karl-Heinz Reuband, *What We Knew: Terror, Mass Murder, and Everyday Life in Nazi Germany: An Oral History* (Cambridge, MA: Basic Books, 2005); Norbert Frei, *1945 und wir. Das Dritte Reich im Bewusstsein der Deutschen* (Munich: C.H. Beck,

thermore, that the National Socialist leadership was to a large extent successful in creating a regime many Germans could relate to, which was one of the main reasons why there was so limited resistance towards the regime. An important part of this is the interpretation of the Third Reich as a society in which two parallel and mutually dependent processes took place. One of them was a process of integration of those whom the National Socialist regime deemed racially valuable. The other was the increasingly radicalized process of exclusion from German society of those who were regarded as racially unfit for the *Volksgemeinschaft*. This exclusionary process above all targeted the Jews but also affected other victims of the National Socialist regime, such as the handicapped and mentally ill. What was important, howhowever, was that the groups in society that were targeted for exclusion were quite easily identified and only constituted a minority of the German population.

Even though the National Socialist idea of a *Volksgemeinschaft* was to a lesser extent an actual political union and more than anything a promise to be realised in the future, it was also an actual process taking place in the Third Reich, in which the population was mobilised for the regime. The ongoing process fits well with this mobilisation aspect as the National Socialists were very much concerned with changing German society in their own image and realised that this had to take form as a consciousness-raising process in which the population was attached to a National Socialist worldview. The in-group of the Third Reich, the "Aryan" Germans that supported the regime or at least were sufficiently indifferent towards it, could be included into a greater national community in a number of ways. One was through the National Socialist Party or a host of other associations such as the Winter Aid *(Winterhilfe)* or the Strength through Joy *(Kraft durch Freude)* programme. The career opportunities and the partial destruction of traditional social hierarchies that transcended possibilities in the Weimar Republic were an important element of integration and inclusion that should be mentioned here. One of the things I have tried to do in this chapter is to show that this way of thinking about inclusion and (re-)integration developed within the National Socialist movement from the early 1920s onwards, and that it was specifically connected to the attempt to attract the working class in the Weimar era.

The interpretation of the dual processes of inclusion and exclusion as essential aspects of the Third Reich and as an important explanation for the absence of serious opposition towards the regime highlights the importance of race as *the* fundamental concept of the Third Reich. How, then, does the question of race correspond to the attempt to appeal to the working class vote in the Weimar era through the insistence on a national community? An answer can only be hinted at here, but in my research on the National Socialist movement in Berlin I rarely encountered explicit references about race or racial characteristics, especially so in the

2005); Peter Longerich, *"Davon haben wir nichts gewusst!" Die Deutschen und die Judenverfolgung 1933-1945* (Munich: Siedler Verlag, 2006); Michael Wildt, *Volksgemeinschaft als Selbstermächtigung. Gewalt gegen Juden in der deutschen Provinz 1919 bis 1939* (Hamburg: Hamburger Edition, 2007); Frank Bajohr and Michael Wildt, eds., *Volksgemeinschaft: Neue Forschungen zur Gesellschaft des Nationalsozialismus* (Frankfurt a.M.: Fischer, 2009).

National Socialist discourse on labour. The National Socialists continued to refer to a German *nation* rather than a German, Nordic or Aryan *race*, and although Jews were frequently singled out as supposed string pullers behind any ill that had befallen Germany, the term *Rasse* hardly ever appeared at all. However, there were numerous references to *Blut* and *Volk*, both of which have distinct racial connotations.

Bibliography

Bons, Joachim. *Nationalsozialismus und Arbeiterfrage. Zu den Motiven, Inhalten und Wirkungsgründen nationalsozialistischer Arbeiterpolitik vor 1933.* Pfaffenweiler: Centaurus-Verlagsgesellschaft, 1995.

Böhnke, Wilfrid. *Die NSDAP im Ruhrgebiet 1920-1933.* Bonn: Verlag Neue Gesellschaft, 1974.

Broszat, Martin. "Die Anfänge der Berliner NSDAP 1926/27". *Vierteljahrshefte für Zeitgeschichte* 8 (1960), 85-118.

Broszat, Martin. *Der Staat Hitlers.* Munich: dtv, 1983.

Brown, Jeremy R. S. "The Berlin NSDAP in the Kampfzeit". *German History* 7 (1989), 241-247.

Brustein, William. *The Logic of Evil: The Social Origins of the Nazi Party, 1925-1933.* New Haven: Yale University Press, 1996.

Büsch, Otto and Wolfgang Haus. *Berlin als Hauptstadt der Weimarer Republik 1919-1933. Mit einem statistischen Anhang zur Wahl- und Sozialstatistik des demokratischen Berlin 1919-1933.* Berlin/New York: Walter de Gruyter, 1987.

Fischer, Conan, ed. *The Rise of National Socialism and the Working Classes in Weimar Germany.* Providence/Oxford: Berghahn Books, 1996.

Friedrich, Thomas. *Die missbrauchte Hauptstadt. Hitler und Berlin.* Berlin: Propyläen, 2007.

Gliech, Oliver C. "Die Spandauer SA 1926 bis 1933. Eine Studie zur nationalsozialistischen Gewalt in einem Berliner Bezirk". In *Berlin-Forschungen III*, edited by Wolfgang Ribbe, 107-205. Berlin: Colloquium Verlag, 1988.

Griffin, Roger. *The Nature of Fascism.* London: Routlegde, 1994.

Hamilton, Richard. *Who Voted for Hitler?* Princeton: Princeton University Press, 1982.

Kele, Max H. *Nazis and Workers. National Socialist appeals to German Labour, 1919-1933.* Chapel Hill: University of North Carolina Press, 1972.

Kellerhoff, Sven Felix. *Hitlers Berlin. Geschichte einer Hassliebe.* Berlin: be.bra verlag, 2005.

Kessemeier, Carin. *Der Leitartikler Goebbels in den NS-Organen "Der Angriff" und "Das Reich".* Münster: Fahle, 1967.

Kissenkoetter, Udo. *Gregor Strasser und die NSDAP.* Stuttgart: DTA, 1978.

Kjøstvedt, Anders G. "Hitler's Metropolis? The National Socialist Movement in Berlin 1925-1933". PhD diss., University of Oslo, 2010.

König, André. *Köpenick unter dem Hakenkreuz. Die Geschichte des Nationalsozialismus in Berlin-Köpenick.* Mahlow: Mein Verlag, 2004.

Kratzenberg, Volker. *Arbeiter auf dem Weg zu Hitler? Die Nationalsozialistische Betriebszellen-Organisation. Ihre Entstehung, ihre Programmatik, ihr Scheitern 1927-1934.* Frankfurt a.M.: Peter Lang, 1989.

Kruppa, Bernd. *Rechtsradikalismus in Berlin 1918-1928.* Berlin: Overall, 1988.

Kühnl, Reinhard. *Die nationalsozialistische Linke 1925-1930.* Meisenheim: Anton Hain, 1966.

Mai, Gunther. "Die Nationalsozialistische Betriebszellen-Organisation: Zum Verhältnis von Arbeiterschaft und Nationalsozialismus". *Vierteljahreshefte für Zeitgeschichte* 31 (1983), 573-613.

Mai, Gunther. "'Verteidigungskrieg' und 'Volksgemeinschaft'. Staatliche Selbstbehauptung, nationale Solidarität und soziale Befreiung in Deutschland in der Zeit des Ersten Weltkrieges (1900-1925)". In *Der Erste Weltkrieg. Wirkung, Wahrnehmung, Analyse*, edited by Wolfgang Michalka, 583-602. Munich: Piper, 1994.

Mai, Gunther. "National Socialist Factory Cell Organisation and the German Labour Front". In *The Rise of National Socialism and the Working Classes in Weimar Germany*, edited by Conan Fischer, 117-136. Providence/Oxford: Berghahn Books, 1996.

Mason, Tim. *Social Policy in the Third Reich. The Working Class and the "National Community"*. Providence/Oxford: Berg Publishers, 1993.

Mühlberger; Detlef. *The Social Bases of Nazism 1919-1933*. Cambridge: Cambridge University Press, 2003.

Reschke, Oliver. *Der Kampf der Nationalsozialisten um den roten Friedrichshain (1925-1933)*. Berlin: Trafo Verlag, 2004.

Reschke, Oliver. *Der Kampf um die Macht in einem Berliner Arbeiterbezirk. Nationalsozialisten am Prenzlauer Berg 1925-1933*. Berlin: Trafo Verlag, 2008.

Reuth, Ralf Georg. *Goebbels. Eine Biographie*. Munich: Piper, 1990.

Ruck, Michael. *Bollwerk gegen Hitler? Arbeiterschaft, Arbeiterbewegung und die Anfänge des Nationalsozialismus*. Cologne: Bund Verlag, 1988.

Röpenack, Arne von. *KPD und NSDAP im Propagandakampf der Weimarer Republik. Eine inhaltsanalytische Untersuchung in Leitartikeln von "Rote Fahne" und "Angriff"*. Stuttgart: Ibidem Verlag, 2002.

Sauer, Bernhard. "Goebbels 'Rabauken': Zur Geschichte der SA in Berlin-Brandenburg". *Berlin in Geschichte und Gegenwart. Jahrbuch des Landesarchivs Berlin* (2006), 107-164.

Schmiechen-Ackermann, Detlef. *Nationalsozialismus und Arbeitermilieus. Der nationalsozialistische Angriff auf die proletarischen Wohnquartiere und die Reaktion in den sozialistischen Vereinen*. Bonn: Dietz, 1998.

Schumann, Hans-Gerd. *Nationalsozialismus und Gewerkschaftsbewegung. Die Vernichtung der deutschen Gewerkschaften und der Aufbau der "Deutschen Arbeitsfront"*. Hanover/Frankfurt a.M.: Norddeutsche Verlagsanstalt, 1958.

Schuster, Martin. "Die SA in der nationalsozialistischen 'Machtergreifung' in Berlin und Brandenburg 1926-1934". PhD diss., Technical University Berlin, 2004.

Stachura, Peter D. *Gregor Strasser and the Rise of Nazism*. London: Harper Collins, 1983.

Stachura, Peter D. "National Socialism and the German Proletariat, 1925-1935: Old Myths and New Perspectives". *Historical Journal* 36 (1993), 701-718.

Szejnmann, Claus-Christian. *Nazism in Central Germany. The Brownshirts in "Red" Saxony*. New York/Oxford: Berghahn Books, 1999.

Szejnmann, Claus-Christian. "The Rise of the Nazi Party in the Working-Class Milieu of Saxony". In *The Rise of National Socialism and the Working Classes in Weimar Germany*, edited by Conan Fischer, 189-215. Providence/Oxford: Berghahn Books, 1996.

Welch, David. "Manufacturing a Consensus: Nazi Propaganda and the Building of a 'National Community'". *Contemporary European History* 2 (1993), 1-15.

Welch, David. *The Third Reich: Politics and Propaganda*. London: Routledge, 1993.

Welch, David. "Nazi Propaganda and the Volksgemeinschaft: Constructing a People's Community". *Journal of Contemporary History* 39 (2004), 213-238.

Wildt, Michael. "Die Ungleichheit des Volkes. 'Volksgemeinschaft' in der politischen Kommunikation der Weimarer Republik". In *Volksgemeinschaft. Neue Forschungen zur Gesellschaft des Nationalsozialismus*, edited by Frank Bajohr and Michael Wildt, 24-40. Frankfurt a.M.: Fischer, 2009.

Finding Fascism:
The Politics of Sir Oswald Mosley, 1929-1932*

Matthew Worley

On September 21, 1931, Sir Oswald Mosley made a life-defining decision. The previous day, he had visited Glasgow. There he spoke under the banner of his recently-formed New Party, calling on the youth of Britain to discard the "old" parties and the "old" ways in order to forge a new movement dedicated to the building of a "modern state of which we can be proud".[1] The meeting, to which between 20,000 and 40,000 people attended, ended in chaos.[2] As communists heckled from the crowd, so Mosley led his bodyguard into the throng and confronted those he accused of disrupting his speech. Disorder reigned; fists, bottles, stones and knives were utilised in a "free fight" that spread across Glasgow Green before Mosley and his entourage escaped in cars assailed by the angry crowd. It was, therefore, in the aftermath of an ugly scene of political violence that Mosley told his comrades that the time had come. "This", he insisted, "forces us to be fascist and [...] we need no longer hesitate to create our trained and disciplined force".[3]

Mosley's decision set in motion arrangements that led eventually to the formation of the British Union of Fascists (BUF) in October 1932.[4] And it was a decision that was not taken lightly. Britain, after all, was at this time in the midst of a severe political and economic crisis. The Labour government, of which Mosley had previously been a member before leaving to form the New Party in February 1931, had collapsed in August 1931, its cabinet divided as to how best respond to the economic problems that had mounted steadily since Wall Street's crash in October 1929.[5] In its place, a national government dominated by the Conservative Party but headed by Labour's erstwhile leader, James Ramsay MacDonald, was in power. Economically, Britain's long-standing structural problems had been compounded by mounting unemployment, budget deficits and anxiety as to the resilience of the country's financial resolve in the face of on-going global upheaval. All around, Brit-

---

* A revised and slightly longer version of this paper has been published as "Why Fascism? Sir Oswald Mosley and the Conception of the British Union of Fascists", *History* 66/1 (2011), 66-81.

1 *The Scotsman*, September 21, 1931.

2 *The Times*, September 21, 1931; Nigel Nicolson, ed., *Harold Nicolson Diaries and Letters, 1930-39* (London: Collins, 1966); *Daily Worker*, September 22, 1931.

3 Nicolson, ed., *Diaries*, September 21, 1931.

4 Upper-case "Fascism" will be used to denote Italian Fascism; lower-case "fascism" for generic fascism.

5 For the New Party, see Matthew Worley, *Oswald Mosley and the New Party* (Basingstoke: Palgrave, 2010).

ain's existing political order appeared to be in flux.[6] For Mosley, at least, Britain stood poised on the edge of an abyss. Decisive action was needed; new methods and new ideas were necessary to "save" Britain and prevent its collapse into bloody class war. Fascism, Mosley came to argue, was the only solution.[7]

This chapter will examine the factors that led Mosley to such a conclusion. With hindsight, perhaps, Mosley's drift to fascism seems relatively straightforward. Here was an egoist and national chauvinist who tried and failed to succeed within the parliamentary system and so adopted a political creed that lent itself to decisive action based on a militarism that befitted a young ex-soldier and member of the landed gentry. Mosley regarded himself as a leader, and he found in fascism a corporate vision that tallied with his own wartime experience and the quasi-feudal memories of his childhood.[8] But it would be wrong to conclude that Mosley was somehow destined to fascism. To do so would be to ignore both the context and the contingent factors that combined to shape Mosley's understanding of the world in the early 1930s. Put bluntly, it took the events of 1929-32 to forge Mosley's own variant of the fascist creed.

The Coming Man?

Oswald Mosley was born in 1896. His father was the (fifth) baronet of Ancoats, a title that Mosley inherited in 1928. Mosley schooled at Winchester College and the military academy in Sandhurst; he served in the Great War (1914-18). Politically, Mosley was inspired by the experience of war and the desire to build a new world that eclipsed the follies of those who had led the British people into four years of unprecedented slaughter. In 1918, aged just 22, he was elected as the Unionist MP for Harrow on an idiosyncratic platform of "socialistic imperialism". From the outset, Mosley sought to mix the collective values of socialism with a deep-seated patriotism; he saw in the state-driven war economy the potential "to build a better and more modern nation".[9]

Not surprisingly, Mosley soon found that his generational politics and plans for economic reform jarred with the outlook of the older "hard-faced men" who dominated the government benches. In 1920, therefore, he crossed the floor of the Commons and stood successfully as an independent candidate in the 1922 and 1923 general elections. He took up Labour Party membership in 1924, so aligning himself with what he believed to be the "forces of progress in their assault against

---

6 Philip Williamson, *National Crisis and National Government: British Politics, the Economy and Empire, 1926-32* (Cambridge: Cambridge University Press, 1992); Robert Skidelsky, *Politicians and the Slump: The Labour Government of 1929-31* (London: Macmillan, 1967). See also David Powell, *British Politics, 1910-35: The Crisis of the Party System* (London: Routledge, 2004).

7 Oswald Mosley, *The Greater Britain* (London: BUF, 1932), 15.

8 Oswald Mosley, *My Life* (London: Thomas Nelson, 1968).

9 Ibid., 90; Robert Skidelsky, *Oswald Mosley* (London: Macmillan, 1975); Stephen Dorril, *Blackshirt: Sir Oswald Mosley and British Fascism* (London: Viking, 2006).

the forces of reaction".[10] Therein, Mosley joined with John Strachey to plot a "revolution by reason" that fused J. A. Hobson's liberal-socialist thesis of underconsumption with Keynes' monetary theories and Labour's implicit but undeveloped notion of economic planning. The objective was to "weave these various aspects of modern thought into one comprehensive whole".[11]

Mosley cut an awkward figure in the Labour Party. He became close to Ramsay MacDonald, served on the party's National Executive Committee (NEC), and proved a popular speaker among the party membership. Simultaneously, as a member of the landed gentry, his lifestyle, demeanour and blatant ambition led many a leading party and trade union figure to treat him with suspicion.[12] Although Mosley declared himself a socialist, he understood socialism as an efficient form of economic administration rather than a means by which to fundamentally realign existing class relations. Even so, he was seen by some to be a rising star within the party and even tipped as a future prime minister.[13] With the election of a Labour government in 1929, Mosley was appointed Chancellor of the Duchy of Lancaster with instructions to assist J. H. Thomas in developing plans to alleviate the growing problem of unemployment.

Three overlapping factors coincided to deflect Mosley's political rise. First, the Great Slump of 1929-32 reaffirmed his conviction that the structural and ideological basis upon which the British economy had long been established was forever lost. As Europe shuddered from the aftershocks of the American crash, so Mosley recognised the extent to which Britain's future was bound up within a competing global market place. He noted the severity of the crisis, its destabilising influence across continental Europe, and the inability of both laissez faire and protectionist economics to offer a solution.[14] Consequently, Mosley – alongside other politicians, economists, business people and intellectuals – began to rethink his approach to Britain's economic future.

Second, Mosley's experience as a government minister undermined his belief in the efficiency of a democratically elected parliamentary government. Not only did Mosley find his plans to tackle unemployment ignored or dismissed by senior col-

---

10 Cited in Skidelsky, *Oswald Mosley*, 127.

11 John Strachey, *Revolution by Reason: An Account of the Financial Proposals Submitted to the Labour Movement by Mr. Oswald Mosley* (London: Parsons, 1925), x. Mosley's original but shorter essay is included in Michael Quill, ed., *Revolution by Reason and Other Essays by Oswald Mosley* (London: Edwin Mellen, 1997).

12 Mosley was by no means the only aristocratic or Tory recruit to Labour, but such members were relatively rare. See Martin Pugh, "'Class Traitors': Conservative Recruits to Labour, 1900-30", *English Historical Review* 113/450 (1998), 38-64; Catherine Ann Cline, *Recruits to Labour: The British Labour Party, 1914-31* (New York: Syracuse University Press, 1963).

13 For examples of Mosley being talked about as a future prime minister, see *Daily Express*, July 12, 1924; *Smethwick Telephone*, February 28, 1931; Norman and Jeanne MacKenzie, eds., *The Diary of Beatrice Webb*, vol. 4: *1924-43: The Wheel of Life* (London: Virago, 1985), December 24, 1928.

14 Oswald Mosley, Untitled Memorandum, November 19, 1930, Parliamentary Archive London, Beaverbrook Papers (BBK/C/254).

leagues in the cabinet and the treasury, but he soon came to regard the archaic traditions of the British parliament ill-suited to tackling the severe economic problems of the day. Most members of parliament were unable to understand the intricacies of economic theory and practice, Mosley argued; the formalities of parliamentary debate and the process by which bills were passed through the Commons were both long-winded and prone to the machinations of party politics.[15] "A cabinet of Caesars", the New Party's Cyril Joad argued in early 1931, "each of whom was endowed with the energy of Napoleon and the vision of Lenin, could not get through the present House of Commons one-tenth of the measures which an adequate treatment of the present crisis demands".[16] As such, Mosley proposed that "an emergency cabinet of not more than five ministers, without portfolio, should be invested with power to carry through the emergency policy".[17] This, in turn, was adapted by the New Party to include the streamlining of the parliamentary process, whereby the government issued orders in council to be subject only to limited parliamentary discussion and accepted or rejected within a specified timeframe.[18]

Finally, Mosley rejected the Labour Party and the wider labour movement as the principal means by which to implement the radical measures that he believed necessary to prevent Britain's decline. This, in part, was a conclusion reached out of personal pique. Despite his best efforts, Mosley had failed to convince the majority of the cabinet, Parliamentary Labour Party (PLP) and wider labour movement that he and his proposals should be adopted in favour of existing party policy. Simultaneously, however, he became increasingly frustrated at the caution that underpinned the British labour movement and the apparent lassitude of MacDonald's government. For Mosley, the Labour government's response to the ensuing crisis of capitalism was akin to the Salvation Army taking to its heels and running away from the day of judgement.[19]

The ramifications of Mosley's break with Labour would prove integral to his eventual adoption of fascism. Most immediately, Mosley had committed the trade unionist's cardinal sin in "splitting" from the party, thereby ensuring that any degree of support that his proposals held within the wider labour movement was quickly overtaken by suspicion and animosity.[20] From the outset, New Party meetings were tense affairs that attracted Labour supporters enraged at Mosley's "treachery" and more than willing to let the speakers know about it. Most famous-

15 Ibid.

16 Cyril E. M. Joad, *The Case for the New Party* (London: New Party, 1931), 5-6.

17 *The Times*, December 8, 1930.

18 Allan Young, et al. *A National Policy: An Account of the Emergency Programme Advanced by Sir Oswald Mosley M.P.* (London: Macmillan, 1931), 45-48; John Strachey and Cyril E.M Joad, "Parliamentary Reform: The New Party's Proposals", *Political Quarterly* 2/2 (1931).

19 Nicolson, ed., *Diaries*, September 12, 1931; James Drennan, *BUF: Oswald Mosley and British Fascism* (London: John Murray, 1934), 238-239.

20 For Mosley's relationship with the Labour Party, see David Howell, "'The Sheik ... A Valentino in Real Life': Sir Oswald Mosley and the Labour Party, 1924-31", *Contemporary British History* 23/4 (2009), 425-443.

ly, the New Party's intervention into the Ashton-under-Lyne by-election in April 1931 was seen to have contributed to Labour losing the seat.[21]

Equally, however, irate Labour supporters were often joined in their heckling of Mosley by small bands of communists. The Communist Party of Great Britain (CPGB) was in 1931 bound to a policy of "class against class" that understood social democracy to be but an adjunct of capitalism and thus a vehicle for "social fascism" in a period of capitalist crisis. Given such reasoning, the CPGB recognised the Labour-incubated New Party to be the "first concrete form of Fascism in embryo we have had in this country" and instructed its members to confront Mosley and his supporters on just those terms.[22] Scuffles and interruptions – often involving communists – subsequently became a feature of New Party meetings, culminating in the violent scenes at Glasgow described above and the full-scale riot that broke out in Birmingham's Rag Market just days before the 1931 general election.[23]

As is well known, Mosley responded to such opposition by pledging to meet force with force, forming both a bodyguard and a team of stewards to protect New Party meetings from disruption. As such, the programmatic nature of Mosley's politics was thus complemented by a physical dimension that purportedly embodied the assertive dynamism of a supposedly modern movement. In the process, the patriotic flavour that Mosley had always added to his politics took on new meaning once divorced from its erstwhile Labour context. Mosley and the New Party began to attract committed nationalists and anti-communists to their cause, many of whom saw little distinction between the CPGB and the Labour Party. By 1932, the focus of Mosley's politics had shifted from reform through Westminster to revolution in the streets.

Taken altogether, these factors combined with the circumstances of the early 1930s to convince Mosley that liberal capitalism was doomed to failure, that parliamentary democracy was ill-equipped to deal with the economic problems of the postwar world, and that the labour movement would never provide the ideological and political ingenuity by which to construct a dynamic nation state. In breaking from Labour in early 1931, Mosley and those who followed him began to search for new political means and methods; they sought a new movement informed by and equipped to shape the modern world.

This is the Modern World

Mosley's politics, whether Labour, New Party or BUF, were built on an economic base. The so-called "Mosley memorandum" presented to the prime minister at the beginning of 1930 recommended a planned, state-directed economic programme that prioritised the development of the home market in preference to Britain's tra-

21 John Strachey, *The Coming Struggle for Power* (London: Gollancz, 1932), 161-162.

22 Minutes of the Central Committee of the CPGB, March 14-15, 1931, Communist Party Archive, People's History Museum Manchester (GB 394 CPGB).

23 *The Times*, October 19, 1931; *Evening Despatch*, October 19, 1931; *Birmingham Post*, November 19, 1931.

ditional reliance on export trade. As with Mosley and Strachey's earlier *Revolution by Reason* (1925), an emphasis was placed on the control and flow of capital rather than the ownership of the means of production, while the idea of a high-wage economy was presented as a means of alleviating poverty while simultaneously stimulating demand.[24]

A shift occurred in mid-to-late 1930 following Mosley's resignation from the government. The instability of the global market led him to argue that import control boards should be formed to "insulate" the British economy. Such an idea was then extended across the British Empire via a mixture of recommended trade agreements, price controls, tariffs and mutual assistance.[25] The empire would thus form a stable – "insulated" – trading bloc through which long-term planning and development could be conceived. Significantly, too, the complex network of boards, committees and departments proposed by Mosley and, successively, the New Party and BUF to plan and direct the economy comprised appointed experts and state delegates, co-ordinating with worker, employer and consumer representatives. It was, therefore, with some justification that Mosley later claimed to have introduced the "germ of the corporate idea" into his politics some time prior to his becoming aware of comparable developments in Italy.[26]

Of course, state planning, imperial preference and a corporate conception of economic management do not in themselves constitute a form of fascism. Notions of planning and corporatism were becoming increasingly varied and widespread in the context of the early 1930s, both in Britain and beyond; the adoption of tariffs and imperial trading were being considered across the political spectrum by 1930-32.[27] What served to tip Mosley's economic programme towards fascism was the means by which he sought to enact it and the reasoning that led him to adapt his reforms and think them so imperative.

Again, we may posit three broadly inter-linking factors to explain this. First, if Mosley believed parliamentary democracy to be "dead", as he told Harold Nicolson and Robert Bruce Lockhart in January 1931, then new means were needed to implement the measures that he felt necessary to revive Britain's ailing economy.[28] To simply *reform* parliament, as he proposed from 1930 through to late 1931, was no longer an option once Mosley extended his critique of parliament to its logical end. Simultaneously, as the economic crisis deepened, so Mosley's disillusionment with parliamentary democracy was compounded by his own drift away from the centre

---

24 Letter from Sir Oswald Mosley to the Prime Minister, containing the memorandum, January 23, 1931, National Archive London, MacDonald Papers (PRO 30/69/445).

25 Oswald Mosley, "Empire Unity – But No Food Taxes", *Daily Herald*, July 7, 1930; Hansard, House of Commons Debates, vol. 241, cols. 1347-50 (July 16, 1930).

26 Oswald Mosley, "Have We A Policy?", *Action*, December 17, 1931, 1-2.

27 Daniel Ritschel, *The Politics of Planning: The Debate on Economic Planning in Britain in the 1930s* (Oxford: Clarendon Press, 1997); idem., "A Corporatist Economy in Britain? Capitalist Planning for Industrial Self-Government in the 1930s", *English Historical Review* 106/418 (1991), 41-65; Luther P. Carpenter, "Corporatism in Britain, 1930-45", *Journal of Contemporary History* 11/1 (1976), 2-25.

28 Nicolson, ed., *Diaries*, January 26, 1931.

of power. As a result, his plans for reform gave way to proposals that envisaged a wholly reconstituted state apparatus based on corporate principles and executive government.[29] In other words, Mosley committed to the construction of a corporate state which he later defined as a "state in which all will possess their function and in which the bungler and the sluggard must go to the wall".[30] It would, he continued, aim to "overcome class war by constituting a continually functioning machinery which reconciles the conflict of interests, and arbitrates and harmonises differences of class"; it would preside over "the self-government of an industrial system, the components of which are welded together in the corporate state to function with the central and directive purpose of a human body"; it would require "the maximum direction from above" and "the maximum self-sacrifice below"; it would replace political liberty, meaning parliamentary democracy, with economic and social liberty, broadly defined as the right to leisure and freedom from material want. To this end, the state would be directed by a five-man executive with wide-ranging powers. Parliament would continue to exist, but reconstituted to represent industrial-economic interests. "Methods of occupational franchise", the New Party's weekly paper *(Action)* suggested, "must be considered".[31]

Second, therefore, Mosley came to believe that new political forces were necessary to enact such fundamental change. Most obviously, as its name implied, the New Party was designed to offer an alternative to the politics and personnel of the "old gang".[32] This, initially, implied taking the "best bits" from the "old parties" to provide a practical and consensual solution to Britain's economic problems.[33] By late 1931, however, amidst the political realignment that took place following the collapse of the Labour government and the formation of a national coalition, Mosley felt able to question the very future of the existing party system. Britain stood on the verge of a devastating crisis, Mosley insisted, from which he believed newer, more modern political movements would necessarily come to the fore.[34] The question was: What form should such a movement take within the British context? Mosley's answer was soon clear. "Communism", he said, would "quickly supersede the woolly-headed and woolly-hearted social democrats of Labour", while "communism's inevitable and historic opponent will arise to take the place of a flabby Conservatism".[35] In Britain, that "opponent" was to be the BUF.

---

29 *Action*, October 8, November 16, December 17, 1931; Mosley, *The Greater Britain*, 26-35.

30 "Election Will Annoy You", *Action*, October 8, 1931, 10-11.

31 Ibid; "Have We A Policy? – Yes!", *Action*, December 17, 1931, 1-2. Mosley offered more detail as to the composition and remit of the corporate state in his *The Greater Britain*, 26-41.

32 Strachey et al., *Why We Left the Old Parties*, passim; William E. D. Allen, *The New Party and the Old Toryism* (London: New Party, 1931); Jimmie MacDougall, *Disillusionment* (London: New Party, 1931).

33 Allen, *The New Party*, 2; Cecil F. Melville, "Political Upheaval: Sir Oswald Mosley", *Fortnightly Review*, May 1931, 658-667.

34 "Have We A Policy?", 1-2.

35 Oswald Mosley, "Old Parties or New?", *Political Quarterly* 3/1 (1932), 27-32; "Have We A Policy?", 1-2.

Consequently, the third factor that conspired to push Mosley to fascism was his conceiving a "new" – or "modern" – movement applicable to the postwar world. A modern mind, Mosley informed readers of the *Sunday Express* in mid-1930, was "a hard, realistic type, hammered into existence on the anvil of great ordeal".[36] This, in turn, needed to be given political expression, something Mosley came to see as impossible within the existing political system. From late 1930, therefore, he began to talk of a "modern movement" designed to reflect the harsh realities of the postwar world. Continental precursors were referenced, ranging from Bolshevism and Fascism to the Young Turk movement and the Kuomintang, all of which were deemed to have been born from a "new generation of men who are weary of words and have learned the harsh dictates of action".[37]

In the end, of course, Mosley chose fascism. Several of his allies commented on "fascist elements" coming into the New Party by the summer of 1931, and Mosley's attraction to the concept of a corporate state served only to bolster his growing admiration for Mussolini's Fascist example.[38] Over the course of late 1930 and 1931, Mosley began to talk more and more of a new psychology, conceiving in his mind a movement that comprised men who "live like athletes for the exacting purposes of a great age".[39] The evolution of the party's fledgling youth movement, too, complemented Mosley's fascist drift. By November, the party's youth organisation had been reconstituted as Nupa, a self-proclaimed "shock movement" of "vibrant nationalism" that Mosley admitted to Nicolson would "correspond to the [...] Schutzstaffel [SS] organisation of the Nazis".[40] Indeed, Nupa formed the basis of the early BUF, with its members housed in barracks and committed to confronting communists in the battle to control Britain's streets.[41]

Fascism, then, appeared to provide Mosley with the means by which to implement the economic policies that he believed essential for Britain's future. It offered Mosley a "constructive alternative" by which to combat communism and replace both liberal capitalism and parliamentary democracy. In the modern world defined by Mosley, "either fascism or communism" would emerge "victorious" from the crisis afflicting liberal capitalism.[42] The formation of the BUF, therefore, was designed to ensure that fascism won the day.

36 Oswald Mosley, "What Are We Fighting For?", *Sunday Express*, May 25, 1930; also quoted in Skidelsky, *Oswald Mosley*, 225.

37 Mosley, Untitled Memorandum, November 19, 1930; *The Times*, November 15, 1930.

38 Nicolson, ed., *Diaries*, June 10, July 23, 1931; *The Times*, July 24 and 27, 1931.

39 Mosley, Untitled Memorandum, November 19, 1930; Cecil F. Melville, *The Truth About the New Party: And Much Else Besides Concerning Sir Oswald Mosley's Political Aims, the "Nazi" Movement of Herr Adolph Hitler and the Adventure in Political Philosophy of Mr. Wyndham Lewis* (London: Wishart, 1931), 31.

40 Nicolson, ed., *Diaries*, January 5, 1932.

41 *Action*, November 12, 1931, 5; Kenneth Young, ed., *The Diaries of Sir Robert Bruce Lockhart, 1915-38* (London: Macmillan, 1973), December 4, 1931.

42 Mosley, *The Greater Britain*, 150-151.

A Question of Choice

Mosley chose to become a fascist. However, such a "choice" was not made randomly nor even instinctively. For some time, Mosley had employed numerous secretaries and researchers to gather facts and draft reports on policy. As well as Strachey, men such as Allan Young, George Catlin, Cecil Melville and George Sutton worked closely with Mosley throughout the 1920s and into the 1930s, providing information that was then discussed with contemporary experts and intellectuals such as John Maynard Keynes, H.G. Wells and George Bernard Shaw. Remembering the 1926 by-election in Smethwick, C.J. Simmons wrote how Mosley's "own private menagerie" moved down from London "en bloc": His secretaries, private research men, a van load of filing cabinets and press cuttings.[43] Four years later Mosley turned his attention to events unfolding on the continent, redirecting his research "menagerie" towards those emergent political movements that offered an alternative to a seemingly moribund liberalism.

As noted above, Mosley initially understood fascism to be a variant of what he termed the "modern movement". Its relevance to Britain, so far as Mosley was concerned, came with the onset of the economic downturn in late 1929, from which time there was much debate as to the potential depth of the ensuing depression and parliamentary democracy's ability to cope in such dire circumstances. The modern movements, it seemed, tallied with Mosley's already-established influences, in particular the political-philosophical writings of Shaw and Wells. To these he soon added Nietzsche and Spengler, so eventually finding in fascism a vitalist, post-liberal creed that recognised the need for a modern and extensive state apparatus. Of course, fascism's ultra-nationalism and emphasis on leadership also appealed to Mosley, as did its militarism and sense of discipline and service.[44] Simultaneously, talk of coups, communism and dictatorship began to inform the late night conversations of some within Britain's political class, as the remit and nature of a twentieth-century state was reassessed amidst the deepening sense of crisis.[45]

To augment their ideas, many of those close to Mosley and, later, the New Party and BUF journeyed overseas to locate policies and strategies applicable to the British context. Both Strachey and Cynthia Mosley visited Soviet Russia in 1930, from where they returned with rather different feelings as to the potential of the Bolshevik model.[46] W.E.D. Allen and Melville shared their experiences of central and eastern Europe with Mosley, examining nationalist politics, Nazism and King Alexander's "experiment towards the modern state" in Yugoslavia.[47] Mosley himself was

43 Charles J. Simmons, *Soap-Box Evangelist* (Chichester: Janay, 1972), 68.

44 Oswald Mosley, "The Philosophy of Fascism", lecture delivered to the English Speaking Union, March 22, 1933, University of Birmingham, Mosley Papers (OMN/B/4/8).

45 Nicolson, ed., *Diaries*, February 15, November 29, 1930, April 29, May 6 and 30, 1931.

46 Aneurin Bevan, E. J. Strachey and Georg Strauss, *What We Saw in Russia* (London: Hogarth Press, 1931); Nicholas Mosley, *Rules of the Game: Sir Oswald and Lady Cynthia Mosley, 1896-1933* (London: Secker and Warburg, 1982), chapter 16.

47 C. F. Melville, "A Balkan Monarch Takes a Chance", *Action*, November 12, 1931, 11.

to visit Italy in January 1932, while at least two New Party delegations travelled to Germany with instructions to examine Nazi methods and techniques.[48]

Not surprisingly, in the context of 1930-31, Russia and Italy were seen by most in the New Party to constitute the "two great modern experiments".[49] Bolshevism's appeal lay primarily in its resort to a planned economy. But Mosley showed only disdain for the materialist analysis that underpinned the Soviet Union and baulked at the idea of the class struggle. Bolshevism, he wrote in January 1931, looked set to "wade cheerfully to its objective of a Soviet State through the blood and starvation of a disgruntled society".[50] Class warfare, he later wrote in *The Greater Britain,* had led Russia only "to the destruction of all science, skill and managerial ability, until, when it begins to feel its feet, it has to buy these same qualities at enormous cost from foreign nations". Transferred to Britain, "half-a-million starving or killed" was deemed the probable scenario.[51]

By contrast, Italian Fascism retained something of an enigmatic quality in 1930-32. With the corporate state existing as much in concept as reality, so English-language studies on the subject were relatively few.[52] Nevertheless, the more Mosley discussed Mussolini's dictatorship, the more its basic premise, particularly its state-directed corporatism and commitment to strong leadership and action, began to tally with his own reading of concurrent debates on-going in Britain. If Soviet communism was deemed inimical to British conditions, then Fascism appeared to provide a working alternative to both untrammelled capitalism and a shaken parliamentary democracy. Fascism had a statist vision that seemed able to facilitate Mosley's economic policy; its emphasis on "action" – up to and including violence – complemented Mosley's reading of a "crisis" that would need to be fought physically as well as intellectually; further, Fascism was imbued with a sense of masculinity that tallied with Mosley's own vision of the warrior-male. Of course, the harsh treatment handed out by Mussolini to his erstwhile socialist comrades had been enough to convince the bulk of the British labour movement that Fascism was no

---

48 Letter from Hobhouse to Thost, December 7, 1931, National Archive London, WED Allen Papers (KV 2/879). Nicolson also travelled to Germany in January 1932; he was not impressed by Nazism. See Nicolson, ed., *Diaries*, January 22 and 24, 1932. Melville, in 1931, wrote of "various" New Party members visiting the Nazis' *Braunes Haus* in Munich. See Melville, *The Truth About the New Party*, 34.

49 Rupert Trouton, "New Economic Policy No. 1", *Action*, November 5, 1931, 4.

50 Mosley, "A New National Policy", 103-104. See also his speech at a meeting in Sheffield in October 1931, *Sheffield Daily Independent*, October 19, 1931, where he said that a communist revolution would mean "slaughter and starvation for thousands".

51 Mosley, *The Greater Britain*, 29-30, 79-80.

52 For English-language books on Fascism, see James Strachey Barnes, *The Universal Aspects of Fascism* (London: Williams & Norgate, 1928); idem., *Fascism* (London: T. Butterworth, 1931); Harold E. Goad, *What is Fascism? An Explanation of its Essential Principles* (Florence: Italian Mail & Tribune, 1929); Tomaso Sillani, ed., *What is Fascism and Why?* (London: Ernest Benn, 1931); Luigi Villari, *The Fascist Experiment* (London: Faber & Gwyer, 1926); idem., *Italy* (London: Ernest Benn, 1929); Corrado Gini, "The Scientific Basis of Fascism", *Political Science Quarterly* 42/1 (1927), 99-115.

friend of the working class. But Mosley was never representative of the British labour movement; by 1932 he recognised the internationalism of socialism, the class focus of Marxism, and the independent ("sectional") interests of trade unionism to be barriers that would need to be broken down – forcefully if necessary – in order to build any brave new world. In Mussolini, Mosley saw a man whose "mind is hard, concentrated, direct – in a word, 'Modern'"; in Fascism, Mosley recognised "the greatest constructive and revolutionary creed in the world".[53]

But what of Germany? Not surprisingly, the rise of Hitler over the early 1930s proved of increasing interest to Mosley. Indeed, the socio-economic disarray of Germany appeared to offer them a premonition of the unfolding crisis in Britain. "In Germany", *Action* reported following the electoral gains made by the Nazis and the German Communist Party in Hamburg in September 1931, "the bleating bourgeois block is dropping out of politics. The same phenomenon is certain, within a measurable time, to occur in England".[54] Consequently, the New Party began to pay ever more attention to events unfolding in the Weimar Republic. From Mosley's perspective, National Socialism offered a classic example of a once marginalised "modern movement" gaining momentum as it moved into a political vacuum born from socio-economic crisis.[55] The Nazi "technique", therefore, was studied and its organisational methods adopted to inform the transition of the New Party to the BUF. Contact was made with Dr Hans-Wilhelm Thost, a journalist stationed in Britain with orders to organise resident Germans into Nazi sections; New Party members visited the *Braunes Haus* in Munich; and the emphasis placed on the New Party's youth organisation from late 1931 was informed by German advice to build a movement from the grass roots.[56] Subsequently, as one astute observer noted in September 1932, the BUF emerged as "Mussolini in policy and Hitlerite in organisation", albeit enveloped in the patriotic wrap of the Union Jack.[57]

Conclusion

Much recent work has chosen to highlight the indigenous roots of British fascism.[58] Indeed, historians have for some time warned against presuming that Britain was

53 *Daily Mail*, February 1, 1932; Mosley, *The Greater Britain*, 15.

54 Nicolson, "Election Will Annoy You", 10-11.

55 Cheyney likened Mosley's election result in 1931 to that of Mussolini in Milan in 1919, whereat the future dictator's defeat was followed one year later by the return of "thirty Fascist candidates". See *Action*, November 26, 1931, 5. See also P.M.M., "Our Leader", *The New Times*, June 1932, 5.

56 Letter from Hobhouse to Thost, December 7, 1931, National Archive London, WED Allen Papers (KV 2/879); James J. Barnes and Patience P. Barnes, *Nazis in Pre-War London, 1933-39: The Fate and Role of German Party Members and British Sympathisers* (Brighton: University of Sussex, 2005); Nicolson, ed., *Diaries*, January 2, 1932.

57 Young, ed., *The Diaries of Sir Bruce Lockhart*, September 29, 1932.

58 Dan Stone, *Breeding Superman: Nietzsche, Race and Eugenics in Edwardian and Interwar Britain* (Liverpool: Liverpool University Press, 2002); Martin Pugh, *Hurrah for the Blackshirts: Fascists and Fascism in Britain Between the Wars* (London: Jonathan Cape, 2005); Gary Love, "'What's the

somehow immune from fascism; that such recourse to coercion or intimidation was simply not the British way.[59] And quite right, too. Fascism's prejudices and ultra-nationalism could be located in British society just as easily as they could elsewhere; the forces that converged to provide fascist "solutions" elsewhere in Europe were not thereby absent from the British context. The reasons as to *why* Britain did not succumb to fascism remain multiple and contentious, but if the failure of British fascism was due in part to the evolution of Britain's political structures, its relative economic prosperity and stability, and the state's management of opposition, then it is too simplistic to say that this was either inevitable or due to some inherent national trait. British fascism was marginal but not wholly detached from British politics; its ideas and points of focus were not alien to Britain.

For this reason, historians such as Gary Love are right to suggest that the BUF could – and did – present itself as a "home-grown movement".[60] Dan Stone's exploration of the "extremes of Englishness" demonstrates clearly the extent to which aspects of fascist ideology fed into contemporary thinking across Britain's intellectual and political milieu. Martin Pugh, like Richard Griffiths before him, can readily claim that British fascism had connections in high places and thus a potential influence beyond its apparent means.[61] My own work, too, has sought to contextualise Mosley's drift to fascism, pointing to contemporary debates on economic planning and corporatism to explain where his ideas came from and how they fitted into arguments that existed well within the political mainstream.[62] Mosley certainly differed from his continental mentors with regard to the priority status afforded to a distinct economic programme.

However, it is suggested here that we must not lose sight of the external influences that also shaped Mosley's thinking, particularly with regard to his conception of fascism as a movement and as a form of state organisation. It is indisputable that Mosley looked to the continent to find an answer to Britain's problems in the early 1930s. Having tried and failed to forge a suitable solution "at home", he looked to what was "working" overseas in order to find whatever policies and strategies may be capable of overcoming a crisis that Mosley saw as integral to Britain's future development. This does not mean that he simply transplanted fascism onto Britain; but that he adopted the fascist label after much deliberation and with very definite reference to the Italian and German examples. Mosley was, after all, somewhat unusual among his continental equivalents in using the "f-word" to name his organisation. Though he was quick to point out that the "modern movement" could take different forms in different countries in accord with their different traditions and

---

Big Idea?' Oswald Mosley, the British Union of Fascists and Generic Fascism", *Journal of Contemporary History* 42/3 (2007), 447-468.

59 For a good overview, see Michael Cronin, ed., *The Failure of British Fascism: The Far Right and the Fight for Political Recognition* (Basingstoke: Macmillan, 1996).

60 Love, "'What's the Big Idea?'", 449.

61 Richard Griffiths, *Fellow Travellers of the Right: British Enthusiasts for Nazi Germany, 1933-39* (Oxford: Oxford University Press, 1983).

62 Worley, *Oswald Mosley and the New Party*, especially chapter 2.

contexts, he chose to launch his British version with the insignia of Italian Fascism (the fasces) and with black-shirted uniforms at the ready. Not dissimilarly, Mosley's model for a corporatist state borrowed from Mussolini's pioneering example, while his extra-parliamentary youth movement took much of its substance from continental precedents. Neither were simply decorations to distinguish a supposedly modern form of popular British ultra-nationalism.

To sum up: The eventual form that Mosley's fascism took sought to build upon a sense of patriotism and service to the nation. It took up national emblems (the Union Jack, the national anthem), presented itself as a future vision for Britain that drew from the best elements of the country's past, and developed its policy from on-going debates that fed into the British political and intellectual mainstream. However, the means by which Mosley wished to achieve his "Greater Britain" were largely modelled abroad. So while it may be possible to argue that Mosley's perspective and the premise of his policies were cultivated at home, then we should also recognise the extent to which his plan of action drew from foreign precedents. In other words, Mosley *found* fascism, adapting it to his own ends whilst using it to inform the crisis scenario that he predicted for Britain but which never quite came.

Bibliography

Barnes, James Strachey. *Fascism.* London: T. Butterworth, 1931.

Barnes, James Strachey. *The Universal Aspects of Fascism.* London: Williams & Norgate, 1928.

Barnes, Patience P. *Nazis in Pre-War London, 1933-39: The Fate and Role of German Party Members and British Sympathisers.* Brighton: University of Sussex, 2005.

Carpenter, Luther P. "Corporatism in Britain, 1930-45". *Journal of Contemporary History* 11/1 (1976), 3-25.

Cline, Catherine Ann. *Recruits to Labour: The British Labour Party, 1914-31.* New York: Syracuse University Press, 1963.

Cronin, Michael, ed. *The Failure of British Fascism: The Far Right and the Fight for Political Recognition.* Basingstoke: Macmillan, 1996.

Dorril, Stephen. *Blackshirt: Sir Oswald Mosley and British Fascism.* London: Viking, 2006.

Drennan, James. *BUF: Oswald Mosley and British Fascism.* London: John Murray, 1934.

Goad, Harold E. *What is Fascism? An Explanation of its Essential Principles.* Florence: Italian Mail & Tribune, 1929.

Griffiths, Richard. *Fellow Travellers of the Right: British Enthusiasts for Nazi Germany, 1933–39.* Oxford: Oxford University Press, 1983.

Howell, David. "'The Sheik ... A Valentino in Real Life': Sir Oswald Mosley and the Labour Party, 1924-31". *Contemporary British History* 23/4 (2009), 425-443. Love, Gary. "'What's the Big Idea?' Oswald Mosley, the British Union of Fascists and Generic Fascism". *Journal of Contemporary History* 42/3 (2007), 447-468.

MacKenzie, Norman and Jeanne, eds. *The Diary of Beatrice Webb*, vol. 4: *1924-43, The Wheel of Life.* London: Virago, 1985.

Melville, Cecil F. *The Truth About the New Party: And Much Else Besides Concerning Sir Oswald Mosley's Political Aims, the 'Nazi' Movement of Herr Adolph Hitler and the Adventure in Political Philosophy of Mr. Wyndham Lewis*. London: Wishart, 1931.

Mosley, Nicholas. *Rules of the Game: Sir Oswald and Lady Cynthia Mosley, 1896-1933*. London: Secker and Warburg, 1982.

Mosley, Oswald. *My Life*. London: Thomas Nelson, 1968.

Mosley, Oswald. *The Greater Britain*. London: BUF, 1932.

Nicolson, Nigel, ed. *Harold Nicolson Diaries and Letters, 1930-39*. London: Collins, 1966.

Powell, David. *British Politics, 1910-35: The Crisis of the Party System*. London: Routledge, 2004.

Pugh, Martin. "'Class Traitors': Conservative Recruits to Labour, 1900-30". *English Historical Review* 113/450 (1998), 38-64.

Pugh, Martin. *Hurrah for the Blackshirts: Fascists and Fascism in Britain Between the Wars*. London: Jonathan Cape, 2005.

Quill, Michael, ed. *Revolution by Reason and Other Essays by Oswald Mosley*. London: Edwin Mellen, 1997.

Ritschel, Daniel. *The Politics of Planning: The Debate on Economic Planning in Britain in the 1930s*. Oxford: Clarendon Press, 1997.

Ritschel, Daniel. "A Corporatist Economy in Britain? Capitalist Planning for Industrial Self-Government in the 1930s". *English Historical Review* 106/418 (1991), 41-65.

Sillani, Tomaso, ed. *What is Fascism and Why?* London: Ernest Benn, 1931.

Simmons, Charles J. *Soap-Box Evangelist*. Chichester: Janay, 1972.

Skidelsky, Robert. *Oswald Mosley*. London: Macmillan, 1975.

Skidelsky, Robert. *Politicians and the Slump: The Labour Government of 1929-31*. London: Macmillan, 1967.

Stone, Dan. *Breeding Superman: Nietzsche, Race and Eugenics in Edwardian and Interwar Britain*. Liverpool: Liverpool University Press, 2002.

Strachey, John. *Revolution by Reason: An Account of the Financial Proposals Submitted to the Labour Movement by Mr. Oswald Mosley*. London: Parsons, 1925.

Strachey, John. *The Coming Struggle for Power*. London: Gollancz, 1932.

Villari, Luigi. *Italy*. London: Ernest Benn, 1929.

Villari, Luigi. *The Fascist Experiment*. London: Faber & Gwyer, 1926.

Williamson, Philip. *National Crisis and National Government: British Politics, the Economy and Empire, 1926–32*. Cambridge: Cambridge University Press, 1992.

Worley, Matthew. *Oswald Mosley and the New Party*. Basingstoke: Palgrave, 2010.

Worley, Matthew. "Why Fascism? Sir Oswald Mosley and the Conception of the British Union of Fascists". *History* 66/1 (2011), 66-81.

Young, Allan, John Strachey, William J. Brown and Aneurin Bevan, *A National Policy: An Account of the Emergency Programme Advanced by Sir Oswald Mosley M.P.* London: Macmillan, 1931.

Young, Kenneth, ed. *The Diaries of Sir Robert Bruce Lockhart, 1915-38*. London: Macmillan, 1973.

Nasjonal Samling's Foreign Office in Germany during the Second World War:
Organisation, Strategies and Cooperation

Nicola Karcher

Introduction

For decades the Norwegian public associated National Socialism and treason with the political party *Nasjonal Samling* (National Unity, NS). Two events triggered this perception: First, party leader Vidkun Quisling attempted a coup and declared himself prime minister on April 9, 1940, the day Germany occupied Norway. Second, a collaboration government was formed a few months later on September 25, which was based on the NS. Quisling failed to form an own government as early as in April and was removed from office a few days later. Nevertheless, Hitler decided to rely on the NS in the course of the summer 1940. Although this particular National Socialist party had been politically entirely insignificant prior to the occupation of Norway, it collaborated with the German occupying power until May 8, 1945.[1]

The NS was symbolically founded on the Norwegian national day on May 17, 1933. It first and foremost perceived of itself as a nationalist unification movement. As such, the party was composed of heterogeneous individuals. Apart from established representatives of the middle class, the industry, the farming community and the military, there were ecclesiastical representatives, proponents of a neopagan and pan-Germanic racism, traditional nationalists and followers of Fascism.[2] Even though the foundation of the NS was beyond any doubt inspired by the success of National Socialism in Germany, and the Norwegian public understood it to be a copy of the NSDAP right from the outset, its programme did not feature any direct links with National Socialism. In fact, Quisling was oriented towards Mussolini's Fascism during the early years of the NS. His party was particularly marked by a radical opposition to Marxism and its struggle against the Norwegian socialist workers' movement. Moreover, the NS created a historical link to the age of the

---

1 The events on April 9, 1940, and the developments in the course of the following weeks are described in a number of studies. See i.e. Hans Fredrik Dahl, *Vidkun Quisling. En fører for fall* (Oslo: Aschehoug 1992); Hans-Dietrich Loock, *Quisling, Rosenberg und Terboven. Zur Vorgeschichte und Geschichte der nationalsozialistischen Revolution in Norwegen* (Stuttgart: Deutsche Verlags-Anstalt, 1970); Magne Skodvin, *Striden om okkupasjonsstyret. Fram til 25. september 1940* (Oslo: Det norske samlaget, 1956).

2 Cf. Christhard Hoffmann, "Die reine Lehre einer politischen Sekte. Antisemitismus in der norwegischen 'Nasjonal Samling'", in *Vorurteil und Rassenhaß. Antisemitismus in den faschistischen Bewegungen Europas*, eds. Hermann Graml, Angelika Königseder and Julianne Wetzel (Berlin: Metropol Verlag, 2001), 255.

Vikings and placed itself within the tradition of the Norwegian heyday of the Middle Ages by using "Nordic" symbols and medieval terminology.[3]

The NS was rather unsuccessful in the ensuing period. It achieved 2.2 per cent of the votes in the parliamentary elections in autumn 1933 and only 1.8 per cent three years later. The heterogeneous political and ideological composition of the NS as well as its lack of success led to a series of internal conflicts, which accelerated the negative trend of the party. At the beginning of 1937, deputy party leader Johan B. Hjort left the party after a protracted power struggle, hence leaving the NS without its most promising politician. Further individuals left the party or were excluded from it in the course of the same year. Hoping that it would be able to reverse this development, the NS finally took the route towards National Socialism. However, this strategy was unsuccessful. Until the German occupation of Norway in 1940, the NS plodded along as a political sect with not more than 1,000 members.[4]

Hence, the collaboration government was based on a party that received insignificant support from the Norwegian population and in no way represented Norwegian politics. Since his attempted coup, Quisling in particular was considered a traitor par excellence. On April 19, 1940, *The Times* used his name as a synonym for a traitor to the nation for the first time. Due to the BBC, the term was broadcasted worldwide and is used until today.[5] The German occupying power reacted to this situation accordingly. It was only in February 1942 that the NS party leader was appointed prime minister of Norway. Even though NS party membership increased to over 40,000 individuals in the course of the occupation, the party remained a political outsider. The majority of the population rejected it, and it was unable to achieve any political success that was not based on coercion. The intended nazification of Norway ultimately failed.[6]

As an effect of the collaboration of the NS with the German occupiers, other forms of collaboration were barely accorded any attention after the war. For decades, Norwegian research on collaboration almost exclusively concentrated on the NS.[7] Therefore, it is all the more remarkable that the activities of the Foreign Of-

3 See Hans Fredrik Dahl, "Fascismen i Norge 1920-1940. Et overblikk", *Kontrast* 31 (1966), 13f.

4 See, among others, Hans Olaf Brevik, *NS – fra parti til sekt* (Oslo: Pax, 1970), 77ff.; Ivo de Figueiredo, "Nasjonal Samling 1937-1940", in *Den norske fascismen. Nasjonal Samling 1933-1940*, eds. Hans Olaf Brevig and Ivo de Figureido (Oslo: Pax, 2002), 113f.; Dag Olav Bruknapp, "Ideene splitter partiet", in *Fra idé til dom. Noen trekk fra utviklingen av Nasjonal Samling*, eds. Rolf Danielsen and Stein Ugelvik Larsen (Bergen et al.: Universitetsforlaget, 1976), 9-47.

5 See *The Times*, April 19, 1940; Hans Fredrik Dahl et al., eds., *Norsk krigsleksikon 1940-1945* (Oslo: Cappelen 1995), http://mediabase1.uib.no/krigslex/q/q1.html#quisling (accessed November 1, 2012).

6 Cf. Hans Fredrik Dahl, Bernt Hagtvet and Guri Hjeltnes, eds., *Den norske nasjonalsosialismen. Nasjonal Samling 1933-1945 i tekst og bilder* (Oslo: Pax, 1982), 109-191.

7 Economic collaboration and the exploitation of Norwegian resources for the wartime economy have barely received attention. Robert Bohn's study *Reichskommissariat Norwegen. "Nationalsozialistische Neuordnung" und Kriegswirtschaft* (Munich: Oldenbourg, 2000), and Fritz Petrick's

fice of the party in Germany has not been considered and examined independently. Especially the fact that on the whole its policy of *Gleichschaltung* and nazification in Norway remained unsuccessful, renders the question all the more relevant how its course of action was received within the Norwegian milieu in Germany. In which sense is it for example possible to assume that Germany-based Norwegians more strongly sympathised with National Socialism and NS collaboration? Was Gleichschaltung of their organisations possibly easier? And was it more likely for the NS to achieve political success among this group of Norwegians?

These are some of the questions this chapter seeks to answer. Based on the results of my PhD thesis, the foreign work of the NS in Germany during the Second World War will be described and examined, with a focus on the attempts to gain supremacy over the local Norwegian milieu and to establish links to various National Socialist authorities.

The Prehistory and Establishment of the NS Foreign Office

The NS member Olaf Willy Fermann represented the party in Germany well before the NS Foreign Office was officially established under the name of *Nasjonal Samlings Utenriksorganisasjon* (NSUO) in autumn 1940. Initially Fermann had been a member of the radical association Norwegian National Socialists in Germany (*Norske Nasjonalsocialister i Tyskland,* NNST), which had been founded in Berlin in summer 1933 and represented the group in northern Germany.[8] However, he left the association for the NS due to internal struggles as early as in autumn 1933. On April 24, 1934, Quisling appointed him *Gauleiter* of his party in Germany and instructed him to build up a foreign office of the NS.[9]

Even though the activities of the NS in Germany were not formalised in the following years, it is worthwhile to briefly outline the prehistory of the NSUO in order to understand its initial situation in 1940. Fermann played a central role as a juncture within Norwegian-German National Socialist networks, since he had extensive contacts to the NS system and was one of the leading figures of the Norwegian milieu in Germany. His contacts to the SS are particularly noteworthy.[10]

---

dissertation "Der 'Leichtmetallausbau Norwegen' 1940-1945. Eine Studie zur Expansions- und Okkupationspolitik des faschistischen deutschen Imperialismus" (PhD diss., University of Greifswald, 1983; in a revised version in Frankfurt a.M.: Peter Lang, 1992) are exceptions.

8 See my article on the NNST: "Norske Nasjonalsosialister i Tyskland 1933-1940. Politisk profil, intern struktur og nettverk", in *Utenfor det etablerte. Aspekter ved Einhart Lorenz' forskning,* eds. Øivind Kopperud, Vibeke Moe and Vibeke Kieding Banik (Oslo: HL-senteret, 2011), 97-110. In addition, see my recently completed PhD thesis, which examines Norwegian-German right-wing networks in the interwar period: "Zwischen Nationalsozialismus und nordischer Gesinnung. Eine Studie zu den rechtsgerichteten Verbindungen norwegisch-deutscher Milieus in der Zwischenkriegszeit" (PhD diss., University of Oslo, 2012), 127-159.

9 See Quisling to Fermann, April 24, 1934, Riksarkivet Oslo (RA), L-sak Olaf Willy Fermann, box 4.

10 On Fermann, see in detail Karcher, "Zwischen Nationalsozialismus und nordischer Gesinnung", 160-172.

Having worked abroad as a businessman within shipping and transport for years, Fermann had temporarily lived in Danzig in the 1920s. This is where he in 1928, via Werner Lorenz, a former Free Corps member *(Freikorps)* and subsequent *SS-Obergruppenführer* and head of the *Volksdeutsche Mittelstelle,* got to know the later *Reichsführer-SS* Heinrich Himmler. Fermann moved from Hamburg to Berlin in 1936, and apart from keeping company with Lorenz and other members of the SS, he also associated with Himmler.[11] Although Quisling and the NS barely seem to have benefitted from this contact in the 1930s, it is beyond debate that Fermann's contact to Himmler was of great significance during the occupation of Norway. As most probably Himmler's closest Norwegian intimate, Fermann was familiar with his plans to colonise the East and accompanied him to the Ukraine in autumn 1941 as a member of the Personal Staff Reichsführer-SS. He had been stationed in Poland earlier on where he, among other places, stayed in Himmler's headquarters. Moreover, he served as an adjutant and translator for the *SS-Hauptsturmführer* Rudolf May, who was assigned to organise the "anti-partisan warfare".[12] On February 16, 1942, Fermann was appointed *Untersturmführer* of the *Waffen-SS*. The same year he became the head of the ideological training of the Germanic SS Norway (*Germanske SS Norge,* GSSN) and the Office of Frontline Soldiers *(Frontkjemperkontoret),* which was responsible for taking care of the Norwegian SS volunteers and their families.[13]

Fermann's commitment as the representative of the NS in Germany during the 1930s was however far less purposeful. He does not seem to have made much of an effort to recruit party members. He himself mentions about twelve members in Hamburg, three to four in Berlin and a few individuals scattered across other German cities until 1940.[14] Since he knew that Himmler was at the very latest from 1937 onwards not interested in collaborating with Quisling and rather relied on the former NS deputy party leader Johan B. Hjort,[15] Fermann used other channels to promote the NS. Among these were in particular his efforts to distribute *Fritt Folk,* the party newspaper of the NS, within the Norwegian milieu in Germany. Together with Thorvald Heyerdahl, the chairman of the Norwegian Club in Berlin and one

---

11 See Dok. 32, January 30, 1945; Dok. bil. 4, February, 1959. L-sak Fermann, box 1 and 7.

12 See Rettsbok [undated], L-sak Fermann, box 5. Most probably it was planned that Fermann take on the leadership of a colony of Norwegian "armed peasants" *(Wehrbauern)* who were meant to be settled on Russian territory as part of Himmler's plans to colonise the East. However, Fermann is said to have turned down the appointment. See the witness statement of Hans Keller, February 19, 1948; witness statement Herbert Noot, February 27, 1948; Rettsbok for Oslo, August 18, 1945. L-sak Fermann, box 4. Also cf. Terje Emberland and Matthew Kott, *Himmlers Norge. SS, Norge og det storgermanske prosjekt* (Oslo: Aschehoug, 2012), 209ff.

13 See Dok. 24/12, February 16, 1942, L-sak Fermann, box 1. Cf. Emberland and Kott, *Himmlers Norge,* 349f.; sine editore, *Vår innsats* (Oslo: Blix Forlag, 1942).

14 See Dok. 123/8 [undated], L-sak Fermann, box 4.

15 See, among others, Dok. 175, September, 1947, L-sak Fermann, box 4; Nicola Karcher, "Schirmorganisation der Nordischen Bewegung. Der Nordische Ring und seine Repräsentanten in Norwegen", *NORDEUROPAforum* 1 (2009), 34f.

of the most influential representatives of the so-called Norwegian colony[16], and cousin of Thor Heyerdahl, the leader of the famous Kon-Tiki expedition in 1947, he opened a bank account in order to support the party in Norway. This account mainly served as a donations account in order to fund and distribute *Fritt Folk* of which Fermann became the official representative in Germany in 1939.[17]Additionally, the account was supposed to have been used to enable leading NS members to visit Berlin.[18] Marketing the NS party newspaper, however, seems to have been unsuccessful. At the beginning of 1940, Heyerdahl complained that *Fritt Folk* had too few subscribers and that they had failed to amass sufficient money for daily appearance. In this context he also criticised the party programme for being imprecise, barely comprehensible and inaccessible to the general public.[19]

Therefore, it does not come as a surprise that the NS, just as in Norway, was barely known and did not achieve a breakthrough within Norwegian circles until 1940. Quisling's party was neither perceived to be the Norwegian version of the NSDAP, nor was it associated with its programme. However, this does not mean that there were no sympathies for National Socialism. Rather, one can assume that an affirmative attitude towards National Socialism existed within the Norwegian milieu in Germany, which however did not translate to an interest in the NS.

The establishment of the collaboration regime in Norway required a clear structuring of the foreign work of the NS. The NSUO, which had been established in autumn 1940, was the only party facility of the NS, officially operating abroad. Contrary to the original plans, it only succeeded in establishing an outpost in Germany. Fermann who had returned to Oslo shortly before the country was occupied, took over the leadership of the NSUO.[20] Since he was unable to conduct the work on the spot, he was dependent on finding reliable liaison people in Germany. To this end, he turned to the former leadership of the NNST, which is remarkable, since he had precipitately left the association in autumn 1933.

While the NNST had disintegrated in the course of the events of September 25, 1940, as a result of the prohibition of all Norwegian parties and was willing to represent the NSUO in Germany,[21] in practice the cooperation proved to be quite complicated. Assuming that they themselves were the "true" representatives of Norwegian National Socialism in Germany, the former NNST leadership, which

---

16 The use of the term "colony" is formally incorrect. However, the term will be used hereafter, because it is the way the Norwegian groups in Germany described themselves.

17 See Dok. 123/8, November 6, 1939, L-sak Fermann, box 1. Also cf. Loock, *Quisling, Rosenberg und Terboven*, 195f.

18 See Audun Rusten to NSUO, January 20, 1941, RA, L-sak Audun Rusten.

19 Thorvald Heyerdahl to *Fritt Folk*, February 12, 1940 [transcript], L-sak Rusten.

20 See Karcher, "Zwischen Nationalsozialismus und nordischer Gesinnung", 166, 172ff. Since Fermann returned to Oslo shortly before the country was occupied, he was accused of having functioned as a kind of "fifth colony" of the German occupying power. However, this allegation could not be verified during his treason lawsuit.

21 See Fermann to Salomon Clausen, October 28, 1940, RA, PA NSUO, box fa-4/Fylkesfører og sekretariat. Also cf. Rapport til Oslo Politikammer, August 12, 1947, RA, L-sak Salomon Clausen.

had taken over the leadership of the NSUO group in Berlin, was only to a limited extent willing to accept orders from Oslo. Fermann in particular and the conflicts of 1933 posed a problem. A letter from 1942 comments on Fermann and his work in the 1930s:

> One should expect of a 'born leader' that he demonstrates his abilities, for instance that he is able to establish an NS group in Hamburg immediately! However, this was not the case. Nor did he [Fermann] bring about an NS group in Berlin. Indeed, in the course of three years in which he lived in Berlin, he did not succeed in convincing a single Norwegian of the trueness of NS ideology![22]

At that time Fermann had already removed the leadership of the NSUO group from the former NNST representatives. According to him, their persistent boycott of the work of the NSUO in Berlin was still responsible "for many of the difficulties with which the group had to cope"[23]. As the conflicts within the NS during the occupation in Norway reveal,[24] Norwegian National Socialism in Germany was anything but homogeneous. Right from the start, the NSUO met upon difficulties in Germany and faced internal conflicts just like in Norway. After Fermann fell ill for several months in autumn 1941 after his trip with Himmler to the Eastern Front, Quisling's "informal foreign minister" Finn Sophus Støren took over the leadership of the NSUO. Fermann's return to his position in 1942 was said not to have run smoothly.[25]

Due to various initial difficulties of this sort, the NSUO only began working in any concrete way from 1942 onwards. Even though it represented itself to the outside as a consulate, its main goal was the Gleichschaltung of the Norwegian milieu in Germany. In addition, it tried to collaborate extensively with German National Socialist institutions.

Structure, Working Method and Networks

The Foreign Office *(Auslandsorganisation)* of the NSDAP, which had been operating as a section of the party since 1931 and was responsible for ideologically mentoring the citizens of the German Reich living abroad, most probably served as a role

22 Rusten to the NSUO group Berlin, May 12, 1942. In addition, see Fermann's reply, May 30, 1942. L-sak Rusten.

23 Fermann to Clausen [undated], L-sak Fermann, box 3.

24 On the internal conflicts in the NS during the occupation, see Øystein Sørensen, *Hitler eller Quisling. Ideologiske brytninger i Nasjonal Samling 1940-1945* (Oslo: Cappelen, 1989). Also cf. my article: "Die Nasjonal Samling während der deutschen Okkupation Norwegens 1940-1945. Nationalismus versus Pangermanismus", in *Jahrbuch für Antisemitismusforschung*, ed. Wolfgang Benz, vol. 16 (Berlin: Metropol Verlag, 2007), 195-216.

25 See Quisling to Fermann, October 16, 1940; Dok. 123/a, December 31, 1948; Dok. 123/14, March 29, 1949. L-sak Fermann, box 3. On Støren, see *Norsk krigsleksikon*, http://mediabase1.uib.no/krigslex/s/s9.html#storen-finn (accessed November 1, 2012).

model for the NSUO.[26] Hence, the NSUO essentially had the same structure and goals. Particularly during the last years of the war, it established itself as the central Norwegian facility in Germany. Even though it did not manage to penetrate entirely the various Norwegian colonies, the NSUO was able to span a tight-knit network of chapters and liaison people in virtually the whole of *Großdeutschland.*

Formally, within the party structure of the NS, the NSUO had the same position as a county *(Fylke),* and its structure was organised accordingly. As a kind of Gauleiter *(Fylkesfører),* Olaf Fermann operated from Oslo, while Germany and Austria together formed the district No. 1 *(krets 1),* Großdeutschland *(Stor-Tyskland).* The latter consisted of five subgroups or districts, respectively. These were Berlin, Hamburg, Dresden, Munich and Vienna. The group leader of Berlin functioned as the country leader of the whole of Großdeutschland at the same time.[27] All the other cities, municipalities or boroughs were subordinate to these districts. The Mark of Brandenburg, Pomerania, Danzig, West Prussia, East Prussia and the Warteland belonged to the district of Berlin. The district of Hamburg was, in addition to the Hanseatic City, comprised of Mecklenburg, East and South Hanover, Brunswick, Magdeburg, Anhalt, Schleswig-Holstein, Weser-Ems, Essen, Düsseldorf, Cologne-Aachen, North and South Westfalia as well as Electoral Hesse. Saxony, Halle-Merseburg, Thuringia, Hesse-Nassau, the Moselland, Lower and Upper Silesia as well as the Protectorate of Bohemia and Moravia belonged to Dresden. The district of Munich was responsible for Munich and Upper Bavaria, Swabia, Franconia, Württemberg-Hohenzollern, Baden, the Westmark, Bayreuth, Main-Franconia as well as Tirol-Vorarlberg. Vienna encompassed Lower and Upper Danube, Styria, Carinthia and Salzburg.[28]

The way the NSUO structured the districts and attempted to gain members even in boroughs without a Norwegian milieu worth mentioning, reveals the desire to completely penetrate Norwegian life in Germany, an undertaking that demanded an enormous organisational effort. Hence, one important task of the country leadership in Berlin was to administrate a register of all Germany-based Norwegians, which was updated whenever possible. The register was a means to comprehensively influence and control this group of citizens. This purpose explains why the administrators of the register were criticised for providing incomplete or incorrect data.[29] The latter was, among other things, an effect of frequent relocations due to the bombing of German cities. Therefore it is not possible to determine exactly how many Norwegians lived in Germany during the war. The numbers on the membership of the NSUO are just as inaccurate and do not completely document

26 On the Foreign Office of the NSDAP, see Donald M. McKale, *The swastika outside Germany.* (Kent: Kent State University Press, 1977).

27 See, among others, NSUO to Direktoratet for spesialorientering, May 11, 1943, L-sak Fermann, box 4.

28 See Redegjørelse om N.S. utenriksorganisasjon [undated], L-sak Fermann.

29 See e.g. Fermann to the NSUO group leadership in Berlin, May 11, 1943, PA NSUO, file Fylkesfører, Korrespondanse 1943. Cf. interrogation Idar Melandsø, July 15, 1946, L-sak Fermann, box 4.

every year. Moreover, the list frequently does not reflect whether it was dealing with transients, such as the numerous Norwegian SS volunteers, or with individuals with a permanent address in Germany.

Therefore, the data available only convey a rough idea of the number of Germany-based Norwegians during the war. For example, in March 1944 113 members were registered for the district of Berlin, 104 for the district of Hamburg, 54 for the district of Dresden, 28 for the district of Munich and 32 for the district of Vienna.[30] The register lists 107 members of the NSUO for the district of Berlin, 101 for the district of Hamburg, 68 for the district of Dresden, 41 for the district of Munich and 32 for the district of Vienna for October of the same year.[31] With regard to the cities themselves, only 43 members were allotted to Berlin, 46 to Hamburg, 16 to Dresden, 14 to Munich and 20 to Vienna. As a result, and taking into consideration a certain margin of error, NSUO membership in Germany as a whole amounted to 349 individuals six months before the end of the war. This number also corresponds with the estimates of the prosecuting body in Fermann's treason lawsuit.[32] Unfortunately, the archives of the NSUO do not provide any reliable information on the total number of Germany-based Norwegians for 1944 or one of the previous years. Fermann himself mentions 1,100 to 1,200 Norwegians for 1943.[33] Disregarding the possible fluctuations between 1943 and 1944, it is fair to say that about every third to fourth Norwegian in the Third Reich was a member of the NSUO. An internal report of the group leadership in Berlin confirms these figures.[34] The initiatives of the NS to attract party members in Germany were therefore far more successful than those in Norway.

The explicit ideological programme of the NSUO becomes evident in Fermann's exclamation on the work of the NS Foreign Office:

> Those of us who are dealing with Norwegians abroad are working on a very much more important basis than those who are leading the battle here at home. It is not our mission to gain a number of members, but to create an understanding [...] in all circles of our fellow countrymen abroad for the big overthrow. It is such that a people cannot become National Socialist, if it does not contain within itself the conditions to experience a new era and to be effective in it. We belong to a people that bear these conditions due to its Nordic blood, which renders it tailor-made for the idealistic attitude towards life of this new era. There is some truth to it that one cannot become NS [Nasjonal Samling], if one does not by birth bear the core within oneself.[35]

30 See rapport NSUO to Fermann, April 13, 1944, L-sak Fermann, box 4.

31 See Medlemsfordelingen i Krets Stor-Tyskland, October 1, 1944, L-sak Fermann, box 4.

32 See Dok. 124 [undated], L-sak Fermann.

33 See Fermann to Næringsdepartementet, July 9, 1943, PA NSUO, file Fylkesfører, Korrespondanse 1943.

34 See Krets Stor Tyskland av Nasjonal Samling [undated], 4, L-sak Fermann, box 3.

35 Fermanns redegjørelse på N.S. Utenriksorganisasjon, September, 1942, L-sak Fermann, box 2.

Since the NSUO was obviously not convinced that "racial intuition" alone would suffice to "convert" their fellow countrymen to National Socialism, the propaganda activities in collaboration with other National Socialist institutions in Germany took on an important part of the work of the NSUO. Apart from the German press that was regularly supplied with materials,[36] the contacts with the Nordic Liaison Agency *(Nordische Verbindungsstelle)* of the Propaganda Ministry of the Reich *(Reichspropagandaministerium)* and the Agency of the Reich Commissioner *(Vertretung des Reichskommissars)* for the occupied Norwegian territories were important.[37] In addition, the cultural events the NSUO organised together with the Nordic Society *(Nordische Gesellschaft)* in Lübeck played a central role.[38]

A number of celebrities in Norwegian cultural life also willingly served propaganda purposes. Among these were the well-known opera singer and Wagner interpreter Beate Asserson; Marie Hamsun, wife of the famous writer and Nobel laureate in literature Knut Hamsun; Christian Leden, the arctic explorer and icon of the *völkisch* Nordic Movement *(Nordische Bewegung);* Karo Espeseth, the scandal author and wife of the German professor for Russian Studies Gerhard von Mende, Alfred Rosenberg's staff member in the Eastern Ministery *(Ostministerium);* the pianist Birger Hammer as well as Gunnar Graarud, the opera singer and professor at the University for Music and Performance Arts in Vienna *(Wiener Musikhochschule).* With the exception of Marie Hamsun, they all resided in the German Reich and were, except for Beate Asserson, members of the NS.[39] The well-known German opera singer Erna Berger got involved in the NSUO, too, and was granted guest membership in the party due to her marriage to the Norwegian engineer Sverre Wiull.[40] The ties with a number of further NS organisations become particularly obvious when looking at Graarud, who was a board member of the Viennese Office of the Nordic Society.[41] Graarud, who considered it "the greatest fortune" of his life "to fight for Hitler's world",[42] had been a member of the NSDAP as early as in 1933 and belonged to the first members of the Norwegian National Socialist NNST.[43] He was the head of the Ostmark Office *(Ostmarkkontor)* of the NSUO in

36 See the letter to Olga Bjoner about the organisation of the NSUO, September 8, 1943, PA NSUO, file F Hirden, 1942-45.

37 See Tyske myndigheter og institusjoner, PA NSUO, box Fb-5/B. Organisasjon.

38 See Nordische Gesellschaft to the NSUO, October 6, 1943, PA NSUO, box Fa-4.

39 See various unsorted membership lists of the NSUO as well as Fermann to Marie Hamsun, March 6, 1941, PA NSUO, box Fa-4. Cf. also Odd Svang Rasmussen to Rusten [undated, most probably end of February 1941], L-sak Rusten.

40 See letter on September 8, 1943 on the organisation of the NSUO, PA NSUO, box Ff-fl/12.

41 Gunnar Graarud to Fermann, April 6, 1941. Cf. also Graarud to Fermann, May 9, 1941. RA, L-sak Gunnar Graarud.

42 Graarud to Gulbrand Lunde, April 29, 1941, L-sak Graarud.

43 See Graarud to NS Riksøkonomiavdelingen, November 17, 1942; Adolf Egeberg jr. to Graarud, July 17, 1933. L-sak Graarud.

Vienna from 1941 onward and the most important supporter on site of the Norwegian SS members. In 1944 he voluntarily joined the *Volksturm.*[44]

Attending to the Norwegian SS volunteers was an integral part of the work of the group. The head office of the NSUO in Berlin served as a contact point for the Norwegian SS members who lived in Germany, and the local Norwegian population was pressured to support this work financially. In addition, the NSUO closely collaborated with the Germanic Headquarters *(Germanische Leitstelle)*[45] in Oslo, which was responsible for recruiting Norwegian volunteers for the SS.[46] In this context Fermann's double function as the head of the NSUO and *Frontkjemperkontoret* had particular effect.

Controlling student life in Germany was another focus of activity.[47] During the war the student organisaton of the NS (*Nasjonal Samlings Studentfylking*, NSSF) and the general student union *(Norsk Studentsamband)* happened to exist alongside each other. However, the group leadership of the NSUO tried to prompt all the students to join the NS, and it extensively influenced the awarding of scholarships.[48] The extent of the Gleichschaltung becomes evident when considering that the leader of the NSSF in Germany, Jan Jansholt, was also head of the general student union, whose ombudsmen, he reported, were all members of the NS. Therefore, the collaboration would materialise automatically, even though there was no direct link.[49] As various letters between the student groups and the NSUO suggest, there was however nothing that can remotely be considered a successful Gleichschaltung. The conflicts between members and non-members of the NS remained a constant centre of conflict.[50]

Furthermore, the NSUO closely collaborated with the Hitler Youth and the Foreign Office of the NSDAP. However, only a few sources could be found that provide details about the nature of this collaboration.[51] Incidentally, the NSUO also attempted to establish contact with other National Socialist and fascist groups, such

44 See Fermann to Graarud, March 28, 1941; Graarud to Fermann, November 3, 1944. L-sak Graarud.

45 On the work of the Germanic Headquarters in Norway, see Malte Gasche, "Norge og prosjektet Germanische Wissenschaftseinsatz. Hans Schwalm og Ahnenerbes fiasko i Norge 1942-1944", in *Jakten på Germania. Fra nordensvermeri til SS-arkeologi*, eds. Terje Emberland and Jorunn Sem Fure (Oslo: Humanist forlag, 2009), 202-226.

46 See Fermann to Idar Melandsø, July 12, 1943, PA NSUO, file Fylkesfører Fermann. Also see Rapport over kretsledelsens arbeid [undated], L-sak Fermann, box 3.

47 On the attempts of Gleichschaltung of university life in Norway, see Jorunn Sem Fure, *Universitetet i kamp 1940-1945* (Oslo: Vidarforlaget, 2007).

48 See Fermann to Quisling, May 15, 1942; Fermann to Samuel Simonsen, April 11, 1942. L-sak Fermann, box 4.

49 See Jan Jansholt to Fermann, May 20, 1944, PA NSUO, box Fb-5/B. Organisasjon. Also cf. letter to Olga Bjoner, September 8, 1943, PA NSUO, file F Hirden, 1942-45. In addition, see RA, L-sak Jan Jansholt.

50 Cf., among others, the correspondence on the conflicts in the student milieu in Munich, RA, L-sak Per Støren (son of the abovementioned Finn Sophus Støren and intermittent group leader of the NSUO in Munich). Cf. also the relevant correspondence in L-sak Fermann.

51 See Rapport over Kretsledelsens arbeid [undated], L-sak Fermann, box 3.

as the foreign agency of the Spanish *Falange*.[52] In addition, there were links to National Socialist Danish and Swedish groups in Germany. However, to date little is known about this cooperation.[53]

Attempts to Bring Norwegian Clubs in Germany Into Line

There is still no scholarly work that entirely documents Norwegian life in Germany in the interwar period and during the Second World War.[54] The Norwegian milieu in various German cities can not be reconstructed comprehensively due to the limited source material available. Moreover, we are dealing with small groups or individuals in most of the cases. Norwegian colonies of note mainly existed in well-known university cities, which had attracted Scandinavian students since the 1880s and increasingly so since the turn of the century. Evidence can be provided for Norwegian clubs with a large membership in Dresden, Berlin and Hamburg, among others. The only clubs that continue to exist to this day are the Norwegian Club in Hamburg and the Norwegian Rowing Club in Berlin.

Since Norwegian life in Germany in the abovementioned cities mainly seems to have taken place in the social surroundings of the respective clubs, the NS Foreign Office concentrated on the Gleichschaltung of them. Therefore, I will discuss the interference of the NSUO on the Norwegian milieu using three case studies: The Norwegian Club in Berlin, the Norwegian Club in Hamburg and the Norwegian Rowing Club in Berlin. They all played central roles within Norwegian life in Germany and all had a club tradition of their own.

In contrast to the Norwegian Rowing Club, which first and foremost was a meeting point for Norwegian students in Berlin, the Norwegian Club in Berlin-Charlottenburg predominantly consisted of individuals that belonged to the established middle class and who in part held key positions in society and were quite well-known.[55] Among these were a number of entrepreneurs, public figures and

52 See Forbindelse med den spanske Falange [most probably of March 8, 1945], PA NSUO, box Fb-5/B. Organisasjon. In particular, the NSUO collaborated closely with the *Nationaal-Socialistiske Beweging der Nederlanden* on issues related to the assistance of SS volunteers. See the letter written by the *Nationaal-Socialistiske Beweging der Nederlanden*, July 1, 1944, L-sak Fermann, box 4.

53 Cf. Rusten to the NSUO, February 15, 1941, L-sak Rusten. Rusten emphasises that the corresponding Danish and Swedish associations had by far more members. Therefore, it was not possible for the NSUO to adopt a dominant position in the cooperation.

54 However, in the last years popular science works have appeared that deal with aspects of Norwegian life in Germany. See e.g. Daniela Büchten, ed., *"Jeg har en koffert i Berlin". Nordmenn i Berlin rundt 1900 og 2000* (Oslo: Nasjonalbiblioteket, 2007); Bernd Henningsen, ed., *Hundert Jahre deutsch-norwegische Begegnungen* (Berlin: Berliner Wissenschaftsverlag, 2005); Sverre Jervell, *Nordmenn i Berlin. Glimt fra Berlins historie* (Oslo: Skyline, 2007); Laila Thuestad, ed., *Berlin – med norske øyne. Dokumentasjon av norsk liv i Berlin i dag* (Laksevåg: Alvheim & Eide, 2006).

55 So far, the Norwegian Club has been mentioned in Terje Emberland und Bernt Rougthvedt's study *Det ariske idol. Forfatteren, eventyreren og nazisten Per Imerslund* (Oslo: Aschehoug, 2004). For a more detailed portrait about the clubs, see Karcher, "Zwischen Nationalsozialismus und nordischer Gesinnung", 184-204.

cultural celebrities as well as artists who frequently happened to be more successful in Norway after having stayed in Berlin. Prominent names were for example the pianist Amalie Christie, the composer Klaus Egge, the actors Gerd Høst and Fridtjof Mjøen, son of the well-known eugenicist Jon Alfred Mjøen, the painter and son of Knut Hamsun, Tore Hamsun, as well as the Norwegian ambassador in Berlin, Arne Scheel.[56] Moreover, the club was one of the first places to go for Norwegians who visited Berlin or who sought contact with the Norwegian milieu without formally belonging to the club.[57] Information on the number of members of the club can only be found for 1937. Therefore, it is not possible to document neither the number of members of the club after 1940, nor the number of those club members who joined the NSUO. Of the 237 members that were registered in 1937, evidence for a membership in the NS can so far only be provided for a handful of individuals.[58]

Thorvald Heyerdahl was the chairman and most important financier of the Norwegian Club from 1933 until its dissolution in 1941. Therefore, the group leadership of the NSUO in Berlin associated all of its actions with Heyerdahl.[59] When describing the attempts of the NSUO to bring the club under their control, the relationship between Heyerdahl and the Berlin NSUO leadership requires special consideration. Fermann described Heyerdahl as one of his most important Norwegian connections in Berlin, and he was also his main contact person when trying to establish the party newspaper *Fritt Folk* in Germany.[60] According to the police investigations that were launched against Heyerdahl after the war, he had been a member of the NS since 1938.[61] Heyerdahl however claimed that despite the fact that Quisling had requested him to join the party due to his social influence in Berlin he had refused to do so. Nevertheless, he is registered on the NSUO membership list of November 27, 1940.[62]

Similar to a number of so-called Norwegian friends of Germany, the occupation of Norway and the events that followed April 9, 1940, initially induced a political turnabout in Heyerdahl's case. Hence, as a reaction to Quisling's attempted coup,

56 See the mailing list of the Norwegian Club, PA Nicola Karcher, fraction of the estate Finn Rafn.

57 See the guestbook of the Norwegian Club, PA Ketil Høst Heyerdahl, estate Gerd Høst Heyerdahl.

58 Cf. the mailing list of the Norwegian Club, PA Karcher. See also various unsorted registers of NSUO members that document club memberships between 1940 and 1945. However, they neither provide information about the time before 1940, nor do they refer to previous registers. I assume that Fermann did not create a register due to the small number of members. See PA NSUO.

59 This becomes evident for e.g. from the letter by Rusten to Heyerdahl on February 2, 1941, L-sak Rusten.

60 See Dok. 123/8 [undated]; cf. also Dok. 32, January 30, 1945. L-sak Fermann, box 3 and 4.

61 See Oslo Politikammer, NS-kartotek, January 4, 1946, RA, henlagt sak Thorvald Emil Heyerdahl.

62 See Liste innmeldte NS-medlemmer i Berlin, November 27, 1940, PA NSUO, box Fd-9, D. Økononomi, file Korrespondanse om medlemskap 1940-45.

Heyerdahl wrote in a telegram to him: "After all that has happened in the last days, I would like to ask you to remove me as a member of the Nasjonal Samling, in case I happen to be on your list."[63] However, Heyerdahl primarily seems to have been at odds with the way Quisling attempted the coup and less so with the fact that the NS had come to power. In summer 1940, he wrote to Fermann:

> That must be a marvelous time: without a king, a government and the parliament, – so without the factors which procrastinate and do not achieve anything! The opportunity ought to be used to create a little bit of dictatorship in various areas, in various organisations [...]. I was often astonished that everybody agrees that one needs a dictatorship in critical times, and why shouldn't this therefore be useful in normal times?[64]

Hence, it is not surprising that Heyerdahl welcomed the reorganisation of Norway on September 25, 1940: "Congratulations to the National Socialist reorganisation of Norway. It took a load off my mind when I heard that we released 'the big thing' for the future, that parties have been dissolved etc. [...]."[65] In November of the same year, he reapplied for membership in the NSUO. However, it is noteworthy that he only appears on the register of members on November 1940 and not for the years to follow. He was either not registered or he left the party immediately.[66]

In the light of the NSUO leadership's attempts to bring the Norwegian Club into line from December 1940 onwards, Heyerdahl's attitude towards the NS changed fundamentally. In the same month the NSUO group leadership in Berlin reported that the Norwegian Club had met illegally despite the assembly ban, it imposed against it. In the course of the meeting the members were said to have "stirred up hatred" against the NSDAP and its *Führer*.[67] In the following months several conflicts arose between the leadership of the NSUO in Berlin and Heyerdahl as the representative of the interests of the Norwegian Club. The conflicts finally led to the dissolution of the club. In several letters to the NS Foreign Office in Oslo, the NSUO group leadership in Berlin tried to document that the club was an "anglophile", "anti-German" and "democratic" institution that was subverting the work of the NS in Germany. They accused Heyerdahl of heading the so-called *Jøssinger* (supporters of England), which according to the NSUO made up the majority in the Norwegian colony.[68]

The conflict finally climaxed when the Norwegian Club hosted a gala to which all Germany-based Norwegians were invited, without having made arrangements

63 Heyerdahl to Quisling, April 10, 1940, henlagt sak Heyerdahl.

64 Heyerdahl to Fermann, July 21, 1940, Norges Hjemmefrontmuseum (NHM), R, 8 I-0009, file 13b, korrespondanse vedr. straffesak mot Olaf Willy Fermann.

65 Heyerdahl to Fermann, September 26, 1940, NHM, R, 8 I-0009, file 13b, korrespondanse vedr. straffesak mot Olaf Willy Fermann.

66 See NS Generalsekretariatet to the NSUO, November 4, 1940, PA NSUO, box Fd-9.

67 See Rusten to the NSUO, December 7, 1940, L-sak Rusten.

68 See e.g. Rusten in a letter to the NSUO group Berlin, May 12, 1942, L-sak Rusten.

with the NSUO group in Berlin.[69] The event was interpreted by the NSUO as an attempt to collectively condemn the German Reich and National Socialism on behalf of the Norwegian milieu.[70] It was an initial confession of failure of NSUO policy that the group leadership did not succeed in preventing the meeting or was not invited to plan the event. The NSUO leadership took note of the dismissive attitude of the Norwegian Club. Fermann reacted clearly in a letter to Heyerdahl:

> According to the information I have, you strongly opposed to our movement in the time after April 9. Your attitude towards an understanding between Germany and Norway [...] is absolutely negative. Your statements and appearance left behind a general expression that you seemed to be happy about every success by English weapons and that you were only waiting for a defeat of our German friends.[71]

Because of the resistance the NSUO leadership met upon in the Norwegian Club, it intended to finally bring it into line and to have an election on a new NS directorate.[72] The club defied this plan by organising private meetings for loyal members only. In doing so, it forestalled the imposed, but at the time not yet implemented, prohibition.[73]

Nevertheless, the Norwegian Club could not, or did not want to entirely reject the collaboration with the NSUO. Hence, it co-organised an elaborately planned propaganda event when the head of the NS propaganda ministry Gulbrand Lunde visited Berlin in March 1941.[74] The club was at least prepared to collaborate to a certain degree during the first year after Norway had been occupied. In the end, though, this seems to have been the only extensive collaboration of its kind. Therefore, the attempt of the NSUO to bring into line the Norwegian Club has to be considered a failure.[75]

---

69 See Heyerdahl to Rusten, January 26, 1941; Rusten to Heyerdahl, January 28, 1941; Meddelse fra Den Norske klubb, January 31, 1941; Heyerdahl to Rusten, February 4, 1941; Rusten to the NS Generalsekretariatet, March 12, 1941. L-sak Rusten.

70 Rusten to the NSUO, February 3, 1941. In addition cf. Rusten to the NSUO, February 6, 1941; Rusten to the NSUO, February 15, 1941. L-sak Rusten.

71 Fermann to Heyerdahl, February 10, 1941, L-sak Rusten.

72 See Fermann to Heyerdahl, March 15, 1941; Rusten to Heyerdahl, March 28, 1941; Rusten to the NSUO, January 26, 1941; Rusten to the NSUO, February 3, 1941; Rusten to the NSUO, February 9, 1941. L-sak Rusten.

73 See note by Bertha Duesberg [undated]; Heyerdahl to the police agent Pettersen, September 6, 1945. Henlagt sak Heyerdahl.

74 See Beretning om Nasjonal Samlings massemöte i Berlin Raadhus, March 22, 1941, L-sak Rusten.

75 However, the arguments did not exclude further collaboration between Heyerdahl and Fermann. They remained in contact during the course of the war, especially for reasons that were related to aiding Norwegians in Germany. Since his brother Fridtjof Heyerdahl was the head of the Norwegian Red Cross, Heyerdahl disposed of an indispensable contact. See more about this, among others, in Fermann's letter to Heyerdahl on June 13, 1942 and his reply on June 20, 1942. NHM, 8 I-0009, file 13b. The fact that Heyerdahl donated 700 RM to

Right from the outset, the Norwegian Club in Hamburg rejected political statements of any kind in its by-laws.[76] Most probably it did so in order to protect itself from internal and external political influences:

> We ought to be grateful to these understanding gentlemen [the management of the club] that they inserted section 2 into the by-laws of the club, which disallows politicisation in the club. Without this section, the club certainly would have ceased to exist quite some time ago.[77]

As a result, the records of the club do not contain any hints towards the relationship to National Socialism in Germany or to the NS. There are not even official political statements for 1933 and 1934 when Olaf Fermann headed the club.

Since there are no registers of members and only lists of participants for various events as well as a guestbook, it is not possible to ascertain how many members the club had in various stages of its development and who was a member of the NS. Apart from Fermann, there is only evidence for the NS membership of a few individual, however important, representatives of the club. Hence, the records of the NSUO confirm that Andreas Lorenzen, one of the leading initiators of the club right from the beginning, was a keen member of the NS despite of his age.[78] Samuel Simonsen, a significant member and important financier of the club was a member of the NS from August 1940 onwards.[79] In addition to Fermann, so far only Nils Haagensen and Odd Svang Rasmussen were documentable members of the NS before 1940. They were both members of the Hamburg department of the NNST during the 1930s. Haagensen was also a member of the NSDAP and prior to that of the Norwegian conservative party *Høyre*.[80] Contrary to Fermann's statement that only about twelve Norwegians had joined the NS in Hamburg prior to 1940, the long-time club members Sigurd Blydt-Hansen and Stein Skraastad reported on the occasion of the 100-year existence of the Norwegian Club in 1989 that to everybody's surprise the NS enjoyed a large clientele. At the same time they

---

the Office of Frontline Soldiers in Berlin in 1942 is worth mentioning in this context. See Oslo Politikammer, ad landssvik Thv. Heyerdahl, October 21, 1946, henlagt sak Heyerdahl.

76 See the individual minutes and by-laws of the club, PA Den Norske Klub i Hamburg.

77 Minutes [undated], ibid.

78 See Svang Rasmussen to the NSUO, March 27, 1941, RA, L-sak Odd Svang Rasmussen. Whether this applies to the time after or even before 1940 has not been documented.

79 See Redegjørelse fra Visekonsul Sam. Simonsen, Hamburg [undated, after 1945], RA, PA Samuel Simonsen.

80 See Spørreskjema (Bilag til søknaden om opptagelse i Nasjonal Samling), January, 1941, L-sak Svang Rasmussen. In addition, see Søknad om opptagelse, September 14, 1940; Ansøkning om optagelse, February 17, 1941. RA, L-sak Nils Haagensen. See Støren to *Hauptsturmführer* Wolff [undated], PA NSUO, Liste over Norske Nasjonalsocialister i Tyskland, box 22.

stressed that the meetings of NS members that had taken place on the premises of the club allegedly did not have any further effects on the club life.[81]

Just as was the case for the Norwegian Club in Berlin, attempts to bring the club into line started in autumn 1940 onwards under the auspieces of Odd Svang Rasmussen as the leader of the Hamburg NSUO group. These endavours were much more successful than those in Berlin. As early as in October Fermann appointed Haagensen who, like Svang Rasmussen, was a member of the club management as a liaison between the NSUO group in Hamburg and the NSDAP. After the NS had initially planned to close down the club completely at the beginning of 1941, it tried to have the club elect Haagensen as chairman in the following weeks.[82] At first Fermann pressured the long-time club manager Johan Pedersen to resign from his office and to use his influence to create a basis for the collaboration with the NS. Fermann particularly aimed at the abovementioned section 2 of the by-laws, which stood in the way of political activities in the club. Almost at the same time he accused Pedersen in a letter of being one of the leading opponents of the NSUO in Hamburg:

> The situation in Hamburg, in the colony, has unfortunately started to go into the direction that fronts have more or less developed. [...]. The relationship is such that there is a part within the colony that adopts a hostile stance [towards the NSUO] and whose attitude is mainly based on the support for its stance from leading figures in the colony. One of the persons I am aiming at is yourself.[83]

Pedersen initially refused to step down. However, he finally had to give in to the pressure and resigned.

During the general assembly that took place on March 26, 1941, Andreas Lorenzen who was also acceptable to the opponents of the NS, was elected chairman. Vice-chairman Nils Haagensen and the secretary Odd Svang Rasmussen were confirmed in office. The treasurer of the club, Sigurd Blydt-Hansen, was the only board member who did not belong to the NS.[84] The controversial section 2 remained in place, however with the modification that political speeches and discussions were allowed to take place. As a result, it became ineffective. Moreover, the club was forced to accommodate the local NSUO group on demand. Svang Rasmussen emphasised that the interests of the NS were completely covered without

81 See Sigurd Blydt-Hansen and Stein Skraastad, *Den Norske Klubb i Hamburg. 1889-1989*. http://www.dennorskeklub.de/76740 (accessed November 1, 2012). See also Dok. 34, March 6, 1946, L-sak Fermann, box 3.

82 See NS Generalsekretariat to the NSUO, October 24, 1940; Fermann to Haagensen, February 3, 1941. PA NSUO, box Fa-4 Fylkesfører og sekretariat. In addition, cf. L-sak Haagensen.

83 Fermann to Pedersen, February 1, 1941, L-sak Fermann, box 3.

84 See Svang Rasmussen to the NSUO, March 27, 1941, L-sak Svang Rasmussen. As the records suggest, the management remained unchanged in the following years. See Svang Rasmussen to Fermann, March 17, 1942, L-sak Svang Rasmussen.

directly having had to bring the club into line. He considered this an important victory for the NS.[85]

Nevertheless, the conflict within the colony seems to have continued during the war. Already in October 1940, Fermann was informed about an "alarming fragmentation"[86]. At the same time Svang Rasmussen disclosed that so far only twelve new members had been gained for the NSUO. He considered the sharp distinction between supporters of the NS and "the others" as the cause of this situation.[87]

However, the political split did not seem to influence the number of members in a longer perspective of time. In the course of the war, the NSUO listed relatively high numbers of members for Hamburg.[88] The collaboration of Norwegians in the so-called Fichte League *(Fichte-Bund)* can be categorised in this context. The latter had been subordinate to Goebbels' Propaganda Ministry since 1933 and was mainly responsible for propaganda directed towards the Nordic countries. The same applies to the establishment of the National Socialist Norwegian Union *(Nordmannslaget)* in the Hanseatic city in May 1940.[89] Both organisations indicate that sections within the Norwegian milieu in Hamburg had turned to National Socialist activities well before the National Socialist reorganisation of Norway in September 1940.

In the light of incomplete membership registers of the NSUO, it is difficult to specify the number of members for Hamburg, too. According to the two existing lists from 1940 to 1945, out of altogether 155 and 135 Hamburg-based Norwegian residents, 53 and 74, respectively, were members of the NSUO.[90] This means that on average every second to third Norwegian in Hamburg was a member of the NS. Most probably decisions to enter the party were based less on ideological convictions than on the increasing function of the NSUO as a kind of Norwegian consulate in Germany. After Simonsen, who had been the vice-consul of the Norwegian consulate general in Hamburg from 1929 to 1940, took over the head of the NSUO in Berlin in 1942, and with that of the district of Großdeutschland, the work of the NSUO increasingly steered into this direction.[91] In the course of the war, issues relating to the supply of Germany-based Norwegians became more and

---

85 See Svang Rasmussen to the NSUO, April 20, 1941, L-sak Svang Rasmussen. Cf. also Protokoll Generalforsamlingen, March 26, 1941, PA Den Norske Klub i Hamburg. In addition, cf. Rusten to the NSUO, February 21, 1941; Svang Rasmussen to Rusten [undated, most probably end of February 1941]. L-sak Rusten.

86 Nicolai Bjønnes to Fermann, October 31, 1940, PA NSUO, box Fa-4.

87 See Svang Rasmussen to Fermann, November 8, 1940, PA NSUO, box Fd-9.

88 See Nordmenn i Hamburg, PA NSUO, box Fd-7, file D.9 Medlemskap 1942-1945. In addition, cf. Liste over norske borgere i Hamburg og omegn, PA NSUO, box Fd-9, D-Økonomi, Korrespondanse om medlemskap 1940-45.

89 On the *Deutsche Fichte-Bund e.V., Reichsbund für Deutschtums-Arbeit* which was founded in 1914, as well as the *Nordmannslaget*, see Karcher, "Zwischen Nationalsozialismus und Nordischer Gesinnung", 197-199.

90 See PA NSUO, box Fd-7, file D.9 Medlemskap; file Fd-9, D-Økonomi, Korrespondanse om medlemskap 1940-45.

91 The club in Hamburg also supported the aid project. Cf. Redegjørelse fra Visekonsul Sam. Simonsen [undated], PA Simonsen.

more vital. Although aid was not tied to a membership in the NS, there are reasons to believe that access to supplies was easier that way.

Everyday club life in the Norwegian Rowing Club in Berlin-Köpenick, which was founded in 1907, was first and foremost shaped by Norwegian students, who were studying at the Technical College Charlottenburg (presently the Technical University Berlin). At the same time the club boasted a high number of socially established members that supported the club formally and economically and who only participated in club life on special occasions.[92] The rowing club mainly served as an important forum for these people to establish social networks within the Norwegian colony in Berlin. In addition, the Norwegian Rowing Club in Berlin-Köpenick maintained close ties to the Norwegian Club in Berlin-Charlottenburg. Apart from his function as the chairman of the Norwegian Club, Thorvald Heyerdahl was in the 1930s head of the rowing club, as well. The significance the rowing club had as an informal representative of Norwegian life in Germany becomes apparent when considering that in part internationally well-known Norwegians who had lived in Germany had been members. Among these were for example the architects Frithjof Platou who was later on responsible for the construction of the Kon-Tiki-Museum in Oslo and Christian von Munthe af Morgenstierne who had designed the first clubhouse as well as the landscape painters and representatives of the *Düsseldorfer Schule* Hans Dahl and Adelsteen Normann, who partly were sponsored by Kaiser Wilhelm II.[93] Normann's son Eilert Adelsteen became a member of the NSUO in 1941, succeeded Samuel Simonsen as head of the NSUO in Berlin in 1943, and continued to perform as such in his private premises in Potsdam until the end of the war.[94]

Similar to the cases of the Norwegian clubs in Berlin and Hamburg, there is so far no evidence for formal links of the rowing club to National Socialist German institutions, and before 1940 there are documentable links to Fermann's NS group in isolated cases only. At any rate, there were most probably no relationships to the active club members, for instance to the students. Since Fermann was anyway interested in another target group for cooperation with the NS, soliciting students does not seem to have had any particular relevance. His contacts primarily focused on influential and established members of the Norwegian milieu in Germany of whom he expected financial support for the party. Accordingly, he had turned, among others, to the former head of the Norwegian Rowing Club Abraham Erichsen, in order to win potential sponsors for the party newspaper *Fritt Folk*.[95] However, nothing indicates that Erichsen actively supported the NS. Fermann had

92 Cf. Daniela Büchten, "De første årene", in *1907-2007. 100 år Norsk Roklub i Berlin*, ed. Norsk Roklub i Berlin (Berlin: self publishing, 2007), 5ff.

93 See the register of members of the Norwegian Rowing Club, PA Norsk Roklub i Berlin. Cf. also Büchten, "De første årene"; Tore Leite, "Klubbhusene i Hessenwinkel", in *1907-2007*, 14ff.

94 See Adelsteen Normann's curriculum vitae, June 20, 1947, L-sak Clausen. In addition, cf. Dok. 119 [undated], L-sak Fermann, box 4.

95 Fermann to Abraham Erichsen, January 13, 1941, PA NSUO, box Ff-Fl/12.

originally assumed that he would agree to promote the work of the NSUO in Berlin. Therefore, there is reason to believe that Erichsen was initially not entirely hostile to the cause.[96] There do not seem to have been any contacts of the rowing club to the NNST worth mentioning. Indeed, only two NNST members can be found on the club's membership list.[97]

There is evidence for direct interference on club life only after the reorganisation of Norway on September 25, 1940, and after the NSUO was formally founded. A first step was the attempt of the NSUO at the beginning of 1941 to reach an agreement with the Norwegian Rowing Club that members of the NS may be admitted to the club. That this was obviously not the case earlier on is documented by the hostile attitude of the bulk of the active club members and is confirmed by Fermann's letter to several leading representatives of the club, such as Erichsen and Heyerdahl, in which he asks for support to change this situation: "The relationship is [...] such that the students in the rowing club strongly reject the NS, and I would like to ask you to assist us in order to change this situation."[98] Fermann's records reveal that Curt Wiig, the chairman of the club and director of the branch office of the *Deutsche Bank* on Unter den Linden was willing to comply to these directives. However, in the course of negotiating the demands of the NSUO in autumn 1941, Wiig refused to admit NS members to the board.[99] It is remarkable that the documents of the NSUO do not reveal any reactions to Wiig's refusal.[100] There are only

---

96 Cf. Fermann to Rusten, December 10, 1941, L-sak Rusten.

97 These were Rusten who was later to become the group leader of the NSUO in Berlin and the pianist Birger Hammer. See register of members of the Norwegian Rowing Club, PA Norsk Roklub i Berlin.

98 Fermann to Erichsen, January 13, 1941, PA NSUO, box Ff-Fl/12. See also Fermann to Consul Jacobsen, January 13, 1941; Fermann to the home secretary of the NS Albert Viljam Hagelin, February 1, 1941. L-sak Fermann, box 3. In addition, see Fermann to Heyerdahl, March 18, 1941 [copy], PA Ebba Sommerfeldt, estate Johan Ludwig Hermansen. In addition, cf. Rusten's letter on March 13, 1941 in which he considers converting the clubhouse into a home for the *Hird* (a kind of SA of the NS), L-sak Rusten.

99 See Dok. 32, January 30, 1945, L-sak Fermann. Cf. Utdrag av endel av Den Norske Roklub i Berlin's akter [undated], PA Sommerfeldt. In addition, cf. Henrik Lystad, "Norsk Roklub i Berlin under den annen verdenskrig", in *1907-2007*, 48. As an effect of the demands of the NSUO, apart from Curt Wiig, the entire management of the club as well as Heyerdahl and Erichsen participated in an emergency meeting of the club. While some members suggested admitting at least a few NS students to the management in order to save the club, Wiig rejected this proposal.

100 Fermann wrote only one letter in April 1942 in which he requests the leader of the NSUO in Germany, Simonsen, to finally force leading club members to issue a political statement. For this purpose, a letter regarding the Norwegian SS volunteers was supposed to be sent to the management of the rowing club in order to provoke a written statement on Bolshevism. If the reply happened to be non-satisfying, the plan was to remove the respective individuals and to create a new board of managers. See Fermann to Simonsen, April 10, 1942, L-sak Fermann, box 1.

documents on the demands of the NSUO group vis-à-vis the club from 1943 onwards that the NSUO tried to enforce by means of the *Waffen-SS* and the *Gestapo*.[101]

In autumn 1943 a meeting between the representative of the NSUO Idar Melandsø and Curt Wiig took place in the Hotel Adlon on Unter den Linden. Theo Findahl, the correspondent of the largest Norwegian newspaper *Aftenposten* was present in order to support the chairman of the rowing club during the negotiations. In the course of the conversation Wiig learned that is was not only Fermann's responsibility, but that Quisling himself stood behind this initiative of the NSUO. As a result of the meeting, the rowing club was obliged to render its premises available to the NSUO for Norwegians who were victims of bombing raids.[102] Until the end of the war the clubhouse served as accommodation for bombed out members of the NSUO.[103] Moreover, the NSUO had considered converting the building into a recreation home for "Germanic" SS volunteers. Due to the local circumstances, these plans did not materialise.[104]

Although the NS was, according to the sources, unable to ideologically penetrate the club, it was by the time the work of the NSUO began, considering its role as a party supportive of the state, at least able to actually intervene into club life. Its propaganda activities were unsuccessful among the active members, which becomes obvious when none of the approximately 40 to 50 members of the rowing club between 1933 and 1945, and who were retroactively registered between 1990 and 1992, were members of the NSUO. With regard to the complete registry that has been preserved, which covers the period from the foundation of the club until presumably 1932 (during this time up to 237 individuals belonged to the club), only a handful of individuals can be verified as members of the NSUO later on.[105] Since it needs to be taken into consideration that a number of registered members had in the meantime either left Berlin, deceased or left the club, the figures are not really representative, especially since new members were not registered after 1933. Looking at the number of members, though, the NSUO did not succeed. As in the case

101 See the statement by the long-standing club member Jørgen Rafn, circular to the members of the rowing club, October 11, 1990, PA, Sommerfeldt.

102 See the interrogation Idar Melandsø, July 15, 1946, L-sak Fermann, box 4. In addition, see Wiig's letter, October 15, 1943, PA Sommerfeldt.

103 See Melandsø to Adelsteen Normann, November 9, 1944, PA NSUO, box Fm-13/Omsorgsavdelingen, file O.1 Omsorgsavdelingen, Kretsen 1944-45. Cf. Melandsø to Wiig, August, 28. 1943, PA NSUO, box Fa-4/Fylkesfører og sekretariat. Cf. rapport NSUO, January 11 until April 15, 1944, as well as rapport NSUO, April 16 until May 31, 1944, PA NSUO, box Fe-11/Propaganda, file E.2 Propaganda, Kretsene 1944-45. In addition, see NSUO, Førermøte på slottet i tiden 1944, L-sak Fermann, box 3.

104 See Fermann to Melandsø, July 20, 1944, PA NSUO, box Fc-6/C. Personal. Cf. Fylkesøkonomilederen to Riksøkonomisjefen, July 3, 1944, PA NSUO, box Fd-7/D. Økonomi. See also rapport from the district of Großdeutschland, October 16, 1944, L-sak Fermann. Cf. Lystad, "Norsk Roklub i Berlin", 48f. In addition, cf. rapport Wiigs [1945], PA Sommerfeldt.

105 See Fortegnelse over nålevende medlemmer, February 20, 1990; May 15, 1990; September 19, 1991; July 7, 1992. PA Sommerfeldt. Also cf. Medlemsfortegnelse over NS Gruppe Berlin [undated], PA NSUO, box Fd-7, D. Økonomi, file D 9 Medlemskap 1942-1945, as well as the register of members of the Norwegian Rowing Club, PA Norsk Roklub i Berlin.

of the Norwegian clubs in Berlin and Hamburg, collaboration between the rowing club and the NSUO only took place with reservations.

Final Considerations

As this chapter shows, in 1940 the NS Foreign Office was established with a clear purpose. While the NSUO increasingly focused on supporting Norwegians in need and assisting the numerous Norwegian SS volunteers that travelled through Germany in the course of the war, the nazification and Gleichschaltung ofNorwegian life in Germany was the main aim. The interferences with varying degrees of success on Norwegian clubs presented here illustrate this goal.

Although the NSUO focused on propaganda as a means to achieve its goal, it was at the same time as a representative of the official Norwegian collaborative party in a position to resort to state reprisal. Consequently, the NSUO leadership was able to intervene extensively into the organisational structure of the Norwegian clubs and either enforced Gleichschaltung or the dissolution of the clubs after voluntary collaboration had only materialised in a few isolated cases.

Fermann expected to win the support of influential representatives of the Norwegian milieu for the NS by employing his principle of "processing individuals" ("Bearbeitung Einzelner")[106]. Thorvald Heyerdahl's conduct as the head of the Norwegian Club in Berlin reveals that this policy ultimately failed. While the latter initially did not have any objections to cooperate with the NS before Norway was occupied and after the country was reorganised in September 1940, he decided to make a turnabout due to the attempts to bring the club into line. Personal animosity played a considerable role in this conflict, and presumably Heyerdahl compensated for his lack of political power by mobilising his personal networks in Berlin. Backed up by his contacts, he tried to demonstrate to the NSUO group leadership who ultimately called the shots in the Norwegian milieu.

As an outpost of the Norwegian collaboration party in Germany, the links of the NSUO to various areas of the German National Socialist party were part of the official policy. The extent of this collaboration and the role it played in the NSUO attempts at Gleichschaltung is to date not comprehensibly accessible. The sources on this problem are far from being complete. It seems certain, though, that Fermann's personal connections, especially to Himmler and the SS, played a considerable role when deciding not only to confer the foreign work of the NS on him, but a number of other tasks of the party, as well.

Nevertheless, Fermann was quite obviously unable to cope with the task of leading the NSUO. His initial decision to entrust the NNST with the local work of the NSUO reveals that the NS Foreign Office encountered serious problems when trying to recruit suitable personnel in 1940. Indeed, the accusation that he was not sufficiently familiar with the situation in Germany was relevant. Ironically, it was the former NNST leadership that held this against him and which itself had seri-

106 Fermann to Rusten, December 10, 1940, L-sak Rusten.

ously marred the work of the NS Foreign Office in Berlin. During its time as the representative of the NSUO in Germany, conflicts such as the one with the Norwegian Club in Berlin developed much more rapidly than would have been the case had the party adopted a diplomatic approach.

Although the NSUO was able to register a relatively high number of members in Germany in the course of the war, it remains debatable to what extent this is an indication of its political vigour. This applies in particular to the Norwegian clubs that were examined here. While the NSUO was with regard to the Norwegian Club in Hamburg able to resort to party members who willingly implemented Gleichschaltung, the Norwegian Club in Berlin eluded the top down intervention by dissolving itself. The Norwegian Rowing Club in Berlin continued to exist during the war, but was at least partially coerced by the NSUO to collaborate. It has to be stressed though, that the official stance of the clubs during the war does not necessarily apply to the attitudes of individual club members.

In essence, one needs to be cautious about generalising Germany-based Norwegians' attitudes towards National Socialism on the basis of the developments described here. Indeed, in the final analysis the ideological penetration of the Norwegian milieu failed. The aid the NSUO provided to victims of bombing raids significantly contributed to an increased party membership. At the same time, the vigour of the NSUO cannot be explained on the basis of its consular tasks alone. Despite the split of the colony in Hamburg, a number of Germany-based Norwegians were willing to collaborate with National Socialists in situations that were not linked to the living conditions in Germany during the war.

As in the case of a number of other pro-German Norwegian circles,[107] the NS politically disqualified itself in large parts of the Norwegian milieu in Germany when it collaborated with the German occupying power. This however did not necessarily apply to the same extent to the National Socialist regime. A large number of Germany-based Norwegians considered Germany a home away from home and was connected to it by family ties, tradition and culture. Therefore, there is reason to believe that there were sympathies for National Socialism within the Norwegian milieu in Germany or at least a kind of loyalty towards the host country that even lasted throughout the war. A direct involvement for National Socialism, however, was more an exception.

Bibliography

Blydt-Hansen, Sigurd and Stein Skraastad. *Den Norske Klubb i Hamburg. 1889-1989.* http://www.dennorskeklub.de/76740 (accessed November 1, 2012).

Bohn, Robert. *Reichskommissariat Norwegen. "Nationalsozialistische Neuordnung" und Kriegswirtschaft.* Munich: Oldenbourg, 2000.

Brevik, Hans Olaf. *NS – fra parti til sekt.* Oslo: Pax, 1970.

107 See e.g. Karcher, "Zwischen Nationalsozialismus und nordischer Gesinnung".

Bruknapp, Dag Olav. "Ideene splitter partiet". In *Fra idé til dom. Noen trekk fra utviklingen av Nasjonal Samling*, edited by Rolf Danielsen and Stein Ugelvik Larsen, 9-47. Bergen et al.: Universitetsforlaget, 1976.

Büchten, Daniela, ed. *"Jeg har en koffert i Berlin". Nordmenn i Berlin rundt 1900 og 2000.* Oslo: Nasjonalbiblioteket, 2007.

Büchten, Daniela. "De første årene". In *1907-2007. 100 år Norsk Roklub i Berlin*, edited by Norsk Roklub i Berlin, 5-10. Berlin: self publishing, 2007.

Dahl, Hans Fredrik. "Fascismen i Norge 1920-1940. Et overblikk". *Kontrast* 31 (1966), 5-17.

Dahl, Hans Fredrik, Bernt Hagtvet and Guri Hjeltnes, eds. *Den norske nasjonalsosialismen. Nasjonal Samling 1933-1945 i tekst og bilder.* Oslo: Pax, 1982.

Dahl, Hans Fredrik. *Vidkun Quisling. En fører for fall.* Oslo: Aschehoug 1992.

Dahl, Hans Fredrik et al., eds. *Norsk krigsleksikon 1940-1945*. Oslo: Cappelen 1995, http://mediabase1.uib.no/pls/apex/f?p=108:23:4297396938218298::NO::P23_SHOWWHAT:1 (accessed November 1, 2012).

Emberland, Terje and Bernt Rougthvedt. *Det ariske idol. Forfatteren, eventyreren og nazisten Per Imerslund.* Oslo: Aschehoug, 2004.

Emberland, Terje and Matthew Kott. *Himmlers Norge. SS, Norge og det storgermanske prosjekt.* Oslo: Aschehoug, 2012.

Figueiredo, Ivo de. "Nasjonal Samling 1937-1940". In *Den norske fascismen. Nasjonal Samling 1933-1940*, edited by Hans Olaf Brevig and Ivo de Figureido, 111-201. Oslo: Pax, 2002.

Fure, Jorunn Sem. *Universitetet i kamp 1940-1945.* Oslo: Vidarforlaget 2007.

Gasche, Malte. "Norge og prosjektet Germanische Wissenschaftseinsatz. Hans Schwalm og Ahnenerbes fiasko i Norge 1942-1944". In *Jakten på Germania. Fra nordensvermeri til SS-arkeologi*, edited by Terje Emberland and Jorunn Sem Fure, 202-226. Oslo: Humanist forlag, 2009.

Henningsen, Bernd, ed. *Hundert Jahre deutsch-norwegische Begegnungen.* Berlin: Berliner Wissenschaftsverlag, 2005.

Hoffmann, Christhard. "Die reine Lehre einer politischen Sekte. Antisemitismus in der norwegischen 'Nasjonal Samling'". In *Vorurteil und Rassenhaß. Antisemitismus in den faschistischen Bewegungen Europas*, edited by Hermann Graml, Angelika Königseder and Julianne Wetzel, 253-273. Berlin: Metropol Verlag, 2001.

Jervell, Sverre. *Nordmenn i Berlin. Glimt fra Berlins historie.* Oslo: Skyline, 2007.

Karcher, Nicola. "Die Nasjonal Samling während der deutschen Okkupation Norwegens 1940-1945. Nationalismus versus Pangermanismus". In *Jahrbuch für Antisemitismusforschung*, vol 16, edited by Wolfgang Benz, 195-216. Berlin: Metropol Verlag, 2007.

Karcher, Nicola. "Schirmorganisation der Nordischen Bewegung. Der Nordische Ring und seine Repräsentanten in Norwegen". *NORDEUROPAforum* 1 (2009), 7-35.

Karcher, Nicola. "Norske Nasjonalsosialister i Tyskland 1933-1940. Politisk profil, intern struktur og nettverk". In *Utenfor det etablerte. Aspekter ved Einhart Lorenz' forskning*, edited by Øivind Kopperud, Vibeke Moe and Vibeke Kieding Banik, 97-110. Oslo: HL-senteret, 2011.

Karcher , Nicola. "Zwischen Nationalsozialismus und nordischer Gesinnung. Eine Studie zu den rechtsgerichteten Verbindungen norwegisch-deutscher Milieus in der Zwischenkriegszeit". PhD diss., University of Oslo, 2012.

Leite, Tore. "Klubbhusene i Hessenwinkel". In *1907-2007. 100 år Norsk Roklub i Berlin*, edited by Norsk Roklub i Berlin, 14-25. Berlin: self publishing, 2007.

Loock, Hans-Dietrich. *Quisling, Rosenberg und Terboven. Zur Vorgeschichte und Geschichte der nationalsozialistischen Revolution in Norwegen.* Stuttgart: Deutsche Verlags-Anstalt, 1970.

Lystad, Henrik. "Norsk Roklub i Berlin under den annen verdenskrig". In *1907-2007. 100 år Norsk Roklub i Berlin,* edited by Norsk Roklub i Berlin, 44-49. Berlin: self publishing, 2007.

McKale, Donald M. *The swastika outside Germany.* Kent: Kent State University Press, 1977.

Fritz Petrick. "Der 'Leichtmetallausbau Norwegen' 1940-1945. Eine Studie zur Expansions- und Okkupationspolitik des faschistischen deutschen Imperialismus". PhD diss., University of Greifswald, 1983 (in a revised version in Frankfurt a.M.: Peter Lang, 1992).

Sine editore. *Vår innsats.* Oslo: Blix Forlag, 1942.

Skodvin, Magne. *Striden om okkupasjonsstyret. Fram til 25. september 1940.* Oslo: Det norske samlaget, 1956.

Sørensen, Øystein. *Hitler eller Quisling. Ideologiske brytninger i Nasjonal Samling 1940-1945.* Oslo: Cappelen, 1989.

Thuestad, Laila, ed. *Berlin – med norske øyne. Dokumentasjon av norsk liv i Berlin i dag.* Laksevåg: Alvheim & Eide, 2006.

Johann von Leers as Part of an International Network of Postwar Fascism*

Martin Finkenberger

Introduction

In August 1957, the weekly magazine *Frankfurter Illustrierte* published a series of sensational articles under the headline "SS Meeting Point in Cairo". A journalist sent to Egypt stridently reported the presence of a large number of former National Socialists, SS and SD members, who were said to have found refuge in Egypt, where "a form of a small branch of the Third Reich" had been revitalised. From there, the reporter claimed, they were recruited by the Soviets, who for their part maintained close relations with President Nasser and supported his anti-Israeli policies. The Germans were allegedly placed in key positions in both the Egyptian military and propaganda apparatus. One of them was said to have been Johann von Leers (1902-1965), who had reportedly taught as a professor at the "University of Breslau" until the end of the war and who was now working under the alias "Euler" in Egypt. According to the *Frankfurter Illustrierte,* his role consisted of "taking part in the construction of an Egyptian National Socialism" – among other things as the "director" of "Radio Cairo" which broadcasted "Goebbels-style attacks" against the West and those Arab nations which did not submit to Nasser's leadership. All these efforts were said to be "part of the big plan to install the Soviet Union as the new leading power in the Middle East".[1]

The now defunct *Frankfurter Illustrierte* was not without influence. It appeared weekly and had a circulation of some 100,000 copies. The above-cited report, however, was a crude mix of a few facts, numerous wild speculations and an outrageous distortion of the truth.[2] It is true that at that time von Leers was living in Cairo, where he worked as a propaganda advisor. However, what the *Frankfurter Illustrierte* served up for its readers was a grotesque exaggeration. Still, this report was a lurid

---

* A German version of this chapter has been published as "Johann von Leers und die 'faschistische Internationale' der fünfziger und sechziger Jahre in Argentinien und Ägypten", *Zeitschrift für Geschichtswissenschaft* 59 (2011), 522-543.

1 "SS-Treffpunkt Kairo", *Frankfurter Illustrierte,* August 17, 1957, 10-11, 28-32; ibid., August 24, 1957 (part II), 16-18, 32-34; ibid., August 31, 1957, 12-16, 31 (part III); ibid., September 7, 1957 (part IV), 32-37. The editors emphasised that an "expert with intimate knowledge of the most important Secret Services and the Middle East" described "for the first time the employment of former SS and SD members in Arab countries". In reality, these articles did nothing more than to compile conventional narratives on the topic which had been circulating widely since 1956.

2 Von Leers actually did serve as a university professor until the end of the war, however, this was in Jena. He also used the name "Euler", but as a pseudonym for various publications between 1949 and 1952 and for his illegal trip from West Germany to Argentina in August 1950.

example of the approach that the West German and international press had taken towards the subject since the late 1940s. The standard theme was the presence of former National Socialists and Wehrmacht officers in foreign nations, especially Egypt.[3] With the appearance of von Leers, however, this narrative admittedly underwent a modification. Unlike the technical and military experts who up until now had found a way to make a living in Egypt, von Leers – who in the summer of 1956 had resettled in Cairo – was a prominent National Socialist propagandist. After a Canadian journalist exposed his role as a member of the Egyptian government's information service, the news attracted worldwide attention.[4] Once the story began circulating internationally, rumours about his whereabouts underwent countless variations in the international press in the following years. Fact and fiction often became indistinguishable from one another. Just to cite a second example: In December 1956 the London *Daily Mail* published a report under the headline "Goebbels' Men Lie for Nasser: The Nazis behind the Egyptian Propaganda War". According to the report, four former employees of Goebbels' Ministry of Propaganda were now active in Nasser's radio station, Voice of the Arabs. Von Leers was identified as one of them. However, not a single fact was given to justify this claim. Another claim from a published report in September 1960 that mentioned von Leers in the same breath as Martin Bormann also belongs in the realm of fantasy. According to that report, Bormann lived in the USA, where he directed a worldwide organisation of neo-Nazis based in South America, Spain, Sweden and West Germany. Von Leers was reportedly one of the directors of this organisation.[5]

The question is, however, what role did he actually play in the international postwar network of right-wing extremists and anti-Semites? An answer seems all the more necessary not only because von Leers was one of the "most productive anti-Semitic publicists of the Nazi movement", as was aptly pointed out in modern historical research more than thirty years ago,[6] but also remained a fanatical anti-

3 Many journal-style reports and other literature have been published on this topic, however, without always showing great care for accuracy. E.g. John O. Rogge, *The Official German Report. Nazi Penetration 1924-1942. Pan-Arabism 1939-Today* (New York/London: Thomas Yoseloff, 1961), 380-381; Robert St. John, *The Boss* (London: Barker, 1960), 153; Michel Bar-Zohar, *Die Jagd auf die deutschen Wissenschaftler (1944-1960)* (Berlin: Propyläen, 1966). More recent publications include Erich Schmidt-Eenboom, *BND. Der deutsche Geheimdienst im Nahen Osten* (Munich: Herbig, 2007), which repeats many of the erroneous statements of the earlier publications. Wolfgang Lotz's *Fünftausend für Lotz. Der Bericht des israelischen Meisterspions* (Frankfurt a.M.: Goverts Krüger Stahlberg, 1973) may be considered a type of splashy literature and colportage. For a critical approach on this subject, see Kurt P. Tauber, *Beyond Eagle and Swastika. German Nationalism since 1945*, vol. 1 (Middletown, CO: Wesleyan University Press, 1967), 242-253.

4 Cf. "Expose of Nazi Jackboots as Force behind Nasser Caused Stevenson Ouster", *Toronto Daily Star*, August 27, 1956. These news were spread in the following days by various newspapers, especially in Europe, North and South America. On the other hand, von Leers' emigration to Cairo was old news to the German Foreign Office and US Secret Services.

5 Cf. the notice in the Israeli newspaper *Yediot Achronot*, September 20, 1960.

6 Erich Goldhagen, "Weltanschauung und Endlösung. Zum Antisemitismus der nationalsozialistischen Führungsschicht", *Vierteljahrshefte für Zeitgeschichte* 24 (1976), 400.

Semite throughout his life. In the 1950s and 1960s he was one of the central protagonists of an "Fascist International".[7] As will be illustrated with examples in the following, this International attempted to establish links with networks from the 1930s and 1940s, at first from Argentina and later from Egypt.

During a study trip to Italy in 1940, von Leers remarked about himself that he was "a convinced hater of Jewry". The journey to Italy had brought him together with leading anti-Semites of the Italian Fascist Party, among them Giovanni Preciosi (1881-1945).[8] How obsessive this hatred was again became evident in his last article, written less than a year before his death, in which he recalled his encounter with Preciosi. In it he summed up that during his "entire life" he had "done research on the Jews" and had studied them "like a bacteriologist studies a dangerous bacillus".[9] Nonetheless, current research has to date largely neglected his biography, the networks in which he was active before and after 1945 and his numerous publications.[10] This can be attributed in part to the difficult nature of the sources, particularly for the years after 1945, for some of which von Leers went underground and deliberately attempted to cover his tracks.[11] To make matters worse, many of his articles appeared in newspapers which can be assigned to the "basement of journalism and literature",[12] particularly in the 1950s and 1960s, which are at the centre of the present discussion.

To assess von Leers' role in the international anti-Semitic network, a concise overview of his biography until 1945, focusing on his work as a propagandist, will be presented. In addition, this chapter briefly sketches the course of his life from

---

7 Hans Jaeger, "Die faschistische Internationale", *Deutsche Rundschau* 78/9 (1952), 993-1003.

8 "Bericht über meine Studienreise nach Italien", undated [1940], Russian State Military Archive Moscow (RGVA), Fond 1283/12b, 42-49, 43. On Preziosi, see *Handbuch des Antisemitismus. Judenfeindschaft in Geschichte und Gegenwart*, vol. 2/2, ed. Wolfgang Benz (Berlin: De Gruyter, 2009), 654-655.

9 Quoted from the translation of an article by von Leers published in Italian in 1964, Politisches Archiv des Auswärtiges Amtes (PAAA), B 82, V 33-88, vol. 444, 86-88.

10 Since the beginning of the 1960s, historical research has touched on von Leers several times in passing, but has ignored him in general. Cf. Hildegard Brenner, "Die Kunst im politischen Machtkampf der Jahre 1933/34", *Vierteljahrshefte für Zeitgeschichte* 10 (1962), 17-42; Joseph Wulf, *Literatur und Dichtung im Dritten Reich. Eine Dokumentation* (Hamburg: Rowohlt, 1966), passim. More recent publications have devoted more attention to his biography, *"Kämpferische Wissenschaft". Studien zur Universität Jena im Nationalsozialismus*, eds. Uwe Hoßfeld et al. (Cologne: Böhlau, 2003), passim; Gregory Paul Wegner, "A Propagandist of Extermination. Johann von Leers and the Anti-Semitic Formation of Children in Nazi Germany", *Paedagogica Historica* 43 (2007), 299-325. A biography which places von Leers in the context of the *völkisch* and anti-Semitic movements of the late 1920s and early 1930s, of National Socialism and the postwar era remains, however, a desideratum.

11 His biography and publications up to 1945 can to some extent be gathered from literary materials in the Bundesarchiv Berlin (BA Berlin), N 2168; RGVA, Fond 1283. For the years after 1945 no such literary remains are known. A symptomatic example of covering up the facts can be found in Ernst Jünger's diary entries of August 25, 1947. Ernst Jünger, *Jahre der Okkupation* (Stuttgart: Klett, 1958), 287-288.

12 Uwe Puschner, *Die völkische Bewegung im wilhelminischen Kaiserreich. Sprache – Rasse – Religion* (Darmstadt: Wissenschaftliche Buchgesellschaft, 2001), 18.

1945 to 1965. Following that, an introductory outline of two propaganda or publicist networks von Leers had been involved with from 1950 to 1965, first in Argentina and then in Egypt, will be given. The focus is on the one hand on the Argentine journal *Der Weg* and the network connected with it, and on the other hand on the Cairo-based attempt to revitalise the "anti-Semitic International" which from 1933 until 1944 had operated through the German flagship publication *Weltdienst*. In the context of his escape to Argentina in 1950, the reasons why von Leers decided to take such a step, thus rejecting any accommodation and integration into postwar society, will be analysed. Finally, the significance of von Leers in this context will be critically examined.

Some Remarks on von Leers' Biography

Johann von Leers was born in 1902 in Vietlübbe in Mecklenburg-Schwerin. He studied law in Berlin and Rostock. For some time in the 1920s he belonged to a Free Corps *(Freikorps)*. After completing his doctoral thesis in 1926, he entered the German Foreign Service to start a career as a diplomat, but he left this position in 1928. One reason for this, given by him when he joined the SS in 1936, was his open "anti-Semitic attitude", which made it difficult for him to work for the government.[13] At this time, he probably already had contact with the Nazi Party. In August 1929 he joined the NSDAP in Berlin. Working closely with *Gauleiter* Joseph Goebbels, prior to falling out with him later, he started his career as a propagandist, speaker and journalist for the newspaper *Der Angriff*, for which he wrote a large number of articles.[14] Von Leers stood out due to a gift for languages, which made it possible for him to learn different foreign languages in a short time.[15] This proved useful later in his life, when he went to South America and Egypt. He also stood out on account of a remarkable rhetorical ability. According to himself, he participated as a propagandist until 1936 in nearly 5,000 meetings – for small audiences, but also for thousands of listeners at rallies. These numbers may be exaggerated, owing to the outspoken propagandistic nature of the articles published in *Der Angriff*. For example, when he appeared before an audience of members of the SA, one article claims, von Leers delivered a

> harsh and powerful speech about our struggle [...] and final victories! Never before had party members been moved so strongly [...]! He told them bluntly that they were not worthy of living for Germany, unless they were prepared to die for her.[16]

---

13 Handwritten Curriculum Vitae, dated June 22, 1936, BA Berlin, BDC, name file von Leers.

14 At least 60 articles can be ascribed to him in the period from January 1930 until August 1931, when he fell out with Goebbels. On the newspaper, see Russel Lemmons, *Goebbels and "Der Angriff"* (Lexington: University Press of Kentucky, 1994).

15 Von Leers tended to exaggerate, thus, the extent of his foreign language skills is debatable. However, it is safe to assume that he was able to communicate in different Romanesque (French, Italian and Spanish), Ugric (Hungarian) and Turkic languages, as well as in English, Japanese and Arabic.

16 *Der Angriff*, December 13, 1930.

The fact remains that von Leers was a well-versed public speaker, who soon gained Goebbels' respect: "Dr. von Leers amused us a lot. He wants to cut off all our enemies' heads. Hopefully he'll soon get an opportunity to do so", Goebbels noted in his diary after a rally in the Berlin district of Spandau in August 1930.[17] Von Leers also displayed a talent for journalism and writing which enabled him to produce a substantial number of works. By 1945, von Leers had written dozens of books, several hundred articles and a large number of essays for National Socialist daily newspapers, as well as for the leading theoretical journals of National Socialist ideology such as *NS-Monatshefte, SS-Leitheft* and *Weltkampf.*

Above all, publications by von Leers strengthened the anti-Semitic ideology for which he tried to provide a pseudo-scientific legitimisation. The headline of one of his first articles in *Der Angriff* – published under the pseudonym "M. Thomas" some weeks before the Reichstag elections in September 1930 – clearly stated his programme: "Dem Weltfeind an den Kragen" (Attacking the World Enemy).[18] His conviction that the "Aryan race" was engaged in a universal struggle with a supposedly omnipresent "world Jewry" is identical with the views of Goebbels and the party ideologist Alfred Rosenberg.[19] But in this article, von Leers let his anti-Semitism and his violent fantasies wander around without limits, and he repeated them in many subsequent articles and reports:

> It is enough! What was the dream of the best of all Germans for decades – the great and strong folk movement which would sweep away the universal pestilence from the German territory – together with all other evils – has today become reality [...]. This election shall be the first punch of the awakening young Germany in the face of this thousand years old shochet [ritual butcherer] of peoples, now torn by fear and anger![20]

Von Leers maintained close contact with prominent National Socialists such as the Reich Minister of Food and Agriculture and convinced *Blut und Boden*-ideologist Richard Walther Darré and Heinrich Himmler. It was their ideology for which he provided pseudo-scientific justification. The origins of these relationships stretched back to the late 1920s. At the time Darré had been assigned the task of developing an agricultural policy apparatus in order to win voters for the NSDAP among the agrarian population in Northern Germany. On the other hand, Himmler, as the deputy leader of the party's propaganda department, coordinated the public ap-

17 Diary entry of August 26, 1930, in *Die Tagebücher von Joseph Goebbels*, ed. Elke Fröhlich, part 1, *Aufzeichnungen 1923-1941*, vol. 2/I: December 1929 to May 1931 (Berlin: De Gruyter, 2005).

18 M. Thomas [pseud. von Leers], "Dem Weltfeind an den Kragen! Warum jeder Sozialist Judengegner sein muss", *Der Angriff*, July 24, 1930.

19 Joseph Goebbels, "Der Jude", *Der Angriff*, January 21, 1928; idem., "Der Weltfeind", *Der Angriff*, March 19, 1928. See also Jeffrey Herf, *The Jewish Enemy. Nazi Propaganda during World War II and the Holocaust* (Cambridge, MA/London: Harvard University Press, 2008), 37-38. Characteristically, a periodical established by Alfred Rosenberg in 1924 for the dissemination of the National Socialist worldview bore the title "Weltkampf". Ernst Piper, *Alfred Rosenberg. Hitlers Chefideologe* (Munich: Karl Blessing Verlag, 2005), 116-121.

20 M. Thomas [pseud. von Leers], "Dem Weltfeind an den Kragen!".

pearances of speakers.[21] Himmler could hardly have failed to notice the talent of such an accomplished writer, journalist and agitator as von Leers, who had held hundreds of public speeches since 1929 and was noted for his verbal aggression when dealing with political opponents. There were also a number of biographical parallels. For example, both Himmler and von Leers were familiar with problems of agrarian policy – although for different reasons. The later *Reichsführer-SS* was even regarded for a time as an "expert on agriculture" in the party.[22] Within the NSDAP both originally belonged to the circle around Gregor Straßer. They disseminated their political convictions in the *Nationalsozialistische Briefe,* the organ of the National Socialist "left-wing".[23] In their analyses of the decline of German agriculture they made use of an anti-capitalist rhetoric,[24] which was based on anti-Semitism. For example, Himmler's conviction that the farmers were the victims of "international Jewish stock exchange capital" and the dictates of the "grain exchange" was in accordance with von Leers' opinion. In addition, Himmler, Darré and von Leers shared a layman's understanding of science and an interest in mythical and prehistorical materials.[25] Therefore, it is not surprising that von Leers was involved in the ideological education of the SS and the Reich Food Estate *(Reichsnährstand).*[26] At the beginning of the 1940s a flood of publications followed which between the lines justified the genocide of the European Jews as a necessary historical act and gave the readers an inkling of the on-going processes of extermination.[27] How closely Leers co-operated with Darré is further revealed in the pseudo-historical work *Odal,* which was comprised of over 700 pages, a short version of which was published under the title *Der deutschen Bauern 1000jähriger Kampf um deutsche Art und deutsches Recht.* In this book von Leers attempted to historically justify the State Hereditary Farm Law *(Reichserbhofgesetz)* of September 1933, in which the *Blut und Boden*-ideology was associated with agrarian policy measures. Both works were without doubt commissioned by Darré, who personally controlled and changed the manuscripts von Leers presented to him.[28]

---

21 See Udo Kissenkoetter, *Gregor Straßer und die NSDAP* (Stuttgart: DVA, 1978), 60; Peter Longerich, *Heinrich Himmler. Biographie* (Munich: Siedler, 2008), 99.

22 Longerich, *Heinrich Himmler,* 109.

23 Johann von Leers, "Außenpolitische Perversität", *Nationalsozialistische Briefe* 5, February 15, 1930; Heinrich Himmler, "Die Lage der Landwirtschaft", *Nationalsozialistische Briefe* 1, April 1, 1926. Cf. Longerich, *Heinrich Himmler,* 93.

24 Ibid., 100.

25 Michael Kater, *Das "Ahnenerbe" der SS 1935-1945. Ein Beitrag zur Kulturpolitik des Dritten Reiches* (Munich: Oldenbourg, 2001), 17-27.

26 Between 1936 and 1940 von Leers published slightly below 30 contributions to the *SS Leitheft.* A selection appeared later in an anthology prepared for schoolchildren: Johann von Leers, *Für das Reich. Deutsche Geschichte in Geschichtserzählungen* (Langensalza/Berlin/Leipzig: Beltz, 1941[1940]). Equally numerous were the contributions he made between 1933 and 1942 to the periodical *Odal,* the organ of the Reich Food Estate.

27 A good example is Johann von Leers, *Die Verbrechernatur der Juden* (Berlin: Verlag Paul Hochmuth, 1944).

28 Johann von Leers, *Odal. Das Lebensgesetz eines ewigen Deutschland* (Goslar: Blut und Boden Verlag, 1936); idem., *Der deutschen Bauern 1000jähriger Kampf um deutsche Art und deutsches Recht* (Go-

Thanks to these contacts, von Leers was able to start an academic career. In 1936 he became a lecturer, and then – in spite of his modest qualifications as a scientist – a professor of "Racial History" at the University of Jena, a stronghold of National Socialist research on racial matters.[29] Himmler's goodwill – at the beginning of 1936 he had assured von Leers how much he "esteemed" his work[30] – and his influence on the appointment procedure in Jena coincided with the intention of influential members of the academic staff to help the university, as one of them wrote, to acquire the "necessary concentration of ideologically and scientifically first class scholars".[31]

In 1945 von Leers was dismissed from the university and imprisoned in a camp in the US-occupied zone. At the end of 1946 he escaped from the camp. Afterwards he went underground for more than three years, living not far from Bonn, which was at that time part of the British-occupied zone. He finally emigrated to Argentina in August 1950. In the spring of 1956 he relocated to Egypt, where he remained until his death in March 1965.

Some Remarks on the Term "Network"

From his arrival in Buenos Aires and until his death in Cairo in March 1965, von Leers was part of an international network of right-wing extremists.[32] However, the term "network" in this context needs clarification. A close look at right-wing extremism in the 1950s and 1960s shows that the term can include different forms of communication and cooperation.[33]

It can, for example, describe a type of non-binding and informal network made up of separate individuals who act in cooperation and trade favours with each other. Such informal networks are based above all on private personal contacts and are mostly defined by the exchange of propaganda and information material. However, there are more institutional structures based on organisations in different nations. These networks also plan longer-lasting political activities. For the most part, how-

---

slar: Blut und Boden Verlag, 1935). See letters from von Leers to Darré, May 15, 1935, May 19, 1935, July 3, 1935, BA Berlin, BDC, name file von Leers. See also the letter from von Leers to Gustav Frenssen, August 31, 1936, where he explained to Frenssen that the "history of the German farmers [had been] commissioned by Darré", Schleswig-Holsteinische Landesbibliothek (SHLB), Frenssen Collection, Cb 21.56: 1020, fol. 1.

29 Cf. *"Kämpferische Wissenschaft"*, eds. Hoßfeld et al.

30 Letter from Himmler to von Leers, January 9, 1936, BA Berlin, BDC, name file von Leers.

31 Letter from Karl Astel to Karl Wolff, Chief of Personal Staff Reichsführer-SS, February 1938 (date uncertain), Archiv des Institut für Zeitgeschichte Munich (IfZ), MA 297.

32 Still convincing for the 1950s and 1960s, although with errors in details, see Tauber, *Beyond Eagle and Swastika*. For earlier literature, see Werner Smoydzin, *Hitler lebt. Vom internationalen Faschismus zur Internationale des Hakenkreuzes* (Pfaffenhofen: Ilmgau, 1966); Horst W. Schmollinger, "Deutscher Block", in *Parteien-Handbuch. Die Parteien der Bundesrepublik Deutschland 1945-1980*, edited by Richard Stöss (Opladen: Westdeutscher Verlag, 1983), 833-837.

33 Cf. Richard Stöss, *Zur Vernetzung der extremen Rechten in Europa* (Berlin: Free University Berlin, 2001).

ever, they demonstrate only a limited level of commitment. Finally, there are independent international organisations with a professional organisation and structure marked by a charter or articles of association, a programme, formal membership, and a board of directors with representatives from different countries. The question is: In what kind of network did von Leers operate?

The network was an informal mutual support group of like-minded people. It revolved around publishing projects that included magazines and printing houses. It was based largely on personal connections and friendships, some of whose origins dated as far back as the 1930s. The members of this network were among the intellectual and ideological trailblazers of National Socialism from the milieu of Himmler, Darré and Rosenberg. They frequently came out of the *völkisch* movement. The main task of this network was to provide an interdependent mutual assistance organisation, including financial aid, based on fundamental political and ideological convictions. One of these convictions was without doubt a fanatical hatred of Jews. The central figures of this mutual support network shared similar life histories after 1945. They frequently believed that they had been treated in a way they deemed unjust and felt that they had been socially excluded and disenfranchised wrongly. Another distinguishing characteristic of members of this network were their loyalty and faithfulness to their political ideals up until 1945. Their denial of any personal responsibility or any sense of individual guilt is also based upon this conviction. The political practices of the National Socialist regime were justified, its crimes were either minimised or even denied, and their own role during the National Socialist period either relativszed or sentimentalised with misty-eyed recollections. In the next section, two elements of this publicist network – the network in Argentina associated with the monthly journal *Der Weg* from 1950 to 1956 and the attempt undertaken from 1955 by a semi-state organisation in Cairo to revitalise the tradition of the National Socialist publication *Welt-Dienst* – will be scrutinised more closely.

The Network Surrounding the Magazine Der Weg

In 1950, von Leers fled from Germany to Argentina. In doing so, he joined a large number of Germans who had escaped to South America as early as in 1946-47. On the number and type of emigrants, the literature offers many different accounts. These accounts are related because of the very heterogeneous makeup of the emigrants.[34] Many of them were driven by economic motives. A significant number also fled in order to evade criminal charges. Prominent names which are usually mentioned in this context include Adolf Eichmann, who worked in the Reich Security Main Office (*Reichssicherheitshauptamt,* RSHA) and was responsible for the administration of the "Final Solution", and Josef Mengele, the Auschwitz doctor.[35]

34 Cf. Holger M. Meding, *Flucht vor Nürnberg? Deutsche und österreichische Einwanderung in Argentinien, 1945-1955* (Cologne/Weimar/Vienna: Böhlau, 1992).

35 Cf. Sven Keller, *Günzburg und der Fall Josef Mengele. Die Heimatstadt und die Jagd nach dem NS-Verbrecher* (Munich: Oldenbourg, 2003), 42-61.

Other less prominent figures were, for example, Erich Priebke and Josef Schwammberger. In many instances they fled through either Italy or Spain to South America. Another escape route went through Denmark. It is certain that this type of exodus was supported by an organised escape network, especially in Italy. In general, however, the escape operation functioned in a highly improvised manner. Historical research has recently proved that a tightly organised escape organisation never existed.[36]

It seems surprising that von Leers fled to Argentina at a relatively late date. Indeed, he and his wife had already considered taking this step as far back as in 1946. However, they lacked the necessary financial means. They also lacked at that time the assistants required to successfully obtain, for example, the necessary false identity documents and visas.

An examination of the reasons for von Leers' decision to emigrate reveals several different motives. First, still clinging to his anti-Semitic ideology, rejecting any kind of accommodation to, and showing deep contempt for, the new system of parliamentarianism and democracy under the control of occupying forces, von Leers obviously could not have any future career prospects in West Germany – either as a journalist and publicist or as a lawyer, a profession he trained for but never actually practised. Moreover, his stock themes were very limited. In his imagination, the Federal Republic seemed to be "a colony of American Jewry", dominated and controlled by "the Jewish communities".[37] Where could he attract public interest for such opinions, if not in foreign countries which gave a home to comrades who shared, at least in parts, these opinions? In any case, the idea that he could work for a serious publication was inconceivable. In addition, the publications of the extreme right, for which he could have worked, hardly existed at this time. *Nation Europa*, for example, which was one of the flagship publications of the extreme right in the Federal Republic, did not appear until 1951. Given these factors, the complaint made by his wife Gesine von Leers during the period of his illegality is not surprising: "It is high time for us to leave, so that uncle Hans can work freely – here, under these circumstances it is impossible", she wrote to the author and writer Klaus Mehnert, with whom von Leers had been in contact since the early 1930s.[38] Additionally, von Leers had to accept a considerable loss of social status and prestige. In 1942 he held the position of a university professor and had a yearly income of approximately 40,000 Reichmarks, living far from the front in an idyllic

36 For recent literature, see Heinz Schneppen, *Odessa und das Vierte Reich. Mythen der Zeitgeschichte* (Berlin: Metropol, 2007); Uki Goñi, *Odessa. Die wahre Geschichte. Fluchthilfe für NS-Kriegsverbrecher* (Berlin: Assoziation A, 2007); Gerald Steinacher, *Nazis auf der Flucht. Wie Kriegsverbrecher über Italien nach Übersee entkamen* (Innsbruck: Studienverlag, 2008).

37 Letter from von Leers to Karl A. Wittfogel, June 7, 1952, Hoover Institution Archives (HIA), Collection K. Wittfogel, Box No. 29.

38 Letter from Gesine von Leers to Klaus Mehnert, November 12, 1948, Hauptstaatsarchiv Stuttgart (HStA), Q 1/30 Bü 9. "Onkel Hans" served as a camouflage for Johann von Leers. On Mehnert's relation with von Leers, see Klaus Mehnert, *Ein Deutscher in der Welt. Erinnerungen 1906-1981* (Stuttgart: DVA, 1981), 118-119.

castle located between Jena and Rudolstadt in Thuringia. In 1948 he suffered such a loss of revenue that he had to sell his antiques. He even had to be thankful just to get 250 Marks for a book manuscript. "Publishers are aware of the financial distress of authors and take advantage of them", Gesine von Leers explained in the letter to Mehnert quoted above.[39] On the other hand, Argentina under President Juan Perón, which became a "favourable destination for emigrants"[40] from 1946, seemed to open up some kind of future prospects: "My husband is now a contributor for the Dürer-Verlag on a regular basis and hopes to get a professorship", Gesine von Leers wrote optimistically about her family's future.[41] Moreover, von Leers' sympathy for the policy under Perón has to be taken into account, even if it was a result of transfiguration and glorification. For him, this policy was not only characterised by its "wonderful boom of all sciences" and "a rich publicist life", but also by the fundamental difference from policy in the Federal Republic and Central Europe: While "the growing democratic cornification of brains [demokratische Gehirnverhornung] in all of the European countries seems to be getting thicker and thicker", von Leers wrote, "a new mental elite of European peoples is gathering here, like in Atlantis".[42] It seems evident that von Leers counted himself among this group, thus uncovering the ideological core of this so-called "elite". The most decisive motive for the emigration, however, was the fact that von Leers remained an incorrigible anti-Semite. He refused to change his way of thinking and was not ready to accept the new political order. He also refused to endorse de-nazification and integrate into the new society. He regarded the policy of large-scale integration by the Adenauer government, whose 1949 Amnesty Law offered a way out to people living illegally, not with criticism, but with outright hostility.[43] The writer Ernst Jünger, whose house von Leers visited incognito in summer 1947, noted in his journal: "I found him unshaken in his views."[44] That was an accurate observation.

---

39 Ibid.

40 Steinacher, *Nazis auf der Flucht*, 12.

41 Letter from Gesine von Leers to Hans Friedrich Blunck, September 10, 1950, SHLB, Blunck Collection, Cb 92.56: 52a, fol. 14. See also the letter from Gesine von Leers to Hans Friedrich Blunck, March 14, 1952, SHLB, Blunck Collection, Cb 92.56: 52a, fol. 15.

42 Letter from von Leers to Gerhard Heberer, August 21, 1953, Niedersächische Staats- und Universitätsbibliothek Göttingen (SUB Göttingen), Heberer Collection. Heberer, who in the 1930s taught at the University of Jena and later became a member of the SS' Ahnenerbe-organisation, obviously did not react to this letter. On Heberer, see Uwe Hoßfeld, *Gerhard Heberer (1901-1973). Sein Beitrag zur Biologie im 20. Jahrhundert* (Berlin: Verlag für Wissenschaft und Bildung, 1997).

43 On the origin and the contemporary debate on this Law in juridical literature, see Norbert Frei, *Vergangenheitspolitik. Die Anfänge der Bundesrepublik und die NS-Vergangenheit* (Munich: C.H. Beck, 1997), 46, 57.

44 Diary entry, August 25, 1947 in Jünger, *Jahre der Okkupation*, 287-288.

The Voyage to Argentina

Using a false passport with the name "Hans Euler", von Leers booked a passage on a ship from Hamburg to Buenos Aires in August 1950. His family followed him a few weeks later. In Buenos Aires he quickly established connections with the journal *Der Weg* and the Dürer Verlag, the publishing house under whose auspices *Der Weg* had been published since 1947. In the years that followed he helped turn the journal – which had begun as a conventional publication for Germans living abroad – into an indoctrination journal in the spirit of the SS.[45]

Der Weg was established in 1947 by Eberhard Fritsch. Fritsch, who was not in relation to Theodor Fritsch, was a firm believer in *völkisch* thought. Until 1945 he taught German at a school in Buenos Aires. In 1946, he took part in establishing a bookstore and the Dürer Verlag. In the beginning the monthly magazine was a national conservative publication with rather sedate views and a circulation of just about 2,000 copies. By 1948, however, we can already see a shift in views. It is necessary, stated Fritsch, that "we can truly call a spade a spade". Only in this way would it be possible to successfully "fill the terrifying vacuum of ideas".[46] As this remark makes clear, the journal was not only intended for Germans living abroad. It also sought readers in West Germany. A considerable number of copies were sent to Germany, where they were circulated through covert distribution channels. In West Germany at that time, the press still operated under strict censorship measures. The expression of extremsit views, such as those in *Der Weg*, was virtually impossible in the late 1940s.

The changes in *Der Weg* were decisively advanced thanks to the efforts of von Leers. In autumn 1950, shortly after his arrival in Buenos Aires, von Leers began contributing to the journal. He published countless pieces both under his own name and under various pseudonyms.[47] As a result, *Der Weg* obtained a sharply anti-Semitic orientation. Many of von Leers' themes were variations on articles that he had already published before 1945 in National Socialist publications. A further development in this direction could be seen in the apologetic treatment of Nazi rule and its crimes. In the pages of *Der Weg* we also find, as far back as the early 1950s, the beginnings of subjects like historical revisionism, which further developed during the 1960s and 1970s. This pertains especially to the question of the scale of the genocide inflicted on the Jews. The number of murdered Jews was relativised, although the Holocaust was not denied completely.

With its new orientation, *Der Weg* enjoyed success at first. At the beginning of the 1950s, its circulation grew to between 20,000 and 25,000 copies. This success was certainly partly due to the fact that its readers were no longer just Germans living abroad, but could be found in West Germany as well. The journal was for some time also a mouthpiece for an "International" – for instance an international

45 Cf. Holger M. Meding, *"Der Weg". Eine deutsche Emigrantenzeitschrift in Buenos Aires 1947 bis 1957* (Berlin: Wissenschaftlicher Verlag, 1997).

46 "Ein Gruß der Schriftleitung", *Der Weg* 12/2 (1948), 842-843.

47 At least three pseudonyms can be attributed to von Leers in this period: "Hans Euler", "Gordon Fitzstuart" and "Felix Schwarzenborn".

movement – of former National Socialists and their European collaborators. On the one hand, this is accounted for by the circle of writers recruited by the journal. On the other hand, *Der Weg* at this time also functioned as a semi-official information bulletin for a federation of different far right European groups.

This draws attention to the circle of authors and contributors to *Der Weg.* Many of them lived in the Federal Republic of Germany or Austria, representing at the same time the whole of European right-wing extremism, its movements and networks. Among the German contributors we discover, besides leading National Socialists who had either received death sentences or were sentenced to long prison terms like the above mentioned Darré or Rosenberg, numerous high-ranking functionaries from the truly National Socialist world of culture and print media. In this context we find, amongst others, Helmut Sündermann, the former deputy press chief of the Third Reich; Peter Kleist, a close associate of Foreign Minister Ribbentrop; Hans Fritzsche, the former head of the department of broadcasting services at Goebbels' Ministry of Propaganda, who himself delivered commentaries on the radio until 1945; and Hans W. Hagen, who was active in *Amt Rosenberg.* None of these authors lived in South America, but due to the lack of alternatives, they wrote more or less regularly for *Der Weg,* where they could publish their memories and justifications of the Third Reich. In addition, there were both well-known and less famous *völkisch* writers and literati writing for the journal, who had achieved high circulation figures for their publications under National Socialism. In this category belongs Hans Grimm, author of the famous novel *Volk ohne Raum* (1926); poets such as Will Vesper or Hans F. Blunck, and Anton Zischka, a well-known author of non-fiction literature. Many of them had at first encountered problems in continuing their journalistic careers after 1945, especially if they had exposed themselves as functionaries of the cultural political sphere. To complete the picture, it is necessary to look at a group of *völkisch* academics who had been removed from their university positions. They included Hans F. K. Günther, famously referred to as "Rassegünther", who belonged to the promoters of von Leers' academic career from 1935 on; and the medical doctor and SS member Lothar Stengel von Rutkowski, who taught "racial hygiene" at the University of Jena until 1945. We should also add representatives of the *völkisch* religious movement such as Jakob Wilhelm Hauer, Herbert Grabert or Mathilde Ludendorff to this category. They all knew each other from the debates of the years 1933-34, when, during the Church Struggle *(Kirchenkampf)* various *völkisch*-religious and pagan groups and currents came together to form the German Faith *Movement (Deutsche Glaubensbewegung).* Its aim at the time was recognition as an official religion and third confession alongside Catholicism and Protestantism.

In addition to these groups, we can also speak of an international network in terms of collaborators and anti-Semites. The international character of *Der Weg* was achieved through contributors from the ranks of former collaborators. They included, for example, supporters of *Action Française* or the Belgian Rexist movement. Some of them also fled to South America. One of them, a Belgian named Willem Sassen (also known as Willem Sluyse), later achieved particular prominence. In the middle of the 1950s, he and Eberhard Fritsch conducted long and detailed interviews with Adolf Eichmann, which they recorded on audio tape. After Eichmann had been kidnapped and sent to Israel, where legal actions were taken against him, Sassen tried to establish a lucrative business based on his tape recordings.[48] The journal also maintained its international character due to the fact that at the time, it served as a semi-official organ for a European post-fascist (as well as post-National Socialist) cluster of parties and organisations. In the literature, this movement is frequently described as the "Malmö International", although it was officially known as the European Social Movement (ESM). It was named after the Swedish city where one of the first meetings was held in 1951. Among the leading members of this short-lived movement, which had already split by 1953, were Per Engdahl and Maurice Bardèche as well as the German representative, Karlheinz Priester, who attempted, without great success, to succeed as a radical right-wing small publisher.[49] Von Leers maintained close contact with all of them. Under the rubric "Convention of Patriots", he even occasionally compiled reports for *Der Weg* about the development of nationalist movements that orbited around the ESM.[50]

Finally, the international character of *Der Weg* is demonstrated by the journals it cited in its articles and which von Leers also utilised. They included, for example, *Common Sense* and *The Cross and the Flag*, both of which were issued by far right extremists in the US, *Defense de l'Occident*, which was published by Maurice Bardèche; and – to quote von Leers – the "excellent information service" *Gothic Ripples*, published by Arnold Spencer Leese.[51] In the 1920s, Leese had dedicated himself to political activities and he drew close to National Socialism in the 1930s.

The journal was quite influential until the middle of the 1950s. It emerged more and more as a platform for former National Socialists and their collaborators who could not and would not accept the new political conditions after the Second World War. *Der Weg* enabled them to maintain and perpetuate a political identity which was formed in the first decades of the 20th century. Most of the contributors declared that all efforts made by the government to stop the policy of denazification since 1949 were not extensive enough. For them it was also vital to revise all judgments, especially those of the allied courts. Moreover, during the period between 1948 and 1954, there was no similar magazine with such an overt connection to National Socialist ideology, and with such a wide range of authors and large circulation.

Especially from the start of the 1950s, anti-Semitism became one of the main

48 Cf. Irmtrud Wojak, *Eichmanns Memoiren. Ein kritischer Essay* (Frankfurt a.M.: Campus Verlag, 2001); Bettina Stangneth, *Eichmann vor Jerusalem. Das unbehelligte Leben eines Massenmörders* (Hamburg: Arche, 2011), 304-399.

49 See Hans Jaeger, "Die Faschistische Internationale", in *Deutsche Rundschau* 78/9 (1952), 993-1003.

50 See e.g. *Der Weg* 5/6 (1952), 351-356; *Der Weg* 6/6 (1952), 423-428; *Der Weg* 7/6 (1952), 496-500.

51 Gordon Fitzstuart (pseud. von Leers), "Das Königreich Davids und die Sassoons", *Der Weg* 9/7 (1953), 607.

topics of the propaganda in *Der Weg*. Of course, this is related to the fact that von Leers joined the magazine at this time. But it must also be taken into consideration that many other contributors were similarly polemical and prolific anti-Semites. Reading the articles of von Leers, we encounter some kind of intellectual deficiency, and a wide range of simplifications and speculations about conspiracy, with perpetuating topical accusations of the 1930s and early 1940s. This is evident in the repeated accusations of an alleged Jewish conspiracy, once through "clandestine wire pullers behind Roosevelt", nowadays by the "United Nations".[52] Both of them were accused of being instruments of "enigmatic powers", aiming to "defeat the German Reich" in order to secure world supremacy for the Jews. This could, according to von Leers, be documented by the fact that Jews were "holding important positions" at the UN.[53] Other articles dealt with "conspiracy against the Reich", the "betrayal" of Hitler or "the crimes of the allied".[54]

Der Weg was successful with this attitude at the end of the 1940s and the beginning of the 1950s, but ran into trouble from the middle of the 1950s. The collapse of the Perón regime and the following economic crisis had already increased the insecurity felt by many Germans who had illegally entered Argentina after the end of the war. Above all, fugitive National Socialists who sought to evade criminal responsibility for their actions and had viewed Argentina as a safe haven abandoned the country. A sense of resignation also spread to members of the group around *Der Weg* and the Dürer Verlag. As a result of the regime change, some of them relocated to other South American nations, while others returned to Europe. Perón's downfall was, however, only the catalyst for this reaction. The decline of *Der Weg* had been evident for some time. A symptom of this decline was the strong drop in circulation from approximately 1953 on, which occurred for different reasons: Executive measures taken against the publication in the Federal Republic of Germany made the distribution of the journal considerably more difficult. These measures also resulted from the radicalisation of the journal by the contributions written by von Leers. He published, under his various pseudonyms, a large number of articles. At times his work made up nearly half of the magazine. Von Leers' boundless output, which was inextricably tied to his fanatical anti-Semitism, constricted the journal intellectually to such a degree that many authors, especially those who were otherwise able to establish themselves successfully in society, now withdrew from it. Finally, internal conflicts on the editorial board and publishing company, which resulted in terrible business payment practices and which only worsened following a financial embezzlement scandal, led to bankruptcy in 1957.

---

52 Felix Schwarzenborn [pseud. von Leers], "Welttyrannei ab 1955?", *Der Weg* 3/6 (1952), 209.

53 Ibid.

54 For some examples see, A. Euler [pseud. von Leers], "Jus rebellionis", *Der Weg* 1/5 (1951), 51-55; Felix Schwarzenborn [pseud. von Leers], "Folterknechte aus Luxemburg", *Der Weg* 5/9 (1955), 325-330; Hans Euler [pseud. von Leers], "Ein Reichsverräter bekennt", *Der Weg* 4/11 (1957), 255-258.

The Network in Cairo

In the light of these considerations it was not surprising that von Leers had to look for a new position. This was offered to him in Egypt. After the 1952 coup d'état against the corrupt regime of King Farouk, which brought Gamal Abd el Nasser to power in 1954-55, well-versed propagandists like von Leers were not only welcome to implement their skills, but were also directly mandated to do so by state authorities. This seems to be clear from the attempt since the middle of the 1950s to resurrect and resume the publicist tradition of the anti-Semitic *Weltdienst*.[55] In the summer of 1956, von Leers therefore relocated from Argentina to Egypt.[56]

The exact circumstances under which von Leers and his family's unusual relocation from Argentina was made possible still remain unclear. The following picture therefore remains incomplete, but upon examination of the relevant sources it becomes obvious that highly influential functionaries in the official Egyptian state apparatus and semi-governmental bodies wanted to make use of von Leers' services. Here it is worth mentioning the Arab League, which had its headquarters in Cairo. Some of their members belonged to the inner circle of the Mufti of Jerusalem, el-Husseini, who stayed in the Third Reich during the Second World War.[57] It was at this time that he and von Leers first became acquainted.

It is evident that von Leers had considered relocating to Cairo as far back as 1954. In 1955, a new dynamic reinforced this idea. At the time, a semi-state organisation in Cairo tried to revitalise the tradition of National Socialist publications. It looked to the former *Weltdienst,* which was published from 1933 to 1944, in an effort to foster worldwide anti-Semitism. Von Leers was regarded as a potential recruit for the new effort. The project was initiated by an Egyptian named Mahmoud Saleh. Saleh and von Leers had reportedly been in contact for many years. Saleh, who purportedly had studied in both Berlin and Paris, although there is limited information available on his past, was no less a fanatical anti-Semite and designated propaganda expert than von Leers. From 1945 to 1946 he was interned in Palestine by the English Mandate regime. At the time, he was reportedly openly pro-German, anti-British, and hostile to Jews.[58] At the beginning of the 1950s, Saleh went to Cairo where he worked as a press correspondent and publicist.[59] Additionally, he proclaimed himself as a "representative of Natinform in Egypt", an independent network of right-wing propaganda experts.[60]

---

55 Letter from Mahmoud Saleh to Theodor Fischer, March 11, 1955, Eidgenössische Technische Hochschule Zurich (ETH Zurich), Fischer Collection.

56 See CIA report "Johann von Leers" [ca. 1960], National Archives Washington (NA), RG 263, box 32.

57 Cf. Klaus Gensicke, *Der Mufti von Jerusalem und die Nationalsozialisten. Eine politische Biographie Amin el-Husseinis* (Darmstadt: Wissenschaftliche Buchgesellschaft, 2007).

58 Letter from the German Embassy in Cairo to the German Foreign Office, March 6, 1960, PAAA, B 82, V3-88, Nr. 250, vol. 1, 64.

59 Letter from Mahmoud Saleh to Theodor Fischer, October 17, 1955, ETH Zurich, Fischer Collection.

60 Letter from Saleh to Fischer, November 12, 1954, ETH Zurich, Fischer Collection. On the network "Natinform", see Tauber, *Beyond Eagle and Swastika,* 243-252; Kevin Coogan, *Dream-*

In 1952 Saleh received the permission as well as funding from the Egyptian regime to open up a propaganda bureau. The kind of propaganda he put out was obvious from the name of the organisation, the Anti-Zionist Community. He viewed the initiation of a campaign against, as he wrote, "American Zionists and Jewish capitalists", as his main task.[61] It was also no accident that his bureau was located in a building where Egyptian civil servants were schooled in anti-Zionism.

In the first half of the 1950s, Saleh entered into written contact with various anti-Semites in Europe. From them he hoped to receive material for planned publications about, in Saleh's words, "Judaism and Zionism from antiquity to modern times".[62] In letters to his correspondence partners, Saleh boasted in 1955 that "for twenty years", namely from approximately the middle of the 1930s, he had worked "to hunt down this evil enemy of mankind".[63] By the "enemy of mankind" Saleh meant the Jews. This phrase is reminiscent of von Leers and one of his first articles that appeared in *Der Angriff*, as mentioned above, with the headline "Attacking the World Enemy". In reference to his own "business credentials", Saleh mentioned, among other things, that before the Second World War he had been a colleague of Lieutenant-Colonel Ulrich Fleischhauer. This name requires an explanation.

Ulrich Fleischhauer was a star of the publicist tradition that Saleh wanted to advance.[64] This self-declared expert and authority on the "Jewish question", issued the journal *Weltdienst* since December 1933 from a small publishing house called U. Bodung-Verlag. The journal was supplemented by a series of books on relevant topics. From the beginning, the *Weltdienst* was published in German, English and French and distributed both in Germany and abroad. Its eventful history and the network of its contributors in Nazi Germany and foreign countries, however, cannot be further examined here.[65] The *Weltdienst*'s mission, as stated on its masthead in the earliest editions, was to "enlighten the badly oriented non-Jews". Its character was that of a journal of cheap anti-Semitic sensationalism. In public, the *Weltdienst*'s editors always stressed the private character of their contributors. However, in reality it maintained close connections to the Nazi Party and the state apparatus. At the end of the 1930s, it came under the control of Amt Rosenberg and moved to Frankfurt. From then on, the journal was significantly expanded. In 1944 it was published in at least 19 languages and reportedly with a circulation of some 300,000

---

er of the Day. Francis Parker Yockey and the Postwar Fascist International (New York: Autonomedia, 1999), 409-416.

61 Letter from Saleh to Fischer, October 17, 1955, ETH Zurich, Fischer Collection.

62 Letter from Saleh to Fischer, November 12, 1954, ETH Zurich, Fischer Collection.

63 Letter from Saleh to Fischer, March 11, 1955, ETH Zurich, Fischer Collection.

64 On Ulrich Fleischhauer, see Magnus Brechtken, *Madagaskar für die Juden. Antisemitische Idee und politische Praxis 1885-1945* (Munich: Oldenbourg, 1998), 44-48; Eckart Schörle, "Internationale der Antisemiten. Ulrich Fleischhauer und der 'Welt-Dienst'", *WerkstattGeschichte* 51 (2009), 57-72.

65 On the history of the *Weltdienst* and the network of its contributors, see Louis W. Bondy, *Racketeers of Hatred. Julius Streicher and the Jew-Baiters' International* (London: Newman Wolsey, 1946); Reinhard Bollmus, *Das Amt Rosenberg und seine Gegner. Studien zum Machtkampf im nationalsozialistischen Herrschaftssystem* (Stuttgart: DVA, 1970); Brechtken, *Madagaskar für die Juden.*

copies. At the same time, the editors had at their disposal an extensive archive and library with specialist literature.

This archive was believed lost since 1945, and Saleh strove to locate the remains and acquire access to them. At the same time, he wanted to recruit staff members with appropriate experience for his cause, including von Leers, with whom he was said to have been in contact for many years.[66] After he arrived in Cairo, von Leers became one of Saleh's clients. There can also be no doubt that Saleh frequently employed von Leers to translate propaganda writings. Von Leers also supplied him with the addresses of nationalist and National Socialist sympathisers, so that the writings of Saleh's organisation could be specifically dispatched to them.[67]

In the Saleh network von Leers was able to utilise his propagandistic experiences from the 1930s and 1940s. The question, though, is what effect the writings he developed and promoted actually had. On this issue, it is worth noting that the number of anti-Semitic tracts which were smuggled into the Federal Republic of Germany in the second half of the 1950s may well have been considerable. Their distribution occurred during a period dubbed "the return of anti-Semitism" that began sometime around 1958.[68] On the one hand, this phase is characterised by a range of lenient libel case judgments involving cases of anti-Semitism, as well as a series of questionable jury decisions taken even though a wave of anti-Semitic graffiti occurred around the turn of the year 1959-60. On the other hand, the period is shaped by an increasing national perception of the failure to come to terms legally with the crimes of National Socialism, which was triggered by the *Einsatzgruppen* trial in Ulm in 1958.

In such a climate, anti-Semitic propaganda, including the work von Leers took part in, attracted considerable attention, even though their content was utterly absurd. This is true among others for pamphlets which connected traditional stereotypes of anti-Semitism with the new anti-Zionism in order to challenge the existence of Israel. One example is the book *Frieden im Orient* by Amed Moawad, which was published in a German language edition in 1956 in Cairo.[69] In his foreword, von Leers touted his "understanding and sympathy" for the Arabs "in their fight for their homeland" and his support for them in the war against Israel, "Zionist propaganda" and the "monstrous power" of the Zionists "in the world press".[70] This also holds true for a series of German-language brochures published in Cairo in the beginning of the 1960s. They were motivated by the legal actions against Adolf Eichmann in Jerusalem in 1961. The brochure "The Eichmann Show Trial

66 See the CIA note, "Activities of Dr Johann von Leers", October 24, 1957, National Archives Washington (NA), RG 263, box 32.

67 Sigfrid Gauch, *Vaterspuren. Eine Erzählung* (Königsstein: Athenäum, 1979), 59-60.

68 Werner Bergmann, *Antisemitismus in öffentlichen Konflikten. Kollektives Lernen in der politischen Kultur der Bundesrepublik 1949-1989* (Frankfurt a.M./New York: Campus Verlag, 1997).

69 A[med] Moawad, *Frieden im Orient* (Cairo: Mondiale Press, 1956); idem., *Sicher ist unsere Heimkehr* (Cairo: Mondiale Press, 1956). Note that the Mondiale-Press published various semi-official books and brochures.

70 Amed Moawad, *Frieden im Orient*, 5-9.

Should Help Finance the Atomic Rearmament against the Arab Lands" bears von Leers's signature.[71] Eichmann was said to be a Zionist Jew who had infiltrated the SS in the 1930s in order to organise the emigration of Jews from Germany into Palestine. According to him, claims about six million Jews who died were a "lie". The case against Eichmann served to encourage the financial extortion of West Germany so that the "criminal robber state Israel" could finance its atomic rearmament against the Arab states. Israel's goal was said to be the creation of a "greater Jewish state from the Euphrates to the Nile". The brochure ended with the claim that the case against Eichmann was said to be "one of the greatest fraud enterprises in World History" and "the overture to a Third World War, unless the people finally recognise the world enemy and disrupter of peace and defang it".[72]

Conclusions

Von Leers played a central role as a writer in the publicist networks grouped around various publishing houses and journals which to some extent constituted an "International", for instance an international movement of right-wing extremism and anti-Semitism in the 1950s and early 1960s. His influence was commented on in cyclical waves by the press and often interpreted as scandalous. Thus, the quoted article in the *Frankfurter Illustrierte* tried to pronounce him as the leader of a Cairo-based SS-group. However, his influence must be critically examined.

It is certainly correct that von Leers hoped to excite the attention of the public through targeted provocations and also that he succeeded in his effort. Also verifiable is his almost endless torrent of correspondence with right-wing extremists and anti-Semites in Europe and North America. However, when one examines these letters more thoroughly, insofar as they are still preserved, the impression arises that there was a fantast at work which drew increasingly further away from reality. It is sometimes difficult to follow his confusing theories about, for example, the connection between ancient Egypt, ancient Germania and the rune stones in Alexandria.[73] It is also telling what acquaintances he aided from his Cairo contact centre. Functionaries of extreme right parties in West Germany such as Adolf von Thadden,[74] who sought him out because they hoped to use him to gain access to Egyptian state functionaries, he simply dismissed – certainly in part because the idea of participating in a parliamentary system was foreign to him.[75] Thus von Leers acted to dissociate himself from organised right-wing extremism in West Germany in the 1950s and 1960s. In contrast he maintained close contacts with numerous right-

71 *Der Eichmann-Schauprozess soll die atomare Aufrüstung gegen die arabischen Länder finanzieren helfen* (Cairo: undated [1961]).

72 Ibid., 15.

73 See the two letters from von Leers to Herman Gauch, undated [July 1958] and August 22, 1958, private archive Martin Finkenberger.

74 On Adolf von Thadden, see Gideon Botsch's contribution to this anthology.

75 See the CIA report, "Activities of Johannes [sic] von Leers", August 5, 1957, NA, RG 263, box 32.

wing fringe figures, such as the wine-dealer and innkeeper Friedrich Lenz, who published pertinent pamphlets in his own small printing house; the medical doctor Herman Gauch,[76] former member of Darré's staff and Himmler's adjutant, who acted in the 1950s as an official for cultural affairs for the German Reich Party *(Deutsche Reichspartei)* in Rhineland-Palatinate; or Wilhelm Landig, a writer and distributor of esoteric pamphlets in 1950s Vienna.[77] Furthermore, von Leers was in contact with Walter Kramer from the beginning of the 1950s. This illegitimate son of the admired "old master" of anti-Semitism, Theodor Fritsch, was the author of at least one essay in *Der Weg.*[78] In 1959 he tried to win over von Leers for publishing a script in Egypt that even a German right-wing printing house, the Druffel-Verlag, refused to accept. Additionally, he also maintained contacts with the shrilling forms of international anti-Semitism, for example Savitri Devi, a native Frenchwoman whose worldview involved a bizarre mix of Hinduism, religious-like deification of Hitler, and glorification of the Cult of Aryans.[79]

Von Leers' dwindling influence can be seen from the character of the publications offering him a forum for his ideas in the late 1950s: *Der Ring,* a journal of the Federal Association of Former Internees and Aggrieved Parties of Denazification *(Bundesverbandes ehemaliger Internierter und Entnazifizierungsgeschädigter)* as well as the short-lived *Nordische Rundschau – Monatsschrift für nationale Freiheit,* which was published in Vienna in 1956, or *Die Plattform* which was issued by a small *völkisch* group in Austria.[80] Writers for these publications attracted a fanatical, but insignifiant, audience. In any case, von Leers could earn hardly any money from them. Incidentally, it is worth noting that the most important journal of right-wing extremists since

---

76 Von Leers had been in contact with Herman Gauch since the 1930s. In his books, Gauch dealt with ancient customs – i.e. *Brauchtum* – and the so-called *Odalsverfassung* of Teutons in ancient times, which was also one of the favoured topics of Johann von Leers. On Gauch's biography, see Gauch, *Vaterspuren;* Josef Ackermann, *Heinrich Himmler als Ideologe* (Göttingen: Musterschmidt, 1970), 110.

77 Landig, a native Austrian, became associated with the National Socialist movement in Austria in the early 1930s. After the failure of the coup d'état in 1934 he fled to Nazi Germany, where he became a member of the SS and worked for the SD. After the war, Landig was a prominent figure in occultist circles of former National Socialists. Between 1971 and 1991 he published a trilogy in the guise of a novel illustrating the construction of flying discs during the war which allegedly had taken Hitler and some of his fellows to South America and the Antarctic shortly before the end of the war. On his biography, see Nicholas Goodrick-Clarke, *Im Schatten der Schwarzen Sonne. Arische Kulte, Esoterischer Nationalsozialismus und die Politik der Abgrenzung* (Wiesbaden: Matrix, 2009), 272-309.

78 Arno Gildemann, "Leibeigene der Finanz", *Der Weg* 3-4/7 (1953), 159-162. Using von Leers as an intermediary, Kramer sent further manuscripts to the journal, which were not published. See the letter from Kramer to von Leers, July 25, 1955, private archive Christoph Knüppel, Kramer Collection.

79 Nicholas Goodrick-Clarke, *Hitler's Priestess. Savitri Devi, the Hindu-Aryan Myth, and Neo-Nazism* (New York/London: New York University Press, 1998); Savitri Devi et al., *100 Jahre Savitri Devi* (Straelen: Regin-Verlag, 2005).

80 Johann von Leers, "Einer wird es sein", *Die Plattform,* April 6, 1957, 1-2; idem., "Muss man am deutschen Volk verzweifeln?," *Die Plattform,* June 6, 1957, 1.

the beginning of the 1950s, the *Nation Europa* from Coburg, which ran many articles about the "liberation war" of both the Arabs and North Africans during the period of decolonisation and conflict in the Near and Middle East, hardly ever published an article by von Leers.[81] It is equally significant that none other than the influential right-wing extremist publisher Gerhard Frey, who interviewed von Leers in Cairo in 1963, reported back about the "truly confusing ideas" of his interlocutor.[82]

Finally, while in Cairo, von Leers reproduced the same pattern of behaviour that he showed in the late 1930s and early 1940s. The underlying basis of his behaviour was frenetic activism, which frequently ended in failure. This is especially true of his attempt in 1957 to revitalise the journal *Der Weg* in Cairo. It also proved true of his attempt to import printing presses from West Germany to Egypt and to create a publishing house for relevant texts. His failure becomes equally evident in the campaign against the Eichmann trial. The assertions he put forward were so far-fetched that even right-wing extremist journals refused to publish contributions from him. Nonetheless, the importance of von Leers should not be underestimated, both as a sloganeer and contact point for like-minded people. However, he certainly cannot be regarded as the leader of a worldwide movement of anti-Semitism, which is how he has occasionally been portrayed.

Bibliography

Ackermann, Josef. *Heinrich Himmler als Ideologe.* Göttingen: Musterschmidt, 1970.

Bar-Zohar, Michel. *Die Jagd auf die deutschen Wissenschaftler (1944-1960).* Berlin: Propyläen, 1966.

Benz, Wolfgang, ed. *Handbuch des Antisemitismus. Judenfeindschaft in Geschichte und Gegenwart,* vol. 2/2. Berlin: De Gruyter, 2009.

Bergmann, Werner. *Antisemitismus in öffentlichen Konflikten. Kollektives Lernen in der politischen Kultur der Bundesrepublik 1949-1989.* Frankfurt a.M./New York: Campus, 1997.

Bondy, Louis W. *Racketeers of Hatred. Julius Streicher and the Jew-Baiters' International.* London: Newman Wolsey, 1946.

Bollmus, Reinhard. *Das Amt Rosenberg und seine Gegner. Studien zum Machtkampf im nationalsozialistischen Herrschaftssystem.* Stuttgart: DVA, 1970.

81 The *Nation Europa* only published two articles by von Leers, apart from one letter to the editors in 1958 and a written declaration by von Leers from early December 1960 in Cairo, where he refuted all accusations against him that had appeared in newspapers in the years before. Cf. Gordon Fitzstuart [pseud. von Leers], "Die schwarzen Yankees", *Nation Europa* 11/2 (1952), 39-41; [Johann] v[on] L[eers], "Marsz, marsz, Dabrowski", *Nation Europa* 6/3 (1953), 23-27. On the history and importance of *Nation Europa*, see Thomas Pfeiffer, *Für Volk und Vaterland. Das Mediennetz der Rechten – Presse, Musik, Internet* (Berlin: Aufbau, 2002), 145-176.

82 Cf. "Die 'Faschistische Internationale' in Kairo. Wenn die Wellen der Weltpresse anrollen", *Deutsche National- und Soldatenzeitung,* May 24, 1963. This article was part of a series of reports by the editor Gerhard Frey, which dealt with, as the journal stated, "the supposed danger of a 'Fascist International' with its seat in Cairo, which has been exaggerated time and again by the world press".

Brechtken, Magnus. *Madagaskar für die Juden. Antisemitische Idee und politische Praxis 1885-1945.* Munich: Oldenbourg, 1998.

Brenner, Hildegard. "Die Kunst im politischen Machtkampf der Jahre 1933/34". *Vierteljahrshefte für Zeitgeschichte* 10 (1962), 17-42.

Coogan, Kevin. *Dreamer of the Day. Francis Parker Yockey and the Postwar Fascist International.* New York: Autonomedia, 1999.

Dörner, Bernward. *Die Deutschen und der Holocaust. Was niemand wissen wollte, aber jeder wissen konnte.* Berlin: Propyläen, 2007.

Finkenberger, Martin. "Johann von Leers und die 'faschistische Internationale' der fünfziger und sechziger Jahre in Argentinien und Ägypten". *Zeitschrift für Geschichtswissenschaft* 59 (2011), 522-543.

Frei, Norbert. *Vergangenheitspolitik. Die Anfänge der Bundesrepublik und die NS-Vergangenheit.* Munich: C.H. Beck 1997.

Gauch, Sigfrid. *Vaterspuren. Eine Erzählung.* Königstein: Athenäum, 1979.

Gensicke, Klaus. *Der Mufti von Jerusalem und die Nationalsozialisten. Eine politische Biographie Amin el-Husseinis.* Darmstadt: Wissenschaftliche Buchgesellschaft, 2007.

Goebbels, Joseph. *Die Tagebücher von Joseph Goebbels.* Edited by Elke Fröhlich, part 1, *Aufzeichnungen 1923-1941*, vol. 2/I: December 1929 to May 1931 (Berlin: De Gruyter, 2005).

Goldhagen, Erich. "Weltanschauung und Endlösung. Zum Antisemitismus der nationalsozialistischen Führungsschicht". *Vierteljahrshefte für Zeitgeschichte* 24 (1976), 378-405.

Goodrick-Clarke, Nicholas. *Hitler's Priestess. Savitri Devi, the Hindu-Aryan Myth, and Neo-Nazism.* New York/London: New York University Press, 1998.

Goodrick-Clarke, Nicholas. *Im Schatten der Schwarzen Sonne. Arische Kulte, Esoterischer Nationalsozialismus und die Politik der Abgrenzung.* Wiesbaden: Matrix, 2009.

Goñi, Uki. *Odessa. Die wahre Geschichte. Fluchthilfe für NS-Kriegsverbrecher.* Berlin: Assoziation A, 2007.

Herf, Jeffrey. *The Jewish Enemy. Nazi propaganda during World War II and the Holocaust.* Cambridge, MA/London: Harvard University Press, 2008.

Hoßfeld, Uwe, Jürgen John, Oliver Lemuth and Rüdiger Stutz, eds. *"Kämpferische Wissenschaft". Studien zur Universität Jena im Nationalsozialismus.* Cologne: Böhlau, 2003.

Jaeger, Hans. "Die faschistische Internationale", *Deutsche Rundschau* 78/9 (1952), 993-1003.

Jünger, Ernst. *Jahre der Okkupation.* Stuttgart: Klett, 1958.

Kater, Michael. *Das "Ahnenerbe" der SS 1935-1945. Ein Beitrag zur Kulturpolitik des Dritten Reiches.* Munich: Oldenbourg, 2001.

Keller, Sven. *Günzburg und der Fall Josef Mengele. Die Heimatstadt und die Jagd nach dem NS-Verbrecher.* Munich: Oldenbourg, 2003.

Kissenkoetter, Udo. *Gregor Straßer und die NSDAP.* Stuttgart: DVA, 1978.

Leers, Johann von. *Der deutschen Bauern 1000jähriger Kampf um deutsche Art und deutsches Recht.* Goslar: Blut und Boden Verlag, 1935.

Leers, Johann von. *Odal. Das Lebensgesetz eines ewigen Deutschland.* Goslar: Blut und Boden Verlag, 1936.

Leers, Johann von. *Für das Reich. Deutsche Geschichte in Geschichtserzählungen.* Langensalza/Berlin/Leipzig: Beltz, 1941.

Leers, Johann von. *Die Verbrechernatur der Juden.* Berlin: Verlag Paul Hochmuth, 1944.

Leers, Johann von. *Kräfte hinter Roosevelt.* Berlin: Theodor Fritsch Verlag, 1942.

Lemmons, Russel. *Goebbels and "Der Angriff"*. Lexington: University Press of Kentucky, 1994.

Longerich, Peter. *Heinrich Himmler. Biographie.* Munich: Siedler, 2008.

Lotz, Wolfgang. *Fünftausend für Lotz. Der Bericht des israelischen Meisterspions.* Frankfurt a.M.: Goverts Krüger Stahlberg, 1973.

Meding, Holger M. *Flucht vor Nürnberg? Deutsche und österreichische Einwanderung in Argentinien, 1945-1955.* Cologne/Weimar/Vienna: Böhlau, 1992.

Meding, Holger M. *"Der Weg". Eine deutsche Emigrantenzeitschrift in Buenos Aires 1947 bis 1957.* Berlin: Wissenschaftlicher Verlag, 1997.

Mehnert, Klaus. *Ein Deutscher in der Welt. Erinnerungen 1906-1981.* Stuttgart: DVA, 1981.

Moawad, A[med]. *Frieden im Orient.* Cairo: Mondiale Press, 1956.

Moawad, A[med]. *Sicher ist unsere Heimkehr.* Cairo: Mondiale Press, 1956.

Pfeiffer, Thomas. *Für Volk und Vaterland. Das Mediennetz der Rechten – Presse, Musik, Internet.* Berlin: Aufbau, 2002.

Piper, Ernst. *Alfred Rosenberg. Hitlers Chefideologe.* Munich: Karl Blessing Verlag, 2005.

Puschner, Uwe. *Die völkische Bewegung im wilhelminischen Kaiserreich. Sprache – Rasse – Religion.* Darmstadt: Wissenschaftliche Buchgesellschaft, 2001.

Rogge, John O. *The Official German Report. Nazi Penetration 1924-1942. Pan-Arabism 1939-Today.* New York/London: Thomas Yoseloff, 1961.

Schmidt-Eenboom, Erich. *BND. Der deutsche Geheimdienst im Nahen Osten.* Munich: Herbig, 2007.

Schmollinger, Horst W. "Deutscher Block". In *Parteien-Handbuch. Die Parteien der Bundesrepublik Deutschland 1945-1980*, edited by Richard Stöss, 807-847. Opladen: Westdeutscher Verlag, 1983.

Schneppen, Heinz. *Odessa und das Vierte Reich. Mythen der Zeitgeschichte.* Berlin: Metropol, 2007.

Schörle, Eckart. "Internationale der Antisemiten. Ulrich Fleischhauer und der 'Welt-Dienst'". *WerkstattGeschichte* 51 (2009), 57-72.

Smoydzin, Werner. *Hitler lebt. Vom internationalen Faschismus zur Internationale des Hakenkreuzes.* Pfaffenhofen: Ilmgau, 1966.

Savitri Devi et al. *100 Jahre Savitri Devi.* Straelen: Regin-Verlag, 2005.

Steinacher, Gerald. *Nazis auf der Flucht. Wie Kriegsverbrecher über Italien nach Übersee entkamen.* Innsbruck: Studienverlag, 2008.

Stangneth, Bettina. *Eichmann vor Jerusalem. Das unbehelligte Leben eines Massenmörders.* Hamburg: Arche, 2011.

Stöss, Richard. *Zur Vernetzung der extremen Rechten in Europa.* Berlin: Free University Berlin, 2001.

Tauber, Kurt P. *Beyond Eagle and Swastika. German Nationalism since 1945*, vol. 1. Middletown, CO: Wesleyan University Press, 1967.

Wegner, Gregory Paul. "A propagandist of extermination. Johann von Leers and the Anti-Semitic Formation of Children in Nazi Germany". *Paedagogica Historica* 43 (2007), 299-325.

Wojak, Irmtrud. *Eichmanns Memoiren. Ein kritischer Essay.* Frankfurt a.M.: Campus Verlag, 2001.

Wulf, Joseph. *Literatur und Dichtung im Dritten Reich. Eine Dokumentation.* Hamburg: Rowohlt, 1966.

Men among the Ruins
The Radical Right in Italy

Elisabetta Cassina Wolff

Introduction

The present chapter deals with the intellectual life of the Italian philosopher Giulio Cesare Andrea (Julius) Evola.[1] Born in 1898, Evola was a leading intellectual figure, albeit through different phases of controversial success, until his death in 1974. He comes to our attention first as a very young poet and painter, interested in Marinetti's futurism, the decadentism of Oscar Wilde and Gabriele D'Annunzio, Nietzsche's irrationalism and the Dada movement. As early as in 1914 Evola was an interventionist, on the side of the *Triplice,* favouring typically Prussian principles such as discipline and hierarchy. After a few years during which he devoted himself to alchemy, esotericism and oriental philosophy, he turned to political philosophy. In 1925 he published an article critical of both Italian Fascism and democracy, entitled "Stato, potenza, libertà" (State, Power, Freedom), in which he expressed his contempt for the masses.[2] Evola started to contribute to Giuseppe Bottai's *Critica fascista,* but he never applied for membership of the Fascist Party. In 1934 the publication of his book *Rivolta contro il mondo moderno* (Revolt against the Modern World)[3], where he advocated the values of Tradition, made him widely known within intellectual circles. From 1934 to 1943 Evola was also responsible for "Diorama Filosofico", the cultural page of *Il Regime Fascista,* a daily owned by Roberto Farinacci. In the same period he published regularly in Giovanni Preziosi's *La Vita Italiana* and Carlo Costamagna's *Lo Stato.* Both *Rivolta* and his various articles in the Fascist press gained him notoriety as the "philosopher of the Tradition".[4]

---

1 For biographical data on Evola, see Francesco Germinario, "Evola, Giulio Cesare", in *Dizionario del fascismo,* eds. Sergio Luzzatto and Victoria de Grazia, vol. I: A-K (Turin: Einaudi, 2002), 497-498; Luca Lo Bianco, "Evola, Giulio Cesare Andrea", in *Dizionario biografico degli italiani* (Rome: Istituto della Enciclopedia Italiana Treccani, 1993), 575-581.

2 The article was published in *Lo Stato democratico,* May 1, 1925. For an analysis of Evola's relation to Fascism after the march on Rome, see Rossi Marco, "Lo Stato democratico (1925) e l'antifascismo antidemocratico di Julius Evola", *Storia contemporanea* 1/XX (1989), 5-43.

3 Julius Evola, *Rivolta contro il mondo moderno* (Milan: Hoepli, 1934). References in the following text are from the 1998 edition.

4 A short but comprehensive presentation of Evola's role in Italian culture until 1945 is to be found in Marco Tarchi, "Julius Evola e il fascismo. Note su un percorso non ordinario", in *Cultura e fascismo. Letteratura arti e spettacolo di un ventennio,* eds. Marino Biondi and Alessandro Borsotti (Florence: Ponte alle Grazie, 1996), 123-142. See also Marco Rossi, "L'avanguardia che si fa tradizione: l'itinerario culturale di Julius Evola dal primo dopoguerra alla metà degli anni Trenta", *Storia contemporanea* 6/XXII (1991), 1039-1090. Other relevant works on Evola are: Gianni Scipione Rossi, *Il razzista totalitario. Evola e la leggenda dell'antisemitismo spirituale* (Soveria Mannelli: Rubettino, 2007); Francesco Cassata, *A destra del fascismo. Profilo politico di*

At the end of the 1930s, Evola's theories on race and Semitism attracted Mussolini's attention. The philosopher published some eighty articles devoted to racial matters, in various Fascist press organs. Three essays were published in the late 1930s and early 1940s: "Tre aspetti del problema ebraico" (Three Aspects of the Jewish Problem)[5] in 1936, "Il mito del sangue" (The Myth of Blood)[6] in 1937 and "Sintesi di dottrina della razza" (Synthesis of the Doctrine of Race)[7] in 1941. During the same period, his articles were published in *La difesa della razza,* a periodical devoted entirely to racial topics and edited by Telesio Interlandi, an intransigent and radical Fascist, racist and anti-Semite.[8]

After July 25, 1943, Evola moved first to Berlin and later to Vienna, where he studied confiscated Freemason and Jewish documents he had received from European SS-officials.[9] Together with Giovanni Preziosi, he was among the party that welcomed Mussolini to Hitler's headquarters in Rastenburg after the *Duce* had been rescued from prison; this confirms how close Evola was to inner Fascist circles. However, Evola kept a distance from the final years of the republican experience of Italian Fascism. In Vienna he was wounded and crippled by a bomb. He did not return to Rome until 1948.

In the present chapter, I have chosen to focus on Evola's unexpected popularity during the 1940s and 1950s among the younger generation of Italian neo-fascists. Unlike other prominent Fascist intellectuals who were largely forgotten in the postwar period, there was an even greater interest in Evola after 1945; in neo-fascist circles during the 1970s he was compared to Marcuse, but "only better".[10] In order to explain such popularity and understand the relationship between Evola and the youngest neo-fascists, I am convinced that we need to look at his analyses of history and of fascism.[11] Only a few years after the end of the Second World War, Evola's analyses appealed to many young Italian neo-fascists. Fascinated by his philosophy, they remained attached to fascism as a "general concept" or as a

---

Julius Evola (Turin: Bollati Boringhieri, 2003); Francesco Germinario, *Razza del sangue, razza dello spirito. Julius Evola, l'antisemitismo e il nazionalismo (1930-43)* (Turin: Bollati Boringhieri, 2001); Paul Furlong, *Social and Political Thought of Julius Evola* (London/New York: Routledge, 2011).

5 Julius Evola, *Tre aspetti del problema ebraico: nel mondo spirituale, nel mondo culturale, nel mondo economico sociale* (Rome: Edizioni Mediterranee, 1936).

6 Julius Evola, *Il mito del sangue* (Milan: Hoepli, 1937).

7 Julius Evola, *Sintesi di dottrina della razza* (Milan: Hoepli, 1941).

8 The entire collection is to be found in Julius Evola, *I testi de "La difesa della razza"*, ed. Piero Di Vona and idem., (Padova: Edizioni di Ar, 2001); *La nobiltà della stirpe (1932-1938). La Difesa della Razza (1939-1942)*, ed. Gian Franco Lami (Rome: Fondazione Julius Evola, 2002).

9 Mauro Raspanti, "Evola a Vienna 1944-45", paper at the conference *Il collaborazionismo intellettuale in Europa*, November 21-22, 1996 (Brescia: Fondazione Luigi Micheletti, 1996), 86; Marco Tarchi, "Julius Evola e il fascismo", op. cit., 138.

10 Comment by Giorgio Almirante, secretary of the neo-fascist party *Movimento Sociale Italiano* (MSI), in 1974. In Giorgio Galli, *La Destra in Italia* (Milan: Gammalibri, 1983), 38.

11 In this context and in my text, "fascism" is conceived both as a general term referring to a supranational phenomenon (written with small letters) and as a specific term referring to the Italian regime 1922-1943 and the Salò republic 1943-1945 (with a capital letter).

universal set of values and ideas. This was in spite of the clear political and military defeat of the Fascist regime. Like Evola, they were only "lonely soldiers", doomed to fight a lost battle. However, they did not abandon fascism and ultimately managed to exercise an influence on the Italian political scene.

Evola's writings from the late 1940s and early 1950s represent a crucial moment in the development of a neo-fascist ideology that cannot be wholly identified with the ideas and projects of Mussolini's regime. On the contrary, they mark the ideological starting point of the postwar political phenomenon that became known as the Radical Right.[12] Evola's definition of "The (Radical) Right" helps us to make a clear distinction between democratic and non-democratic political ideologies. It also enables us to distinguish between the different currents within Italian neo-fascism. Evola was a real *maître à penser;* but we may question the moral influence of his intellectual contribution.

Evola played a role in postwar Italian political culture and was a central figure in the Italian neo-fascist community of the time.[13] However, we also come across his ideas when we analyse the different movements of the extreme right in today's Europe. As well as being widely read in Italy, where we see a renewed interest in his works, Evola's books have been translated into other languages. In the past, he had readers in Spain, Portugal, France, and Latin America, and nowadays in post-1989 Eastern Europe and Russia.

The 1951 FAR Trial

Postwar Italy was a country devastated by the Mussolinian wars and three years of civil war in its northern regions. In 1951, we find Evola in a courtroom. This was the year of the so-called FAR trial.[14] A group of neo-fascists were accused of being responsible for a series of demonstrations and terrorist attacks that had occurred in

---

12 In Italian historiography the notion of the Radical Right was introduced by Giorgio Galli, *La crisi italiana e la Destra internazionale* (Milan: Mondadori, 1974), who referred to the studies of Talcott Parsons. Later on, the historian Franco Ferraresi defined the Radical Right in ideological terms: Opposition to any democratic political system and, more generally, to the process of modernisation (rationality, science, individualism). See Franco Ferraresi, *Minacce alla democrazia: la destra radicale e la strategia della tensione in Italia nel dopoguerra* (Milan: Feltrinelli, 1995), 24. In Italian historiography, "Radical" is often synonymous with "Extreme", though in my view it is important to make a distinction, at least *in theory*. The Radical Right refers to ideological opposition, i.e. to anti-democratic thought without direct involvement in practical political action; the Extreme Right refers to violent and armed opposition, i.e. to anti-democratic attitudes transferred into political action. In practice, in the Italian context, where neo-fascist militants were engaged in both ideological and political activity, the distinction is less relevant. In the present chapter, I consistently use the term "Radical Right".

13 For an exhaustive bibliography on Evola, see Renato del Ponte, "Julius Evola: una bibliografia 1920-1994", *Futuro Presente* 6 (1995), 27-70.

14 For details about the trial, see Marco Iacona, "Julius Evola e le vicende processuali legate ai FAR (1951-1954)", *Nuova Storia Contemporanea* 3 (2009), 129-152. See also Antonio Carioti, *Gli orfani di Salò. Il 'Sessantotto nero' dei giovani neofascisti nel dopoguerra. 1945-1951* (Milan: Mursia, 2008), 224-254.

the two previous years.[15] The majority of the 36 accused were young men who had been volunteers in the Italian Social Republic of Salò (*Repubblica Sociale Italiana,* RSI, 1943-45) and connected to clandestine neo-fascist organisations after the war. Many of them were openly engaged in political activity within the legal (neo-fascist) Italian Social Movement (*Movimento Sociale Italiano,* MSI) founded in December 1946 by Salò veterans and/or they were prolific writers published in the fascist-oriented Italian press. The magistrates believed that the terrorist actions promoted by the so-called "Black Legion" were inspired by the clandestine Revolutionary Action Fasces (FAR), which had been active between 1946 and 1947. However, no connection between the FAR and the young men in the dock was proven. The philosopher Julius Evola was also arrested in May 1951 and imprisoned for six months, in spite of the fact that he sat in a wheelchair. During the trial, he was introduced to the public as a *maestro* and accused of being the ideologue behind the group and the subversive neo-fascist community. It was claimed that Evola's writings inspired young, ignorant and naive men to commit violent and terrorist acts against the republican Italian state. The prosecutors accused him of "ideological complicity". He was also accused of having contributed to the re-establishment of the dissolved Fascist Party in the form of the Black Legion, a crime according to law no. 1546 of December 3, 1947 (art. 1). In addition, he was accused of praising Fascism, which was also a crime according to the same law (art. 7).[16]

Evola's Message to the Young in Postwar Italy

The way Evola came in contact with the young neo-fascists in Italy was casual and unplanned. While he was still recovering in an Italian hospital after the wartime bomb injury, Evola was contacted by a small group of Italian neo-fascists. These were people who had been too young to have served in the war, although a number of them had enlisted in the RSI before the end of the conflict (among them were Pino Rauti, Enzo Erra, Fausto Gianfranceschi, Primo Siena, Silvio Vitale, Roberto Mieville and Giulio Caradonna). Some of these individuals had, incredibly enough, first discovered Evola's books whilst serving sentences in Italian prisons for having been involved in clandestine (neo-fascist) activities.[17] When they were released they found his address in the telephone catalogue. They had been especially struck by Evola's work from 1934, *Rivolta contro il mondo moderno.*

Probably influenced by authors such as Oswald Spengler, René Guénon and Alfred Rosenberg, Evola described in *Rivolta* his conception of Tradition as a spiritual energy that is made up of factors that remain unchanged over the centuries: The

---

15 Nicola Rao, *Neofascisti! La Destra italiana da Salò a Fiuggi nel ricordo dei protagonisti* (Rome: Settimo Sigillo, 1999), 53-59.

16 The crime of "praise of Fascism" was intended to suppress activity connected to the Fascist regime. Article 7 of the law read: "Whoever publicly exalts, by means of the press or in other manner, persons or ideologies characteristic of Fascism, or publicly performs demonstrations of a Fascist nature, is punished by incarceration from six months to three years."

17 Rao, op. cit., 39-52.

ideas of Authority, Hierarchy and Order, the primacy of quality over quantity, the differentiated personality, corporative solidarity in the social field, justice that recognises difference and inequality. He also praised traditional values: Honour, courage, loyalty, obedience and sacrifice. Finally, he interpreted history as an inevitable process of caste regression.[18] In *Rivolta* Evola described all the stages of the historical regression; from civilizations dominated by the warrior caste, such as the ancient Romans, to civilizations where the merchant caste had acquired power. The transition from so-called traditional civilizations to modern ones was accomplished, in his view, when the power system based on hierarchy was replaced with a system based on contract, and when traditional values were challenged by other values such as individualism and materialism. In the book's conclusion, he referred to two dominant modern and equally anti-traditional and materialistic civilizations in the West: American liberal democracy and Soviet communism.[19]

The book, deeply pessimistic, was not a success in the Italy of the 1930s, at a time when Fascism was still predominantly vitalist, futurist and modern. However, Evola was recognised by those European intellectuals who propagated the political-philosophical ideas of Tradition[20] and, outside his country, considered as the most important Italian theoretician of the Conservative Revolution.[21]

The pessimism of *Rivolta* had a completely different impact on the young neo-fascists who read the book after the war. The traditional values Evola cherished were exactly those values that had convinced them to fight side by side with the Germans after the fall of the Fascist regime. In the wake of the disintegration of the Fascist state, with the consequent "betrayal" of Italy's German allies and the alliance with the American "invaders", thousands of Italians' instinctive (and non-political) sense of honour and loyalty had been offended.[22] When some of these postwar neo-fascists visited Evola and started to follow his "lessons" in his apartment in Rome, they experienced a widening of their intellectual horizons. They had only previously heard of Giovanni Gentile, Alfredo Oriani and Gioacchino Volpe, and their analysis of the global conflict had been narrowly nationalist; Italy had participated in order to win prestige and gain new land for her proletarians. Evola offered an interpretation of history that gave a new legitimation and a new dimension to the fight against the Allies. The young neo-fascists abandoned the rhetorical nationalism of the Fascist regime and began to identify with a larger "nation", one that was founded on other values than those imposed by its conquerors. Was it

---

18 Julius Evola, *Rivolta contro il mondo moderno* (Rome: Edizioni Mediterranee, 1998), 306-321.

19 Ibid., 379-398.

20 Francesco Cassata, *La difesa della razza. Politica, ideologia e immagine del razzismo fascista* (Turin: Giulio Einaudi Editore, 2008), 151-189; Renato Del Ponte, "Gli orizzonti europei del tradizionalismo nel *Diorama filosofico* (1934-1943)", in *Delle rovine e oltre. Saggi su Julius Evola*, eds. Mario Bernardi Guardi and Marco Rossi (Rome: Pellicani, 1995), 167-197.

21 Armin Mohler, *Die Konservative Revolution in Deutschland 1918-1932* (Stuttgart: Chr. Belser, 1950), 21, 241-242; Marcello Veneziani, *La rivoluzione conservatrice in Italia. Genesi e sviluppo della "ideologia italiana" fino ai nostri giorni* (Carnago: SugarCo, 1994), 214.

22 A testimony by Pino Rauti in Francesco Giorgino and Nicola Rao, *L'un contro l'altro armati* (Milan: Mursia, 1995), 146-147.

possible – they asked – to interpret the victory of the modern and materialistic civilizations of the Allies as the ultimate stage in the decline of Tradition? Was there something they could do in order to reverse this decline?

What also fascinated the young neo-fascists who came in contact with Evola were his erudition and his connections. They learned about the élite guards of Nazism, the SS, José Antonio Primo De Rivera's Spanish Falange and Corneliu Zelea Codreanu's Romanian Legion of the Archangel or Iron Guard. They heard, for the first time, the names of Knut Hamsun and Vidkun Quisling, Leon Degrelle, Drieu La Rochelle, Robert Brasillach, Maurice Bardèche and Charles Maurras.[23]

These young neo-fascists were all active in the MSI, but they did not really feel at home there. At the end of the 1940s, the MSI was divided into two main factions. There was a left-wing radical faction concerned with corporative democracy and social issues such as socialisation, the policy of developing worker participation in management and profit-sharing ("national socialists"). There was also a moderate, nationalist and conservative centrist faction, where many former Fascist *gerarchi* operated; this wing was engaged with European integration and political alliances with other parties on the right ("political realists").[24] The young intransigent neo-fascists despised both factions for their political and ideological commitment to the democratic process. And of course they despised the Italian democratic system which, in their opinion, was characterised by parliamentary anarchy and the inability of the Christian-democratic governments to make decisions. They clustered around Julius Evola and formed a third faction, which was defined as an intellectualist-aristocratic radical right-wing faction ("radical elitists").[25] Evola was flattered by the interest of his youthful disciples and, in 1949, decided to contribute to the ideological elaboration of a "new" fascism. However, he made no political commitment to the MSI.

On June 20, 1949, Evola published his first postwar article, under the pseudonym "Arthos", in *La Sfida* (The Challenge, 1948-49), a magazine edited by the young neo-fascist Enzo Erra. The other contributors were young neo-fascists who went on to play a role in Italian politics in the following decades. In May-July 1950 three articles appeared in *Imperium* (1950-51, 1954), another magazine edited by Enzo Erra. The publication's name was inspired by one of Evola's key-words, *imperium:* The authority and power to command.

Evola's two most important political texts appeared a few months before the FAR trial. A booklet significantly entitled *Orientamenti* (Guidelines)[26] was written during the last months of 1950 and published in *Imperium*. The anonymous *Carta della gioventù* (For a Charter of Youth)[27] was published in March-April 1951 in

23 A testimony by Pino Rauti in Rao, op. cit., 42-43.

24 Elisabetta Cassina Wolff, "Starting from the End. Fascist Ideology in Post-War Italy (1945-1953)" (PhD diss., University of Oslo, 2008), 251.

25 Giorgio Pini, "Prima le idee", *Meridiano d'Italia*, October 7, 1951; VI/39 in Cassina Wolff, op. cit., 251.

26 Julius Evola, *Orientamenti* (Padova: Ar, 2000 [1950]).

27 Anonymous [Julius Evola], "Per una Carta della Gioventù", *Cantiere*, March-April 1951, II/3.

Cantiere (Building Yard, 1950-52), edited by the young Primo Siena, who also revealed the identity of the author of the article.[28] At the same time, Evola's articles were published in a considerable number of fascist-leaning publications close to the MSI. Later on, he was to revise and publish these articles in two single volumes: *Gli uomini e le rovine* (Men among the Ruins)[29] from 1953 and *Il fascismo. Saggio di un'analisi critica dal punto di vista della Destra* (Fascism. A critical Essay Viewed from the Right)[30] from 1964.

The opening of *Orientamenti* is in line with Evola's previous literary works:

> [...] it is useless to give oneself illusions through the chimeras of whatever optimism: today we find ourselves at the end of a cycle. For centuries [...] a multiplicity of processes have destroyed all normal and legitimate order among men [...]. And the movement of this fall, its speed, its vertiginousness, has been called 'progress'.[31]

In the postwar period, Evola's philosophy was still focused on a total rejection of the historicist belief in the progress of mankind – the so-called "myth of progress".[32] Concepts such as decadence and sickness were also central to his work. Evola wrote about the disease of modernity that had affected European civilization since the liberal revolutions in England, the Enlightenment and rationalism, liberalism, democracy, socialism and communism. All of these were "toxins",[33] products of modernity that had poisoned culture, science, literature and sociology – Darwinism, historical materialism, psychoanalysis, existentialism and relativism. Evola revitalised the idea of Tradition with its "constant factors"[34] (Hierarchy, Authority, Order) and gave further clarification to the concept of *Imperium*.[35] The theoretical and ideological meaning of *Imperium* is linked to the concept of state and Evola reads the history of the Western world through the centuries as the slow and inexorable "decline of the idea of the state".[36]

---

28 Primo Siena, "Genesi di un documento evoliano", in *Idee per una Destra*, ed. Alessandro Barbera (Rome: Fondazione Julius Evola, 1997), 61-64.

29 Julius Evola, *Gli uomini e le rovine* (Rome: Edizioni Dell'ascia, 1953). References are from a recent edition: *Gli uomini e le rovine e Orientamenti* (Rome: Edizioni Mediterranee, 2002a).

30 Julius Evola, *Il fascismo. Saggio di un'analisi critica dal punto di vista della Destra* (Rome: Volpe, 1964). The second edition, *Il fascismo visto dalla destra*, had an appendix entitled *Note sul Terzo Reich* (Rome: Volpe, 1970). References are from a recent edition: *Fascismo e Terzo Reich* (Rome: Edizioni Mediterranee, 2001).

31 Julius Evola, op. cit. 2000 [1950], 17.

32 "Arthos" [Evola], "La 'Storia' e il suo senso", *Meridiano d'Italia*, October 30, 1949; *I testi del Meridiano d'Italia* (Padova: Ar, 2002b), 42.

33 Julius Evola, op. cit. 2000 [1950], 31.

34 Julius Evola, "La 'Tradizione'", *Meridiano d'Italia*, May 4, 1952, op. cit. 2002b, 123-125.

35 Julius Evola, "Il senso dell'imperium", *Imperium*, May 1950, I/1; idem., "Impero e civiltà", *Imperium*, June 1950, I/2; idem., "'Imperium', simboli e persone", *la Rivolta Ideale*, January 18, 1951, *I testi de la Rivolta Ideale* (Padova: Ar, 2003), 50-51.

36 Evola, "Il senso dell'imperium".

In the years that followed the global conflict, Evola was able to elaborate upon his interpretation of history and to provide new arguments for neo-fascists who were eager to justify their wartime commitment. The conflict had seen the ultimate, desperate and unsuccessful attempt on the part of Fascist Italy, Nazi Germany and Imperial Japan to restore the principle of authority in the struggle against a coalition of democracies. The young neo-fascists adopted Evola's interpretation of the Second World War not as a nationalistic war, but as an ideological one; a real clash of civilizations, a clash between two interpretations of life and the world.[37] Moreover, Evola wrote that sacrifice, courage and honour were the attributes of the traditional warrior; these were the traits of the "legionary spirit" of those "who were capable of choosing the hardest way, who were capable of fighting in the knowledge that the battle was materially lost".[38] Reading this passage, one is struck that it was the young volunteers of the RSI that Evola had in mind. And the young neo-fascists did not hesitate to identify themselves with those lonely and courageous legionaries.

In *Orientamenti*, Evola also posed other questions:

> The only thing that matters is this: today we are in the middle of a world of ruins. We should ask ourselves: are there still any men remaining on their feet among the ruins? Is there anything they must do, anything they can still do?[39]

Again, the young neo-fascists felt they were personally involved. They were attracted to Evola's concept of Real Men *(uomini very)*. This concept was linked to the notion of "legionary spirit" and the necessity to counter the decline of modern society through the political action of a minority who possessed the qualities needed for this task. In an article significantly entitled "Towards the *Élite* of an Ideal Front",[40] Evola wrote that Italy needed to select those individuals who could "remain on their feet among the ruins" and keep them apart from the "broken men". According to Evola, the leaders of men are those who follow the values of Tradition and epitomise and exhibit Tradition in their actions. Leaders have strong characters and they can *command.*

When the article was published, the young neo-fascists were unaware of the subtle continuity from Evola's 1930s and early 1940s texts, which were wholly dedicated to issues of race and anti-Semitism, to his 1950s concept of the "unbroken men". Evola's anti-Semitism before the war was set out in a "totalitarian way".[41] According to the philosopher, the Jewish problem had to be studied in its three dimensions: The social-economic and political, the cultural-ethical and the spiritual.

---

37 Rao, op. cit., 41.

38 Evola, op. cit. 2000 [1950], 19.

39 Ibid., 18.

40 "Arthos" [Evola], "Verso l' 'élite'di un fronte ideale", *Meridiano d'Italia,* September 18, 1949, op. cit. 2002b, 37-38, appendix.

41 Julius Evola, "Andare avanti sul fronte razzista", *La difesa della razza,* February 20, 1941, IV/8.

Semitism, according to Evola, was not *only* biologically and racially founded. It was primarily an instinct, an attitude, a vision of the world and life, a style, a way of being and thinking and a spiritual category. As such, it represented a total antithesis to the values of Tradition and Aryanism. Hebraism was a life-style that precisely corresponded to the "worst" and "most decadent" traits of the modern spirit, traits such as equality, democratism, sensuality and materialism. Moreover, it was synonymous with the "bourgeois element". However, during the 1930s Evola had no intention to undermine German racism based on the myth of blood. The latter was, yet without any scientific fundament, an "idée-force"[42] which was able to create action and in this function it had to be praised.

Evola had been concerned with Aryanism, with how to select a super-race capable of again dominating the world. His "spiritual" racism during the regime time was to be instrumental in bringing about a "process of racist selection"[43] that would enable a "purification"[44] of the Italian race. Leading this purified Italian race would be an imaginary Fascist Order of the Italian Empire *(Ordine Fascista dell'Impero Italiano),* politically and militarily modelled on Heinrich Himmler's SS.[45]

During the trial in 1951, and in three articles published at the end of that year[46] – the only ones dealing with racism in the postwar period –, Evola tried to minimise his intellectual role as ideologue of Italian Fascist racism. He declared in the court that his doctrine on racism during the regime had been based on the concept of "spiritual race", an interior reality, measured by taking into account qualities such as the dignity of the individual, character, manhood and sensibility to traditional values. It was a spiritual racism opposed to "the materialistic and vulgarly anti-Semitic racism"[47] that had been formulated in Germany. In other words, Evola tried to present his Italian spiritual racism as different and respectable, compared to the German biological one, and even as a theory that had a "subordinated and secondary"[48] role within the whole of his philosophy. His defence seemed convincing to the court who judged Evola in 1951, but recent studies have demonstrated the impact of Evola's theories on Italian culture and politics during the regime.[49] In

---

42 Ibid.

43 Ibid.

44 Ibid.

45 Julius Evola, *Sintesi di dottrina della razza* (Padua: Edizioni di Ar, 1994 [1941]), 144, 170-171.

46 Julius Evola, "Mussolini e il razzismo", *Meridiano d'Italia,* December 16, 1951, VI/49; idem., *I testi del Meridiano d'Italia* (Padova: Ar, 2002), 105-106; idem., "Il mito della nuova Italia", *Meridiano d'Italia,* December 23, 1951, VI/50, idem., op. cit., 107-108; idem., "Sangue e spirito", *Meridiano d'Italia,* December 30, 1951, VI/51, idem., op. cit., 109-111.

47 Julius Evola, "Autodifesa", idem., *Fascismo e Terzo Reich,* 171. The article "Autodifesa" was first published in *L'Eloquenza* 12, November-December 1951, which reproduced the speech Evola gave to the court.

48 Evola, "Autodifesa", 171.

49 On Julius Evola's racism, see Mauro Raspanti, "I razzismi del fascismo" in *La menzogna della razza. Documenti e immagini del razzismo e dell'antisemitismo fascista,* ed. Centro Studi F. Jesi (Bologna: Grafis, 1994), 73-89; Francesco Germinario, *Razza del sangue, razza dello spirito. Julius Evo-*

truth, his spiritual racism was not at all milder or even *better* than the German biological racism which inspired the *Manifesto* against the Jews in 1938, as the scholar Francesco Cassata points out in his remarkable work on the Italian philosopher.[50]

In the postwar period, the issue of race disappeared from Evola's writings. However, Evola's main intellectual concerns, based on anthropological pessimism, elitism and contempt for the weak, for men and women of lesser intellectual capacity, or lesser strength of character, for all representatives of modern society who believe in values such as democracy and equality, remained unchanged. The doctrine of the Aryan-Roman "super-race" was simply transformed into a doctrine of the "leaders of men" and the Fascist Order of the Italian Empire was simply relabelled the *Order* or "male society", with reference no longer to the SS, but to the medieval Teutonic Knights or the Knights Templar.

Once the unbroken men have been selected, they need to be organised as an elite. To Evola, the distinction between *party* and *movement* was important.[51] Those who belong to a party simply pursue a *programme* of practical and contingent social and economic objectives. On the other hand, those who belong to a movement have a *vision of life*, a *style*. Furthermore, a movement has "real leaders"[52] who are not necessarily party leaders or MPs. Evola was totally opposed to the Italian postwar political system, which he regarded as being one in which petty politicians were merely engaged in pursuing their own interests. Evola openly called for action to defend the country from communism, which he feared would bring about final national decadence. Although he considered communism to be a greater danger than Americanism, he believed that both ideologies threatened Western civilization. They shared a number of values: Conformism, democratic levelling, utilitarianism and the myth of production.

Evola denied that his words were intended to stir up revolt. During the 1951 trial, he stated that no-one could realistically believe that in postwar Italy, given the international situation, there existed the conditions for an anti-democratic revolution or a *coup d'état* inspired by traditional values.[53] Nonetheless, only a few months before he had stated that if the established authority was to face a crisis, the *Order* of real men should be in a position to counter the communist threat by gathering all the forces of the Right (the MSI, the monarchist and the liberal parties) in order

---

la, l'antisemitismo e il nazionalismo (1930-43) (Turin: Bollati Boringhieri, 2001); Rossi, *Il razzista totalitario.*

50 Francesco Cassata, "Il razzismo totalitario alla prova del fuoco", in idem., *A destra del fascismo. Profilo politico di Julius Evola* (Turin: Bollati Boringhieri, 2003), 226-270; idem., "Antisemitismo e cospirazionismo (1933-1943)", idem., op. cit., 271-320.

51 Evola, op. cit. 2000 [1950], 20; idem., "Partito e movimento", *Meridiano d'Italia*, January 7, 1951, op. cit. 2002b, 89-91; idem., "Uomini dei partiti e uomini dei movimenti", *la Rivolta Ideale*, April 19, 1953, op. cit. 2003, 92-93; idem., "Considerazioni antielettorali", *la Rivolta Ideale*, June 21-28, 1953, op. cit. 2003, 94-95.

52 Julius Evola, "Partito e movimento", *Meridiano d'Italia*, January 7, 1951, op. cit. 2002b, 90.

53 Evola, "Autodifesa", 168.

to take over the running of the country.[54] He had also stated that the communist forces in Italy were "well financed and well organised"[55] and therefore what mattered was "to set up selected, thoroughly trained and well directed teams, ready to take action precisely and straight away at the right moment".[56]

In the meanwhile, it was necessary that these organised elites were instilled with an idealistic motivation. To Evola and to the young neo-fascists, it was evident that fascism, as an idea independent of the historical contingency of the Italian Fascist regime and its military defeat, remained valid. In Evola's view, fascism contains four key concepts, or *idées-forces:* The concept of the Right, the idea of the Nation, the myth of Rome and the idea of the Corporation. Let us focus on the first two. From a purely ideological point of view, Evola identifies fascism with the Right. By the "Right" he does not mean capitalism, liberalism, bourgeois reaction or a conservatism based on class economic interests. Evola's idea of the Right is a conception of life and of the state that is inspired by the principles of Tradition. During his trial, Evola openly declared that he defended ideas such as monocracy, hierarchy and aristocracy/elitism not because they belonged to a Fascist doctrine elaborated during the regime, but because they belonged to a "previous and superior" European tradition. The Fascist regime may have borrowed these ideas, but it did not invent them. Evola informed the court that he was defending a traditional conception of the state that, at least until the French Revolution, was a universal one. He placed himself in the ranks of the great authors of the past who had written or acted in accordance with traditional principles: Aristotle, Plato in *The Republic,* Dante in *De Monarchia,* De Maistre, Donoso Cortés, Metternich and Bismarck. He insisted on labelling himself as an anti-democratic thinker, and firmly denied that he was a Fascist.[57]

His concept of Right is further connected to the idea of the Nation. In Evola's understanding, the Nation has nothing to do with the concept of homeland defined in terms of territory, ethnicity or language. Rather, it is a "qualitative and anti-democratic myth".[58] The "spiritual Nation"[59] is made up of all those who identify with the idea of the Right/fascism, who cherish the same view of life, who abide by the same inner rule. It consists of all those who believe in Tradition and belong to the same *Order.* Given that fascism promotes the concept of a spiritual nation, it attracts interest beyond limits of time and space.

---

54 "Arthos" [Evola], "Verso l' 'élite' di un fronte ideale", *Meridiano d'Italia,* September 18, 1949, op. cit. 2002b, appendix 4.

55 Ibid.

56 Ibid.

57 Evola, "Autodifesa", 172-174. See also Julius Evola, "Carta d'identità", *La Torre,* February 1, 1930, 1, now in idem., op. cit. 2001, 117-118; idem., "Il coraggio di dirsi antidemocratici non equivale necessariamente a dichiararsi fascisti", *la Rivolta Ideale,* January 17, 1952, op. cit. 2003, 56-58.

58 "Arthos" [Evola], "Doppio volto del nazionalismo", *Meridiano d'Italia,* November 13, 1949, op. cit. 2002b, 46.

59 Julius Evola "Idea e patria", *Meridiano d'Italia,* March 19, 1950, op. cit. 2002b, 65.

In analysing the genesis of the Italian Radical Right, the concepts of state and revolution also deserve our attention. Reinforcing the authority of the state is a major goal of Evola's political doctrine.[60] Evola rejected, as absolute "nonsense", the idea that an authoritarian state could be democratic. He advocated a pre-Enlightenment monarchic state, rooted in the aristocracy.[61] Moreover, Evola was convinced that the first task for the real state was to jettison all the "nonsense" associated with the French Revolution: Universal suffrage, parliaments, political parties, trade unions etc. The only acceptable form of representation was that based on orders or corps, genuine corporatism.[62] As far as the concept of revolution is concerned, Evola saw it as subversion and chaos, the overthrow of all order.[63] What is important is "restoration". According to Evola, fascism as a universal political phenomenon means restoring the values and principles of Tradition. To him, "reactionary" is a positive term. If fascism has to be considered revolutionary, it must be a revolution that has restoration as its goal, a revolution that first destroys all the forms and institutions of modernity, such as democracy, before re-establishing the aristocratic and hierarchic idea.[64]

This vision of fascism had important consequences for interpretations of the Fascist regime (Fascism) and Nazism. It also coloured Evola's (and the young neo-fascists') evaluation of the MSI in postwar Italy. In *Orientamenti,* during the trial in 1951, and later on in press articles, Evola criticised the Italian version of "historical fascism". The Fascist regime had been totalitarian, tending to centralise all power in a single individual's hands, rather than attempting to establish a hierarchical system within an organic state. Hierarchy had degenerated into hierarchism *(gerarchia versus gerarchismo).* For Evola, the fact that the state must hold absolute power does not mean that it is free to interfere with all aspects of life, as the Fascist state did.[65] He also criticised Fascism for its rhetorical nationalism, for the idea of the single party, a contradiction in itself, for its *petit-bourgeois* moralism, for its compromises with the Catholic Church, and for its Bonapartist and populist tendencies. Evola also opposed Giovanni Gentile's concept of the ethical state, as long this meant a paternalistic and demagogic one rather than a community where every individual is well aware of his role, duties and rights. He opposed demagogy and dictatorship, as well as many aspects of the Fascist corporations, which he viewed as unnecessary bureaucratic machines that kept class conflict alive. Evola's most critical remarks, however, were directed towards the Salò republic and Mussolini's late conversion to a sort of "national socialism", involving socialisation and worker participation in

60 Evola, op. cit. 2000 [1950], 29.

61 Julius Evola, "Il senso dell'imperium"; idem., "Impero e civiltà", *Imperium,* June 1950, I/2; idem., *Gli uomini e le rovine,* 71-80.

62 Evola, op. cit. 2000 [1950], 26-27.

63 "Arthos" [Evola], "Reazione e Rivoluzione", *la Rivolta Ideale,* October 20, 1949, op. cit. 2003, 32.

64 Evola, op. cit. 2002a, 61-69.

65 Evola, "Autodifesa", 174-176; Evola, op. cit. 2000 [1950], 27-29. See also "Ignitus" [Evola], "Il fascismo e Carnelutti", *Meridiano d'Italia,* March 9, 1952, op. cit. 2002b, 115-117.

management and profit-sharing. Evola dismissed this as a dangerous form of demagogic Marxism. It is true that he approved of the Fascists' intention to re-enforce the authority of the state, by affirming its supremacy over both the people and the nation. On the whole, however, Evola found Fascism insufficiently radical and absolute.

Evola's evaluation of Nazism is in line with his critique of Fascism. It was not only in his postwar writings that he expressed his misgivings; he also did so in articles written in the 1930s.[66] He was most critical of what he conceived as fundamental elements in the Nazi experience: Pan-Germanism, ethnic nationalism, irredentism, the idea of a "national socialism", biological racism, social Darwinism, Hitler's megalomania, and the myth of the *Volk* as superior to the state, the abolition of the Prussian state and *Junker* tradition, the proletarian features of labour policy. In his opinion, the Nazi regime, as well as Fascism, was characterised by a demagogic and populist dictatorship whose discourse on racial purity obscured other more noble goals such as the construction of a new Europe, based on principles of order and hierarchy.

As far as the Italian neo-fascist party founded in 1946 is concerned, Evola asked whether the MSI could be regarded as the legitimate representative of Italian Fascism, and whether this party had the power and the will to attract all of the forces that were "truly right-wing, that is, forces of order, authority, reconstruction, and tradition".[67] He recognised that the MSI had the intention of preserving the positive Fascist legacy; however, he doubted whether it could truly represent the Right. In fact, he claimed that a true Right did not exist in Italy. In Evola's opinion, the MSI was too democratic. It was too keen to respect the rules of democracy, just as Fascism had been too liberal. Evola had little sympathy for the party's left-wing representatives, nor for the republican formulae of "social nationalism", "national socialism" or even "corporative democracy", concepts that were extensively discussed in postwar neo-fascist circles.[68] He argued that they actually distanced Italian neo-fascism from the Right and brought it nearer to crypto-Marxism.[69]

In an article published only a few months before he was arrested in 1951, Evola exhorted the MSI to be more intransigent and to move to "action".[70] What kind of action? Violent, extra-parliamentary political action against the system? Evola did not go into detail. However, he acknowledged that adopting an uncompromising ideological stance would expose the MSI to two dangers. On the one hand, there

66 See Julius Evola, "Note sul Terzo Reich", in idem., op. cit. 2001, 179-229; idem., "Osservazioni critiche sul razzismo nazional-socialista", *La Vita italiana*, November 1933, now in idem., op. cit. 2001, 233-237; idem., "Sulle differenze fra la concezione fascista e nazista dello Stato", *Lo Stato*, April 1941, now in idem., op. cit. 2001, 247-254.

67 "Arthos" [Evola], "Questa inesistente Destra", *la Rivolta Ideale*, November 17, 1949, op. cit. 2003, 36.

68 Cassina Wolff, op. cit., 139-184.

69 "Arthos" [Evola], "Questa inesistente Destra", *la Rivolta Ideale*, November 17, 1949, op. cit. 2003, 36.

70 Julius Evola, "Partito e movimento", *Meridiano d'Italia*, January 7, 1951, op. cit. 2002b, 90.

would be the danger from within, the risk that factions would break away. On the other, there would be the external danger of being banned by the constitutional and democratic parties. Consequently, the best strategy was to wait. One month before his arrest, Evola published an article entitled "For a Charter of Youth". This text, which listed the cardinal points of a (neo-fascist) doctrine that should and could inspire the young, became a political and ideological manifesto for the neo-fascists of the 1950s.[71] Evola exhorted the young to rise, to be reborn internally, to organise themselves in an order. He urged them to "have character" and fight in order to realise the (neo-fascist) Idea. He insisted that the party system and quantitative democratic representation had to be rejected. He concluded that the political strategy of the New Right had to focus on the establishment of a spiritual and national movement to train future cadres for the country's ruling class. He also mentioned Europeanism, which was understood as support for setting up a bloc of European national states within which Italy might play a role as a Latin and Roman nation. That entailed withdrawing plans for a federal parliament and backing the development of a hierarchical system in Europe – based on the values of Tradition, on the idea of fascism/the Right – where each state was supposed to contribute according to its own competences and individuality.

The Outcome of the FAR Trial

Of the 36 accused at the FAR trial, 23 were released, while 13 were sentenced to a few months imprisonment for having re-established the dissolved Fascist Party (Black Legion) and for praising Fascism. Evola was acquitted of all charges, as were the young neo-fascists of *Imperium*.[72] As far as the accusation of the re-constitution of a Fascist Party was concerned, Evola's stance was interpreted as a personal position in favour of "an ethical, heroic and spiritual attitude".[73] His references to a legionary attitude were given a spiritual interpretation and not understood as indirect incitements to rebellion or violence. Enzo Erra, editor of *Imperium,* was accused of being the principle proponent of the intransigent anti-democratic faction of the MSI. However, because he was one of Evola's most fervent disciples, he was also released, it being argued that his engagement was confined to the philosophical sphere.[74] Moreover, Evola was absolved of the charge of praising Fascism. The judges did not consider that the anti-democratic ideas expressed by Evola – monocracy, hierarchy and aristocracy – were necessarily Fascist. They agreed with Evola that although the regime adopted such ideas and often referred to them, they belonged to older currents of thought. The distinction between the ideology of the Italian regime (Fascism) and the universal, anti-democratic philosophy of fascism as a generic concept was not seriously discussed at the trial.

71 Evola, "Per una Carta della Gioventù".
72 Iacona, op. cit., 144.
73 Evola, "Autodifesa", 168.
74 Iacona, op. cit., 148.

In fact, Evola's position was only normative and included a harsh critique of the Fascist regime. Nonetheless, it is difficult to say that he did not praise fascism. Consequently, the result of the trial was an absolution of both Fascism and the anti-democratic tradition. To explain the outcome of the trial and the tolerance towards both Evola and the volunteers of Salò, we have to consider the climate in Italy at the beginning of the 1950s. The "purge" of Fascists in postwar Italy had been much less thorough than had been the case in other European countries, and the state machinery, including the judiciary, had remained more or less untouched since the time of the regime.[75]

The Consolidation of the Italian Radical Right

Evola declared at the trial that his relationship with the young neo-fascists was a solely intellectual one; they had shared political and ethical doctrines, as well as a spiritual vision of life inspired by traditional values. He added that he was impressed by their insistence that any political action had to be preceded by internal spiritual revolution.[76]

In fact, Evola's influence was both intellectual and political. We first see this in the appearance of a number of popular journals published during the 1950s; these were either edited by his disciples or clearly inspired by Evola's traditionalist philosophy. As far as his political influence is concerned, the young neo-fascists, organised as an independent group within the MSI, emerged as significant political actors. In 1952, the "leftist" faction of the party was considerably weakened, while members of the youthful faction on the Right (Enzo Erra, Pino Rauti, Primo Siena, Enzo Vitale) climbed the party hierarchy.

By that time, Erra, in line with Evola, recognised the contrast between (his group's) anti-democratic neo-fascist theory and the MSI's formal, democratic organisational structure:

> Nowadays we feel, however, that within the Movement we vote too much, and too often. Above all, we are afraid that now we have acquired a taste for voting and for being elected.[77]

However, Erra shared Evola's conclusion that such a conflict between theory and practice was inevitable, primarily because there was no qualified and select minority

---

75 The "purge" of Fascists was stated by the decree of December 28, 1943, and by the Royal Lieutenant's decree no. 159 of July 27, 1944, under the Badoglio government of national unity. For details, see Giuseppe Parlato, *Fascisti senza Mussolini. Le origini del neofascismo in Italia, 1943-1948* (Bologna: Il Mulino, 2006), 193-210; Mimmo Franzinelli, *L'amnistia Togliatti. 22 giugno 1946, colpo di spugna sui crimini fascisti* (Milan: Oscar Mondatori, 2006); Claudio Pavone, *Alle origini della Repubblica. Scritti su fascismo, antifascismo e continuità dello Stato* (Turin: Bollati Boringhieri, 1995), 123-159.

76 Evola, "Autodifesa", 167.

77 Enzo Erra, "Bloccare la democrazia", *Asso di bastoni*, January 20, 1952, V/3.

able to direct the party from above. He stated that internal party democracy was a necessary stopgap solution, since a qualified and selected minority capable of leading the party was not yet available.[78]

The MSI did well in the 1953 elections, winning 5.8 per cent of the vote for the Chamber of Deputies and returning 29 deputies and 9 senators. However, the overall result was disappointing. In 1956, the centrist faction finally gained control of all the party's organs, and of its group in parliament. On the right, Pino Rauti left the party to form the New Order movement (*Ordine Nuovo,* ON), taking with him the radical Evolian group. Two years earlier, he had founded the New Order Study Centre *(Centro Studi Ordine Nuovo)* with the aim of diffusing the ideas of the right-wing youth faction through lectures and other cultural events. Both the movement and the popular journal *Ordine Nuovo* (New Order, 1955-1965) were expressions of an internal opposition that set young neo-fascists against the moderate party leadership. From this time, it is important to make a clear distinction between the MSI and those movements which abandoned the party in order to carry out revolutionary acts, sometimes violent ones, against the democratic system. The Italian scholar Piero Ignazi states that the term "Radical Right" is an appropriate label for these illegal extremist neo-fascist (and terrorist) groups.[79]

The ON movement kept a distance from the MSI until 1969, when Rauti decided to re-join the party. In the meanwhile, it maintained relations with European neo-Nazism and with the Italian secret services.[80] ON was among those "historic groups" of the extra-parliamentary Italian Radical Right that represented the *trait d'union* between the right-wing neo-fascism of the 1940s and the right-wing terrorism of the 1980s.[81] ON, which boasted a national membership of about 10,000[82] was most concerned with ideological-doctrinal discussions, dissemination of radical right doctrine and research. It published theoretical journals such as *Ordine Nuovo,* and bulletins such as *Noi Europa, periodico per l'ordine nuovo* (We Europe, Bulletin for the New Order, 1966-1968) and *Civiltà* (Civilization, 1973-75), while other groups engaged in violent actions in the streets. In the case of the ON, Evola's philosophy played a central role. This was confirmed by one of its leaders: "Our work since 1953 has been to transpose Evola's teaching into direct political action."[83]

---

78 Ibid.

79 Piero Ignazi, "La cultura politica del Movimento Sociale Italiano", *Rivista Italiana di Scienza Politica* XIX/3 (1989), 431-465; idem., "The Changing Profile of the Italian Social Movement", in *Encounters with the Contemporary Radical Right,* eds. Peter H. Merkl and Leonid Weinberg (Boulder, CO: Westview Press, 1993), 75-93.

80 Franco Ferraresi, "The Radical Right in Post-war Italy", *Politics and Society* 1/16 (1988), 71-119. See also Franco Ferraresi, "La destra eversiva", in *La destra radicale,* eds. Franco Ferraresi and Marco Revelli (Milan: Feltrinelli, 1984), 62-71.

81 Franco Ferraresi, "Julius Evola: tradition, reaction, and the radical right", *European Journal of Sociology* 28 (1987), 135.

82 Ferraresi, op. cit. (1988), 81.

83 Clemente Graziani, *Processo a Ordine Nuovo, processo alle idée* (Rome: Edizioni di ON, 1973), 27, 30, as referred to by Franco Ferraresi, op. cit. (1988), 84.

From the mid-1960s to the mid-1970s the Italian Radical Right was linked to the so called "strategy of tension". The *Piano Solo* plot of 1964, the bomb explosion in Milan's Piazza Fontana in December 1969, Junio Valerio Borghese's 1970 coup attempt, the 1974 Brescia bombings and the 1974 massacre on the Munich-Rome Italicus train were all important parts of this strategy. The aim was to force the Italian state to take more authoritarian measures. These actions showed striking similarities to Evola's calls for action, especially the several failed *coups d'état,* in which the neo-fascists belonging to ON had a prominent role.

During the 1980s, the Italian Radical Right abandoned terrorist violence, but maintained its organisational and cultural profile. We find examples of this in the activities of such organisations as the secret Masonic lodge P2 *(Propaganda 2)* and the New Right *(Nuova Destra).* The latter was, and still is, more of a cultural movement than a political one and Evola's ideological influence is present, but no longer so dominant. The New Right, which identified with the French *Nouvelle Droite* and with the German Conservative Revolution (Jünger, Spengler, Schmitt, von Salomon), revised Evola's anti-Fascism and anti-Nazism. While presenting fascism as a third way between capitalism and communism, the New Right stressed that the longing for a "third way" originated in the Conservative Revolution during the Weimar Republic. It was from here that a philosopher like Evola, not easily impressed by official Fascist or Nazi propaganda, took his inspiration.

Conclusion

At the end of the 1950s Evola abandoned any political engagement. He no longer believed that political action could rescue Italy – and the Western world – from atrophy and degeneration. Italy was experiencing an "economic miracle" and showed all the traits of a society in decline, one in which materialistic values and consumerism prevailed over traditional ones.[84] He concluded that the Right was incapable of reversing such a degenerative process. Evola's work from 1961, *Cavalcare la tigre* (Ride the Tiger)[85], shows a subjective interiority and an existential detachment from the world.

However, for at least two generations of Radical Right militants, he remained a cult figure, *the* ideologue, *the* sage and *the* guru, as he had been *il maestro* for the young Italian neo-fascists. The concepts that were to be found in his 1953 book, *Gli uomini e le rovine,* had a central place in the universe of the Radical Right: Tradition, unbroken men, legionary spirit, aristocracy, hierarchy, élite rule, political warriors, holy war. Giulio Salierno's autobiography has a chapter dealing with the 1950s in Rome, where he was a young MSI militant. Here he describes the fascination that Evola exerted on him and his friends; the chapter is entitled "Il maestro".[86] Salierno spent fifteen years in prison, from 1953 to 1968, after having

84 Ferraresi, op. cit. (1987), 131.

85 Julius Evola, *Cavalcare la tigre* (Milan: Scheiwiller, 1961).

86 Giulio Salierno, "Il maestro", in idem., *Autobiografia di un picchiatore fascista* (Turin: Einaudi, 1976), 136-146.

committed a murder. He had intended to kill the partisan and communist Walter Audisio, who had ordered the execution of Mussolini in 1945. However, this plan ended with a banal, non-political act of violence for which he was convicted. "Violence is the only possible and reasonable solution", Evola once said.[87] This cynical remark, together with the development of the Italian Radical Right, make it difficult to swallow any claim that Evola's teachings were merely influential on a metapolitical level.

Bibliography

Baillet, Philippe. "I rapporti di Evola con il fascismo e il nazionalsocialismo. Una proposta di lettura". *Futuro Presente* 6 (1995), 133-147.

Bernardi Guardi, Mario and Marco Rossi. *Delle rovine e oltre. Saggi su Julius Evola.* Rome: Antonio Pellicani Editore, 1995.

Biondi, Marino and Alessandro Borsotti, eds. *Cultura e fascismo. Letteratura arti espettacolo di un ventennio.* Florence: Ponte alle Grazie, 1996.

Carioti, Antonio. *Gli orfani di Salò. Il "Sessantotto nero" dei giovani neofascisti nel dopoguerra. 1945-1951.* Milan: Mursia, 2008.

Cassata, Francesco. *A destra del fascismo. Profilo politico di Julius Evola.* Turin: Bollati Boringhieri, 2003.

Cassata, Francesco. *La difesa della razza. Politica, ideologia e immagine del razzismo fascista.* Turin: Giulio Einaudi Editore, 2008.

Chiantera-Stutte, Patricia. *Julius Evola. Dal Dadaismo alla rivoluzione conservatrice (1919-1940).* Rome: Aracne, 2002.

de Turris, Gianfranco and Bruno Zoratto, eds. *Julius Evola nei rapporti con le SS.* Rome: Fondazione Julius Evola, 2000.

de Turris, Gianfranco. *Elogio e difesa di Julius Evola. Il Barone e i terroristi.* Roma: Edizioni Mediterranee, 1997.

de Turris, Gianfranco. *Testimonianze su Evola.* Roma: Edizioni Mediterranee, 1973.

Del Ponte, Renato. "Gli orizzonti europei del tradizionalismo nel *Diorama filosofico* (1934-1943)". In *Delle rovine e oltre. Saggi su Julius Evola,* edited by Bernardi Guardi, Mario and Marco Rossi, 167-197. Rome: Pellicani, 1995.

Del Ponte, Renato. "Julius Evola: una bibliografia 1920-1994". *Futuro Presente* 6 (1995), 27-70.

Evola, Julius. *Rivolta contro il mondo moderno.* Rome: Edizioni Mediterranee, 1998 [1934].

Evola, Julius. *Tre aspetti del problema ebraico: nel mondo spirituale, nel mondo culturale, nel mondo economico sociale.* Rome: Edizioni Mediterranee, 1936.

Evola, Julius. *Il mito del sangue.* Milan: Hoepli, 1937.

Evola, Julius. *Sintesi di dottrina della razza.* Milan: Hoepli, 1941.

Evola, Julius. *Sintesi di dottrina della razza.* Padua: Edizioni di Ar, 1994 [1941].

Evola, Julius. *Orientamenti.* Padova: Ar, 2000 [1950].

Evola, Julius. *Gli uomini e le rovine e Orientamenti.* Rome: Edizioni Mediterranee, 2002 [1953].

Evola, Julius. *I testi de la Rivolta Ideale.* Padova: Ar, 2003.

87 Ibid., 143.

Evola, Julius. *I testi del Meridiano d'Italia.* Padova: Ar, 2002.

Evola, Julius. *Fascismo e Terzo reich.* Rome: Edizioni Mediterranee, 2001 (Original edition: *Il fascismo. Saggio di un'analisi critica dal punto di vista della Destra.* Rome: Volpe, 1964).

Evola, Julius. *Cavalcare la tigre.* Milan: Scheiwiller, 1961.

Ferraresi, Franco and Marco Revelli, eds. *La destra radicale.* Milan: Feltrinelli, 1984.

Ferraresi, Franco. "Julius Evola: tradition, reaction, and the radical right". *European Journal of Sociology* 28 (1987), 107-151.

Ferraresi, Franco. "The Radical Right in Post-war Italy". *Politics and Society* 16/1 (1988), 71-119.

Ferraresi, Franco. *Minacce alla democrazia: la destra radicale e la strategia della tensione in Italia nel dopoguerra.* Milan: Feltrinelli, 1995.

Franzinelli, Mimmo. *L'amnistia Togliatti. 22 giugno 1946, colpo di spugna sui crimini fascisti.* Milan: Oscar Mondatori, 2006.

Galli, Giorgio. *La crisi italiana e la Destra internazionale.* Milan: Mondadori, 1974.

Galli, Giorgio. *La Destra in Italia.* Milan: Gammalibri, 1983.

Germinario, Francesco. "Evola, Giulio Cesare". In *Dizionario del fascismo*, vol. 1: A-K, edited by Sergio Luzzatto and Victoria de Grazia, 497-498. Turin: Einaudi, 2002.

Germinario, Francesco. *Razza del sangue, razza dello spirito. Julius Evola, l'antisemitismo e il nazionalismo (1930-43).* Turin: Bollati Boringhieri, 2001.

Graziani, Clemente. *Processo a Ordine Nuovo, processo alle idée.* Rome: Edizioni di ON, 1973.

Hansen, H. T. "Julius Evola e la Rivoluzione Conservatrice tedesca". *Studi Evoliani* 1 (1998), 144-188.

Iacona, Marco. "Julius Evola e le vicende processuali legate ai FAR (1951-1954)". *Nuova Storia Contemporanea* 3 (2009), 129-152.

Ignazi, Piero. "La cultura politica del Movimento Sociale Italiano". *Rivista Italiana di Scienza Politica* XIX/3 (1989), 431-465.

Ignazi, Piero. "The Changing Profile of the Italian Social Movement". In *Encounters with the Contemporary Radical Right*, edited by Peter H. Merkl and Leonid Weinberg, 75-93. Boulder, CO: Westview Press, 1993,

Jesi, Furio. *Cultura di destra.* Milan: Garzanti, 1979.

Lo Bianco, Luca. "Evola, Giulio Cesare Andrea". In *Dizionario biografico degli italiani*, 575-581. Rome: Istituto della Enciclopedia Italiana Treccani, 1993.

Mohler, Armin. *Die Konservative Revolution in Deutschland 1918-1932.* Stuttgart: Chr. Belser, 1950.

Parlato, Giuseppe. *Fascisti senza Mussolini. Le origini del neofascismo in Italia, 1943-1948.* Bologna: Il Mulino, 2006.

Pavone, Claudio. *Alle origini della Repubblica. Scritti su fascismo, antifascismo e continuità dello Stato.* Turin: Bollati Boringhieri, 1995.

Rao, Nicola. *Neofascisti! La Destra italiana da Salò a Fiuggi nel ricordo dei protagonisti.* Rome: Settimo Sigillo, 1999.

Raspanti, Mauro. "I razzismi del fascismo". In *La menzogna della razza. Documenti e immagini del razzismo e dell'antisemitismo fascista*, edited by Centro Studi F. Jesi, 73-89. Bologna: Grafis, 1994.

Rauti, Pino. *Le idee che mossero il mondo.* Rome: Edizioni Europa, 1976.

Romualdi, Adriano. *Julius Evola: l'uomo e l'opera.* Roma: Giovanni Volpe Editore, 1968.

Rossi, Gianni Scipione. *Il razzista totalitario. Evola e la leggenda dell'antisemitismo spirituale.* Soveria Mannelli: Rubettino, 2007.

Rossi, Marco. "L'avanguardia che si fa tradizione: l'itinerario culturale di Julius Evola dal primo dopoguerra alla metà degli anni Trenta". *Storia contemporanea* 6/XXII (1991), 1039-1090.

Salierno, Giulio. *Autobiografia di un picchiatore fascista.* Turin: Einaudi, 1976.

Siena, Primo. "Genesi di un documento evoliano". In *Idee per una Destra,* edited by Alessandro Barbera, 61-64. Rome: Fondazione Julius Evola, 1997.

Tarchi, Marco. "Julius Evola e il fascismo. Note su un percorso non ordinario". In *Cultura e fascismo. Letteratura arti e spettacolo di un ventennio,* edited by Marino Biondi and Alessandro Borsotti, 123-142. Florence: Ponte alle Grazie, 1996.

Veneziani, Marcello. *Julius Evola tra filosofia e tradizione.* Rome: Ciarrapico, 1984.

Veneziani, Marcello. *La rivoluzione conservatrice in Italia. Genesi e sviluppo della 'ideologia italiana' fino ai nostri giorni.* Carnago: SugarCo, 1994.

Wolff, Elisabetta Cassina. "Biological Racism and Anti-Semitism as Intellectual Contructions in Italian Fascism. The Case of Telesio Interlandi and *La difesa della razza*". In *Racial Science in Hitler's "New Europe", 1938-1945,* edited by Anton Weiss-Wendt and Rory Yeomans. Lincoln: University of Nebraska Press, forthcoming 2013.

Wolff, Elisabetta Cassina. "Starting from the End. Fascist Ideology in Post-War Italy (1945-1953)". PhD diss., University of Oslo, 2008. Publication in Italian: *L'inchiostro dei vinti. Stampa e ideologia neofascista (1945-1953).* Milan: Mursia, 2012.

Continuities within Germany's "National Opposition"
From the Deutsche Reichspartei to the Nationaldemokratische Partei Deutschlands, 1949-2010*

Gideon Botsch

Introduction

Looking at the extreme right in Germany from a historical perspective, we see a picture of apparent discontinuity and cyclical developments:[1] Phases of unprecedented popular success and dramatic "chains of events"[2] alternate with the rapid decline and extensive disintegration of extreme right-wing organisations and networks. Hitherto, in terms of organisation and members, the radical nationalist camp has not been able to become firmly established within the political culture of the German Federal Republic. Partly for this reason, contemporary history has all but abandoned research into the issue of continuity and the development of the extreme right with regard to aspects of historical heredity. General accounts of the emergence and development of the extreme right or radical nationalism in the Federal Republic are mostly written on the premise of a historical cut-off point in 1989-90.[3]

---

* A German version of this essay has been published as "Parteipolitische Kontinuitäten der 'Nationalen Opposition'. Von der Deutschen Reichspartei zur Nationaldemokratischen Partei Deutschlands", *Zeitschrift für Geschichtswissenschaft* 59 (2011), 113-137.

1 See, e.g., Richard Stöss, *Rechtsextremismus im Wandel* (Berlin: Friedrich Ebert Foundation, 2007); Armin Pfahl-Traughber, *Rechtsextremismus in der Bundesrepublik* (Munich: C.H. Beck, 2000); Gideon Botsch, *Die extreme Rechte in der Bundesrepublik. 1949 bis heute* (Darmstadt: Wissenschaftliche Buchgesellschaft, 2012).

2 See Peter Dudek and Hans-Gerd Jaschke, *Entstehung und Entwicklung des Rechtsextremismus in der Bundesrepublik. Zur Tradition einer besonderen politischen Kultur*, vol. 1 & 2 (Opladen: Westdeutscher Verlag, 1984), here vol. 1, 177f; see also 30ff., 172ff.

3 See among others, Lutz Niethammer, "Nach dem Dritten Reich ein neuer Faschismus? Zum Wandel der rechtsextremen Szene in der Geschichte der Bundesrepublik", in *Die verkannte Gefahr. Rechtsradikalismus in der Bundesrepublik*, ed. Paul Lersch (Reinbek: Rowohlt, 1981), 105-127; Dudek and Jaschke, *Entstehung und Entwicklung;* Richard Stöss, *Die extreme Rechte in der Bundesrepublik. Entwicklung – Ursachen – Gegenmaßnahmen* (Opladen: Verlag für Sozialwissenschaften, 1989); Thomas Assheuer and Hans Sarkowicz, *Rechtsradikale in Deutschland. Die alte und die neue Rechte* (Munich: C.H. Beck, 1990), cited here from the current edition of 1992; Uwe Backes and Eckard Jesse, *Politischer Extremismus in der Bundesrepublik Deutschland*, vol. 2: *Analyse* (Cologne: Wissenschaft und Politik, 1989), 44-96; Detlev Peukert and Frank Bajohr, *Rechtsradikalismus in Deutschland. Zwei historische Beiträge* (Hamburg: Ergebnisse Verlag, 1990). For an internal perspective, see Holger Apfel, "Die Geschichte der Nationaldemokratischen Partei Deutschlands (NPD)", in *Alles Große steht im Sturm. Tradition und Zukunft einer nationalen Partei. 35 Jahre NPD – 30 Jahre JN*, ed. Holger Apfel (Stuttgart: Deutsche Stimme Verlag, 1999), 34-59.

Any interest in the historical progression of the extreme right and hence in the question of continuity and discontinuity is even explicitly denied. Richard Stöss, for example, stresses that

> when we deal with the development of the NPD today, we do so primarily not from the standpoint of contemporary history [...]. The fundamental facts are well known and have been set out at length in the literature.[4]

The tendency to assume the continued validity of past findings has caused a core of extreme right-wing organisations and members to be overlooked. They have provided a degree of continuity and stability beneath the surface of discontinuity described above. In the 1980s and early 1990s, the republic's oldest extreme right-wing party, the National Democratic Party of Germany (*Nationaldemokratische Partei Deutschlands,* NPD) appeared, as well as its predecessor, the German Reich Party (*Deutsche Reichspartei,* DRP), to be a failed political option, leading a sect-like existence not only in relation to the nationwide political scene, but also to the narrower world of the extreme right, the future of which was generally assumed to be one of organisational stagnation.[5]

In metaphorical terms, the historical path, which the NPD took, seemed to break down from 1970 into a number of minor byways and tracks, several of which came to nothing. In 1990, all the evidence seemed to support this. Today, more than twenty years later, it appears a section of the path was overlooked. A surprising picture emerges of a narrow central path that continued even during this stage of disintegration and which some of the byways mentioned above ultimately joined.

With reference to research literature, we will now attempt to trace the party-political continuities within the "national opposition" in Germany, which endured below the surface of discontinuity. Our focus will be the NPD and its historical forerunners.

By describing itself as "national opposition", the "discrete political culture" of the radical right distanced itself from mainstream society. Being fundamentally oppositional, radically nationalist and professing no loyalty to the system, the extreme right wing parties should be seen as distinct from those nationalist, conservative and right-wing forces which have opened up to the political system of the Federal Republic and become democratised in the mid-term. In this respect, the source term "national opposition" is of particular relevance for contemporary history and the analysis and investigation of the extreme right.

The term "national opposition" goes back further than the National Socialist era to the radical nationalism of the Wilhelmine Empire, which began to gain ground

4 Richard Stöss, "Die NPD – Erfolgsbedingungen einer Rechtsextremen Partei", *Jahrbuch für Antisemitismusforschung* 14 (2005), 41-59, citation here, 41.

5 See, e.g., Armin Pfahl-Traughber, *Rechtsextremismus. Eine kritische Bestandsaufnahme nach der Wiedervereingung* (Bonn: Bouvier, 1993), 74f.

in the 1890s. From 1919, "national opposition" became the catchword and motto of the broad anti-republican network with which the NSDAP is also associated.

"The National Right" – Attempts to Amalgamate in the 1940s

The direct predecessor parties of the German Reich Party sprang from a drive to harness those radical nationalist tendencies, which had been partly suppressed or subdued under National Socialism.[6] The German Conservative Party (*Deutsche Konservativen Partei*, DKP) was set up as an attempt to revive the party apparatus of the old German National People's Party (*Deutschnationale Volkspartei*, DNVP) in northern and north-western Germany. The German Reconstruction Party (*Deutsche Aufbaupartei*, DAP) was set up by former members of the German *Völkisch* Freedom Party (*Deutschvölkische Freiheitspartei*, DVFP)[7], an off-shoot of the DNVP. The DKP and the DAP remained confined to the British sector and subjected to considerable restrictions enforced by the local licensing practice. In March 1946 a fusion took place. The third element which ultimately went to make up the DRP, the National Democratic Party (*Nationaldemokratische Partei*, NDP), was a direct continuation of the DNVP-sympathetic Hessian Farmers' Association (*Hessischer Bauernbund*, later to become the *Hessischer Landbund*) in Upper Hesse. The cooperation between the DKP-DRP and the NDP began in June 1948, when the two parties formed the Association of the National Right *(Arbeitsgemeinschaft Nationale Rechte)*.

Initially, the DKP-DRP and NDP attempted to distance themselves from National Socialism, and to represent the continuation of authoritarian, traditionalist and conservative lines of development. Corporatist and monarchist influences played a part in this, to varying degrees. The parties' basic economic and socio-political orientation partly corresponded with that of the traditional Protestant elites and partly with that of the rural, agricultural and urban, merchant middle classes. In the process of gathering and consolidating these forces, they were joined by an additional element: The remaining die-hard National Socialists. These were mostly relatively young and frequently in socially unstable circumstances, coming

6 On the following, see Manfred Jenke, *Verschwörung von rechts? Ein Bericht über den Rechtsradikalismus in Deutschland nach 1945* (Berlin: Colloquium Verlag, 1961), 55ff.; Kurt P. Tauber, *Beyond Eagle and Swastika. German Nationalism since 1945*, 2 vols. (Middletown, CO: Wesleyan University Press, 1967), here: vol. 1, 47ff., 727ff; Horst W. Schmollinger, "Die Deutsche Konservative Partei – Deutsche Rechtspartei", in *Parteien-Handbuch. Die Parteien der Bundesrepublik Deutschland 1945-1980*, ed. Richard Stöss (Opladen: Westdeutscher Verlag, 1983), cited here from the special edition in vol. 4 (Opladen: Westdeutscher Verlag, 1986), 982-1024; Richard Stöss, "Die Nationaldemokratische Partei", in ibid., 1892-1921; Dudek and Jaschke, *Entstehung und Entwicklung*, vol. 1, 182ff.; Stöss, *Die extreme Rechte*, 102ff.; Backes and Jesse, *Politischer Extremismus*, 49ff; Oliver Sowinski, *Die Deutsche Reichspartei 1950-1965. Organisation und Ideologie einer rechtsradikalen Partei* (Frankfurt a.M. et al.: Peter Lang, 1998), 23ff. For an internal perspective see, Adolf von Thadden, "Die Entwicklung der Nationalen Rechten nach 1945", in *Kongress-Protokoll 1989. Das Ende der Nachkriegszeit*, ed. Gesellschaft für freie Publizistik e.V. (Berg: Gesellschaft für freie Publizistik e.V., 1990), 43-69.

7 On the DVFP, see Stefanie Schrader's contribution to this anthology.

from the lower social classes or, more often, having become disenfranchised with the end of the war, whether as displaced persons, ex-prisoners of war or former functionaries in National Socialist organisations and institutions.[8] They were fiercely critical of the "socially reactionary" line of the veteran German nationalist party elite. In Lower Saxony the Association of Independent Germans (*Gemeinschaft unabhängiger Deutscher,* GuD) around Fritz Dorls, Franz Richter (alias Fritz Rößler), Otto-Ernst Remer and Gerhard Krüger joined the local German Right Party *(Deutsche Rechtspartei).* In Hesse, the NDP was joined by the equally Nazi-oriented circle around Karl-Heinz Priester in Wiesbaden. In the light of spectacular election results for the NDP in April 1948 in Wiesbaden in Hesse (24.4 per cent; 3.4 per cent in all of Hesse) and for the German Right Party in November in the district of Gifhorn in Lower Saxony (30.7 per cent; in Wolfsburg nearly 70 per cent;[9] in all of Lower Saxony 3.8 per cent), which were all credited to the neo-Nazi wing, these forces began to demand greater representation. Hence the DKP-DRP and the NDP initially maintained their stance of remaining open to the Nazi-oriented wing despite considerable internal tension. It was not until after the general election that they disassociated themselves from the die-hard National Socialists. The DKP-DRP expelled the most prominent GuD activists who went on to form the openly neo-Nazi Socialist Reich Party (*Sozialistische Reichspartei,* SRP) in October 1949.[10] A short time later, the group around Karl-Heinz Priester left the NDP of its own accord, first joining the SRP but eventually going separate ways.[11]

On account of its strong regional base in Lower Saxony, the DKP-DRP managed to gain five seats in the first Federal German parliament. Heinrich Leuchtgens, the leading figure in the NDP, was voted into parliament as a candidate for the Free Democratic Party (*Freie Demokratische Partei,* FDP) in Hesse but then went over to those members of parliament making up the "National Right" as had been previously arranged.[12] This group was too small to survive as a parliamentary faction, however, and soon disintegrated. The "National Right" had failed on the parliamentary level.

---

8 See Horst W. Schmollinger, "Die Sozialistische Reichspartei", in *Parteien-Handbuch,* ed. Stöss, 2326ff.; Werner Kaltefleiter, *Wirtschaft und Politik in Deutschland. Konjunktur als Bestimmungsfaktor des Parteiensystems* (Cologne/Opladen: Westdeutscher Verlag, 1966), 131ff.

9 On Wolfsburg, see Jenke, *Verschwörung,* 58ff.; Schmollinger, "DKP-DRP", 1014; Dudek and Jaschke, *Entstehung und Entwicklung,* 191ff.

10 See Otto Büsch and Peter Furth, *Rechtsradikalismus im Nachkriegsdeutschland. Studien über die "Sozialistische Reichspartei" (SRP)* (Berlin/Frankfurt a.M: F. Vahlen, 1957); Jenke, *Verschwörung,* 73ff.; Tauber, *Beyond Eagle,* 689ff.; Schmollinger, "SRP"; Dudek and Jaschke, *Entstehung und Entwicklung,* 64ff.; Norbert Frei, *Vergangenheitspolitik. Die Anfänge der Bundesrepublik und die NS-Vergangenheit* (Munich: dtv, 1999), 326ff.; Henning Hansen, *Die Sozialistische Reichspartei (SRP). Aufstieg und Scheitern einer rechtsextremen Partei* (Düsseldorf: Droste Verlag, 2007).

11 See Hans Frederik, *Die Rechtsradikalen* (Munich: Inning, undated [1964]), 69ff.; Tauber, *Beyond Eagle,* passim.

12 Members of the group were: Fritz Dorls (later SRP), Heinz Frommold, Heinrich Leuchtgens (later DP), Herwarth Miessner (later FDP), Franz Richter alias Fritz Rößler (later SRP), Adolf von Thadden.

The typical centrifugal forces, which in later years regularly stretched parties of the national opposition to breaking point, despite their limited number of members, were already apparent in this period. These forces pulled the national opposition in two directions: The fundamentalist element caused one wing of each party to capitulate and withdraw in resignation or seek other forms of political participation. They gradually became assimilated to the system of parliamentary democracy. Meanwhile, a radical wing, which was mostly oriented toward historical National Socialism, pushed for greater radicalisation. This had a negative impact on the strategy of maintaining legality and inevitably led to the exclusion and departure of members in the mid-term. Generally, it was those who were particularly open to mobilisation that dropped out. When these centrifugal forces caused the breakdown of the planned "nationalist alliance", in the winter of 1949-50 the DKP-DRP was left in the precarious situation of either "leading a marginal existence in the bourgeois spectrum of the party system or a fringe existence in the heterogeneous camp of the 'national opposition'".[13]

The German Reich Party

While the more moderate nationalists turned toward the *Bürgerblock*, the conservative-liberal alliance of Chancellor Konrad Adenauer,[14] and a neo-Nazi party was constituted, the remaining amalgamation-oriented forces within the "national opposition" were compelled to cooperate more closely. A few months after the SRP had broken up, the regional association of the German Right Party in Lower Saxony, around Hans-Heinrich Scheffer and Adolf von Thadden, founded the German Reich Party together with the NDP in January 1950. Their intention was to "domesticate each of the internal opposition groups as well as improve their position in negotiations toward the goal of inner-party – though controversial – fusion with the [...] DP [...]".[15] In other words, the new party aimed to counteract the negative effect of the centrifugal forces. There was considerable internal dissent to overcome. But the two merging partners making up the DRP,

> despite their organisational weaknesses and different political orientations, [were] practically forced together by their view that a German-nationalist party line to compete with the SRP, such as the executive of the DKP/DRP represented, would lead to failure. In con-

13 Schmollinger, "DKP-DRP", 1024.

14 See Manfred Rowold, *Im Schatten der Macht. Zur Oppositionsrolle der nicht-etablierten Parteien in der Bundesrepublik* (Düsseldorf: Droste Verlag, 1974); Richard Stöss, "Einleitung. Struktur und Entwicklung des Parteiensystems der Bundesrepublik – Eine Theorie", *Parteien-Handbuch*, vol. 1, ed. Stöss, 209ff.; Eckhard Fascher, *Modernisierter Rechtsextremismus? Ein Vergleich der Parteigründungsprozesse der NPD und der Republikaner in den sechziger und achtziger Jahren* (Berlin: Köster, 1994), 20ff., 30ff.

15 Schmollinger, "Die Deutsche Reichspartei", in *Parteien-Handbuch*, vol. 2, ed. Stöss, 1112-1191, citation here, 1113.

> trast, they strove for a synthesis, or at least an alliance of German nationalist and national socialist traditions.[16]

In broad terms, the history of the German Reich Party appears to have been determined by the attempt to reinforce its organisational structure with the aim of transferring it to a more comprehensive coalition party of the national opposition. The founding of the NPD, which was largely initiated by DRP functionaries and supported by the DRP apparatus, marked the birth of this coalition movement in the mid-1960s. For this reason, it is certainly factually legitimate to refer to the DRP in its early years as a "forerunner to the NPD".[17]

The DRP holds a key position in the party-political development of the extreme right in the Federal Republic. Not only did it

> supply the organisational infrastructure and human resources of the NPD [in 1964]; the various currents of the 'national opposition' came together in it in 1950; all those scattered elements remaining from failed attempts to merge groupings of the extreme right are gathered in it, representatives of the nationalist-conservative wing as well as former National Socialists.[18]

In retrospect, their "very existence [… becomes their] reason for being".[19]

In contrast to other extreme right-wing groups, however, it did not emerge as a consequence of personal ambition, the bureaucratic self-preservation strategies of egotistical political associations or a drive for programmatic delimitation. On the contrary, it was influential members of the apparatus and the party leadership who upheld the coalition policy. In this respect, the DRP differs from other nationalist groups in that it "is not one of the small doctrinaire leader orders and is always collectively led …; and that it always lays the greatest emphasis of its activities on consolidating the organisation and producing propaganda with public appeal".[20] It is remarkable that the founding of the DRP was apparently perceived quite realistically not as the conclusion of the nationalist alliance, but merely as a transitional stage.

---

16 Schmollinger, "DRP", 1114.

17 Dudek and Jaschke, *Entstehung und Entwicklung*, 181; see also Sowinski, *Die Deutsche Reichspartei*, 7ff. This view of the DRP is set out in i.a. Werner Smoydzin, *NPD. Geschichte und Umwelt einer Partei. Analyse und Kritik* (Pfaffenhofen: Ilmgau Verlag, 1967), 81ff.; Lutz Niethammer, *Angepasster Faschismus. Politische Praxis der NPD* (Frankfurt a.M.: Fischer, 1969), 55ff.; Reinhard Kühnl, Rainer Rilling and Christine Sager, *Die NPD. Struktur, Ideologie und Funktion einer neofaschistischen Partei* (Frankfurt a.M: Suhrkamp, 1969), 23ff.; Hoffmann, *Die NPD*, 47. The DRP is portrayed independently in Jenke, *Verschwörung*, 231ff. and passim; Tauber, *Beyond Eagle*, 740ff.; Schmollinger, "DRP"; Dudek and Jaschke, *Entstehung und Entwicklung*, 181ff.; see also Rowold, *Im Schatten*, 209ff.; Backes and Jesse, *Politischer Extremismus*, 55ff.; Stöss, *Die extreme Rechte*, 133ff.; Assheuer and Sarkowicz, *Rechtsradikale*, 14ff.

18 Dudek and Jaschke, *Entstehung und Entwicklung*, 181.

19 Niethammer, *Angepasster Faschismus*, 56.

20 Ibid., 55f.

Adolf von Thadden[21], party functionary in Lower Saxony and the last chairman, embodies this course, which enjoyed broad support in the DRP.

Regarding the question of continuity, the DRP is significant for being transitory in nature while – the reverse of the same coin – also guaranteeing continuity through its organisation. According to Rowold, the "DRP apparatus constitutes the actual continuum of right-wing radicalism in the Federal Republic to a much greater extent than, for example, intellectual forces or ideological traditions".[22] This, however, is only the case because and insofar as the DRP managed to maintain its apparatus, some of its staff and its basic politico-ideological message of radical nationalism beyond the 1950s, which were a difficult time for the extreme right, and to adapt and reapply them in the context of a broader-based alliance.

This underlying conception of the DRP not as the final goal of the national opposition's coalition policy but as its starting point or medium also determines a fundamental aspect of the political practice of this party, which consists of endless negotiation and conciliation to secure alliance options. Conclusive agreement over which path to take was never reached, not least because the programmatic and structural openness of the DRP "enabled the various tendencies within the party to act against the predominant ideology, aims and practice of the time".[23]

Although attempts to amalgamate temporarily lost momentum, efforts to consolidate were renewed whenever elections (especially to the federal parliament, the *Bundestag*) were on the horizon: "The party becomes integrated by the fact that, wherever possible, it participates in elections and for the sake of this greater, barely defined goal, becomes an election campaign group."[24] One result of this was the fluctuation which defined the party's development in the 1950s. While the DRP was also open in the first phase of its existence[25] to former National Socialists who held on to their old convictions, the SRP had distinctly greater success rallying their support. Still quite strongly influenced by conservative German nationalism at this point, the DRP focused primarily on concentrating the forces to the right of the CDU/CSU by integrating smaller parties of the *Bürgerblock*.

After the SRP was banned in 1952 and the parties of the national opposition faced complete defeat at the federal election in 1953, a "slack period"[26] began for the radical right which left the DRP in the paradoxical situation which was to characterise the second phase of its development: On the one hand, it was forced out on to the politically irrelevant fringe of German politics while, on the other hand, it

21 See Schmollinger, "DRP", 1115, footnote 7; Werner Treß, "Thadden, Adolf von", in *Handbuch des Antisemitismus. Judenfeindschaft in Geschichte und Gegenwart*, vol. 2/2: *Personen*, ed. Wolfgang Benz (Berlin: DeGruyter Saur, 2009), 822-824.

22 Rowold, *Im Schatten*, 213.

23 Schmollinger, "DRP", 1117; see also Dudek and Jaschke, *Entstehung und Entwicklung*, 257ff.

24 Niethammer, *Angepasster Faschismus*, 55.

25 See Schmollinger, "DRP", 1113ff.; Niethammer, *Angepasster Faschismus*, 55ff.; Sowinski, *Die Deutsche Reichspartei*, 17ff.

26 Frederik, *Die Rechtsradikalen*, 30ff.; see also Stöss, *Die extreme Rechte*, 121f.

became a hegemonial force[27] within the "national opposition" by offering "numerous party leaders, who felt primarily committed to extreme right-wing ideological traditions, [...] adequate scope for action pursuing their anti-democratic points of view".[28] At the same time, the DRP managed to gain ground in southern and south-western Germany, where previously the rival German Community (*Deutsche Gemeinschaft*, DG) had predominated.[29]

The price of this hegemony was the programmatic opportunism which became a defining feature of the party. Whereas during Allied occupation, the forerunner parties of the DRP had tried to occupy a position distanced from National Socialism, and in its early years the DRP remained relatively open to the anti-bolshevist orientation towards the West, in 1953 it supported a neutral, reunified Germany. This opportunism in policy – which was also a defining feature of the NPD's later phases of success – was not aimed at the mass of the electorate but at a narrow dissident minority which remained socially and politically isolated. It should not, therefore, be confused with a populist right-wing catch-all policy, such as has gained relevance in various European countries since the 1980s.[30] The DRP's opportunism, in contrast, reacted to the prevailing mood in nationalist circles and was closely connected to a peculiarity of DRP policy which is frequently highlighted in the literature: Its relatively open and indeterminate nature. According to Niethammer, the DRP was

> not bound to a particular programme, a definable ideology or a permanent stratum of supporters, but stands only quite approximately for a general mentality [...], [it] distances itself from its original social circumstances and reproduces as an institution.[31]

It had certainly learnt a lesson from previous phases of radical nationalist policy, when debates over the parties' aims had led to bitter protests, divisions and the formation of sects.

When in the late 1950s and early 1960s the first cracks in Adenauer's conservative-liberal alliance appeared, the DRP – relying on the support of the Nazi-oriented section of its following – was able to further broaden its coalition base, not least by means of altering its programme. The group around von Thadden and publisher Waldemar Schütz created its own mouthpiece, the newspaper *Deutsche Wochenzeitung*, independently from the party leadership, and engineered a gradual policy change, causing the neutralists around party leader Heinrich Kunstmann to leave.

---

27 See Schmollinger, "DRP", 1150; Sowinski, *Die Deutsche Reichspartei*, 32ff.

28 Schmollinger, "SRP", 2331.

29 See Richard Stöss, "Die Deutsche Gemeinschaft", in *Parteien-Handbuch*, ed. Stöss, 876-900.

30 See Armin Pfahl-Traughber, *Volkes Stimme? Rechtspopulismus in Europa* (Bonn: Dietz Verlag, 1994); Cas Mudde, *Populist Radical Right Parties in Europe* (Cambridge: Cambridge University Press, 2007).

31 Niethammer, *Angepasster Faschismus*, 56; see also Schmollinger, "DRP", 1117ff.; Dudek and Jaschke, *Entstehung und Entwicklung*, 208ff.; Sowinski, *Die Deutsche Reichspartei*, 211ff.

As isolated as the DRP was in terms of society as a whole, within the "national opposition" it maintained its hegemonial position in spite of its inherent instability. It had a reliable foundation in the Nazi-oriented elements – who had no realistic political alternative – from which it could venture to increase its influence. It now re-emphasised its old anti-bolshevist stance, which it had never quite abandoned, thus appealing to a section of the nationally-oriented conservative camp which was disturbed by the federal government's cautious steps toward détente.

The "national opposition" hoped to benefit from the frictions within the *Bürgerblock* which put an end to Adenauer's "chancellor democracy" in the 1960s. At the same time, they also took advantage of a new development within nationalist circles. Since the late 1950s, a young generation of followers had grown up who were organised in radically nationalist youth groups and associations and were looking for a political outlet for their activist energy. This activism, however, soon plunged the DRP into a crisis when it became implicated in a wave of anti-Semitic slogan-daubing from December 1959. The initial act which precipitated this "extreme right chain of events" was committed by two members of the DRP.[32] This incident certainly undermined the DRP's chances of success at the federal election in 1961; the younger extreme right elements went on to become some of the supporters, members and activists of the NPD, which was founded in 1964.

The Establishment of the NPD

The NPD seems at first to have been set up as little more than a renewed attempt by the DRP to pursue its alliance policy. Nevertheless, the establishment of the NPD stands in marked contrast – and this seems to have been a precondition for the party's early successes – to previous attempts by the "national opposition" to amalgamate. After several failed attempts to negotiate a consolidation of extreme right forces in the run-up to the 1965 federal election, due to the usual disputes, rivalries and differences of opinion concerning policy, strategy, practice, organisation and personnel, the amalgamation-friendly core of the DRP initially tried to proceed with local alliances. After years of unfruitful consolidation attempts, it seemed to be dawning on those concerned that, as von Thadden concluded some years before his death: "No party merger ever took place that would have worked."[33]

For this reason, a formal merger or association of existing parties was avoided this time. Instead, from 1963, working groups were formed and independent lists of candidates drawn up at local and regional levels. The founding of the party itself, which took place in autumn 1964, was portrayed to the outside world as the initiative of a large number of individuals who were ready for a new start. This appearance of readiness was amplified by the authorisation of dual membership which is "perfectly normal for an electoral pact"[34] but in this case specifically benefited the

32 See Dudek and Jaschke, *Entstehung und Entwicklung*, 266ff.

33 Cited from von Thadden, *Die Entwicklung*, 69.

34 Rowold, *Im Schatten*, 228.

DRP. In this way, the party apparatus and membership could be brought into the NPD as its most important asset while at the same time "a retreat to the old positions of the Reich Party remained an option".[35] As soon as the NPD was established and the DRP functionaries could be sure that they had the apparatus under control, this reservation became superfluous. The DRP was dissolved in favour of the NPD in 1965, from which point the statutes no longer permitted dual membership.

Behind the scenes, the establishment of the new party was to such an extent initiated, enforced and engineered by the DRP that it seems as if "the actual process of fusion" was simply "disguised".[36] But the amalgamation-friendly group – known by critics within the "national opposition" as the "Thadden clique" – was actually concerned with more. An indication of this is evident in their willingness to retreat into the background and allow prominent leadership positions to be taken by figures without any serious history of National Socialism, who were not associated with the parties and postwar organisations of the national opposition. This strategy was personified by the founding leader, Fritz Thielen.[37] He came from the All-German Party *(Gesamtdeutsche Partei)* which had emerged from those parts of the DP and GB/BHE which had not been swallowed by the Christian Democratic Union (*Christlich Demokratische Union,* CDU) or the FDP, and whose regional association in Bremen had been reformed as the German Party in Bremen *(Deutsche Partei in Bremen).*[38] This made Thielen a suitable candidate for the party leadership of the NPD. Later, von Thadden explained: "Without him, the NPD would simply have been the DRP under a new name."[39] This statement illustrates the approach that the "Thadden clique" took to staff policy, which was mainly "to place middle class, conservative, politically non-incriminated figures in representative positions on all levels of the party and at the same time to control the party apparatus".[40] In fact, they were conceded even more authority, influencing the party's aims, choice of name and strategic orientation.

It appears as if the founders of the NPD actually intended to move out of their self-imposed isolation in fundamental opposition and offer constructive parliamentary opposition; as if they were even prepared to tolerate middle class conservative governments and perhaps even participate in coalitions.[41] But the programmatic and strategic openness which characterised the early NPD, perhaps even more so

35 Ibid.

36 Ibid.; also Niethammer, *Angepasster Faschismus*, 66f.

37 See Horst W. Schmollinger, "Die Deutsche Partei (DP)", *Kurzporträt*, in *Parteien-Handbuch*, ed. Stöss, 1086, fn. 364.

38 See Richard Stöss, "Die Gesamtdeutsche Partei (GDP or GPD)", in *Parteien-Handbuch*, ed. Stöss, 1460-1477; Rowold, *Im Schatten*, 213ff.

39 Cited from Kühnl et al., *NPD*, 45.

40 Rowold, *Im Schatten*, 220f.

41 See Horst W. Schmollinger, "Die Nationaldemokratische Partei", in *Parteien-Handbuch*, ed. Stöss, 1967f.; Hoffmann, *Die NPD*, 117f.

than its forerunner party, also guaranteed the integration of the still existent neo-Nazi elements in the NPD.

Rise and Disillusion

The NPD arrived too late for the federal election in 1965, polling only 2 per cent of the votes. In Hamburg the following year it still only gained 3.9 per cent. A party conference was held in Karlsruhe in June 1966, at which nationalist ideologist Ernst Anrich, a close ally of von Thadden, gave a highly controversial speech, eliciting greater public interest in the party. In November it broke the 5 per cent hurdle for the first time in Bavaria and in the following two years it gained seats in all the local state elections that were held, namely in Hesse, Bremen, Lower Saxony, Rhineland-Palatinate, Schleswig-Holstein and finally Baden-Württemberg.[42] It was able to markedly increase its membership, considerably extend its organisation and set up a number of subsidiary organisations.

The NPD was also able to defend the hegemony which the DRP had achieved within the radical nationalist camp. While the German Freedom Party (*Deutsche Freiheitspartei,* founded in 1961 when the neutralists left the DRP) tried to establish a rival party together with the German Community *(Deutsche Gemeinschaft)* and other neutralist-oriented groups under the name Action Group of Independent Germans (*Aktionsgemeinschaft Unabhängiger Deutscher,* AUD), it failed to gain the support of the electorate.[43] Von Thadden wrote: "The NPD was the 'alliance' for the simple reason that apart from it there was nothing else of relevance on the right wing of the party spectrum. Of course there were always individual speciality merchants."[44]

But the rise of the NPD was by no means smooth and straightforward. Niethammer aptly describes the party's organisation as a "consolidation despite crises".[45] Conflicts over the party leadership were a major source of dispute and resulted in Thielen being forced out in 1967. Von Thadden then took over as party leader himself.[46]

The openness and opportunism within the right-wing spectrum which the DRP had practised also determined the character of NPD policy.[47] Set up as an electoral pact, the NPD did not initially have a programme at all but – similarly to the early

42 See Erwin K. Scheuch, Thomas A. Herz and Hans D. Klingemann, eds., *Die NPD in den Landtagswahlen 1966-1968* (Cologne: Institut für vergleichende Sozialforschung, 1969); Christoph Kopke, "Die NPD in Baden-Württemberg und ihre Fraktion im Stuttgarter Landtag 1968-1972", in *Ulm – die Gedenkstätte und der Nationalsozialismus. Festschrift zur Verabschiedung von Silvester Lechner in den Ruhestand,* ed. Dokumentationszentrum Oberer Kuhberg Ulm (Ulm/Münster: Klemm & Oelschläger, 2009), 73-85.

43 See Richard Stöss, "Die Aktionsgemeinschaft Unabhängiger Deutscher", in *Parteien-Handbuch,* ed. Stöss, 310-335.

44 Cited from von Thadden, "Die Entwicklung", 65.

45 Niethammer, *Angepasster Faschismus,* 66ff.

46 See Dudek and Jaschke, *Entstehung und Entwicklung,* 300ff.; Hoffmann, *Die NPD,* 274ff.

47 See Schmollinger, "NPD", 1929ff.; Dudek and Jaschke, *Entstehung und Entwicklung,* 300ff.; Hoffmann, *Die NPD,* 274ff.

DRP and SRP – just a kind of open agenda: The NPD "manifesto". Ernst Anrich's Karlsruhe speech[48] became a key policy document until the party programme was presented at the NPD conference in Hanover in late 1967. While this once again remained largely noncommittal, the NPD's "political encyclopaedia", which was published under the considerable influence of Anrich by Waldemar Schütz, another close friend of von Thadden, was adopted as a central programmatic document.

What actually constitutes the element of continuity in this history is the removal of the DRP's apparatus and body of functionaries to the NPD:

> Without the tight, disciplined organisation of the DRP, the NPD would not have been able to get off the ground. Without the absolute authority of the DRP's leadership, its members would not have acted with the level of commitment that they did.[49]

The DRP apparatus formed a stable framework for the party to hold on to throughout the disintegration processes which took place in 1969-71 and beyond. Most importantly, the DRP provided experience on the organisational level and enduring networks, especially since it officially continued to exist in the amalgamation phase. The DRP, then, had channels of communication at its disposal through which it could influence the NPD but which the other alliance partners had absolutely no control over.[50] At the same time, von Thadden had moved control of the NPD organisation into his own hands when it was founded. The "Thadden clique" secured its supremacy on the party's executive boards and committees. Not unusually, "on the local executive boards [...] the central departments such as finance, organisation, press and propaganda, often even the party's arbitration, were occupied by men who had proven themselves as DRP functionaries, frequently in the same offices".[51] The NPD also inherited DRP premises. The party newspaper was another "legacy"[52] of the DRP. The organ which had previously appeared under the name *Der Reichsruf* was published from January 1965 as the NPD party newspaper under the name *Deutsche Nachrichten*. The newspaper's group of shareholders was "almost identical with the former DRP leadership, hence continues [...] the line of the former Reich Party, which was a sound failure on the political stage, in a new guise and by new means".[53]

---

48 Excerpts are recorded in Fred H. Richards, *Die NPD. Alternative oder Wiederkehr?* (Munich/Vienna: Olzog, 1967), 112ff.; Hans Maier and Hermann Bott, *NPD. Struktur und Ideologie einer "nationalen Rechtspartei"* (Munich: Piper, 1968), 88ff.; see also Niethammer, *Angepasster Faschismus,* 79ff. On Anrich, see Werner Treß, "Anrich, Ernst", in *Handbuch des Antisemitismus,* vol. 2/1, ed. Benz, 23-26.

49 Quoted from von Thadden, *Die Entwicklung,* 67.

50 See Niethammer, *Angepasster Faschismus,* 67.

51 Ibid.

52 Ibid., 70.

53 Heribert Kohl, "Die 'Deutschen Nachrichten'. Eine politologisch-soziologische Analyse des publizistischen Organs der NPD", *Politische Vierteljahresschrift* 8 (1967), 272-292, citation here, 272; Friedrich J. Bröder, *Ein Sprachrohr des Rechtsradikalismus. Die Deutschen Nachrichten. Eine*

In spite of these continuities, the NPD can "not exclusively be regarded as the successor party to the DRP".[54] It was not created as a renamed, regrouped or reformed version of an already existing organisation but as a new party. This is clearly illustrated by its voters. The NPD tapped into new sections of the electorate in terms of geography, social strata and age group and managed "to cross the boundaries of its traditional, extreme right-wing strongholds. It reached regions and sections of the electorate in which its precursor parties had had no success".[55] There was a particularly striking shift in support for the nationalist camp from mainly rural northern Germany to the South and South West, where it was backed by urban, and frequently, working class voters. "The social structure of the NPD electorate had [...] in the late sixties [...] come to resemble all of society in the Federal Republic [...]: its electorate was broadly socially diverse."[56]

At the peak of its electoral success, the NPD provided an arena for political activity to two younger generations who had been born during and after the period of National Socialist rule as well as to the older generation which had lived through National Socialism as adults.[57]

These younger supporters took on an additionally radical dimension which echoed the activism of their political opponent on the left, the extra-parliamentary opposition, and brought them into conflict with the "conservative" party line. In view of growing public resistance, the NPD radicalised its image. As violent forms of protest were increasing in the course of student revolt, the NPD frequently allowed its events to end in disturbances too. But it was also the NPD's inability to deal with democratic dispute which caused the situation to ultimately implode. Not only did the party screen itself off from public exchange, it approved violence against counter-protestors and built up a militant "guard service" (*Ordnerdienst,* OD). Von Thadden's 1969 election campaign, known as the "German Journey" *(Deutschlandfahrt),* sparked fierce protests nearly all over the country. At one point, the head of the OD fired shots at protestors, further damaging the public image of the party. This may have cost the NPD the crucial votes it needed to gain a seat in the federal parliament.[58] In the event, it gained only 4.3 per cent of the votes. The disintegration which now occurred was the effect of opposing centrifugal forces which could no longer be contained after the party's election defeat.

Studie zur Propagandatechnik und –methode (Mainz: Hase & Koehler, 1969); Hoffmann, *Die NPD*, 429ff.

54 Cited from Kaltefleiter, *Wirtschaft und Politik*, 137.

55 Schmollinger, "NPD", 1956.

56 Ibid., 1981.

57 See Niethammer, *Angepasster Faschismus*, 245ff.

58 See Schmollinger, "NPD"; Dudek and Jaschke, *Entstehung und Entwicklung*, vol. 1, 327ff., vol. 2, 129ff.; Hoffmann, *Die NPD*, 117ff.

Crisis and "Second Springtime"

Since its political ambitions had foundered at the federal election in 1969, the NPD briefly played the "resistance" card. A "resistance campaign" *(Aktion Widerstand)*, initiated in October 1970 after several months' preparation by the NPD and its smaller, radically nationalist alliance partners. However, it proved to be a disastrous mistake by the party leadership.[59] The basic elements of radical nationalism in the 1970s were present in the campaign: Attempted convergence with the CDU and "floating" nationalist conservative circles; a new activism which imitated the left-wing protest movement in form and appearance; the emergence of small, violent, proto-terrorist groups, some of which were openly neo-Nazi; efforts to "intellectualise" the movement and modernise its public image.

The tensions, frictions and conflicts over aims which arose in the context of the "resistance campaign" accelerated a process which had already begun with the election defeat in 1969: The nationalist alliance movement which was organised by the NPD fell apart again.[60] This disintegration could be observed on all levels: Supporters, members, functionaries and leadership all began to drift apart. Membership fell steadily from 1970. The party failed to achieve electoral success on either a federal or a regional level. It could only rely on the support of isolated local strongholds. It did not even attempt to stand for a number of major ballots. The party newspaper, *Deutsche Nachrichten,* had to be closed down.

A dramatic leadership crisis ensued in the NPD.[61] A steady stream of party functionaries who stood for a more moderate, conservative course had left the party since the 1970 conference in Wertheim. The following year, at the party conference in Holzminden, things came to a head. Unexpectedly, even for his closest associates, von Thadden resigned as leader of the NPD. Siegfried Pöhlmann, who had been one of von Thadden's severest critics within the party for some time, could not rally enough support behind him. The delegates elected Martin Mußgnug[62] as leader, one of the younger party members who was nevertheless influenced by the DRP apparatus and whom von Thadden had proposed as his successor.

While most NPD voters went over to the CDU, which had adopted a more radical profile in opposition, the party's active supporters and members went different ways.[63] Some NPD supporters sought entry into the conservative party spectrum in

---

59 See Lutz Niethammer, "Integration und 'Widerstand'. Die NPD und die Umgruppierung der Rechten", *Gewerkschaftliche Monatshefte* 22 (1971), 136-153; Christoph Kopke, "'Aktion Widerstand' – historischer Brennpunkt und Wendepunkt. Die 'nationale Opposition' zwischen Sammlung und Zersplitterung, 1969-1971", in *Die 1970er Jahre als schwarzes Jahrzehnt. Politisierung und Mobilisierung zwischen christlicher Demokratie und extremer Rechter,* eds. Massimiliano Livi, Daniel Schmidt and Michael Sturm (Frankfurt a.M.: Campus Verlag, 2010), 249-262.

60 See Schmollinger, "NPD"; Hoffmann, *Die NPD,* 134ff.

61 See Schmollinger, "NPD"; Hoffmann, *Die NPD,* 148ff.

62 See Hoffmann, *Die NPD,* 397ff.

63 For an overview of developments in the 1970s, see Wolfgang Benz, ed., *Rechtsradikalismus: Randerscheinung oder Renaissance?* (Frankfurt a.M.: Fischer, 1980); Lersch, *Die verkannte Gefahr;* Dudek and Jaschke, *Entstehung und Entwicklung;* Stöss, *Die extreme Rechte,* 140ff.

the mid-term, especially the CDU, or became involved in the citizens' initiative groups and interest groups on the right wing of the CDU and the leagues of refugees and expellees.[64] This group demonstrated a degree of overlap with those party supporters who had found a new political home in the German People's Union (*Deutsche Volksunion,* DVU) of nationalist Munich publisher Gerhard Frey. Others followed von Thadden-critic Siegfried Pöhlmann into the Campaign for the New Right (*Aktion Neue Rechte,* ANR) and tried from there to effect the renewal and modernisation of radical nationalism. These currents, which concentrated on influencing public opinion and political culture in a "meta-political" way in the long and mid-term, came together under the somewhat vague label of the New Right *(Neue Rechte).*[65] During the course of the 1970s, the first proto-terrorist paramilitary groups *(Wehrsportgruppen)* were formed as well as the related neo-Nazi groups with only a weak or no link to the generation with first-hand experience of National Socialism.

By seeking an independent, clearly defined NPD identity, distinct from other parts of the "national scene" or the extreme right, the party further isolated itself within the nationalist camp. The "Wertheim manifesto" of 1971, the revised edition of the controversial "political encyclopaedia" and the Düsseldorf programme of 1973 were all pointers along a path toward greater programmatic autonomy. For some years from the mid-1970s, the party was characterised by "programmatic attempts at making its mark" which were "mostly driven by members of the NPD subsidiary organisation Young National Democrats (*Junge Nationaldemokraten,* JN), who were partly influenced by revolutionary nationalist positions among the New Right".[66]

The Young National Democrats became the NPD's most dynamic branch in the 1970s, contributing significant motivation and ideas toward the party's programme, practice and outward appearance. Established across the country by 1970, in the ensuing years it set about styling itself, like its parent party, as a "third force", or "third position", between the "imperialist" and "occupation" super powers, the United States and the Soviet Union. It combined a rebellious attitude with political instruction. It also maintained close links with the youth associations League of Patriotic Youth (*Bund Heimattreuer Jugend,* BHJ) and Viking Youth (*Wiking Jugend,* WJ), as well as with paramilitary and neo-Nazi circles, "revolutionary nationalist" circles and the conservative nationalist scene.

The alliance project, inherited from the DRP and its forerunner parties, and their original justification, had been laid on ice for the time being. The NPD nar-

64 See Rowold, *Im Schatten;* Stöss, "Einleitung". See also Astrid Dypvik's contribution to this anthology.

65 See Günter Bartsch, *Revolution von rechts? Ideologie und Organisation der Neuen Rechten* (Freiburg: Herder, 1975); Margret Feit, *Die "Neue Rechte" in der Bundesrepublik. Organisation – Ideologie – Strategie* (Frankfurt a.M.: Campus Verlag, 1987); Wolfgang Gessenharter and Thomas Pfeiffer, eds., *Die Neue Rechte – eine Gefahr für die Demokratie?* (Wiesbaden: VS Verlag für Sozialwissenschaften, 2004).

66 Schmollinger, "NPD", 1928.

rowed its support base considerably. On the one hand, it passed "incompatibility" resolutions, cutting off the most active and dynamic sections of its following, the pro-Nazi and the "revolutionary nationalist" currents, to whom the party seemed increasingly "reactionary". At the same time, the rift between the NPD and the more "conservative" circles grew, much of which went on to join the DVU.

In the crisis-riddled history of the "national opposition", the 1970s were the most critical decade: "At no point [...] in the history of the Federal Republic was right-wing extremism as insignificant [...] as in the seventies."[67] The state of the NPD should certainly be seen in the context of the general political situation. A "progressive spirit" prevailed in which political and cultural processes worked toward overcoming the limitations of national boundaries and easing political tensions. This and the more radical CDU in opposition left little scope for a "national opposition". Even the NPD bore the decade's sociological imprint to some extent, going through "extreme cultural diversification" accompanied by "withdrawal to small islands of identity-seeking".[68] Schmollinger speaks of a "fall of the NPD into insignificance".[69] Nevertheless, even this phase of the NPD's history should not be interpreted solely as one of decline. On the contrary, in retrospect it becomes clear that a core group, which maintained links with the nationalist camp, used the crisis to find answers to the new situation and the changing world and to experiment with different forms and programmatic content.

Had the NPD and its organisation not continued to exist, it would not have been possible to reintegrate the far right's divergent lines of development about a quarter of a century later. In the 1980s, a slow, very hesitant process of consolidation began, on a low level and again prone to crises. But the NPD recognised relatively early on that the coming decade offered scope for combining politics to the right of the CDU with discussion of the "immigration question" and charging it with extreme right-wing content. From the dawn of the new decade, subdivisions of the NPD cautiously resumed efforts toward political alliance at a grass roots level and experimented quite successfully with electoral lists and civil initiatives "for stopping immigration" *(Bürgerinitiativen für Ausländerstopp)* in some local authority districts.[70] At the federal election in March 1983, the NPD was again only able to poll a tiny percentage of the votes; however, since its total had fallen from 0.55 per cent in 1972 to 0.32 per cent in 1976 and a mere 0.18 per cent in 1980, the result of 0.23 per cent in 1983 was welcomed as an increase, albeit minimal. The NPD's 0.8 per cent at the European elections in 1984 was an acclaimed improvement. When the party gained 0.6 per cent at the federal election in January 1987, it decided to

---

67 Hoffmann, *Die NPD*, 137.

68 Werner Faulstich, "Gesellschaft und Kultur der siebziger Jahre: Einführung und Überblick. Die 1970er-Jahre – Inventur einer Umbruchzeit", *Zeithistorische Forschungen/Studies in Contemporary History*, online edition, 3 (2006), http://www.zeithistorische-forschungen.de/16126041-Material-3-2006 (accessed July 7, 2010).

69 Schmollinger, "NPD", 1928.

70 See ibid., 1942.

seek political allies once again. In April, arrangements were made with the DVU, which had now been permitted to stand for election, to prevent candidates competing for the same seat and in some cases to stand together under the name *Liste D.* In this way, the DVU gained over 3 per cent of the votes in Bremen in September 1987 and was able to install a direct candidate from Bremerhaven. Despite the stiff competition from The Republicans (*Die Republikaner,* REP), a party founded in 1983, things seemed to be looking up for the NPD in the late 1980s, and the REP's electoral success in Berlin in January 1989 could be read as proof of a growing extreme right-wing potential among the electorate.

The Post-Mußgnug NPD

The year 1989-90 was by all accounts a chequered one for the NPD. It had always persisted in its territorial claims for Germany beyond the existing Federal Republic and German Democratic Republic and had always expected the question of the constitution or system of government to be reopened for debate in the event of reunification. Its hopes for radically changing the way the country was run in a supposedly constitutional way rested on the preamble to Germany's *Grundgesetz* (Basic Law). When, in the event, the former GDR joined the Federal Republic, the NPD was disappointed. But the extreme right was glad to see the hated regime in East Germany go and in the nationalistically charged celebrations of the months following November 9, 1989, it recognised the potential for a radically nationalist mass movement and the opportunity to finally become active in "Middle Germany" *(Mitteldeutschland),* as East Germany was called in non-recognition of the Oder-Neisse border. However, in 1990 no established extreme right-wing party was able to benefit directly from the political changes. While conservative or nationally-oriented voters favoured the CDU and their East German coalition partners, and extreme right-wing voters did the same in the hope for speedy unification, the NPD – the "veterans' party" – was left without the dynamism and activist force which only the militant neo-Nazi scene could provide.[71]

As soon as attempts to cooperate with the GDR bloc- or satellite-party National Democratic Party Germany (*Nationaldemokratische Partei Deutschlands,* NDPD) failed, branches of the Middle German National Democrats (*Mitteldeutsche Nationaldemokraten,* MND) were set up in spring 1990, and which assumed the name of their West German parent party and officially merged with it on unification. The gradual build-up of subdivisions in the former GDR could not disguise the fact that the NPD had helplessly looked on at a crucial turning point in contemporary German history and not been able to gain any advantage from the widespread mood of na-

71 See Robert Harnischmacher, ed., *Angriff von Rechts. Rechtsextremismus und Neonazismus unter Jugendlichen Ostberlins. Beiträge zur Analyse und Vorschläge zu Gegenmaßnahmen* (Rostock: Hanseatischer Fachverlag für Wirtschaft, 1993); Pfahl-Traughber, *Rechtsextremismus. Eine kritische Bestandsaufnahme;* Richard Stöss, *Rechtsextremismus im vereinten Deutschland* (Berlin: Friedrich Ebert Foundation, 2000); Britta Bugiel, *Rechtsextremismus Jugendlicher in der DDR und in den neuen Bundesländern von 1982-1998* (Münster: Lit Verlag, 2002).

tionalism or sudden increase in racialist and politically motivated attacks by members of extreme right-wing youth subcultures. Mußgnug's NPD had kept the organisational apparatus alive but in order to develop a new dynamic the party had to change. This became clear after two regional elections in Western Germany in early 1990 – Saarland and Lower Saxony – at which the NPD polled a disastrous 0.2 per cent of the vote. The party was not permitted to stand for the first free East German parliamentary elections in March 1990. The results of the regional elections in the new federal states provided a taste of the bitter defeat to come: In re-unified Germany's first federal election, the NPD polled only 0.3 per cent of the votes.

Thus the NPD found itself in an extremely critical state at precisely the moment when nationalist and racialist sentiments were at a peak.[72] Backed by von Thadden and other senior DRP and NPD activists, Mußgnug had begun negotiations as early as the late 1980s with the aim of creating a new, politically untarnished "united right" *(Vereinigte Rechte)*. The NPD was increasingly regarded as a problem. Old DRP functionaries seem to have sunk back into habits developed during the founding phase of the NPD and ignored the transitory character that distinguished the DRP from the outset from the temporarily successful "national alliance party" that was the NPD. In addition, there was no team used to working together to provide an organisational foundation such as the DRP brought into the NPD in 1964-65. The quasi-official party history of 1999 describes the negotiations of 1989-90 in these mocking terms: "In all seriousness most of those present spoke of a new beginning but, seen symbolically, it was a gathering of 25 years of NPD party history with a few participants who, starting out from the NPD, had been through all possible factions."[73]

Once the impression was conveyed that the group around Mußgnug wanted to sacrifice the NPD, the "most intact and tried and tested organisation"[74] of the "national opposition", for the sake of negotiating a "grand right", mistrust within the party grew. In the face of election defeat, financial irregularities and his increasing isolation on the board, Mußgnug was induced to resign in December 1990. Walter Bachmann temporarily took over as party leader before former JN chairman and long-term Mußgnug critic Günter Deckert[75], who had only recently returned to the NPD, was elected in 1991. His appointment was in line with the decision not to transfer the NPD as a party into the new formation, founded in 1991 as the German Alliance – United Right *(Deutsche Allianz – Vereinigte Rechte)* but a short time later renamed German League for Nation and Homeland (*Deutsches Liga für Volk und Heimat*, DLVH) following a legal dispute. The party apparatus was behind Deckert.

In the recent literature on the NPD, Deckert's leadership is still viewed as the final stage of a supposedly "old" NPD; as the last phase of a continuous process of

72 See Hoffmann, *Die NPD*, 253.

73 Cited from Apfel, "Die Geschichte", 51.

74 Cited from Karl-Heinz Vorsatz in *Deutsche Stimme*, in Hoffmann, *Die NPD*, 255.

75 See Hoffmann, *Die NPD*, 399f.

decline which was not reversed until Deckert was replaced by Udo Voigt.[76] By the same token, the NPD under Voigt is described as a "new NPD".[77] In terms of historical continuity, this interpretation is problematic. The first signs of a revised policy were shown under Deckert and resolutely continued by Voigt. It would be more appropriate to identify the early 1990s as a new phase in the history of the NPD.

Under Deckert, trends which had influenced the DRP and NPD for many years, but were abandoned during Mußgnug's leadership, were revived again. Priority was given to maintaining the legality and organisational apparatus of the NPD, requiring frequent participation in elections to secure party status. This was then the basis for making offers of integration, amalgamation and alliance, as can be proven to have taken place during Deckert's term in office.

At the same time, the NPD needed to distinguish itself more than before from the DVU, REP and DLVH. Deckert's course of radicalisation in the 1990s should be seen in this context. At times he made a single-issue party out of the NPD, devoting it solely to the backward-looking questions of contemporary German history which were relevant to its own circles, but hardly appealing to the outside world. Alongside leadership problems and financial scandals, this narrow political horizon which steered the party leaders into repeated conflicts with the law, certainly cost Deckert the party leadership. But it was also probably the recipe for successfully gaining a more striking public image. Henceforth it was not only one of several racialist, extreme-right, populist parties which courted favour with disenchanted floating voters by addressing popular resentments, but could claim to be the true representative of the "national opposition". In this way, Deckert probably gained some credibility for the party, preparing the ground for the later integration of the neo-Nazi spectrum.

The demarcation resolutions which for many years prevented the party's expansion in this field, but which had also largely protected it from state prosecution, were increasingly circumvented after Deckert became party leader. The JN took the role of blockade runners. When a state offensive to ban neo-Nazi groups was launched in late 1992, it released waves of new members for the NPD, who formed the real potential for the party's revival. The nazification of broad sections of the party can be seen to have occurred in the following stages: In 1993, the party's "incompatibility resolutions" were abolished. Members of banned neo-Nazi groups such as the Free German Workers' Party (*Freiheitliche Deutsche Arbeiterpartei*, FAP) were invited to join the NPD. When Wiking Youth was banned in 1994, its members were advised to join the JN. In 1997, a section of the association named *Die*

---

76 See Eckhard Jesse, "Biographisches Porträt: Udo Voigt", *Jahrbuch Extremismus and Demokratie* 18 (2006), 207-219.

77 See Marc Brandstetter, *Die NPD im 21. Jahrhundert. Eine Analyse ihrer aktuellen Situation, ihrer Erfolgsbedingungen und Aussichten* (Marburg: Tectum-Verlag, 2006); Harald Bergsdorf, *Die neue NPD. Antidemokraten im Aufwind* (Munich: Olzog, 2007); Armin Pfahl-Traughber, *Der "zweite Frühling" der NPD. Entwicklung, Ideologie, Organisation und Strategie einer rechtsextremistischen Partei* (St. Augustin: Konrad Adenauer Foundation, 2008), 23ff.

Nationalen (The Nationalists) merged with the NPD. In the 1990s, these "nationalists" were

> an important motor, considerably stimulating the organisation of members of this scene in explicitly political groups. Viewed in retrospect, they had perhaps an even more important function: during the crisis of the 'national opposition' in the mid-1990s, when organisational structures were broken up by state intervention and the NPD was not yet accepted as a substitute organisation in the neo-Nazi spectrum …, [die Nationalen] ensured there was a minimum degree of continuity and provided a nation-wide organisational framework.[78]

In 2000, Holocaust-denier and political desperado Horst Mahler[79] joined the NPD; a signal which garnered much public interest. Meanwhile, neo-Nazi "comradeship" *(Kameradschaft)* networks and the JN cooperated on campaigns and individual actions in the new federal states under the soubriquet National and Social Activists of Middle Germany (*Nationale und Soziale Aktivisten Mitteldeutschland,* NSAM) which were only locally visible but had a profounder impact. After proceedings to ban the NPD failed, several leading neo-Nazis publicly announced their allegiance with the NPD and even joined the party executive. Since then, all levels of the NPD have been infiltrated by neo-Nazis.

Udo Voigt and the Renaissance of the NPD

In 1996, to mark the beginning of his term in office, Udo Voigt introduced a new party programme which guaranteed a high degree of openness and flexibility in keeping with the internal opportunism described above. Voigt's lack of interest in naming concrete aims and objectives is illustrated by the fact that he generally allowed ambitious party members to do what they liked in the party's working groups and committees and his rhetoric tended to echo their often contradictory statements. On the basis of the 1996 programme, a series of additional programmatic documents were drawn up by both federal and regional groups.[80] This did not stop the programmatic debate but neither did it lead to the paralysis of party policy. The new party programme, which came into force in June 2010, incidentally points in a similar direction.

In 1997 Voigt drew up a statement of principles. One element of this conception is the "three pillar concept" which a number of studies have since attempted to analyse and interpret.[81] However, the three – and later four – pillars are by no

---

78 Kopke, *Die NPD,* 61.

79 See Gideon Botsch, Christoph Kopke and Werner Treß, "Mahler, Horst", in *Handbuch des Antisemitismus,* vol. 2/2, ed. Benz, 509-510.

80 See Hoffmann, *Die NPD,* 329ff.; Brandstetter, *Die NPD,* 107ff.

81 See Brandstetter, *Die NPD,* 109ff.; Pfahl-Traughber, *Der "zweite Frühling",* 42ff.; Robert Philippsberg, *Die Strategie der NPD. Regionale Umsetzung in Ost- und Westdeutschland* (Baden-Baden: Nomos, 2009); Christoph Schulze, "Das Viersäulenkonzept der NPD", in *Strategien der extremen Rechten. Hintergründe – Analysen – Antworten,* eds. Stephan Braun, Alexander Geisler and

means stringently expressed but presented in standardised terms. Mostly they speak of a "fight for the streets" and a "fight for minds" as well as a "fight for voters" and "for parliaments" and, in the fourth pillar, a "fight for the organised will". Rather than interpreting the concept as a clear directive for action from the party leadership and measuring its success along those lines, it seems more relevant to discuss its political function first. After all, Voigt is not really concerned with deciding "Germany's fate" at the ballot box, on the streets or on a meta-political level. Rather, his concept is intended to continue the alliance principle of the old DRP and early NPD and to facilitate the integration of different currents in the NPD. The "three pillar concept" is then a vehicle to signalise to all the currents within the "national opposition", every group and every individual, that they can operate by their own specific means in their own chosen field under the umbrella of the NPD. The disintegration of the previous phase had not been due to purely ideological reasons but had been the articulation of differences over which course to take. While the neo-Nazi and some of the revolutionary nationalist subsets stand for street-oriented activism, the "New Right" – viewed as the "intellectual far right" – intends to exert a meta-political influence on the country's intellectual and political culture; other currents, meanwhile, stand for developing classic party political activities and using election campaigns and parliamentary debates as propaganda platforms. It was Voigt's task to combine these divergent options for action in the context of the NPD.

The NPD's new dynamic was initially subdued by the possibility of a ban and the consequent petitions filed 2001-2003. When the federal government made it clear, however, that it was not prepared to dispute the Constitutional Court's ruling that the state was too implicated in the NPD to start proceedings – a number of informants were working for federal offices –, the floodgates opened. Now the NPD outshone all areas of the "national opposition" with newly won confidence. It opened up wholeheartedly to supporters of the neo-Nazi spectrum while also making election arrangements with the DVU, which were recorded in a "pact for Germany". In this way, the NPD became a flagship of the "national opposition" in Germany. In 2004 it entered the Saxon state parliament and in 2006, the state parliament of Mecklenburg-West Pomerania. In 2009 it was able to continue its parliamentary faction for a second term in the Saxon state parliament for the first time in its history, and two years later in Mecklenburg-West Pomerania. It only narrowly missed entering the state parliament in Thuringia in 2009 and in Saxony-Anhalt in 2011. The NPD apparently has a stable following in East Germany willing to vote for it at state parliament elections.

The peak of the NPD's powers to mobilise support seems to have been reached for the time being in 2006. Since then, the NPD has lost some momentum while still remaining the most dynamic and strongest – the hegemonial – force in the "na-

Martin Gerster (Wiesbaden: Nomos, 2009), 92-108; Eckhard Jesse, "Die Vier-Säulen-Strategie der NPD. Eine Analyse zu Anspruch und Wirklichkeit ihrer Umsetzung", *Jahrbuch für Extremismus- und Terrorismusforschung* 2008, 178-192.

tional camp", causing difficulties for all the other extreme right and right-wing populist groups and parties.[82] In late 2010, DVU and NPD arranged their party fusion, but in fact the DVU joined the NPD. Meanwhile, the NPD has not managed to outgrow its political subculture status on a federal level in the last decade, but has become firmly rooted in a number of federal states. And it has managed to achieve a new integration of divergent currents within the "national opposition". The future will show whether these are just short-term successes or whether the NPD can defend its regained hegemony.

Results and Prospects

From a retrospective, historical perspective, the NPD's renaissance in the last ten years can be analysed as a process in which the disintegration of the "national opposition" in the Federal Republic, which took place a decade previously, was reversed and lines of development from the period prior to 1969 were resumed. Had the organisation and apparatus of the NPD not survived the crisis of the 1970s, this renewed success would not have been possible. Describing the Voigt-era NPD as a "new NPD" fails to acknowledge the significance of the long organisational continuity in the party. Just because the NPD changed does not mean it became a new party. Indeed, some striking features of the party's more recent development can be seen to stem from knowledge of past successes and defeats in the party's long history. This experience can be traced back to the forerunner party DRP and hence to the long tradition of the "national opposition" in recent and contemporary German history.

Five aspects of the party's history deserve particular emphasis:

1) Over long stretches of their development, the DRP and NPD stood for the attempted consolidation of the diverse trends in the "national opposition". The opposing forces within the national camp, however, rendered these consolidation attempts precarious and ultimately caused them to fail. It remained a balancing act between opening up on the one hand to neo-Nazi tendencies and putting the party's legal status at risk, and maintaining a more conservative profile on the other hand, at the risk of alienating the most dynamic and active section of the following.
2) In order to prepare the ground for these amalgamation attempts, the party programme was kept open and arbitrary and characterised by a high degree of opportunism toward far right tendencies. Periods of greater programmatic definition, such as in the mid-1950s to a certain extent and very distinctly in the 1970s, were more detrimental to the hegemonial position of the DRP and NPD.
3) The growth and development of the DRP's and NPD's organisational apparatus constitutes a central aspect of the party history. Up to a certain point,

82 Kopke, *Die NPD*, 101ff.

maintaining this apparatus was an end in itself and party policy defined by this function. This apparatus which the NPD took over from the DRP, moreover, represents "the actual continuum of right-wing radicalism in the Federal Republic".[83]

4) Looking back on over six decades of development of the "national opposition", the 1970s appear to be the real decade of deviation. This decade was not only the most critical but also the least typical phase in the development of radical nationalism. It should not, however, be rashly interpreted as marking a conclusion or historical decline. Analogously to the social, cultural and political history of the Federal Republic in general, it was a decade of transition, change and "criticism and crisis" for the radical right, too.
5) Regardless of the changes within the "national opposition" – and hence within the NPD –, analysis of the current state of the extreme right and their future prospects should not obscure the findings of contemporary historical research. Tendencies within the "national camp" can be better understood against the background of specific historical paths. The party history is an important resource not least for the NPD itself.

Bibliography

Apfel, Holger. "Die Geschichte der Nationaldemokratischen Partei Deutschlands (NPD)". In *Alles Große steht im Sturm. Tradition und Zukunft einer nationalen Partei. 35 Jahre NPD – 30 Jahre JN*, edited by Holger Apfel, 34-59. Stuttgart: Deutsche Stimme Verlag, 1999.

Assheuer, Thomas and Hans Sarkowicz. *Rechtsradikale in Deutschland. Die alte und die neue Rechte.* Munich: C.H. Beck, 1992.

Backes, Uwe and Eckard Jesse. *Politischer Extremismus in der Bundesrepublik Deutschland*. 3 vols. Cologne: Wissenschaft und Politik, 1989.

Bartsch, Günter. *Revolution von rechts? Ideologie und Organisation der Neuen Rechten.* Freiburg: Herder, 1975.

Benz, Wolfgang, ed. *Rechtsradikalismus: Randerscheinung oder Renaissance?* Frankfurt a.M.: Fischer, 1980.

Bergsdorf, Harald. *Die neue NPD. Antidemokraten im Aufwind.* Munich: Olzog, 2007.

Botsch, Gideon, Christoph Kopke and Werner Treß. "Mahler, Horst". In *Handbuch des Antisemitismus. Judenfeindschaft in Geschichte und Gegenwart*, vol. 2/2, edited by Wolfgang Benz, 509-510. Berlin: De Gruyter Saur, 2009.

Botsch, Gideon. "Parteipolitische Kontinuitäten der 'Nationalen Opposition'. Von der Deutschen Reichspartei zur Nationaldemokratischen Partei Deutschlands". *Zeitschrift für Geschichtswissenschaft* 59 (2011), 113-137.

Botsch, Gideon. *Die extreme Rechte in der Bundesrepublik. 1949 bis heute.* Darmstadt: Wissenschaftliche Buchgesellschaft, 2012.

Brandstetter, Marc. *Die NPD im 21. Jahrhundert. Eine Analyse ihrer aktuellen Situation, ihrer Erfolgsbedingungen und Aussichten.* Marburg: Tectum-Verlag, 2006.

83 Cited from Rowold, *Im Schatten*, 213.

Bröder, Friedrich J. *Ein Sprachrohr des Rechtsradikalismus. Die Deutschen Nachrichten. Eine Studie zur Propagandatechnik und -methode.* Mainz: Hase & Koehler, 1969.

Bugiel, Britta. *Rechtsextremismus Jugendlicher in der DDR und in den neuen Bundesländern von 1982-1998.* Münster: Lit Verlag, 2002.

Büsch, Otto and Peter Furth. *Rechtsradikalismus im Nachkriegsdeutschland. Studien über die "Sozialistische Reichspartei" (SRP).* Berlin/Frankfurt a.M.: F. Vahlen, 1957.

Dudek, Peter and Hans-Gerd Jaschke. *Entstehung und Entwicklung des Rechtsextremismus in der Bundesrepublik. Zur Tradition einer besonderen politischen Kultur,* 2 vols. Opladen: Westdeutscher Verlag, 1984.

Fascher, Eckhard. *Modernisierter Rechtsextremismus? Ein Vergleich der Parteigründungsprozesse der NPD und der Republikaner in den sechziger und achtziger Jahren.* Berlin: Köster, 1994.

Faulstich, Werner. "Gesellschaft und Kultur der siebziger Jahre: Einführung und Überblick. Die 1970er-Jahre – Inventur einer Umbruchzeit". *Zeithistorische Forschungen/Studies in Contemporary History*, online edition, 3 (2006), URL: http://www.zeithistorische-forschungen.de/16126041-Material-3-2006 (accessed July 7, 2010).

Feit, Margret. *Die "Neue Rechte" in der Bundesrepublik. Organisation – Ideologie – Strategie.* Frankfurt a.M.: Campus Verlag, 1987.

Frederik, Hans. *Die Rechtsradikalen.* Munich: Inning, undated [1964].

Frei, Norbert. *Vergangenheitspolitik. Die Anfänge der Bundesrepublik und die NS-Vergangenheit.* Munich: dtv, 1999.

Gessenharter, Wolfgang and Thomas Pfeiffer, eds. *Die Neue Rechte – eine Gefahr für die Demokratie?* Wiesbaden: VS Verlag für Sozialwissenschaften, 2004.

Hansen, Henning. *Die Sozialistische Reichspartei (SRP). Aufstieg und Scheitern einer rechtsextremen Partei.* Düsseldorf: Droste Verlag, 2007.

Harnischmacher, Robert, ed. *Angriff von Rechts. Rechtsextremismus und Neonazismus unter Jugendlichen Ostberlins. Beiträge zur Analyse und Vorschläge zu Gegenmaßnahmen.* Rostock: Hanseatischer Fachverlag für Wirtschaft, 1993.

Jenke, Manfred. *Verschwörung von rechts? Ein Bericht über den Rechhtsradikalismus in Deutschland nach 1945.* Berlin: Colloquium Verlag, 1961.

Jesse, Eckhard. "Biographisches Porträt: Udo Voigt". *Jahrbuch Extremismus und Demokratie* 18 (2006), 207-219.

Jesse, Eckhard. "Die Vier-Säulen-Strategie der NPD. Eine Analyse zu Anspruch und Wirklichkeit ihrer Umsetzung". *Jahrbuch für Extremismus- und Terrorismusforschung* 2008, 178-192.

Kaltefleiter, Werner. *Wirtschaft und Politik in Deutschland. Konjunktur als Bestimmungsfaktor des Parteiensystems.* Cologne/Opladen: Westdeutscher Verlag, 1966.

Kohl, Heribert. "Die 'Deutschen Nachrichten'. Eine politologisch-soziologische Analyse des publizistischen Organs der NPD". *Politische Vierteljahresschrift* 8 (1967), 272-292.

Kopke, Christoph."'Aktion Widerstand' – historischer Brennpunkt und Wendepunkt. Die 'nationale Opposition' zwischen Sammlung und Zersplitterung, 1969-1971". In *Die 1970er Jahre als schwarzes Jahrzehnt. Politisierung und Mobilisierung zwischen christlicher Demokratie und extremer Rechter,* edited by Massimiliano Livi, Daniel Schmidt and Michael Sturm, 249-262. Frankfurt a.M.: Campus Verlag, 2010.

Kopke, Christoph. "Die NPD in Baden-Württemberg und ihre Fraktion im Stuttgarter Landtag 1968-1972". In *Ulm – die Gedenkstätte und der Nationalsozialismus. Festschrift zur Verabschiedung von Silvester Lechner in den Ruhestand,* edited by Dokumentationszentrum Oberer Kuhberg Ulm, 73-86. Ulm/Münster: Klemm & Oelschläger, 2009.

Kühnl, Reinhard, Rainer Rilling and Christine Sager. *Die NPD. Struktur, Ideologie und Funktion einer neofaschistischen Partei.* Frankfurt a.M.: Suhrkamp, 1969.

Maier, Hans and Hermann Bott. *NPD. Struktur und Ideologie einer "nationalen Rechtspartei".* Munich: Piper, 1968.

Mudde, Cas. *Populist Radical Right Parties in Europe.* Cambridge: Cambrigde University Press, 2007.

Niethammer, Lutz. *Angepasster Faschismus. Politische Praxis der NPD.* Frankfurt a.M.: Fischer, 1969.

Niethammer, Lutz. "Integration und 'Widerstand'. Die NPD und die Umgruppierung der Rechten". *Gewerkschaftliche Monatshefte* 22 (1971), 136-153.

Niethammer, Lutz. "Nach dem Dritten Reich ein neuer Faschismus? Zum Wandel der rechtsextremen Szene in der Geschichte der Bundesrepublik". In *Die verkannte Gefahr. Rechtsradikalismus in der Bundesrepublik*, edited by Paul Lersch, 105-127. Reinbek: Rowohlt, 1981.

Peukert, Detlev and Frank Bajohr. *Rechtsradikalismus in Deutschland. Zwei historische Beiträge.* Hamburg: Ergebnisse Verlag, 1990.

Pfahl-Traughber, Armin. *Der "zweite Frühling" der NPD. Entwicklung, Ideologie, Organisation und Strategie einer rechtsextremistischen Partei.* St. Augustin: Konrad Adenauer Foundation, 2008.

Pfahl-Traughber, Armin. *Rechtsextremismus in der Bundesrepublik.* Munich: C.H. Beck, 2000.

Pfahl-Traughber, Armin. *Volkes Stimme? Rechtspopulismus in Europa.* Bonn: Dietz Verlag, 1994.

Pfahl-Traughber, Armin. *Rechtsextremismus. Eine kritische Bestandsaufnahme nach der Wiedervereingung.* Bonn: Bouvier, 1993.

Philippsberg, Robert. *Die Strategie der NPD. Regionale Umsetzung in Ost- und Westdeutschland.* Baden-Baden: Nomos, 2009.

Richards, Fred H. *Die NPD. Alternative oder Wiederkehr?* Munich/Vienna: Olzog, 1967.

Rowold, Manfred. *Im Schatten der Macht. Zur Oppositionsrolle der nicht-etablierten Parteien in der Bundesrepublik.* Düsseldorf: Droste Verlag, 1974.

Scheuch, Erwin K., Thomas A. Herz and Hans D. Klingemann, eds. *Die NPD in den Landtagswahlen 1966-1968.* Cologne: Institut für vergleichende Sozialforschung, 1969.

Schmollinger, Horst W. "Die Deutsche Partei (DP)". In *Parteien-Handbuch. Die Parteien der Bundesrepublik Deutschland 1945-1980*, edited by Richard Stöss, 1025-1011. Opladen: Westdeutscher Verlag, 1983.

Schmollinger, Horst W."Die Deutsche Reichspartei". In *Parteien-Handbuch. Die Parteien der Bundesrepublik Deutschland 1945-1980*, edited by Richard Stöss, 1112-1191. Opladen: Westdeutscher Verlag, 1983,.

Schmollinger, Horst W. "Die Sozialistische Reichspartei". In *Parteien-Handbuch. Die Parteien der Bundesrepublik Deutschland 1945-1980*, edited by Richard Stöss, 2274-2336. Opladen: Westdeutscher Verlag, 1983.

Schmollinger, Horst W. "Die Deutsche Konservative Partei – Deutsche Rechtspartei". In *Parteien-Handbuch. Die Parteien der Bundesrepublik Deutschland 1945-1980*, edited by Richard Stöss, 982-1024. Opladen: Westdeutscher Verlag, 1983.

Schmollinger, Horst W. "Die Nationaldemokratische Partei". In *Parteien-Handbuch. Die Parteien der Bundesrepublik Deutschland 1945-1980*, edited by Richard Stöss, 1922-1995. Opladen: Westdeutscher Verlag, 1983.

Schulze, Christoph. "Das Viersäulenkonzept der NPD". In *Strategien der extremen Rechten. Hintergründe – Analysen – Antworten*, edited by Stephan Braun, Alexander Geisler and Martin Gerster, 82-108. Wiesbaden: Nomos, 2009.

Smoydzin, Werner. *NPD. Geschichte und Umwelt einer Partei. Analyse und Kritik*. Pfaffenhofen: Ilmgau Verlag, 1967.

Sowinski, Oliver. *Die Deutsche Reichspartei 1950-1965. Organisation und Ideologie einer rechtsradikalen Partei*. Frankfurt a.M. et al.: Peter Lang, 1998.

Stöss, Richard, ed. *Parteien-Handbuch. Die Parteien der Bundesrepublik Deutschland 1945-1980*. Opladen: Westdeutscher Verlag, 1983.

Stöss, Richard. "Die Aktionsgemeinschaft Unabhängiger Deutscher". In *Parteien-Handbuch. Die Parteien der Bundesrepublik Deutschland 1945-1980*, edited by Richard Stöss, 310-335. Opladen: Westdeutscher Verlag, 1983.

Stöss, Richard. "Die Deutsche Gemeinschaft". In *Parteien-Handbuch. Die Parteien der Bundesrepublik Deutschland 1945-1980*, edited by Richard Stöss, 867-900. Opladen: Westdeutscher Verlag, 1983.

Stöss, Richard. *Die extreme Rechte in der Bundesrepublik. Entwicklung – Ursachen – Gegenmaßnahmen*. Opladen: Verlag für Sozialwissenschaften, 1989.

Stöss, Richard. "Die Gesamtdeutsche Partei (GDP or GPD)". In *Parteien-Handbuch. Die Parteien der Bundesrepublik Deutschland 1945-1980*, edited by Richard Stöss, 1470-1477. Opladen: Westdeutscher Verlag, 1983.

Stöss, Richard. "Die Nationaldemokratische Partei". In *Parteien-Handbuch. Die Parteien der Bundesrepublik Deutschland 1945-1980*, edited by Richard Stöss, 1892-1921. Opladen: Westdeutscher Verlag, 1983.

Stöss, Richard. "Die NPD – Erfolgsbedingungen einer Rechtsextremen Partei". *Jahrbuch für Antisemitismusforschung* 14 (2005), edited by Wolfgang Benz, 41-59.

Stöss, Richard. "Einleitung. Struktur und Entwicklung des Parteiensystems der Bundesrepublik – Eine Theorie". In *Parteien-Handbuch. Die Parteien der Bundesrepublik Deutschland 1945-1980*, edited by Richard Stöss, 17-309. Opladen: Westdeutscher Verlag, 1983.

Stöss, Richard. *Rechtsextremismus im vereinten Deutschland*. Berlin: Friedrich Ebert Foundation, 2000.

Stöss, Richard. *Rechtsextremismus im Wandel*. Berlin: Friedrich Ebert Foundation, 2007.

Thadden, Adolf von. "Die Entwicklung der Nationalen Rechten nach 1945". In *Kongress-Protokoll 1989. Das Ende der Nachkriegszeit*, edited by Gesellschaft für freie Publizistik e.V., 43-69. Berg: Gesellschaft für freie Publizistik, 1990.

Tauber, Kurt P. *Beyond Eagle and Swastika. German Nationalism since 1945*, 2 vols. Middletown, CO: Wesleyan University Press, 1967.

Treß, Werner. "Anrich, Ernst". In *Handbuch des Antisemitismus. Judenfeindschaft in Geschichte und Gegenwart*, vol. 2/1, edited by Wolfgang Benz, 23-26. Berlin: De Gruyter Saur, 2009.

Treß, Werner. "Thadden, Adolf von". In *Handbuch des Antisemitismus. Judenfeindschaft in Geschichte und Gegenwart*, vol. 2/2, edited by Wolfgang Benz, 822-924. Berlin: De Gruyter, 2009.

Wise Women and Germanic Faith: Imagining Witches in Current German Right-Wing Extremism

Felix Wiedemann

The *Walpurgisnacht,* the night before May Day, is a very popular event in present-day Germany. As in other Central European countries, it falls at that time of year when spring is starting to usher in the early vestiges of summer, and given that it precedes a holiday, people like to take the opportunity to go out and enjoy the weather. For most revellers, of course, the mythological meaning of this night holds no meaning: As is well known, *Walpurgis* romantically commemorates the "holy night of the witches", a myth which some believe to stem from pre-Christian or even pre-historic roots.[1] Every year especially regional papers and journals draw upon this mythology, and articles are published on the supposed roots of *Walpurgis* as well as on the brutal persecution of (overwhelmingly) women who were regarded as witches and burned at the stake in Early Modern Europe. This issue has been of special importance for feminists since the Women's Liberation movement used the witch as a symbol for the fight against suppression and misogyny. Furthermore, the stories about mysterious "wise women" and their alleged magical practices have always aroused the curiosity of esoteric groups and circles. Hence, at the end of the 20th century the so-called modern witch cult became established as part of the wider field of the international new religious and neo-Pagan currents, and advanced to become a rather fashionable topic of research in anthropology and religious studies.[2]

---

1 However, it seems clear that this myth is much more modern than archaic, in this respect it belongs to the "invented traditions" as characterised by Eric Hobsbawm and Terence Ranger in *The Invention of Tradition* (Cambridge: Cambridge University Press, 1983). See on the myth of *Walpurgis* the short remarks by Thomas P. Becker, "Mythos Walpurgisnacht. Anmerkungen aus historischer Sicht", *EZW-Materialdienst* 70 (2007), 142-148.

2 On neo-Pagan witch cults, see above all Ronald Hutton, *The Triumph of the Moon. A History of Modern Pagan Witchcraft* (Oxford: Oxford University Press, 1999). In addition, see Margot Adler, *Drawing Down the Moon. Witches, Druids, Goddess Worshippers, and Other Pagans in America Today* (London: Penguin, 1986); Tanya Luhrmann, *Persuasions of the Witch's Craft. Ritual Magic and Witchcraft in Present-day England* (London: Blackwell, 1989); Helen A. Berger, *Witches. Contemporary Neo-Paganism and Witchcraft in the United States* (Columbia: University of South Carolina Press, 1999); Sabina Magliocco, *Witching Culture: Folklore and Neo-Paganism in America* (Philadelphia: University of Pennsylvania Press, 2004). For Germany: Oliver Ohanecian, *Wer Hexe ist, bestimme ich. Zur Konstruktion von Wirklichkeit im Wicca-Kult* (Schenefeld: Eb-Verlag, 2005); Kathrin Fischer, *Das Wiccatum. Volkskundliche Nachforschungen zu heidnischen Hexen im deutschsprachigen Raum* (Würzburg: Ergon, 2007). As mentioned above, a large body of research on neo-Pagan witch cult has emerged in the last two decades, and we could easily refer to twenty

However, the interest in witches by right-wing movements is probably less known. This can already be demonstrated by taking a glimpse at the *Deutsche Stimme,* the party organ of the National Democratic Party of Germany (*Nationaldemokratische Partei Deutschlands,* NPD). One can find some articles on the supposed Pagan tradition of *Walpurgis* here each spring. For example, in 2005 it contained an article by Ingmar Kolb, vice chairman of the right-wing German People's Union (*Deutsche Volksunion,* DVU), who now also advises the Saxon parliament faction of the NPD. In a seemingly innocuous way the author mentions the alleged Pagan roots of *Walpurgis* and gives a fanciful description of ritual conventions as natural and cheerful events. Finally, he encourages us to enrich our existence by re-orientating our life according to the holy rules of nature and ecology. At first glance, the article appears weird rather than nationalist or even racist. Only in the second part of the text which deals with the witch trials does the actual agenda of the author become more obvious: He blames the Church for this bloody persecution and calls it an intended "campaign of destruction against Paganism" and the authentic "faith of the Germanic people".[3]

An even stranger example for the popularity of witches among right-wingers is the mead (honey-wine) *Hexenelixir,* promoted and available on the online shop of *Deutsche Stimme.*[4] Even though this is just a label, it indicates the positive connotation of the term "witch" in current right-wing extremism and, last but not least, evokes similar product names in the feminist movement of the 1970s and 1980s.[5]

As I intend to demonstrate in the following, references like these are far from isolated; on the contrary, the whole subject seems to be of some importance in right-wing discussions on religion and history. This interest raises the question of its ideological and historical background: Why do German right-wingers and neo-Nazis care about supposed magical traditions and remote historical incidents such as the European witch trials, and what are their ideological and political motives? Is this a new, maybe tactically motivated phenomenon in order to appeal to younger and especially female supporters, or has the whole issue been of interest for right-wing movements before? Hence, I want to analyse the representations and interpretations of witchcraft and the witch trials in current German right-wing extremism and show that this interest indeed has a longer history. Preceding this, however, it is necessary to delineate the ideological background of right-wing neo-Paganism as well as the history of using the witch hunts for political, religious and social purposes in the 19th and 20th centuries.

---

or more books, however, in my view, the importance of these currents is rather overestimated.

3 Ingmar Kolb, "Die Hexen zu dem Brocken ziehen. Zur Walpurgisnacht vereinigen sich Sonne und Erde zur Feier der Fruchtbarkeit", *Deutsche Stimme* 4 (2005), http://www.deutsche-stimme.de/index.html (accessed April 30, 2010).

4 See http://www.ds-versand.de/product_info.php?info=p4935_Honig-Met-mit-exotischer-Fruchtmischung--Hexenelixir--0-75-ltr--Flasche.html (accessed April 30, 2010).

5 See Felix Wiedemann, *Rassenmutter und Rebellin. Hexenbilder in Romantik, völkischer Bewegung, Neuheidentum und Feminismus* (Würzburg: Königshausen & Neumann, 2007), 255-333.

The Modern Myth of the Witch

Ever since the witch trials came to an end in late 18th century Europe, these incidents have provoked a wide range of explanations, speculations and allegations. Until the middle of the 20th century both the scholarly and the popular discourse on witches largely followed two chief narratives: The *rationalist-anticlerical* and *the romantic* approach.[6]

Rationalist-anticlerical interpretations regarded witchcraft and sorcery as non-existent and believed all the stories about evil women and black magic to have been just products of a poor imagination or, more precisely, fraud and folly. In this context, the pathologising term *Hexenwahn* (witch-craze) became established as an expression for the superstitious belief in witches as well as for the persecution in Early Modern Europe. From the perspective of the 19th century, the witch-craze appeared as the epitome of the Dark Ages: A horrible incident, which had luckily been overcome by reason and progress, but had to be remembered as a symbol or reminder of the danger posed by irrationalism and superstition. Therefore, it was crucial for the rationalist authors of the time to explain why a non-existent crime such as witchcraft or black magic could have provoked such a heavy persecution and, most importantly, to identify those who were really responsible. With regard to the latter, these authors did not hesitate to provide a decisive answer and blamed the Catholic Church. First, for the dissemination of irrationalism and paving the way for superstition, and second, for executing the witch trials. Through these means, the whole theme had already become established in the 19th century as an important historical argument of religious criticism and anticlericalism.[7] The overall object in this context was to demonstrate the sole responsibility of the Church for the witch trials.

Consequently, the rationalist narrative produced some topoi, assertions and arguments, which became key elements in what can be called the modern myth of the witch. Mentioning the femaleness of the victims in order to evoke special moral indignation was surely the most important: In this sense, the (Catholic) Church was accused of its supposed genuine hatred toward women, whereas Christian misogyny was predominantly derived from its alleged roots in the Old Testament. Another important figure was the orientalisation of superstition by assigning the central fea-

---

6 See on this distinction, William E. Monter, "The Historiography of European Witchcraft: Progress and Prospects", *The Journal of Interdisciplinary History* 2 (1972), 435-452; in addition Roy Porter, "Witchcraft and Magic in Enlightenment, Romantic and Liberal Thought", in *Witchcraft and Magic in Europe*, vol. 5: *The Eighteenth and Nineteenth Centuries*, eds. Bengt Ankarloo and Stuart Clark (London: Athlone Press, 1999), 191-282; Wolfgang Behringer, "Geschichte der Hexenforschung", in *Wider alle Hexerei und Teufelswerk. Die europäische Hexenverfolgung und ihre Auswirkungen auf Südwestdeutschland*, eds. Sönke Lorenz and Jürgen Michael Schmidt (Ostfildern: Thorbecke, 2004), 485-668; Wiedemann, *Rassenmutter und Rebellin*, 33-116.

7 See Jörg Haustein, "Von der Instrumentalisierung zur historischen Erkenntnis – die Auseinandersetzung um den Hexenwahn im 19. Jahrhundert", in *Realität und Mythos. Hexenverfolgung und Rezeptionsgeschichte*, eds. Katrin Moeller and Burghart Schmidt (Hamburg: Dobu, 2003), 163-177.

tures of the witch-craze to an alien background: Superstition, fanaticism and the hatred toward women were said to have their roots in the Ancient Near East. However, ascribing the justification of the persecution to the Old Testament,[8] meaning the Hebrew Bible, at the same time offered scope for anti-Jewish statements. This kind of argument had already been noticeable among opponents of the witch trials during the Enlightenment, but in the 19th century it became more and more established in the wake of rising anticlericalism.[9]

Whereas the rationalist authors regarded the belief in witches as the embodiment of unreason and lunacy and as a result of Church-supported superstition, the central feature of the romantic approach, on the other hand, was the deep fascination with the seemingly archaic legends about the mysterious women who had been persecuted as witches. Most important in this regard was the presentation of the witches as descendants of Germanic "wise women", as lengthily described by the famous romanticist Jacob Grimm: In his *Deutsche Mythologie* (1835) the "wise women" appeared as venerated priestesses and healers, and he ascribed their assumed high status to a specific "Germanic veneration of women".[10] Moreover, Grimm considered witchcraft as an important vestige of an aboriginal "natural cult of our ancestors".[11]

Another important element of the romantic narrative was the combination of the myth of the wise women with the myth of matriarchy.[12] Most influential in this context was the famous book *Das Mutterrecht* (1861) by the Swiss historian Johann Jakob Bachofen, even though he never mentioned the witches himself.[13] But since the book was filled with stories on the rites of seemingly archaic priestesses, it was well suited to Grimm's wise women.

Last but not least, the romantic interpretation of witchcraft became more and more adopted by European occultism in the late 19th century. In doing so, the wise women were not only believed to have been Germanic priestesses, but also appeared as bearers of occult powers which had enabled them, for instance, to predict

---

8 In this regard the notorious verse in the book of Exodus (Ex 22.18) was particularly emphasised: "Thou shalt not suffer a witch to live."

9 See, e.g., the most important treatise against witch trials *De Crimine Magiae* (1701) by Christian Thomasius (1655-1728), who traced the belief in witches to alleged "Jewish-rabbinical" roots. Christian Thomasius, *Vom Laster der Zauberei. Über die Hexenprozesse. De Crimine Magiae. Processus Inquisitorii contra Sagas* (Munich: dtv, 1986), 37.

10 Jacob Grimm, *Deutsche Mythologie*, vol. 1 (Wiesbaden: Matrix, 2003), 329. On witches, see in particular 861-924, on women in general 328-362. On Grimm's method and nationalist ambitions, see Beate Kellner, *Grimms Mythen. Studien zum Mythosbegriff und seiner Anwendung in Jacob Grimms "Deutscher Mythologie"* (Frankfurt a.M.: Peter Lang, 1994).

11 Grimm, *Deutsche Mythologie*, 483.

12 See on the myth of matriarchy Cynthia Eller, *The Myth of Matriarchal Prehistory. Why an Invented Past Won't Give Woman a Future* (Boston: Beacon Press, 2000).

13 Johann Jakob Bachofen, *Myth, Religion and Mother Right. Selected Writings*, trans. Ralph Manheim, ed. Joseph Campbell (Princeton: Princeton University Press, 1992).

the future or to communicate with the dead.[14] It was in this wider new religious context that the romantic narrative became more and more charged with the kind of anticlericalism, hatred toward Christianity and not least anti-Jewish stereotypes that actually had its roots in the rationalist tradition.

This highlights that the rationalist and the romantic narrative were far from incompatible. Based upon the same strategy of blaming and identifying others, they had one thing in common: Regardless of whether accused of having disseminated superstition or of having suppressed a supposedly pre-Christian wisdom, the Church always appeared as the main culprit. Following this, the accusation could be extended to the Christian religion as a whole, including its roots in Judaism. Thus, the history of European witchcraft was established as a controversial issue long before the turn of the 20th century. The two chief narratives comprised a range of topoi, assertions and arguments, which facilitated the connection with different political, ideological and religious positions of the time.

Völkisch Neo-Paganism and the Preoccupation with Witches

Against the backdrop of this wider preoccupation with witches and witch hunts, nationalistic and right-wing currents became increasingly interested in this subject. At the turn of the 20th century the so-called *völkisch* movement[15] emerged out of a very heterogeneous intellectual and political context. Since the desire to overcome the deep denominational gaps and rivalries and to find a unified national faith for all Germans had always belonged to the key issues of nationalist thinking, *völkisch* ideologues tried to construct a religious tradition suited to the national or "racial" heritage: A kind of ethnic or racial religion, for which they coined the term *arteigene Religion*.[16] Even if the vast majority of the *völkisch* movement did not intend to substitute Christianity, a more radical neo-Pagan wing rejected the Christian religion completely and tried to "revitalise" or "resurrect" the faith of the ancient Germanic people, who were believed to have been the direct ancestors of the present-day

---

14 The research on new religious and occult movements in the first half of the 20th century has increased in the last two decades. See i.e. Corinna Treitel, *A Science for the Soul. Occultism and the Genesis of the German Modern* (Baltimore/London: Johns Hopkins University Press, 2004); Thomas Nipperdey, *Religion im Umbruch. Deutschland 1870-1918* (Munich: C.H. Beck, 1988); Ulrich Linse, *Geisterseher und Wunderwirker. Heilssuche im Industriezeitalter* (Frankfurt a.M.: Fischer, 1996); Diethard Sawicki, *Leben mit den Toten. Geisterglauben und die Entstehung des Spiritismus in Deutschland 1770-1900* (Paderborn: Schöningh, 2002).

15 On the *völkisch* movement see, among others, Uwe Puschner, *Die völkische Bewegung im wilhelminischen Kaiserreich. Sprache – Rasse – Religion* (Darmstadt: Wissenschaftliche Buchgesellschaft, 2001); Stefan Breuer, *Die Völkischen in Deutschland. Kaiserreich und Weimarer Republik* (Darmstadt: Wissenschaftliche Buchgesellschaft, 2008).

16 On *völkisch* religion, see Uwe Puschner, "Weltanschauung und Religion – Religion und Weltanschauung. Ideologie und Formen völkischer Religion", *Zeitenblicke* 5 (2006), http://www.zeitenblicke.de/2006/1/Puschner (accessed April 30, 2010); Stefanie von Schnurbein and Justus H. Ulbricht, eds., *Völkische Religion und Krisen der Moderne. Entwürfe "arteigener" Glaubenssysteme seit der Jahrhundertwende* (Würzburg: Königshausen & Neumann, 2001).

Germans. Of course, in doing so they were far from breaking new ground: Notions about an original "Germanic faith", mostly derived from medieval Scandinavian sources, had long been established in the nationalist discourse.[17]

Although the relationship between the *völkisch* movement and the National Socialist German Workers' Party (*Nationalsozialistische Deutsche Arbeiterpartei*, NSDAP) was anything but uncomplicated, some *völkisch*-religious ideas advanced to become official tenets in party organisations which were led by staunch adversaries of Christianity, such as the so-called philosopher of the Nazi Party, Alfred Rosenberg, or *Reichsführer-SS* Heinrich Himmler. Initially, most *völkisch* neo-Pagan groups welcomed the Third Reich and sniffed a chance to realise their religious ideas. However, the Nazi regime was not inclined to risk the alliance with the churches in favour of some marginal religious groups: After a crackdown against so-called sectarian groups by the Gestapo in 1937 most *völkisch* groups were banned; in some cases their leaders were even arrested and deported to concentration camps.[18] Hence, the *völkisch* hopes for a revival of Germanic Paganism were more or less doomed to failure. However, for several reasons the popular notions of witches proved to be very useful for both *völkisch* and Nazi purposes.[19] Referring to this, it is significant that these authors continued to reproduce the traditional difference between the rationalist and the romantic approach as delineated above.

Since the Catholic Church belonged to the declared enemies of *völkisch* nationalism, it is hardly surprising that neo-Pagans were particularly attracted to the anticlerical impact. *Völkisch* authors could simply draw upon the popular anticlerical accounts with their flowery depictions of brutal and lecherous clerics. Nevertheless, they introduced new elements and tried to link the witch hunts with central *völkisch* issues. Most obvious in this regard was the nationalist and racist framework. Even though references to Germany as the centre of persecution or to the "Germanic descent" of the victims was already noticeable in older anticlerical pamphlets, the integration of the witch hunts into the *völkisch* master narrative of an everlasting fight between different races was definitely new: Accordingly, the witch trials were depicted as an intended and surreptitious assault on the Germanic peoples and their racial heritage. Thereby, some *völkisch* authors drew upon the rationalist narrative and constructed a kind of rationalist Paganism – "rationalist", of course, only according to their self-conception: They believed the original Germanic Paganism

---

17 See Klaus Böldl, *Der Mythos der Edda. Nordische Mythologie zwischen europäischer Aufklärung und nationaler Romantik* (Tübingen: Francke, 2000); Julia Zernack, "Germanische Altertumskunde, Skandinavistik und völkische Religiosität", in *Völkische Religion*, eds. Schnurbein and Ulbricht, 227-253.

18 See Wolfgang Dierker, *Himmlers Glaubenskrieger. Der Sicherheitsdienst der SS und seine Religionspolitik 1933-1945* (Paderborn: Schöningh, 2002), 200-210; Treitel, *A Science for the Soul*, 220-242.

19 On the Nazi interest in witches, see Barbara Schier, "Hexenwahn und Hexenverfolgung. Rezeption und politische Zurichtung eines kulturwissenschaftlichen Themas im Dritten Reich", *Bayrisches Jahrbuch für Volkskunde* (1990), 43-117; Sönke Lorenz et al., *Himmlers Hexenkartothek. Das Interesse des Nationalsozialismus an der Hexenverfolgung* (Bielefeld: Verlag für Regionalgeschichte, 2000); Katarzyna Leszczynska, *Hexen und Germanen. Das Interesse des Nationalsozialismus an der Geschichte der Hexenverfolgung* (Bielefeld: transcript, 2009).

to have been a religion without "mysticism", "occultism" and "cultic elements" and claimed that a gap between knowledge and religion could not have evolved among the ancient Germans. Consequentially, the "witch-craze" appeared as a product of the seemingly imposed Christian superstition, which had only been overcome by the rebirth of "German rationalism" during the Reformation.

In the 1930s this position was propagated most extensively by Alfred Rosenberg who had already referred to the "witch-craze" in his infamous *Mythus des 20. Jahrhunderts* (1930) in order to demonstrate the negative role of Christianity in German history.[20] Later, he used the party machinery for his anticlerical campaign and initiated several studies on the alleged corrosion of the Germanic faith by the Christian dissemination of superstition and "witch-craze". Last but not least, Hitler's view seemed to be quite similar: He is said to have suggested the inception of a special museum in order to revere all the "great men", who once "had eliminated these superstitions and constructed a new scientific world view".[21]

But rationalism was by no means the only possibility of *völkisch* and Nazi authors to refer to witches and the witch hunts. Given the importance of popular belief and superstition in nationalist imaginations of the Germanic past, the adaptation of the romantic narrative was not surprising. If the rationalist approach was used for the construction of a "rationalist" Pagan religion, the romantic narrative, on the other hand, corresponded with more romantic views of the Germanic past, for instance focused on seemingly Germanic cults and the supposed wisdom of the ancestors. Himmler, for instance, repeatedly speculated about the "old knowledge and the old teachings" which the wise women had continued to adhere to after Christianisation. According to him, German women appeared as the true bearers and mediators of Paganism to modern times.[22]

Furthermore, the esoteric interpretations of witchcraft in contemporary occultism were adopted by *völkisch* authors as well. Again, they added new elements to the esoteric accounts and tried to integrate them in an all-embracing view on history. According to the so-called ariosophy *(Ariosophie)*, the most important branch of contemporary *völkisch* occultism, witches had not only been bearers of occult powers, but also keepers of the secrets of racial breeding.[23] Consequently, the witch trials appeared as an alien attack on the racial future of the Germanic peoples. The precursor of this kind of interpretation was the founder of ariosophy, Guido List, who described Germanic witchcraft as sexual cult in order to guarantee racial selection and traced the Witches' Sabbath to supposed gatherings of a female priest-

---

20 See Alfred Rosenberg, *Der Mythus des 20. Jahrhunderts. Eine Wertung der seelisch-geistigen Gestaltenkämpfe unserer Zeit* (Munich: Eher, 1935).

21 Adolf Hitler, *Monologe im Führerhauptquartier 1941-1944. Die Aufzeichnungen Heinrich Heims*, ed. Werner Jochmann (Hamburg: Knaus, 1980), 286-287.

22 Himmler's speech in Tölz, February 18, 1937, in Heinrich Himmler, *Geheimreden 1933-1945 und andere Ansprachen*, eds. Bradley F. Smith and Agnes F. Peterson (Frankfurt a.M.: Propyläen, 1974), 103.

23 On ariosophy, see Nicholas Goodrick Clarke, *Occult Roots of Nazism: Secret Aryan Cults and Their Influence on Nazi Ideology* (London: Tauris, 2004).

hood. Moreover, due to his radical anticlericalism, List branded the witch trials as the "main strike against the occult character of the Germanic woman".[24]

As Grimm had already done, this concept of the allegedly venerated Pagan women could be easily contrasted with the supposed patriarchal and misogynist Christian tradition. This is precisely why the whole issue proved to be highly attractive for right-wing and *völkisch* women. Although the *völkisch* movement was overwhelmingly male dominated, during the Weimar Republic some right-wing women tried to combine *völkisch* nationalism and racism with demands for more gender equality and constituted a kind of *völkisch* feminism.[25] A key element of this ideology was the assumption of an original equality between men and women among the Germanic people before the rise of patriarchal Christianity. Accordingly, the witch trials were said to have been the last and most brutal chapter in the long Christian war of destruction against the aboriginal Germanic gender order. Like in the feminist movement of the 1970s, witches served as positive role models, and *völkisch* women identified themselves strongly with the "wise women". Marie Adelheid Reuß zur Lippe, for instance, declared in 1934 the solidarity of "German Pagan women of the present" with their medieval sisters, who had been "persecuted, tortured and burned" as witches: "We pledge that their innocent blood has not been spilled in vain. They will live in us."[26]

Besides anticlericalism, anti-Semitism was another driving force behind the *völkisch* interpretation. This ideological pattern resulted from the close connection between anticlericalism and anti-Semitism in radical German nationalism. Both the Roman Church and the Jews appeared as "supranational powers" and natural enemies of the nationalist and racial world order. Since it was commonplace among *völkisch* neo-Pagans to regard Christianity as a mere continuation of Judaism, or even as an insidious invention of the Jews to enslave all other peoples, references to the alleged Jewish roots of the witch trials aimed primarily at the Jewish origins of Christianity. In this sense, Uriel Tal's expression can be used to term this type of anti-Semitism "anti-Christian anti-Semitism".[27]

It is obvious that *völkisch* authors drew heavily upon older schemes and patterns of argumentation. For proponents of *völkisch* rationalism, for instance, deriving the "witch-craze" from oriental roots was the most important aspect, since in the *völkisch* discourse "Oriental" or "Near Eastern" just served as synonyms for "Jewish". In this sense, *völkisch* women were especially eager to trace the roots of the witch trials to an alleged Jewish hatred against women. Accordingly, the witch trials advanced to become a "Jewish" assault on Germanic women and their important role

---

24 Guido List, *Der Übergang vom Wuotanismus zum Christentum* (Berlin: Guido von List-Verlag, 1926), 101f.

25 See Christiane Streubel, *Radikale Nationalistinnen. Agitation und Propaganda rechter Frauen in der Weimarer Republik* (Frankfurt a.M.: Campus Verlag, 2006).

26 Marie Adelheid Prinzessin zur Lippe, *Nordische Frau und nordischer Glaube* (Berlin: Adolf Klein, 1934), 19.

27 See Uriel Tal, *Christians and Jews in Germany. Religion, Politics and Ideology in the Second Reich 1870-1914* (London: Cornell University Press, 1975), 223-289.

as healers and priestesses.[28] The witch hunts were also integrated in anti-Semitic conspiracy theories. The best example of this was given by Heinrich Himmler in a keynote speech about the role and duties of the SS in 1935: The leader of the SS ranked the "tragedy" of the witch trials among the never-ending "war of the Jews against all peoples", and even though he identified the Church as the manifest executor, he was deeply convinced that "our eternal enemy, the Jew" had orchestrated this tragedy behind the scenes "with his bloody hands".[29] Last but not least, Himmler's deep preoccupation with witches culminated in an extensive research project, the so-called Mission H: He instructed the Security Service of the SS (*Sicherheitsdienst,* SD) to detect and record all witch trials which had been carried out in Early Modern Germany. Accordingly, between 1935 and 1944 the SD combed through more than 250 archives and libraries and recorded the results on almost 30,000 filing cards.[30]

References to the Witch-Craze in Current Right-Wing Extremism

While neo-Germanic mythology at first seemed to be widely discredited after the defeat of Nazism in 1945, Pagan themes and symbols never disappeared from the right-wing and neo-Nazi discourse. But overall, *völkisch* neo-Paganism in the post-war years was a marginal phenomenon and restricted to a few splinter groups. This applied also to romantic interpretations of Pagan witchcraft, a subject, which was at the time generally of marginal scholarly and public interest only.

Nevertheless, unlike witch*craft* the witch *hunt* remained highly symbolically charged and therefore has never lost its utility for political purposes. Thus, the witch *trials* remained a strong metaphor for unjustified persecution and judicial murder in public discourses, and have been repeatedly compared with proceedings, which are believed to be show trials. Maybe the most famous example of this is Arthur Miller's use of the Salem witch hunts of 1692 as a means to criticise the persecution of communists and left-wingers during the McCarthy era in his play *The Crucible* (1953).[31]

Significantly, the same strategy was applied by former Nazis and right-wingers to denounce the unpopular Nuremberg Trials, and the persecution of German war criminals as a whole, as an imposed and unjustified victors' justice. I only want to give a few examples here: In 1993 the convicted Holocaust denier Germar Rudolf published an article entitled "The medieval witch trial and its counterpart in our

28 See e.g. Margarethe Kurlbaum-Sieber[t], "Nur das jüdische Gesetz nahm dem Weibe das Priestertum", in *Deutsche Frauen an Adolf Hitler*, ed. Irmgard Reichenau (Leipzig: Adolf Klein, 1933), 54-58.

29 Heinrich Himmler, *Die Schutzstaffel als antibolschewistische Kampforganisation* (Munich: Eher, 1936), 5.

30 See Lorenz et al., eds., *Himmlers Hexenkartothek*.

31 Arthur Miller, *The Crucible. A Play in Four Acts* (London: Penguin, 2000).

own time", in which he equated the Nuremberg Trials with the witch trials.[32] This kind of political use is still common among right-wing extremists and has been used to denounce other political adversaries as well. Thus, recently the *Deutsche Stimme* compared a declaration by the Council of the German Protestant Church against the rise of right-wing extremism, racism and anti-Semitism with the medieval clerical struggle against heretics and witches.[33] The last example I want to give here is the overall attack on the supposedly left-wing-dominated political culture and the alleged suppression of the freedom of speech in Germany by the former functionary of the right-wing party The Republicans (*Die Republikaner,* REP), Hans Rustemeyer. He draws the following comparison:

> For centuries the witch-craze rushed over Europe. Every sceptic was regarded as a wizard himself. A trick which is still successfully used, though today no one speaks about Satanists, but dissidents are denounced as fascists.

Furthermore, the author regards his book as an "antidote to superstition" which makes it appear scientific.[34]

Like their *völkisch* predecessors, right-wing extremists and neo-Nazis try to integrate the witch hunts into an imagined history of German suffering. In this way, the famous neo-Nazi and former NPD functionary Jürgen Rieger declares the burned "witches and heretics" as victims of the "forced Christianisation" of the Germanic people and ranks them together with the victims of allied bombing and the expellees after the Second World War among the heroic victims of German history.[35] Here, it becomes evident that anticlericalism, radical rejection of Christianity and a more or less openly expressed anti-Christian anti-Semitism continue to be the main motives for right-wingers and neo-Nazis to refer to the witch hunts. Rieger, who died in 2009, was not only a political key figure and an important financier of neo-Nazism for the last thirty years, but also leader of a neo-Germanic Pagan group. Accordingly, the denigration of Christianity was a central issue for him. Moreover, it is generally observed that the expression of radical anti-Christian attitudes have become more and more important in right-wing extremism during the last few decades. In the 1960s, for instance, the NPD clearly adhered to the conservative ideology of the Christian Occident, and references to Christianity as the most suitable faith for the German people were beyond dispute. However, the situation has thoroughly changed with the radicalisation of the party since the late

---

32 Werner Kretschmer [pseud. of Germar Rudolf], "Der mittelalterliche Hexenprozess und seine Parallelen in unserer Zeit", quoted in Leszczynska, *Hexen und Germanen,* 115.

33 Michael Grunzel, "Hexen, Ketzer, Deutsche", *Deutsche Stimme,* December 22, 2009, http://www.deutsche-stimme.de/ds/?p=2711 (accessed April 30, 2010).

34 See the blurb of his recent book *Herrschaft der Lüge* on http://www.ds-versand.de/product_info.php?info=p1392_Rustemeyer--Hans--Herrschaft-der-Luege.html (accessed April 30, 2010).

35 Jürgen Rieger, *Wege und Ziele der Artgemeinschaft,* extract on http://asatru.de/nordzeit (accessed April 30, 2010). More on the *Artgemeinschaft* below.

1990s and with its successful anchoring in the highly un-denominational eastern parts of Germany.[36]

Furthermore, during the last two decades music has become more and more important as a vehicle of right-wing ideology, including anticlericalism and anti-Christian anti-Semitism.[37] Hence, the presence of the witch in lyrics by right-wing bands is hardly surprising. In one of the most popular songs of the famous neo-Nazi band *Landser*, entitled "Walvater Wotan", for example, the witches are mentioned as "German women" who were "burned in their thousands as witches". The context here is clearly anti-Christian anti-Semitism – one line above the total destruction of Christianity by Germanic Wotan is promulgated: "Pray to your Jewish god, he doesn't hear you, you Christian pig."[38]

Anti-Christian attitudes are also widespread among right-wing women who, even though anti-feminism still dominates in current right-wing extremism, definitely played a more important role than in the *völkisch* movement of the 1920s and 1930s.[39] For these women, the witch trials are as attractive as they were for their *völkisch* forerunners. Accordingly, it is not difficult to find websites of right-wing women and proponents of a so-called "national feminism"[40] who continue to use the witch hunts in exactly the same way. A significant example is the Community of German Women (*Gemeinschaft deutscher Frauen*, GDF), an organisation of "girls, women and mothers" who want to "take part in building the national community", and is said to be one of the most important female groups in current right-wing extremism. Based on the assumption that the racially determined estimation of women *(artgemäße Frauenwertung)* had been decomposed by "Jewish Christendom", they enlarge on the "witch-craze". At this point, they obviously resort to depictions of the wise women as elaborated by feminists in the 1970s and 1980s, and continue with a lengthy discussion of the role of the Germanic women as priestesses, healers, midwives and so on.[41]

---

36 See Toralf Staudt, *Moderne Nazis. Die neuen Rechten und der Aufstieg der NPD* (Cologne: Kiepenheuer & Witsch, 2006), 96-98.

37 See in general *RechtsRock. Bestandsaufnahme und Gegenstrategien*, eds. Christian Dornbusch and Jan Raabe (Münster: Unrast, 2006).

38 *Landser*, "Walvater Wotan" (CD 1996). *Landser* is said to have been the most important neo-Nazi band of the 1990s. In 2003 it was declared a criminal organisation by a Berlin court and the musicians were sentenced to imprisonment.

39 See on women in current right-wing extremism: *Braune Schwestern? Feministische Analysen zu Frauen in der extremen Rechten*, ed. Antifaschistisches Frauennetzwerk, Forschungsnetzwerk Frauen und Rechtsextremismus (Münster: Unrast, 2005); Renate Bitzan, ed., *Rechte Frauen. Skingirls, Walküren, Feine Damen* (Berlin: Elefanten Press, 1997); Michaele Köttig, *Lebensgeschichten rechtsextrem orientierter Mädchen und junger Frauen: Biografische Verläufe im Kontext der Familien- und Gruppendynamik* (Gießen: Psychosozial-Verlag, 2004).

40 This was the slogan of the female right-wing group *Mädelring Thüringen*, which was recently dissolved.

41 See the homepage of the *Gemeinschaft deutscher Frauen*, http://www.g-d-f.de/ (accessed April 30, 2010).

Regarding the references to witches in current right-wing extremism given so far, political motives seem to be dominating: Either the persecution serves as a metaphor in political debates or this incident is used to denounce the Church or the Christian religion as a whole. Accordingly, right-wing authors draw mostly upon the traditional rationalist-anticlerical narrative. Nevertheless, references by right-wing women as well as articles in the *Deutsche Stimme* on *Walpurgis* show that the romantic narrative has never disappeared from right-wing discourse. On the contrary, romantic interpretations, accompanied by a new interest in supposedly Pagan traditions, have definitely become more important among right-wing extremists during the last few decades. This reappearance of the wise women is, of course, far from being restricted to right-wing groups, but reflects general tendencies in the wider cultural and religious landscape since the 1960s. Thus, in order to understand more recent right-wing references to witches and the witch hunt, these contexts should be taken into account.

Völkisch Neo-Paganism and the Ideologues of the New Right

As mentioned above, during the postwar years the interest in Pagan traditions was restricted to a few splinter groups, which were clearly rooted in the tradition of *völkisch* neo-Paganism. The best example for this is the *Artgemeinschaft,* a still-existing group and one of the biggest neo-Germanic organisations, which is said to have 150 members. The group was founded in 1951 by Wilhelm Kusserow, who had been a proponent of *völkisch* neo-Paganism since the 1920s. Thirty years later Kusserow was replaced by the above-mentioned neo-Nazi Jürgen Rieger, who remained the leader of the group until his death in 2009. The *Artgemeinschaft* never changed its distinct *völkisch* and racialist ideology.[42] Accordingly, their concepts of Germanic Paganism and their interpretations of the witch trials strictly followed in the steps of those from the 1920s and 1930s: Rieger and his followers claimed the victims of the persecution to have been mostly women of the Nordic race and lamented the loss of "good blood".[43]

However, I want to give two examples here to show how other proponents of old *völkisch* neo-Paganism also tried to integrate new elements into their constructions of the supposed Germanic religion in order to appeal to new adherents.

One of the most important reservoirs of *völkisch* neo-Paganism in the aftermath of the Second World War was the German Unitarian Religious Community (*Deutsche Unitarier Religionsgemeinschaft,* DUR), which was actually a free-Protestant denomination, which has been taken over by *völkisch* neo-Pagans.[44] The leading fig-

42 See Stefanie von Schnurbein, *Religion als Kulturkritik. Neugermanisches Heidentum im 20. Jahrhundert* (Heidelberg: Winter, 1992), 120ff; Franziska Hundseder, *Wotans Jünger. Neuheidnische Gruppen zwischen Esoterik und Rechtsradikalismus* (Munich: Heyne, 1998), 44-58.

43 See i.e. Gudrun Heinkes, "Was bedeutet uns die Frau und Mutter?", *Nordische Zeitung. Die Stimme des Artglaubens* 68/4 (2000), 73-78.

44 See in general Ulrich Nanko, "Religiöse Gruppierungen vormaliger 'Deutschgläubiger' nach 1945", in *Antisemitism, Paganism, Voelkish Religion/Antisemitismus, Paganismus, völkische Religion,*

ure and ideological mastermind of this organisation was Sigrid Hunke, who was at the same time a popular author on the history of religions, as well as on the Islamic and Arab world. However, she had a clear National Socialist background and became an important figure of the emerging intellectual movement of the New Right since the late 1960s.[45] Her depiction of an all-European, pre-Christian *Ur-Religion* in her chief work *Europas eigene Religion* (1969) which strongly influenced the French *Nouvelle Droite* can be seen as a kind of modernisation of older neo-Pagan concepts.[46] She did not only make ideological contributions, but also joined organisations of the New Right like the Thule Seminar, an offshoot of the French Nouvelle Droite. In doing so, Hunke just sold old wine in new skins: She simply replaced "Germanic Paganism" with "Paganism" and limited the anti-Christian anti-Semitism which had permeated throughout her earlier writings to a few but univocal allusions.[47] Within the *völkisch* tradition she pursued the ideology of *völkisch* rationalism and feminism. On this account, her books always told the same story of an eternal fight between the seemingly rational European *Ur-Religion* and the irrationalism of Christianity. Her main target in this context was the so-called Christian "dualism", meaning the separation of body and soul, man and God, immanence and transcendence, politics and religion, which she intended to substitute by the pantheistic "unitarism" of European Paganism. Accordingly, the "concordance of faith and knowledge", or the fundamental unity of the spiritual and the natural, respectively, was the central element of her model of the *Ur-Religion*.[48] Exactly this figure was later adopted by Alain de Benoist, the ideological mastermind of the French Nouvelle Droite, in his neo-Pagan manifesto *Comment peut-on être païen* (How Can One be a Pagan?, 1981) and used as an argument against the so called "Jewish-Christian de-sacralisation of the world".[49]

---

ed. Hubert Cancik and Uwe Puschner (Munich: Saur, 2004), 121-134; on the DUR, see Peter Kratz, *Die Götter des New Age. Im Schnittpunkt von "Neuem Denken", Faschismus und Romantik* (Berlin: Elefanten Press, 1994), 285-372.

45 See on Hunke Horst Junginger, "Sigrid Hunke. Europe's New Religion and its Old Stereotypes", in *Antisemitism, Paganism, Voelkisch Religion*, eds. Cancik and Puschner, 151-162; Felix Wiedemann, "'Allahs Sonne' und 'Europas eigene Religion'. Die Verschränkung von Arabophilie und Neuheidentum in der rechtsextremen Ideologie Sigrid Hunkes", *Zeitschrift für Geschichtswissenschaft* 57 (2009), 891-912.

46 See Sigrid Hunke, *Europas eigene Religion. Die Überwindung der religiösen Krise* (Munich: Bastei-Lübbe, 1981). On her influence on the French Nouvelle Droite, see Miro Jennerjahn, *Neue Rechte und "Heidentum". Zur Funktionalität eines ideologischen Konstrukts* (Frankfurt a.M.: Peter Lang, 2006).

47 Most important in this sense was the replacement of the Jews by the ancient Hurrians as the main root of Christian dualism. See Hunke, *Europas eigene Religion*, 27-33.

48 See Hunke, *Europas eigene Religion*, 399-411. However, her own concept with its sharp distinction between Paganism and Christianity is, of course, itself highly "dualistic".

49 Alain de Benoist, "Paganische Sakralität und jüdisch-christliche Entsakralisierung der Welt", in *Welche Religion für Europa? Ein Gespräch über die religiöse Identität der Völker Europas*, ed. Demetrios Theraios (Bern et al.: Peter Lang, 1992), 41-86; Alain de Benoist, *Comment peut-on être païen. Un recours aux racines – une spiritualité pour notre temps* (Paris: Albin Michel, 1981).

Furthermore, from the very beginning the history of gender relations belonged to Hunke's main subjects, and she always remained strictly within the narrative of *völkisch* feminism when dealing with the subject. Accordingly, she depicted a – now supposedly all-European – gender equality in ancient times and blamed the Christian religion of having destroyed an erstwhile high estimation of women by introducing the fateful "dualism" between men and women. Similar to her precursors in the 1930s, the "witch-craze" stood out as one of the main pieces of historical evidence for the process of degradation of European women. Accordingly, Hunke held the Church alone responsible for the persecution and followed the rationalist narrative in her version of *völkisch* feminism: The "witch-craze" appeared as a fateful result of "forcing European women into the Jewish-oriental strait jacket".[50]

Another proponent of *völkisch* neo-Paganism who experienced a kind of revival in his later years was the former president of the *SS-Ahnenerbe* Herman Wirth.[51] This was mainly due to the fact that he had already introduced some elements into his construction of the supposed pre-Christian *Ur-Religion,* which became fashionable again in the course of the proliferation of alternative spirituality in the 1970s. Most important in this context was the use of the myth of matriarchy: Wirth described the supposed original religion of the Nordic ancestors as a form of cultic matriarchy, dominated by female priestesses. Thus, the attractiveness of the wise women seemed to be quite logical, and accordingly his books were replete with references to witches.[52] After the war he maintained his concept, but whereas he had been nearly isolated in the postwar years, the situation began to change with the emergence of alternative and new religious movements from the late 1960s onwards. He seized the opportunity and focused on Pagan matriarchy in his writings: Again, he described several holy places which had served as ritual and cultic sites for Pagan priestesses who had later been persecuted by the patriarchal Church. Most important in this context was his interpretation of the *Externsteine,* a bizarre rock formation in northern Germany which is believed to be a special "place of power" in the esoteric scene: According to Wirth, the *Externsteine* were the most important spiritual place of the so-called European *Ur-Religion,* and he linked it with the assumed rites of the wise women.[53] It was obvious that he intended to appeal to

50 Sigrid Hunke, "Von der Verteufelung der Frau", *Unitarische Blätter* 34 (1983), 111. See also Hunke, *Am Anfang waren Mann und Frau. Vorbilder und Wandlungen der Geschlechterbeziehungen* (Hildesheim: Olms, 1987).

51 See on his biography Ingo Wiwjorra, "Herman Wirth – Ein gescheiterter Ideologe zwischen 'Ahnenerbe' und 'Atlantis'", in *Historische Rassismusforschung. Ideologien, Täter, Opfer,* eds. Barbara Dankwarth et al. (Hamburg: Argument, 1995), 90-112.

52 See e.g. Herman Wirth, *Was heißt deutsch? Ein urgeistesgeschichtlicher Rückblick zur Selbstbesinnung und Selbstbestimmung* (Jena: Diederichs, 1930), 11, 45, 61.

53 See Herman Wirth, *Der Neue Externsteinführer* (Vienna: Volkstum Verlag, 1969); idem., *Die Frage der Frauenberge – eine europäische Gegenwartsfrage. Eine Denkschrift* (Marburg: Eccestan-Verlag, 1972).

new adherents outside traditional *völkisch* circles, a strategy which was quite successful, in so far that his interpretations, in some cases, are popular even today.[54]

Right-Wing Neo-Pagan Groups

Besides the continued activities of ideologists who still had a *völkisch* and National Socialist background, a second wave of neo-Germanic Paganism emerged along with the proliferation of alternative and non-Christian spirituality in the late 1960s. Generally, the newly established groups tried to integrate some concepts of the new religious discourse into what they believed to have been the aboriginal Germanic religion. The political background and direction of these currents have always been rather diffuse and heterogeneous.[55] Nevertheless, right-wing groups still exist, and some of them clearly stand within the tradition of *völkisch* neo-Paganism.[56] Thus, a general assessment seems to be rather difficult, and each group should be examined closely.

The best-known right-wing neo-Germanic association established in the 1970s are the Armanen Order *(Armanen-Orden)* and the related Working Community of Nature Religious Tribes of Europe (*Arbeitsgemeinschaft naturreligiöser Stammesverbände Europas,* ANSE), which both still exist today.[57] As especially the name of the latter indicates, these groups emphasise the "natural" and "native" character of the Pagan faith instead of the "racial" one. This shift of terms is clearly a reference to the broader alternative and neo-religious current. Thus, the Armanen Order, for example, uses Jungian archetypes to assign each people to a different innate faith and character. Nevertheless, from the very beginning both groups have tried to revitalise the racist tradition of ariosophy, and to combine *völkisch* occultism with newer elements of esotericism. This affects, of course, especially the view on the witches who appeared here not only as wise women and healers, but also as bearers of occult *völkisch* powers. Furthermore, like Herman Wirth, the ANSE in particular uses

---

54 See Luitgard Löw, "Völkische Deutungen prähistorischer Sinnbilder. Herman Wirth und sein Umfeld", in *Völkisch und national. Zur Aktualität alter Denkmuster im 21. Jahrhundert*, eds. Uwe Puschner and Ulrich Großmann (Darmstadt: Wissenschaftliche Buchgesellschaft, 2009), 214-232.

55 See Schnurbein, *Religion als Kulturkritik;* for more recent developments, see Matthias Pöhlmann, ed. *Odins Erben. Neugermanisches Heidentum. Analysen und Kritik* (Berlin: EZW, 2006); René Gründer, *Germanisches (Neu-)Heidentum in Deutschland* (Berlin: Logos, 2008); Ann-Laurence Maréchal, "Ausdifferenzierungsprozesse neugermanisch-heidnischer Religiosität", in *Fluide Religion. Neue religiöse Bewegungen im Wandel. Theoretische und empirische Systematisierungen*, eds. Dorothea Lüddeckens and Rafael Walthert (Bielefeld: transcript, 2010), 189-214.

56 See on right-wing neo-Paganism in general, Friedrich-Wilhelm Haack, *Wotans Wiederkehr. Blut-Boden und Rasse-Religion* (Munich: Claudius, 1981); Mattias Gardell, *Gods of the Blood. The Pagan Revival and White Separatism* (Durham/London: Duke University Press, 2003); Nicholas Goodrick-Clarke, *Black Sun. Aryan Cults, Esoteric Nazism and the Politics of Identity* (New York: New York University Press, 2003).

57 See on these groups in detail Schnurbein, *Religion als Kulturkritik*, 21-80. Gründer (in *Germanisches Heidentum*, 92) estimates the number of members of the group at 100.

the myth of matriarchy to explain the allegedly central role of the wise women and to depict the witch trials as bloody assault of patriarchal Christianity on the cult of the "Great Mother" in Germanic Paganism.[58] Last but not least, the female leader of ANSE, Sigrun von Schlichting, believes herself to be a reincarnated witch who was burned at the stake during the Middle Ages.[59]

In 1985 members of the Armanen Order, of which some had a neo-Nazi background, established the Berlin Pagan Community *(Heidnische Gemeinschaft)*.[60] Although the group later dissociated itself from racism and right-wing extremism, the *völkisch* roots of its convictions remained clearly discernible in its early publications. Most obvious was the defamation of Christianity as an "oriental religion of the desert" *(Wüstenreligion)*. Nevertheless, the group definitely placed more emphasis on the ecological and seemingly female character of Paganism than traditional *völkisch* groups. In doing so, they intended to appeal to new adherents beyond the right-wing scene. For this purpose they adopted not only central themes of the contemporary new social movements, but also their way of political agitation: They published leaflets on witches and the witch trials which were designed and written in a quite similar way to those in the feminist movement. Accordingly, the witch trials were depicted as a bloody attempt to "keep up the domination of patriarchy".[61]

Another group, which emerged out of the milieu of the Pagan Community is the Berlin-located Germanic Faith Community *(Germanische Glaubensgemeinschaft)*. The group also distances itself from Nazism and right-wing extremism, but nevertheless sees itself in a direct tradition to a clearly *völkisch* organisation with the same name of a group which was established before the First World War. Accordingly, the head of the group, Géza von Neményi, represents a very orthodox view on Germanic Paganism and continues to connect religion with ethnic origin and the Germanic faith to Germanic descent.[62] The persecution of the so-called wise women plays a vital role in Neményi's writings: In order to link his ideas with the wider new religious discourse, he refers to the esoteric concept of archaic shamanism and presents the wise women as the female shamans of Germanic Paganism. Moreover, he believes that it was the secret convents of the witches as occult rites that were the real target of the persecution.[63] Last but not least, the group has a "real" witch among its members, Catrin Wildgrube, who works as a Germanic "seeress" and has published some books on being a witch. But actually, her depictions must be re-

58 See the leaflet *Armanischer Thruden Ring* (1981), reprinted in Haack, *Wotans Wiederkehr*, 129.

59 She mentioned her alleged experience in a letter to the organisers of a large historical exhibition on the witch trials in 1987 (reprinted in the journal of the group *Irminsul. Stimme der Armanenschaft* 20/2 [1988]).

60 On the history of this group, see Schnurbein, *Religion als Kulturkritik*, 142-158.

61 See the leaflet *Hexen – weise Frauen*, http://www.runenstein-net.de/ (accessed December 31, 2007). A general problem of an online-based research on this current is the permanent change of websites and addresses. Accordingly, some of the texts and articles mentioned in the following have already disappeared.

62 See his main work: Géza von Neményi, *Götter, Mythen, Jahresfeste. Heidnische Naturreligion* (Holdenstedt: Kersken Canbaz, 2004).

63 Ibid., 137, 183.

garded more as part of the general esoteric literature than of right-wing neo-Paganism in the strict sense.[64]

In the early 1990s the connection between right-wing neo-Paganism, on the one hand, and the wider new religious and esoteric current, on the other, was especially represented by the Arun publishing house. Its programme used to include new editions of old *völkisch* literature as well as books by proponents of international neo-Paganism; however, in the last few years openly right-wing books have increasingly been taken out of the programme.[65] The founder of the publishing house, Stefan Ulbrich, personifies the link between right-wing extremism and esotericism in his own biography: Being a part of the neo-Nazi milieu of the 1980s, he changed to the so-called intellectual New Right, and finally to neo-Paganism. His influential main work *Im Tanz der Elemente* includes a lengthy chapter on witches, which he describes – strictly in the way of *völkisch* romanticism – as "heirs of Pagan priestesses", endowed with special occult powers and responsible for the holy cult of sexual reproduction.[66]

Furthermore, in the last decade several new groups have been founded which now occupy the hybrid status between right-wing extremism and the wider new religious current. I only want to refer to the Working Group Naudhiz *(Arbeitskreis Naudhiz)* here, a small Bavarian neo-Germanic group, which intends to maintain and preserve religious diversity on earth as well as a "racial" one, and thus clearly adheres to the right-wing concept of ethno-pluralism.[67] The witch trials belonged to the most important historical issues of the group's radical anticlerical propaganda in the early years of its existence. Accordingly, they accused the Church of having conducted several genocides in history, including the witch trials, which were termed as an attempt to eliminate the German people.[68] However, maybe due to a lawsuit, the activities of the group on the internet has become less radical during the last few years, and references to witches are now restricted to romantic interpretations of assumed Germanic traditions such as *Walpurgis*.[69]

Another example of a neo-Germanic interpretation with a clear right-wing agenda is the seemingly innocuous website *Naturglaube.de*. Nevertheless, there can be no doubt about its ideological agenda: Christianity is accused of having desacralised the German landscape and is, as a consequence, held responsible for modern pollution. Along with the denigration of nature, the natural faith of the people as well as the Germanic high esteem of women is said to have been devalued and destroyed. It is in this context that one can find the reference to witches

---

64 See Catrin Wildgrube, *Die Welt der Hexen* (Holdenstedt: Kersken Canbaz, 2003).

65 See http://www.arun-verlag.de/ (accessed April 30, 2010).

66 Björn [Stefan] Ulbrich, *Im Tanz der Elemente. Kult und Ritus der naturreligiösen Gemeinschaften* (Engerda: Arun, 1995), 49ff.

67 See http://www.naudhiz.info/ (accessed December 31, 2007).

68 This interpretation was originally part of a radical anti-Christian text, titled "Völkermord im Zeichen des Kreuzes" which disappeared from the Internet in 2007.

69 See http://www.naudhiz.info/V4/Willkommen.html (accessed April 30, 2010).

in the manner of the traditional *völkisch* narrative: The wise women as bearers of Germanic faith were eliminated by an alien power.[70]

As mentioned above, the whole field of neo-Germanic Paganism is by no means homogenous and has become more and more differentiated in the last two decades. Some observers regard groups with an open right-wing agenda as rather marginal in today's neo-Germanic Paganism. According to these studies, younger groups have left their *völkisch* background behind and developed a kind of "universalistic" Paganism. Thus, they considered themselves as part of a global movement.[71] Nevertheless, right-wing neo-Pagan groups still exist, and it remains to be seen if this direction will really gain the upper hand.

Nothing New Under the Black Sun

In view of the long history of using the witch trials for nationalist and *völkisch* purposes, referring to this subject in current right-wing extremism is by no means a new phenomenon. Additionally, the mode of interpretation, for instance the assertions, arguments, allusions and images, remain strictly within the frame of older *völkisch* and Nazi accounts. The dominant ideological motive is still anticlericalism and a radical rejection of Christianity, embedded in a wide range of mostly diffuse and contradictory constructions of Germanic Paganism. Within this general framework different aspects can be emphasised: The politically oriented organisations used the witch trials as a propaganda tool only to denounce political and ideological adversaries. The still-existing right-wing esoteric scene, however, describes the "wise women" as bearers of occult powers of the ancient Germanic people in order to combine contemporary esotericism with right-wing nationalism and racism. And finally, for right-wing women the witches represent heroic victims of patriarchy, which is still traced back to seemingly foreign Jewish-Christian roots.

But the main reason why right-wingers – like their *völkisch* and National Socialist predecessors – still refer to witches and the witch hunt is the seemingly innocuous character of the whole subject: As shown above, stories about the mysterious figure of the witch and her gruesome persecution have not ceased to fascinate people; thereby anticlerical, romantic and esoteric interpretations are, of course, far from being restricted to right-wing currents. Thus, referring to the witches simply provides an opportunity to convey fragments of nationalist and racist ideology in a seemingly harmless way, and by doing so to appeal to new adherents beyond the right-wing scene in a narrower sense.

70 See http://www.naturglaube.de (accessed April 30, 2010).

71 Maréchal, *Ausdifferenzierungsprozesse;* Gründer, *Germanisches (Neu-)Heidentum.* Gründer, 92, lists the membership of the most important neo-Germanic groups, which amount to no more than 900 people for the whole of Germany.

Bibliography

Adler, Margot. *Drawing Down the Moon. Witches, Druids, Goddess Worshippers, and Other Pagans in America Today*. London: Penguin, 1986.

Antifaschistisches Frauennetzwerk. Forschungsnetzwerk Frauen und Rechtsextremismus, ed. *Braune Schwestern? Feministische Analysen zu Frauen in der extremen Rechten.* Münster: Unrast 2005.

Johann Jakob Bachofen, *Myth, Religion and Mother Right. Selected Writings*, trans. Ralph Manheim, ed. Joseph Campbell. Princeton: Princeton University Press, 1992.

Becker, Thomas Peter. "Mythos Walpurgisnacht. Anmerkungen aus historischer Sicht". *EZW-Materialdienst* 70 (2007), 142-148.

Behringer, Wolfgang. "Geschichte der Hexenforschung". In *Wider alle Hexerei und Teufelswerk. Die europäische Hexenverfolgung und ihre Auswirkungen auf Südwestdeutschland*, edited by Sönke Lorenz and Jürgen Michael Schmidt, 485-668. Ostfildern: Thorbecke 2004.

Benoist, Alain de. *Comment peut-on être païen. Un recours aux racines – une spiritualité pour notre temps.* Paris: Albin Michel, 1981.

Benoist, Alain de. "Paganische Sakralität und jüdisch-christliche Entsakralisierung der Welt". In *Welche Religion für Europa? Ein Gespräch über die religiöse Identität der Völker Europas*, edited by Demetrios Theraios, 41-86. Bern et al.: Peter Lang, 1992.

Berger, Helen A. *Witches. Contemporary Neo-Paganism and Witchcraft in the United States.* Columbia: University of South Carolina Press, 1999.

Bitzan, Renate, ed. *Rechte Frauen. Skingirls, Walküren, Feine Damen.* Berlin: Elefanten Press, 1997.

Böldl, Klaus. *Der Mythos der Edda. Nordische Mythologie zwischen europäischer Aufklärung und nationaler Romantik.* Tübingen: Francke, 2000.

Breuer, Stefan. *Die Völkischen in Deutschland. Kaiserreich und Weimarer Republik.* Darmstadt: Wissenschaftliche Buchgesellschaft, 2008.

Hubert Cancik and Uwe Puschner, eds. *Antisemitism, Paganism, Voelkisch Religion/ Antisemitismus, Paganismus, völkische Religion.* Munich: Saur, 2004.

Dierker, Wolfgang. *Himmlers Glaubenskrieger. Der Sicherheitsdienst der SS und seine Religionspolitik 1933-1945.* Paderborn: Schöningh, 2002.

Dornbusch, Christian and Jan Raabe, eds. *RechtsRock. Bestandsaufnahme und Gegenstrategien.* Münster: Unrast, 2006.

Eller, Cynthia. *The Myth of Matriarchal Prehistory. Why an Invented Past Won't Give Woman a Future.* Boston: Beacon Press, 2000.

Fischer, Kathrin. *Das Wiccatum. Volkskundliche Nachforschungen zu heidnischen Hexen im deutschsprachigen Raum.* Würzburg: Ergon, 2007.

Gardell, Mattias. *Gods of the Blood. The Pagan Revival and White Separatism.* Durham/London: Duke University Press, 2003.

Goodrick-Clarke, Nicholas. *Black Sun. Aryan Cults, Esoteric Nazism and the Politics of Identity.* New York: New York University Press, 2003.

Goodrick-Clarke, Nicholas. *Occult Roots of Nazism: Secret Aryan Cults and Their Influence on Nazi Ideology.* London: Tauris, 2004.

Grimm, Jacob. *Deutsche Mythologie.* 2 vols. Wiesbaden: Matrix, 2003.

Gründer, René. *Germanisches (Neu-)Heidentum in Deutschland.* Berlin: Logos, 2008.

Haack, Friedrich-Wilhelm. *Wotans Wiederkehr. Blut-Boden und Rasse-Religion.* Munich: Claudius, 1981.

Haustein, Jörg. "Von der Instrumentalisierung zur historischen Erkenntnis – die Auseinandersetzung um den Hexenwahn im 19. Jahrhundert". In *Realität und Mythos. Hexenverfolgung und Rezeptionsgeschichte,* edited by Katrin Moeller and Burghart Schmidt, 163-177. Hamburg: Dobu, 2003.

Heinkes, Gudrun. "Was bedeutet uns die Frau und Mutter?". *Nordische Zeitung. Die Stimme des Artglaubens* 68/4 (2000), 73-78.

Himmler, Heinrich. *Die Schutzstaffel als antibolschewistische Kampforganisation.* Munich: Eher, 1936.

Himmler, Heinrich. *Geheimreden 1933-1945 und andere Ansprachen,* edited by Bradley F. Smith and Agnes F. Peterson. Frankfurt a.M.: Propyläen, 1974.

Hitler, Adolf. *Monologe im Führerhauptquartier 1941-1944. Die Aufzeichnungen Heinrich Heims,* edited by Werner Jochmann. Hamburg: Knaus, 1980.

Hobsbawm, Eric and Terence Ranger, eds. *The Invention of Tradition.* Cambridge: Cambridge University Press, 1983.

Hundseder, Franziska. *Wotans Jünger. Neuheidnische Gruppen zwischen Esoterik und Rechtsradikalismus.* Munich: Heyne, 1998.

Hunke, Sigrid. *Europas eigene Religion. Die Überwindung der religiösen Krise.* Munich: Bastei-Lübbe, 1981.

Hunke, Sigrid. *Am Anfang waren Mann und Frau. Vorbilder und Wandlungen der Geschlechterbeziehungen.* Hildesheim/Zürich/New York: Olms, 1987.

Hunke, Sigrid, "Von der Verteufelung der Frau". *Unitarische Blätter* 34 (1983), 111-114.

Hutton, Ronald. *The Triumph of the Moon. A History of Modern Pagan Witchcraft.* Oxford: Oxford University Press, 1999.

Jennerjahn, Miro. *Neue Rechte und "Heidentum". Zur Funktionalität eines ideologischen Konstrukts.* Frankfurt a.M.: Peter Lang, 2006.

Junginger, Horst. "Sigrid Hunke. Europe's New Religion and its Old Stereotypes". In *Antisemitism, Paganism, Voelkisch Religion/Antisemitismus, Paganismus, völkische Religion,* edited by Hubert Cancik and Uwe Puschner, 151-162. Munich: Saur, 2004.

Kellner, Beate. *Grimms Mythen. Studien zum Mythosbegriff und seiner Anwendung in Jacob Grimms "Deutscher Mythologie".* Frankfurt a.M.: Peter Lang, 1994.

Köttig, Michaela. *Lebensgeschichten rechtsextrem orientierter Mädchen und junger Frauen: Biografische Verläufe im Kontext der Familien- und Gruppendynamik.* Gießen: Psychosozial-Verlag, 2004.

Kratz, Peter. *Die Götter des New Age. Im Schnittpunkt von "Neuem Denken", Faschismus und Romantik.* Berlin: Elefanten Press, 1994.

Kurlbaum-Sieber[t], Margarete. "Nur das jüdische Gesetz nahm dem Weibe das Priestertum". In *Deutsche Frauen an Adolf Hitler,* edited by Irmgard Reichenau. Leipzig: Adolf Klein, 1933.

List, Guido. *Der Übergang vom Wuotanismus zum Christentum.* Berlin: Guido von List Verlag, 1926.

Leszczynska, Katarzyna. *Hexen und Germanen. Das Interesse des Nationalsozialismus an der Geschichte der Hexenverfolgung.* Bielefeld: transcript, 2009.

Linse, Ulrich. *Geisterseher und Wunderwirker. Heilssuche im Industriezeitalter.* Frankfurt a.M.: Fischer, 1996.

Lorenz, Sönke, Dieter R. Bauer, Wolfgang Behringer and Jürgen Michael Schmidt, eds. *Himmlers Hexenkartothek. Das Interesse des Nationalsozialismus an der Hexenverfolgung.* Bielefeld: Verlag für Regionalgeschichte, 2000.

Luhrmann, Tanya M. *Persuasions of the Witch's Craft. Ritual Magic and Witchcraft in Present-day England.* London: Blackwell, 1989.

Maréchal, Ann-Laurence. "Ausdifferenzierungsprozesse neugermanisch-heidnischer Religiosität". In *Fluide Religion. Neue religiöse Bewegungen im Wandel. Theoretische und empirische Systematisierungen*, edited by Dorothea Lüddeckens and Rafael Walthert, 189-214. Bielefeld: transcript 2010.

Monter, William E. "The Historiography of European Witchcraft: Progress and Prospects". *The Journal of Interdisciplinary History* 2 (1972), 435-452.

Magliocco, Sabina. *Witching Culture: Folklore and Neo-Paganism in America*. Philadelphia: University of Pennsylvania, 2004.

Miller, Arthur. *The Crucible. A Play in Four Acts*. London: Penguin, 2000.

Nanko, Ulrich. "Religiöse Gruppierungen vormaliger 'Deutschgläubiger' nach 1945". In *Antisemitism, Paganism, Voelkish Religion/Antisemitismus, Paganismus, völkische Religion*, edited by Hubert Cancik and Uwe Puschner, 121-134. Munich: Saur 2004.

Neményi, Géza von. *Götter, Mythen, Jahresfeste. Heidnische Naturreligion*. Holdenstedt: Kersken Canbaz, 2004.

Nipperdey, Thomas. Religion im Umbruch. Deutschland 1870-1918. Munich: C.H. Beck, 1988.

Ohanecian, Oliver. *Wer Hexe ist, bestimme ich. Zur Konstruktion von Wirklichkeit im Wicca-Kult*. Schenefeld: Eb-Verlag, 2005.

Pöhlmann, Matthias, ed. *Odins Erben. Neugermanisches Heidentum. Analysen und Kritik*. Berlin: EZW, 2006.

Porter, Roy. "Witchcraft and Magic in Enlightenment, Romantic and Liberal Thought". In *Witchcraft and Magic in Europe*, vol. 5: *The Eighteenth and Nineteenth Centuries*, edited by Bengt Ankarloo and Stuart Clark, 191-282. London: Athlone Press, 1999.

Reuß zur Lippe, Prinzessin Marie Adelheid. *Nordische Frau und nordischer Glaube*. Berlin: Adolf Klein, 1934.

Rosenberg, Alfred. *Der Mythus des 20. Jahrhunderts. Eine Wertung der seelisch-geistigen Gestaltenkämpfe unserer Zeit*. Munich: Eher, 1935.

Puschner, Uwe. *Die völkische Bewegung im wilhelminischen Kaiserreich. Sprache – Rasse – Religion*. Darmstadt: Wissenschaftliche Buchgesellschaft, 2001.

Puschner, Uwe. "Weltanschauung und Religion – Religion und Weltanschauung. Ideologie und Formen völkischer Religion". Zeitenblicke 5 (2006), http://www.zeitenblicke.de/2006/1/Puschner (accessed 30 April, 2010).

Puschner, Uwe and Ulrich Großmann, eds. *Völkisch und national. Zur Aktualität alter Denkmuster im 21. Jahrhundert*. Darmstadt: Wissenschaftliche Buchgesellschaft 2009.

Sawicki, Diethard. *Leben mit den Toten. Geisterglauben und die Entstehung des Spiritismus in Deutschland 1770-1900*. Paderborn: Schöningh, 2002.

Schier, Barbara. "Hexenwahn und Hexenverfolgung. Rezeption und politische Zurichtung eines kulturwissenschaftlichen Themas im Dritten Reich". *Bayrisches Jahrbuch für Volkskunde* (1990), 43-117.

Schnurbein, Stefanie von. *Religion als Kulturkritik. Neugermanisches Heidentum im 20. Jahrhundert*. Heidelberg: Winter 1992.

Schnurbein, Stefanie von and Justus H. Ulbricht, eds. *Völkische Religion und Krisen der Moderne. Entwürfe "arteigener" Glaubenssysteme seit der Jahrhundertwende*. Würzburg: Königshausen & Neumann, 2001.

Schnurbein, Stefanie von. "Religion of Nature or Racist Culture? Contemporary Neogermanic Pagan Movements in Germany". In *Antisemitism, Paganism, Voelkish Religion/Antisemitismus, Paganismus, völkische Religion*, edited by Hubert Cancik and Uwe Puschner, 135-150. Munich: Saur, 2004.

Staudt, Toralf. *Moderne Nazis. Die neuen Rechten und der Aufstieg der NPD.* Cologne: Kiepenheuer & Witsch 2006.

Streubel, Christiane. *Radikale Nationalistinnen. Agitation und Propaganda rechter Frauen in der Weimarer Republik.* Frankfurt a.M.: Campus Verlag, 2006.

Tal, Uriel. *Christians and Jews in Germany. Religion, Politics and Ideology in the Second Reich 1870-1914.* London: Cornell University Press, 1975.

Thomasius, Christian. *Vom Laster der Zauberei. Über die Hexenprozesse. De Crimine Magiae. Processus Inquisitorii contra Sagas.* Munich: dtv, 1986 [1701/1705].

Treitel, Corinna. *A Science for the Soul. Occultism and the Genesis of the German Modern.* Baltimore/London: Johns Hopkins University Press, 2004.

Ulbrich, Björn [Stefan]. *Im Tanz der Elemente. Kult und Ritus der naturreligiösen Gemeinschaften.* Engerda: Arun, 1995.

Wiedemann, Felix. *Rassenmutter und Rebellin. Hexenbilder in Romantik, völkischer Bewegung, Neuheidentum und Feminismus.* Würzburg: Königshausen & Neumann, 2007.

Wiedemann, Felix. "'Allahs Sonne' und 'Europas eigene Religion'. Die Verschränkung von Arabophilie und Neuheidentum in der rechtsextremen Ideologie Sigrid Hunkes", *Zeitschrift für Geschichtswissenschaft* 57 (2009), 891-912.

Wirth, Herman. *Was heißt deutsch. Ein urgeistesgeschichtlicher Rückblick zur Selbstbesinnung und Selbstbestimmung.* Jena: Diederichs, 1930.

Wirth, Herman. *Der Neue Externsteinführer.* Vienna: Volkstum Verlag, 1969.

Wirth, Herman. *Die Frage der Frauenberge – eine europäische Gegenwartsfrage. Eine Denkschrift.* Marburg: Eccestand, 1972.

Wildgrube, Catrin. *Die Welt der Hexen.* Holdenstedt: Kersken Canbaz, 2003.

Wiwjorra, Ingo. "Herman Wirth – Ein gescheiterter Ideologe zwischen 'Ahnenerbe' und 'Atlantis'". In *Historische Rassismusforschung. Ideologien, Täter, Opfer,* edited by Barbara Dankwarth, 90-112. Hamburg: Argument 1995.

Zernack, Julia. "Germanische Altertumskunde, Skandinavistik und völkische Religiosität". In *Völkische Religion und Krisen der Moderne. Entwürfe "arteigener" Glaubenssysteme seit der Jahrhundertwende,* edited by Stefanie von Schnurbein and Justus H. Ulbricht, 227-253. Würzburg: Königshausen & Neumann 2001.

A Voice of the Extreme Right?

The Role of the Bund der Vertriebenen and its Leader Erika Steinbach in the Postwar German Public Discourse

Astrid Sverresdotter Dypvik

Introduction

For more than 60 years, the Federation of Expellees (*Bund der Vertriebenen*, BdV) has played a changing but nonetheless central part in the German debate on the Hitler era, at times by defining the debate, at other times being the topic of discussion. The organisation started as a social and political movement for Germans expelled from Central and Eastern Europe after the end of the Second World War. Since then, it has undergone quite a development in the German public. Starting in the 1950s as a mainstream organisation working for the interests of the expellees, the BdV was gradually marginalised in the German public in the late 1960s. This was due to the change in the political climate created by the *Ostpolitik* of Chancellor Willy Brandt from 1969, and the *Vergangenheitsbewältigung* that began in the 1960s: German society's process of coming to terms with the crimes committed during the Second Word War. Since 2000, however, the BdV has re-entered mainstream political discourse.

Whether this new version of the BdV is in fact politically transformed or just a superficially changed organisation with new slogans covering the same old political program, has been the topic of a heated debate in Germany during the last years. The central question of this debate is whether the BdV and its leader, Erika Steinbach, will manage to integrate the history of the German expellees with the European postwar history, not as a counterpart to the Holocaust, but merely as part of the events following the capitulation of the German *Wehrmacht* and the ethnic cleansing of Europe after 1945.[1]

An underlying question in this debate that will be discussed in this chapter is whether the BdV and Erika Steinbach may be called a voice of the extreme right in the historical debate in Germany. In order to answer this question, this chapter will first provide a brief description of the BdV, Erika Steinbach and the history of the German expellees, before explaining the unique role the question of the expellees has played at the various stages of the German process of coming to terms with its past. The chapter will also briefly discuss the German extreme right, with emphasis on the National Democratic Party of Germany (*Nationaldemokratische Partei Deutsch-*

---

1 This question is formulated by the former chairperson of the Centre against Expulsions (*Zentrum gegen Vertreibungen*, ZgV), Peter Glotz, in Peter Glotz, "Der Kampf gegen das Verbrechen der Vertreibung", *Die Politische Meinung* 417/8 (2004), 15-18.

lands, NPD),[2] which is the largest political organisation on the far right in contemporary Germany. In this context I will compare the rhetoric of the BdV and the NPD with regards to the expulsion, as well as certain other central topics of the German occupation during the Second World War.

The term "expellees" refers to people of German nationality who were expelled from – or fled – the former German territories east of the current German-Polish border (the Oder-Neisse border) and from areas in Czechoslovakia, Hungary, Romania and Yugoslavia in 1945 and the following years. The individuals expelled from these territories were mainly German citizens. Others were in fact citizens of the countries from which they were expelled, thus constituting a German minority in these countries.[3] The number of expellees is uncertain, but the fact that in 1950 the two German states had accepted 11.2 million refugees gives an impression of the proportions of the expulsion.[4] The number of casualties is still disputed; a demographic study by Gerhard Reichling supported by the German government estimates that almost two million people perished during the expulsion (a number that also includes German casualties in Soviet labour camps),[5] while other estimates are lower. The debate on the numbers of casualties is indeed politicised. Historians and writers close to the BdV tend to conclude with higher numbers of casualties and missing individuals than historians and writers critical of the BdV.[6] Although the exact number of the casualties is contested, all historians agree that the death rate among the expellees was high. This can partly be explained by the fact that the expulsion was indeed brutal in some areas, particularly in Czechoslovakia.

One example is the massacre in Ústí nad Labem (Aussig an der Elbe) in northern Bohemia. The massacre took place on July 31, 1945, at the end of the Potsdam Conference, and followed an explosion in a munitions factory. The explosion was blamed on the *Werewolf*, an alleged German underground movement that still was loyal to Hitler, and was used as a pretext for attacking the remaining Germans in the city. A mob mainly consisting of Czech paramilitaries gathered on the city's main square and started attacking Germans, who were easy to identify, as they were already forced to wear white armbands when moving outside. One group of Germans was ordered to march onto the bridge crossing the Elbe and then to jump into the river. The mob opened fire on persons coming up for air. The number of victims in this massacre is still disputed. According to survivors, between 2,000 and 2,700 individuals were murdered.[7] However, there are few other sources supporting

---

2 On the NPD in detail, see Gideon Botsch's contribution to this anthology.

3 Section xiii of the Potsdam declaration states that the expulsion should take place in an "orderly and humane manner".

4 K. Erik Franzen and Hans Lemberg, *Die Vertriebenen – Hitlers letzte Opfer* (Munich: Ullstein, 2002), 324.

5 Gerhard Reichling, *Die deutschen Vertriebenen in Zahlen* (Bonn: Kulturstiftung der deutschen Vertriebenen, 1995), 36, table 7.

6 Bernadetta Nitschke, *Vertreibung und Aussiedlung der deutschen Bevölkerung aus Polen 1945 bis 1949* (Munich: Oldenbourg, 2003), 269-282.

7 Norman Naimark, *Fires of Hatred – Ethnic Cleansing in Twentieth Century Europe* (Cambridge, MA: Harvard University Press, 2001), 127.

these claims. The number of people being reported as missing after the massacre is much lower. German historians estimate that about 220 persons were killed in the massacre,[8] while Czech historians have even lower estimates, claiming that between 43 and 100 persons were killed.[9]

The story of the detention camp Lambinowice (Lamsdorf) is one of the most notorious examples on the Polish side of the Oder-Neisse border. During the Second World War, Lambinowice was a Wehrmacht camp for prisoners of war from the Soviet Union. After the liberation by the Red Army, it was turned into a camp for German civilians who were to be deported from the area. The mortality rate among the inmates of this camp was high; some historians claim that one out of nine died due to harsh treatment, lack of food and poor hygienic conditions.[10]

The violence committed against the expellees can partly be explained by the fact that the war itself had led to a brutalisation of society. Another important explanatory factor is that the German occupation had fostered hatred against Germans, including civilians. In addition to this, the areas in Eastern Europe were impoverished and partly devastated by the brutal occupation, and living conditions were in general very harsh. Within this context, displaced persons were even more vulnerable than the general population to disease, hunger, and the intense cold of the winters of 1944 and 1945.[11]

The German Postwar Debate

In Germany, the postwar expulsion of Germans from Central and Eastern Europe has played an interesting and changing part in the complex process of dealing with the past. In order to understand how the story of the expulsion could play this role, an introduction to the German postwar debate is necessary. The historian Norbert Frei analysed the West German process of dealing with the past and identified four main phases.[12] These four phases are connected to the postwar generations in West German society. New generations have always played a crucial role for the debate on the crimes committed during the Second World War.

The first phase is the period immediately after the war, 1945-1949. During these years, re-educating citizens from Nazi ideology and raising awareness of the wide range of crimes committed by Germans during the war were put on the public agenda by the US military administration. It is important to note that this process was not initiated by the Germans themselves, but by the occupational forces in what would later become the Federal Republic of Germany (FRG), as part of the

8 Theodor Schieder, ed., *Dokumentation der Vertreibung der Deutschen aus Ost-Mitteleuropa*, 2 vols. (Munich: dtv, 2004).

9 Naimark, *Fires of Hatred*, 18.

10 Edmund Nowak, *Lager im Oppelner Schlesien im System der Nachkriegslager in Polen (1945-1950)* (Opole: Zentrales Kriegsgefangenenmuseum Lamsdorf-Oppeln, 2003).

11 Naimark, *Fires of Hatred*, 27, 117.

12 Norbert Frei, *1945 und wir. Das Dritte Reich im Bewusstsein der Deutschen* (Munich: C.H. Beck, 2005).

Allies' programs of creating a new and democratic Germany. The West German response to such re-education was reluctant. In general, the re-education and judicial persecution of German war criminals was not seen as a response to war crimes of an unprecedented scale, but as part of a justice imposed by the war's victors upon the defeated. Germans born in the years around 1905 had a particular interest in this reluctance, as their generation had been strongly represented among the elites of the Hitler regime.[13]

The next phase, 1949-1960, may be summed up by the term *Vergangenheitspolitik*, (Politics of History), the political discourse of the new democratic West Germany and of the era of the west-oriented Chancellor Konrad Adenauer. During this period, outside pressure upon the Germans had eased, convicted war criminals were given amnesties, and people with former careers in the Nazi regime, who had been excluded from their profession in 1945, were allowed to return to their previous occupation. Integration and the wish to "let the past be the past" was the main official policy of the Adenauer era. However, the contemporary political and cultural debate was far more ambiguous. The fact that the diary of the Jewish teenager Anne Frank was widely read in Germany from the 1950s onward is an example of this; the book demands unconditional empathy with Holocaust victims. Still, such concerns were not the main tendency. In the political discourse, a privileged position was granted to the German expellees, who, along with the victims of allied bombing, were seen as innocent Germans who had to carry their nation's defeat upon their own shoulders. This privileged position also explains why the writing of the history of the expulsion was to be one of the largest and most ambitious academic projects in postwar Germany, with contributions from many of the country's most respected historians.[14]

The third phase in the West German process of dealing with its past is the discourse of the *Vergangenheitsbewältigung* (Dealing with the Past), which Frei dates from the 1960s to the 1980s. It involved a reaction to the previous era's harmonic understanding of the past. The most outstanding feature in this era's discourse is a change of focus: Now, the crimes committed by the Nazis in the name of the German people were put to the centre of attention. Trials of key Nazi officials, such as the Eichmann trial in Jerusalem in 1961-1962, and the Auschwitz trial in Frankfurt in 1963-1965, were followed closely by the media and made a great impact on the West German public. Writers such as Martin Walser and Günter Grass were important in articulating and forming this new discourse, as were a new generation of young, radical students born after 1945. Moral allegations and accusations against the generation born around 1905, which constituted the elite of the Hitler regime, were a central part of this discourse. Frei states that within this new

13 See e.g. Michael Wildt's study, *Generation des Unbedingten. Das Führungskorps des Reichssicherheitshauptamtes* (Hamburg: Hamburger Edition, 2003), which shows the strong involment of this generation in the Reich Security Main Office (*Reichssicherheitshauptamt*, RSHA).

14 Mathias Beer, "'Ein der wissenschaftlichen Forschung sich aufdrängender historischer Zusammenhang'. Von den deutschen Schwierigkeiten 'Flucht und Vertreibung' zu kontextualisieren", *Zeitschrift für Geschichtswissenschaft* 51/1 (2003), 59-64.

debate, there was not much room for German victims.[15] German historian Bernd Faulenbach has a more dramatic choice of words, stating that the expulsion ended up in the shadow of the Holocaust.[16] Still, the history of the expulsion was far from forgotten; the topic was subject to serious academic research also in the 1960s and 1970s.[17] But among the younger generation, the history of the expulsion was considered a symbol for the right-wing movement. Chancellor Willy Brandt's foreign policy may be the clearest manifestation of this new discourse. The treaties of Moscow and Warsaw meant a de facto recognition of the Oder-Neisse border. They were also the first acceptance of the effects of the expulsion, although the treaties stated that a final settlement could only be recognised by a united Germany. The effect of the two treaties on West Germany's foreign relations was that the tension between the West German state and Poland and Russia was eased. Within West German society, however, the effect was different: It made Willy Brandt the number one enemy for the BdV and the far right. With their slogan "Waiver is treason" they accused Brandt of having betrayed Germany's true borders.

The fourth and final phase starts in the 1980s and continues into the present. Frei calls this the phase of *Vergangenheitsbewahrung* (Preserving the Past). The harsh disputes of the 1960s and 1970s are over by now, and the struggles and contested debates have been replaced by a culture of remembering. This does not mean that the days of conflict and polarised debates are gone, but rather that the gap between the two sides of the still on-going debate is somewhat diminished. In East Germany, the situation for the expellees was very different than in West Germany. Being geographically closer to the new border, the Soviet Occupation Zone, later to become the German Democratic Republic (GDR), had a higher percentage of expellees in the population than its western neighbour. The expulsion was accepted as a fact by the leadership of the communist party only after some pressure from Moscow. The strategy of the political leadership of the GDR was to integrate the expellees in society as soon as possible, and then put a lid over the whole situation. Any organisation of the expellees, whether with political or cultural aims, was considered revanchist and strictly forbidden.[18] There were no changes in the political debate over the East German expellees until the 1990s, when unification became the dominating discourse of the unified Germany.

Within this current discourse, the expellees have experienced a revival in the public sphere. In 2003, German historian Karl Schlögel claimed that his fellow German historians were avoiding contact with the topic of postwar flight and expulsion, because they were afraid to receive applause from the so-called "wrong

---

15 Frei, *1945 und wir*, 13.

16 Bernd Faulenbach, "Die Vertreibung der Deutschen aus den Gebieten jenseits von Oder und Neisse. Zur wissenschaftlichen und öffentlichen Diskussion in Deutschland", *Aus Politik und Zeitgeschichte* 51/52 (2002), 44-54.

17 Edgar Wolfrum, "Zwischen Geschichtsschreibung und Geschichtspolitik. Forschungen zu Flucht und Vertreibung nach dem Zweiten Weltkrieg", *Archiv für Sozialgeschichte* 36 (1996), 500-522.

18 Franzen and Lemberg, *Die Vertriebenen*, 267-292.

side", meaning the BdV and people associated with the BdV. Such applause would, according to Schlögel's analysis, stigmatise historians as nationalist or even revanchist. His argument is sharply formulated and not entirely correct, because the renowned historian Wolfgang Benz, for example, published a book with contributions from a wide range of historians with positions at German universities in 1985.[19] Still, it points to one important fact: Both the BdV and the expulsion itself were to some extent considered a symbol of right-wing politics. This gradually changed after 2000. The book *Im Krebsgang* by Günter Grass, published in 2002, is generally considered as a milestone of this change of discourse. Following its publication, there was a boom in literature about the expulsion, including academic publications. For example, two editions of the academic journal *Zeitschrift für Geschichtswissenschaft* dealt exclusively with the topic of the expulsion (in 2003 and 2005, both edited by the historians Jürgen Daniel and Philipp Ther).[20] The expulsion was also the topic of a wide range of publications aimed at the general public, such as the book *Die Flucht* by K. Erik Franzen (2002) and the TV-productions by the successful director Guido Knopp.

Finally, the highly controversial debate about the establishment of the Centre against Expulsions *(Zentrum gegen Vertreibungen*, ZgV), which will be treated more thoroughly later in this chapter, and where the BdV played a central role, contributed to bring public attention to the expulsion. German historian Ute Frevert describes this increase in publications and public attention as a "memory boom".[21] The renewed interest does not, however, mean a general acceptance of the BdV. Many of the writers and academics that contributed to the so-called memory-boom distanced themselves explicitly from the organisation, Günter Grass being one of the most prominent examples of this.[22]

The BdV and the Discourse on the Expellees

The BdV was founded in 1957 as an umbrella organisation covering varius organisations within the expellee movement, whose histories date back to the 1940s. The objectives of these organisations under the BdV umbrella were diverse. One branch of the movement worked for the political interests of the expellees in West Germany, while other branches mainly worked to maintain the cultural heritage of the Germans from Eastern and Central Europe. The core of the organisation was the

19 Wolfgang Benz, ed., *Die Vertreibung der Deutschen aus dem Osten – Ursachen, Ereignisse, Folgen* (Frankfurt a.M.: Fischer, 1985). Another example is Philipp Ther and Ana Siljak, eds., *Redrawing Nations. Ethnic Cleansing in East-Central Europe, 1944-1948* (Lanham: Rowman & Littlefield, 2001).

20 *Zeitschrift für Geschichtswissenschaft* 51/1 (2003); 53/10 (2005).

21 Ute Frevert, "Geschichtsvergessenheit und Geschichtsversessenheit revisited. Der jüngste Erinnerungsboom in der Kritik", *Aus Politik und Zeitgeschichte* 40/41 (2003), 6-13.

22 Doris Schäfer-Noske, "Günter Grass gegen Berlin als Standort für Zentrum gegen Vertreibungen", *Deutschlandradio*, http://www.dradio.de/dlf/sendungen/interview_dlf/154568/ (accessed September 10, 2012).

so-called *Landsmannschaften*, groups organised according to the expellees' geographical location prior to the exodus. Consequently, there is one Landsmannschaft for the Sudeten Germans, and one for the Silesians etc. Demands central to the BdV in the 1950s were a non-acceptance of the new border between East Germany and Poland, compensation from the countries in the east for the loss of values during the expulsion, the right to return to their former territories, and the persecution of crimes committed against German civilians. These political objectives were not particularly disputed in the era of the *Vergangenheitspolitik*. Rather, they were supported by the political mainstream, the party of the chancellor, the Christian conservative CDU, and partly also by the social democratic SPD, although the support from the social democrats was not as wholehearted as the support from the Christian conservatives. The political program of the BdV was well tailored for the political discourse of the Adenauer era.

Then, in the 1960s and 1970s, the *Vergangenheitsbewältigung* represented an entirely new way of thinking about the past, individual and collective guilt, and responsibility. However, in the midst of this changing political discourse in Germany, the BdV did not change. During the 1960s and 1970s, the days of being part of the political mainstream were over for the expellee movement, and it gradually turned into a political subculture. The organisation was criticised for fighting yesterday's lost battles. Indeed, the BdV's reputation among the new generation was not increased by the organisation's own political program, which stated that the BdV wanted to stop "the cold de-Nazifying". Nor did it help that several key people within the movement had held high positions in Nazi Germany. Some prominent examples were known as early as in the 1960s and 1970s; more recent research has shown that there is far more to this story than has been publicly known. An investigation by the German news magazine *Der Spiegel* in 2006 showed that among 200 individuals holding high positions within the BdV movement before 1982, over one third had been members of the NSDAP, and that the number of former SS members within the BdV was approximately three times higher than in the general German population.[23]

The BdV stuck to its political program, and members continued to publish books about the atrocities of the expulsion, such as *Die Flucht* by Edgar Günter Lass in 1964. In this process, the movement came to be less representative of the wider group of expellees. This can be explained by two factors. Firstly, the success of the economic integration of the expellees: Many had reached an acceptable level of integration and were therefore no longer in need of an organisation working for their cause. A survey conducted in 1965 showed that less than one per cent of the former expellees were in fact members of the Landsmannschaften of the BdV and that the organisation failed to win the support of the younger generation.[24]

---

23 Hans Michael von Kloth and Klaus Wiegrefe, "Unbequeme Wahrheiten", *Der Spiegel*, August 2006, 46-48.

24 Dietrich Strothmann, "'Schlesien bleibt unser' – Vertriebenenpolitiker und das Rad der Geschichte", in *Die Vertreibung der Deutschen aus dem Osten*, ed. Wolfgang Benz, 267ff.

Today, in the era of the *Vergangenheitspolitik*, we see yet another version of the BdV. The leaders and members of the current organisation were either expelled as children or they are children of expellees. The organisation itself claims to have two million members, but this number is disputed. A report by the German news program *Tagesschau* claims that the correct number is 550,000.[25] This assertion is supported by the historian Matthias Stickler, author of several academic articles about the expellees.[26] The Federal Refugees Act *(Bundesvertriebenengesetz)* which is the law regulating the expellees' rights, states that the BdV is entitled to economic support by the state; consequently, a fair amount of the organisation's budget stems from the German government, which points to society's acceptance of its cause. The leader of the BdV since 1998, Erika Steinbach, has been the key figure in the recent renewal of the organisation. The BdV used to be an organisation mainly dominated by elderly men, so her being both younger (born in 1943) and female in itself constitutes a visual change. But some claim that the organisation's renewal may also be seen on the political level. Before we turn to this aspect, some remarks on Steinbach's biography must be made as it illustrates some of the dilemmas which the expellees' movement faces in German political life today.[27]

Erika Steinbach was born in 1943, in the small town of Ramel in West Prussia. After the first partition of Poland in 1772, Ramel became a part of Prussia. As a result of the Versailles Treaty, from 1920 onwards it was returned to Polish supremacy, but with the German occupation of Poland in 1939, the town came under German control again. Neither her father nor her mother were originally from West Prussia. In fact both of them were from the westernmost part of Germany. Erika Steinbach's father was a German occupation soldier from Hanau in Hesse. Her mother, who was born in Bremen, came to Ramel as an assistant to the German *Luftwaffe*. Steinbach thus has a very short family history in the eastern provinces. This fact led to allegations from Polish critics that she is not a "real" expellee. According to the act regulating the rights of expellees, she is indeed so, as this law states that everyone who was forced to leave his home in Eastern Europe after 1945 because he had German nationality, is an expellee. Steinbach's political career started in 1990, when she became a Member of Parliament for the CDU, a position that she still holds today.[28]

The most outstanding change concerns the organisation's political rhetoric. Under Erika Steinbach's leadership, the BdV no longer writes and talks exclusively about the history of the German postwar expellees. For example, during the Balkan wars of the 1990s, Steinbach and the BdV expressed their solidarity with the victims of ethnic cleansing. In doing so, she also underscored that the German expellees had themselves been victims of ethnic cleansing 50 years ago. This was the first

25 "550,000 Mitglieder statt zwei Millionen?", http://www.tagesschau.de (accessed January 5, 2010).

26 "Verwirrung um Mitgliederzahl", *Der Spiegel*, January 6, 2010.

27 See Astrid Dypvik, "Ein posisjon bortanfor. Bund der Vertriebenen og diskusjonen om Zentrum gegen Vertreibungen 2005-2007" (MA thesis, University of Oslo, 2007), 55-67.

28 Ibid.

time the organisation explicitly expressed solidarity with other persecuted peoples. Their critics argued that the BdV did this only to move itself back into the centre of public attention and once again be able to highlight their own experience.[29] Others have seen the move as a genuine political renewal. In combination with Steinbach's considerable talent for networking, this new rhetoric earned the BdV many new supporters.

This new universalistic approach to expulsion and ethnic cleansing has been a defining feature of the organisation's main political goal for the past decade, namely, the establishment of a state-sponsored museum in Germany where the expulsion of Germans is the central topic. For this purpose, the BdV created the foundation ZgV.[30] The name suggests that the centre's ambition is universal, for instance to describe the horrors of expulsions in general and not only the horrors of the expelled Germans. The centre's statutes explicitly state this ambition.

Another important part of the BdV's political renewal is that the organisation no longer explicitly refuses to recognise the current German-Polish border as it was drawn after the war. The organisation also states that it does not demand compensation for economic and material losses during the expulsion from the countries that expelled them, but some individual members still do demand such compensation. This naturally puts the BdV's leadership in a tight spot when trying to convince its critics on its position in this case.

The most prominent example of the BdV's new supporters was the social democrat Peter Glotz, who himself was an expellee, born in the town of Eger in Bohemia. He was considered one of the greatest intellectuals among his generation of politicians. From 2000 until his death in 2005, Glotz was the co-chairman of the ZgV, together with Erika Steinbach. Other heavyweight supporters won by the BdV for the new museum are the former GDR civil rights activist, pastor and since March 2012 President of Germany, Joachim Gauck, the German-Jewish writer Ralph Giordano and journalist Helga Hirsch.

As previously noted, criticism has been voiced against this reformed BdV, most of which is based on the distrust that the renewal is in fact real and not just a political strategy for gaining new supporters.[31] The criticism has so far concentrated on the following points: Firstly, that the BdV has never officially repudiated any of its former statements or in any way distanced itself from its own history. Secondly, Erika Steinbach belongs to the national-conservative faction of the CDU and is consequently distrusted by people from the political left. Her political patron in the CDU, Alfred Dregger, was the most prominent member of the CDU's so-called "Stahlhelm fraction". This party fraction strongly supports the German military

29 Jorunn Sem Fure, *Gutes Zuhause, aber keine Heimat. War and Post-War Experience, Narrative Strategies and Memory of the German Expellees from the Eastern German Provinces after 1945* (Saarbrücken: VDM Verlag, 2009), 189ff.

30 This foundation is not to be confused with the Memorial against Expulsion *(Gedenkstätte gegen Vertreibungen)*, founded by the German government.

31 Eva Hahn and Hans Henning Hahn, "Peter Glotz und seine Geschichtsbilder. Aus aktuellem Anlass", *Zeitschrift für Geschichtswissenschaft* 52/1 (2003), 72-80.

and criticises the program of the *Vergangenheitsbewältigung*.[32] Steinbach has herself made political statements and choices that are arguably within the "Stahlhelm fraction's" political program. When the German-Polish border treaty was ratified in the lestag in 1991, Erika Steinbach and 22 other members of parliament voted against it. By doing so, they officially disputed that the Oder-Neisse-line was the border between Germany and Poland. This naturally attracted a great deal of interest in Poland. We find another example in 1997, when Steinbach was a founding member of the association Voice of the Majority *(Stimme der Mehrheit)*. This was an association with typical right-wing populist objectives concerning immigration and welfare. Among the organisation's objectives were to stop "the epidemic misuse of social welfare and asylum" and to prevent further asylum seekers from entering the country. Moreover, Erika Steinbach introduced the term "national masochism" to the German language to describe the refusal of the political left to discuss both the expulsion and other German victims of the Second World War. The last example to be mentioned here is also from 1997, when Steinbach was at the forefront of protests against a museum exhibition on the war crimes committed by the German Wehrmacht in Eastern Europe during the war. The exhibition, entitled "Verbrechen der Wehrmacht" (Crimes of the Wehrmacht) was developed by the Hamburg Institute for Social Research, and presented in Germany's largest cities. The researchers were rightly criticised for some minor mistakes and inaccuracies in the exhibition. But some of the critics, among them Steinbach, went a lot further and also criticised the idea and the objectives of the exhibition. Steinbach described it as a "harassment of German soldiers".[33] For this statement she gained support from the far right faction of the CDU, the extreme right and criticism from the left.

A third element in the criticism against the "new" BdV is that critics refuse to believe that the organisation has any real concern for other persecuted peoples. This is often an underlying criticism that is not explicitly stated. When looking at the statutes of the ZgV, 75 per cent of the text describes the struggle and suffering of the German expellees, while other stories of ethnic cleansing are only mentioned in a list of examples of the same phenomenon. This has in turn fostered criticism of the BdV for being biased and not representing anything new after all.[34]

The BdV under Erika Steinbach's leadership does indeed have some new rhetorical elements, because it connects to the discourse of ethnic cleansing, a phenomena that got a lot of attention as an effect of the civil war in former Yugoslavia. The connecting of the history of expulsion to the discourse of a universally condemned practice such as ethnic cleansing has been understood as a political renewal by a group of new supporters. But there are numerous examples of Erika Steinbach placing herself within in the CDU's far right fraction and thereby also representing the "old" BdV. The renewal may therefore be understood as a mere tactical ad-

32 Samuel Salzborn, *Grenzenlose Heimat. Geschichte, Gegenwart und Zukunft der Vertriebenenverbände* (Berlin: Elefanten Press, 2000); idem., *Heimatrecht und Volkstumskampf. Außenpolitische Konzepte der Vertriebenenverbände und ihre praktische Umsetzung* (Hanover: Offizin Verlag, 2001).

33 "Gegenveranstaltung zu 'Hetzausstellung'", *Frankfurter Allgemeine Zeitung*, March 9, 1997.

34 Among the critics were the historians Samuel Salzborn and Eva and Hans Henning Hahn.

justment, leaving many critics unconvinced. In my opinion these two lines of rhetoric, the "old" and the "new", can be explained as a way of addressing two different crowds; some statements are made for the old crowd of traditional supporters to show that the BdV still represents their cause, others are made for the new public to convince them that the BdV is a transformed organisation.[35]

The Federation of Expellees and the Extreme Right

What then, are the connections between the BdV and the extreme right in Germany? None, according to the BdV, but is this correct? Before this comparison is drawn any further, it must be stated that the expulsion and questions concerning it are not generally an issue considered to distinguish German right-wing extremism from other political groups. An example of this is the 2003 publication *Vom Rand zur Mitte* about the prevalence of extreme right-wing positions in Germany. In this study, informants were asked several political questions that in combination were supposed to unveil extreme right-wing positions. None of the questions concerned the history of the expulsion.[36]

Still, there is one point in this analysis that is important to bring into our discussion. The two researchers who conducted the study, Elmar Brähler and Oliver Decker, noted that statements typical of the BdV such as "one should not be ashamed of being German", often reflects an extreme right-wing worldview.[37] The extreme right in Germany is heterogeneous. It consists of many small groups and political parties. The most successful of these groups in Germany today is the NPD. The party has no representatives in the Bundestag, but several representatives in the state parliaments of Saxony and Mecklenburg-West Pomerania in addition to some local parliaments. As a comprehensive analysis of the various far right views on the Nazi past would exceed the limits of this chapter, I will only focus on the politics of the NPD, the largest group on the right-wing scene, when comparing the BdV and the far right. An affiliation with the NPD does not exclude membership or affiliation with other right-wing organisations. Another reason for focusing on the NPD is that the party has in recent years shown a growing interest in the topic of the expulsion.

The NPD naturally has a political program and a general worldview that concerns many other issues than the German past and the expellees. The most prominent feature of NPD politics is a strong criticism of current asylum and immigrant policies.[38] The expulsion, on the other hand, plays a significant role in the party's political rhetoric. Over the last few years, the NPD has tried to position itself as a party more loyal to the expellees' cause than the CDU, which historically has been

35 Dypvik, "Ein posisjon bortanfor".

36 Oliver Decker and Elmar Brähler, *Vom Rand zur Mitte – Rechtsextreme Einstellungen und ihre Einflussfaktoren in Deutschland* (Berlin: Friedrich Ebert Foundation, 2006).

37 Decker and Brähler, *Vom Rand zur Mitte.*

38 Thoralf Staud, *Moderne Nazis – Die neuen Rechten und der Aufstieg der NPD* (Cologne: Kiepenhauer & Witsch, 2005).

their closest political ally. In recent years the NPD has made a point of engaging in the conflict between the BdV and the German government over the details in the establishment of the new ZgV. In September 2010, the NPD published a leaflet with the message "Expellees – we are your party".[39] In 2009, the NPD tried to stage themselves as the only party actually taking the expulsion issue seriously. In the same year, the NPD suggested in the Saxon parliament that the state of Saxony should establish a museum of the expulsion in the town of Görlitz, which lies by the river Neisse on the German-Polish border. It is the German half of a former city split in two after 1945, with Görlitz on the German side and Zgorzelec on the Polish side of the border.[40] The NPD suggested that the museum should be called a *Zentrum gegen Vertreibungen* for Saxony, named after the project that the BdV has worked with for years on a national level. At the same time the NPD has been working for the construction of memorials of the expulsion in several locations. For many years the party worked for a memorial of the expulsion in the town of Neubrandenburg in Mecklenburg-West Pomerania to commemorate the expulsion that took place in the town. The campaign finally succeeded in December 2009.[41]

In press statements and other texts from the NPD about the expulsion, there are six points that are of special interest for our analysis. First, the NPD gives its wholehearted support to the projects of the BdV. Second, the NPD claims that remembering the expulsion is an expression of loyalty to the German people. In a statement concerning a monument of the expellees in Friedland in Mecklenburg-West Pomerania, the NPD wrote that the expulsion was a part of German history that "certain groups" in the country wanted to forget about and that Germany must always remember the crimes committed against its people. This is particularly important for the NPD and its sympathisers.[42] Third, the NPD claims that the expulsion is connected with the Holocaust in the sense that the Holocaust is preventing people from understanding the expulsion in full. The party does not officially deny the Holocaust (which is forbidden under German law), but trivialises it by making comparisons to other historical incidents, and in effect stating that the incidents in question are just as bad, or even worse, than the Holocaust. This can be observed in the NPD's annual marches to mourn the 1945 allied bombing of Dresden, referred to as a "bombing Holocaust". A fourth point has to do with respect: The BdV claims that its critics are treating the expellees as second-rank vic-

39 "Heimatvertriebene und Spätaussiedler – Eure Partei ist die NPD!", NPD, http://www.npd.de/html/714/artikel/detail/1839/ (accessed September 10, 2012).

40 "Unsere Oberlausitz, Petition beantwortet, alles zum Besten?", NPD, http://www.unsere-oberlausitz.de/index.php?option=com_content&task=view&id=35&Itemid=35 (accessed September 10, 2012).

41 "Gedenksteineinweihung in Neubrandenburg", NPD, http://www.npd-mv.de/index.php?com=news&view=article&id=1752&mid=2 option=com_content&task=view&id=35&Itemid=35 (accessed September 10, 2012).

42 "Denkmal für die Vertriebenen in Friedland eingeweiht", NPD, http://www.npd-mv.de/index.php?com=news&view=article&id=1636&mid=2 (accessed September 10, 2012).

tims; the NPD thus demands respect for the victims of the expulsion.[43] Fifth, the position of the NPD concerning the past is that the Germans should not apologise to its neighbouring countries for the crimes committed during the Second World War.[44] And sixth, the NPD wants to restore the German state within what it calls the "historical borders" of Germany, without specifying if this means the borders of 1938, 1914 or 1871, and to give lost land back to the former German owners.[45] Consequently, the party disputes the Oder-Neisse border. As we have seen, this is a position the BdV no longer officially promotes.

In an analysis of the similarities between the thoughts of the BdV and the NPD, the term *topos* is necessary. This chapter will employ the term in the way developed by Ruth Wodak, who defines a topos as "recurrent argumentation schemes that are intended to make the audience draw a particular inference".[46] These are arguments that points to a specific political tradition and worldview, and that tends to be frequently referred to in the debates. Based on the six features of the NPD's view of the expulsion, we may identify the topos of the NPD on this topic. Firstly, we find a topos concerning remembrance: The expulsion must not be forgotten. Secondly, there is a national topos: The expulsion is important because these are crimes committed against the German people. Thirdly, there is a topos on forgetting: "The others" (meaning the left, the politically correct) are trying to make the public forget about the expulsion. The fourth topos concerns the Holocaust: It is a topos of trivialisation. The genocide of the European Jews is no singular crime. It can be compared, for instance to the bombing of Dresden, and these crimes may even be described in the same language. The fifth topos is a topos of loyalty: Remembering the expulsion is something that a loyal German should do out of concern for his own people.

What topoi do the BdV then employ to legitimise its views on German history? The Holocaust indeed plays an interesting role in the organisation's rhetoric. A traditional topos for the BdV has been that the expulsion should not be viewed in relation to the brutal Nazi occupation of the countries in Central and Eastern Europe. But at the same time, the BdV argues that it may be compared to the Holocaust and seen as a historical parallel to the genocide of the European Jews. In the debate over the museum on the expulsion, the BdV insisted that the new museum should be located close to the Memorial to the Murdered Jews of Europe, the large monument situated right by the parliament building and the Brandenburg Gate in Berlin's city centre. According to Erika Steinbach, the topics are related.

---

43 "Denkmal für die Vertriebenen in Friedland eingeweiht", NPD, http://www.npd-mv.de/index.php?com=news&view=article&id=1636&mid=2 (accessed September 10, 2012).

44 Press release from NPD Saxony, January 10, 2006.

45 "Außenpolitische Gründsätze", NPD, http://www.npd.de/html/1/artikel/detail/1697 (accessed September 10, 2012).

46 Ruth Wodak, "History in the making: the making of history", *Journal of Language and Politics* 5/1 (2006), 136.

Furhermore, she compared the Polish internment camp in Lambinowice, where German civilians were imprisoned after the war, with the Holocaust. On several occasions Steinbach called Lambinowice a "death camp" *(Vernichtungslager)* for Germans.[47] Nevetheless, in German political vocabulary, this term is reserved exclusively for the Holocaust. The language concerning the Holocaust is a matter of heated debates in Germany, and Steinbach has more than once been asked why she chooses to use this word. There is no reason to believe that she is not aware that her way of using the term does not follow a common understanding of it, and that she does not know that her way of using it implies that Lambinowice was simply a small-scale Auschwitz. Such a statement is of course a great exaggeration. There is no doubt that the Lambinowice camp was an internment camp with a high death rate and that the inmates' suffering was immense, but it was by no means part of a planned and systematically executed genocide against Germans. Hence a parallel to the Holocaust is simply misleading. As a message to a specific audience, on the other hand, it is clearly successful, as the audience in question enjoys listening when someone trivialises the Holocaust. This topos of comparison and trivialisation held by the BdV is also prominent within the NPD.

Looking at another example of the rhetoric and practice of the BdV with regards to the Holocaust, we find a slightly different meaning. On assignment from the former Minister of Culture, Michael Naumann, the historian Agnete von Specht evaluated museums run by BdV's member organisations, the Landsmannschaften. She concluded that three of the four museums presented crimes of the Nazi era incompletely and one-sidedly. In addition, it was documented that BdV members exerted pressure on the museums' staff in order to prevent them from imparting information about the Nazi regime's crimes.[48] The suffering caused by the expulsion was not to be presented in its historical context, but as a singular historical incident only, and the suffering of the Germans was to be made the most important point. In this way, the topos is that the expulsion is to be presented alone and outside context. This might seem to contradict the topos concerning the Holocaust, but that is actually not the case. In the rhetoric of the BdV, the Holocaust may be used as a parallel to emphasise the Germans' hardship during the expulsion. But the expulsion itself should not be explained in a historical context, as this might imply that the expulsion was not an act of unprecedented violence, and that there is a historical explanation for what happened. It is even possible to find examples of BdV members using revanchist topoi in their descriptions of the Holocaust. On November 9, 2001, the leader of BdV in Thuringia, Paul Latussek, claimed that there were many misunderstandings concerning the Holocaust, and that the truth about the victims had to be revealed. He was ousted from the BdV leadership right away, which does not accept open denial of the Holocaust. It is in-

47 Rainer Eckert, "Flucht und Vertreibung: Eine genauso notwendige wie überfällige Diskussion", *Deutschland Archiv* 37/1 (2004), 8.

48 See "Bestandsaufnahme der nach §96 BVFG vom Bund institutionell geförderten Landes- und Spezialmuseen". This report was written for the *Beauftragte der Bundesregierung für Kultur und Medien* in 1999.

teresting to note, however, that Latussek's ties to the right-wing movement were already well-known. He had published articles in a wide range of right-wing magazines such as *Junge Freiheit,* an independent right-wing newspaper, and *National-Zeitung – Deutsche Wochenzeitung,* which was established by the right-wing party German People's Union (*Deutsche Volksunion,* DVU) and which the German Federal Office for the Protection of the Constitution *(Bundesamt für Verfassungsschutz)* refers to as extreme. Despite these activities, he held a prominent position in the national leadership of the organisation until he made his comments on Auschwitz. For these he was sentenced to a fine by a German court for hate-speech. Nevertheless he kept his position in the BdV-organisation Landsmannschaft Silesia.[49]

The topos of remembrance frequently occurs in the rhetoric of the BdV, including the call for Germans to remember the victims of the expulsion. As in the case of the NPD, these victims are regarded as martyrs by the BdV. Their suffering should be remembered, and it will, as the BdV views it, be healed through the construction of a memorial or a museum. Statements such as "to heal the wrongs of the expulsion" and to "demand justice for the victims" is typical BdV rhetoric on the issue.[50] The topos of remembering is indeed typical for all supporters of a Museum of Expulsion, whereas the connection drawn between national responsibility, recasting the victims as martyrs, and aggressive criticism of the political left, which is accused of not wanting to remember, is typical only for the BdV and the NPD. An interesting topos in the rhetoric of the BdV is that "the government does not work for us" (for instance the Germans), they work for "foreigners". In 2003, Steinbach criticised Chancellor Gerhard Schröder for being "afraid of the neighbouring countries" and for showing greater compassion for Czechs and Poles than for Germans.[51] Here a national topos can be observed. Germans are responsible for remembering the suffering of other Germans, and crimes committed against Germans are of specific interest. The quote also implies that Schröder was not loyal to his own people. This topos is very similar to the NPD's national topos of the expulsion as an important topic for so-called "loyal Germans".

Conclusion

The BdV renewed its political rhetoric on universal human rights in recent decades, as shown in a previous section of this chapter. But as I argued above, the organisation still has not given up the topoi that once made it publicly disputed. First, they still do not place the expulsion within the political and historical context in which it took place. Second, the BdV has made it clear that it is not concerned with crimes perpetrated by Germans, but rather with crimes committed against Germans.

---

49 Dypvik, "Ein posisjon bortanfor", 57; http://www.thueringer-allgemeine.de/web/zgt/politik/detail/-/specific/Landsmannschaft-der-Schlesier-trennt-sich-von-Thueringer-Landesgruppe-1229912778 13 (accessed September 10, 2012).

50 Dypvik, "Ein posisjon bortanfor", 86ff.

51 "Der Kanzler hat Angst vor den Nachbarn", *Frankfurter Allgemeine Zeitung,* August 18, 2003.

Third, we may find positions of the extreme right in the rhetoric of the BdV, such as the trivialisation of the Holocaust, claims that the government are not loyal to "real Germans", that the Poles must compensate Germans for properties lost during the expulsion, and that the border between Poland and Germany is not an acceptable border. May we conclude that the BdV is a voice for the extreme right in the historical debate in Germany? Claiming that the expulsion must be remembered and that its history is a blind spot in the *Vergangenheitsbewältigung* is not in itself an extreme right-wing position. Interest in the history of the expulsion is an accepted position in the political mainstream in Germany. Moreover, the universalistic approach to the question of ethnic cleansing is more typical of the political mainstream than of the extreme right. But the BdV also holds positions that they only share with the extreme right, which moves them away from the political mainstream. This refers specifically to the topoi of the trivialisation of the Holocaust, the linking of victimisation and suffering, the national rhetoric, and the accusations against those who are "disloyal to the German people" and who "want to forget". Here both the rhetoric and the political positions are similar for the BdV and the extreme right. In this sense one may say that the BdV speaks with the same voice as the exreme right. To modify this statement, it appears to be clear that the extreme right is trying to be the new voice of the BdV, as organisations such as the political party NDP are gradually making the expulsion an important symbolic question. In this way, the NDP seems to have a strategy of trying to win over BdV members and sympathisers, thinking that the CDU no longer is a strong enough supporter of the interests of the BdV. Rather than the BdV being the voice of the extreme right, the extreme right and the NPD in particular may be seen as the new voice of the BdV.

Bibliography

Beer, Mathias. "'Ein der wissenschaftlichen Forschung sich aufdrängender historischer Zusammenhang'. Von den deutschen Schwierigkeiten 'Flucht und Vertreibung' zu kontextualisieren". *Zeitschrift für Geschichtswissenschaft* 51/1 (2003), 59-64.

Benz, Wolfgang, ed. *Die Vertreibung der Deutschen aus dem Osten – Ursachen, Ereignisse, Folgen.* Frankfurt a.M.: Fischer, 1985.

Brähler, Elmar and Oliver Decker. *Vom Rand zur Mitte – Rechtsextreme Einstellungen und ihre Einflussfaktoren in Deutschland.* Berlin: Friedrich Ebert Foundation, 2006.

Dypvik, Astrid. "Ein posisjon bortanfor. Bund der Vertriebenen og diskusjonen om Zentrum gegen Vertreibungen 2005-2007". MA thesis, University of Oslo, 2007.

Eckert, Rainer. "Flucht und Vertreibung: Eine genauso notwendige wie überfällige Diskussion". *Deutschland Archiv* 37/1 (2004), 14-19.

Franzen, K. Erik and Hans Lemberg. *Die Vertriebenen – Hitlers letzte Opfer.* Munich: Ullstein, 2002.

Faulenbach, Bernd. "Die Vertreibung der Deutschen aus den Gebieten jenseits von Oder und Neisse. Zur Wissenschaftlichen und öffentlichen Diskussion in Deutschland". *Aus Politik und Zeitgeschichte* 51/52 (2002), 44-54.

Frei, Norbert. *1945 und wir. Das Dritte Reich im Bewusstsein der Deutschen.* Munich: C.H. Beck, 2005.

Frevert, Ute. "Geschichtsvergessenheit und Geschichtsversessenheit revisited. Der jüngste Erinnerungsboom in der Kritik". *Aus Politik und Zeitgeschichte* 40/41 (2003), 6-13.

Fure, Jorunn Sem. *Gutes Zuhause, aber keine Heimat. War and Post-War Experience, Narrative Strategies and Memory of the German Expellees from the Eastern German Provinces after 1945*. Saarbrücken: VDM Verlag, 2009.

Glotz, Peter. "Der Kampf gegen das Verbrechen der Vertreibung". *Die Politische Meinung* 417/8 (2004), 15-18.

Hahn, Eva and Hans Henning Hahn. "Peter Glotz und seine Geschichtsbilder. Aus aktuellem Anlass". *Zeitschrift für Geschichtswissenschaft* 52/1 (2003), 72-80.

Naimark, Norman. *Fires of Hatred – Ethnic Cleansing in Twentieth Century Europe*. Cambridge, MA: Harvard University Press, 2001.

Nitschke, Bernadetta. *Vertreibung und Aussiedlung der deutschen Bevölkerung aus Polen 1945 bis 1949*. Munich: Oldenbourg, 2003.

Nowak, Edmund. *Lager im Oppelner System der Nachkriegslager in Polen (1945-1950)*. Opole: Zentrales Kriegsgefangenenmuseum Lamsdorf-Oppeln, 2003.

Reichling, Gerhard. *Die deutschen Vertriebenen in Zahlen*. Bonn: Kulturstiftung der deutschen Vertriebenen, 1995.

Salzborn, Samuel. *Heimatrecht und Volkstumskampf. Außenpolitische Konzepte der Vertriebenenverbände und ihre praktische Umsetzung*. Hanover: Offizin, 2001.

Salzborn, Samuel. *Grenzenlose Heimat. Geschichte, Gegenwart und Zukunft der Vertriebenenverbände*. Berlin: Elefanten Press, 2000.

Schieder, Theodor, ed. *Dokumentation der Vertreibung der Deutschen aus Ost-Mitteleuropa*, vol. 1 and 2. Munich: dtv, 2004.

Staud, Thoralf. *Moderne Nazis – Die neuen Rechten und der Aufstieg der NPD*. Cologne: Kiepenhauer & Witsch, 2005.

Strothmann, Dietrich. "'Schlesien bleibt unser' – Vertriebenenpolitiker und das Rad der Geschichte", in *Die Vertreibung der Deutschen aus dem Osten – Ursachen, Ereignisse, Folgen*, edited by Wolfgang Benz, 265-276. Frankfurt a.M.: Fischer, 1985.

Ther, Philipp and Ana Siljak, eds. *Redrawing Nations. Ethnic Cleansing in East-Central Europe, 1944-1948*. Lanham: Rowman & Littlefield, 2001.

Wildt, Michael. *Generation des Unbedingten. Das Führungskorps des Reichssicherheitshauptamtes*. Hamburg: Hamburger Edition, 2003.

Wodak Ruth. "History in the making: the making of history". *Journal of Language and Politics* 5/1 (2006), 125-154.

Wolfrum, Edgar. "Zwischen Geschichtsschreibung und Geschichtspolitik. Forschungen zu Flucht und Vertreibung nach dem Zweiten Weltkrieg". *Archiv für Sozialgeschichte* 36 (1996), 500-522.

Contributors

Kerstin Bornholdt (*1973) is Associate Professor at the University College Telemark, Norway. She studied Scandinavian studies, political science and German literature in Kiel, Berlin and Bergen, receiving a PhD from the University of Oslo in 2011 ("Between Exhausting Sports and Swinging Rhythm. An Inquiry into Medical Knowledge Production about Women's Sports and Women's Gymnastics in Norway, Denmark and Germany in the Interwar Years"). Her recent publications include "Erst der sporttreibende Mensch ist der hundertprozentige Mensch? Zur Aushandlung von Gesundheits- und Körperkonzepten im medizinischen Sportdiskurs der Zwischenkriegszeit", in *Gesundheit/Krankheit. Kulturelle Differenzierungsprozesse um Körper, Geschlecht und Macht in Skandinavien,* eds. Lill Ann Körber and Stefanie von Schnurbein (Berlin: Nordeuropa-Institut/Berliner Beiträge zur Skandinavistik 16, 2010), and "'Sportskvinne av i dag' – Fra mellomkrigstidens debatt om kvinnekroppens foranderlighet", *Fortid* 7/2010, 56-62.

Gideon Botsch (*1970) works as a researcher at the Moses Mendelssohn Centre for European-Jewish Studies at the University of Potsdam and is the managing editor of the *Zeitschrift für Religions- und Geisteswissenschaften.* He studied political science at the Free University Berlin, where he received his PhD in 2003 with a work on the History of Political Science and the Study of International Relations in Second World War Germany (published as *Politische Wissenschaft im Einsatz. Die Deutschen Auslandswissenschaften 1940-1945,* Paderborn: Schöningh, 2006). His recent publications include *Die extreme Rechte in der Bundesrepublik Deutschland. 1949 bis heute* (Darmstadt: Wissenschaftliche Buchgesellschaft, 2012); "From Skinhead-Subculture to Radical Right Movement: The development of a 'National Opposition' in East Germany", *Contemporary European History* 21/4 (2012), 553-573; "Die historisch-fiktionale Gegenerzählung des radikalen Nationalismus. Über den rechtsextremen Zugriff auf die deutsche Geschichte", *Jahrbuch für Politik und Geschichte* (2011), 27-40.

Astrid Sverresdotter Dypvik (*1977) works as a journalist in the daily Norwegian newspaper *Nationen.* She studied history and German in Oslo and Leipzig, and received her MA from the University of Oslo in 2007 ("Ein posisjon bortanfor – Bund der Vertriebenen og diskusjonen om opprettinga av Zentrum gegen Vertreibungen 2002- 2005"). She has worked in several major Norwegian newspapers, including *Dagbladet, Dag og Tid* og *Morgenbladet.* Her recent publications include *Det var DDR – forteljingar om eit nedlagt land* (Oslo: Det norske Samlaget, 2012), and "Både offer og forbrytar – Er det mogleg å skriva ei historie om tyske offer utan å gløyma dei tyske brotsverka?", *Fortid* 2/2006.

Martin Finkenberger (*1969) is writing a dissertation at the Free University Berlin about the anti-Semitic propagandist Johann von Leers as part of right-wing extremist networks in the postwar period. He studied political science and history in Würzburg and Berlin. His recent publications include "Der völkische Antisemit Johann von Leers in den religionspolitischen Auseinandersetzungen 1933/34", in *Die völkisch-religiöse Bewegung im Nationalsozialismus. Eine Beziehungs- und Konfliktgeschichte,* eds. Uwe Puschner and Clemens Vollnhals (Göttingen: Vandenhoeck & Ruprecht, 2012), 375-398; together with Horst Junginger, eds., *Im Dienste der Lügen. Herbert Grabert (1901-1978) und seine Verlage* (Aschaffenburg: Alibri, 2004); and "Herbert Grabert: Religionswissenschaftler – Revisionist – Rechtsextremist", *Bausteine zur Geschichte der Universität Tübingen* 9 (1999), 55-100.

Nicola Karcher (*1979) works as a researcher at the University of Oslo. She studied history, philosophy and political science in Berlin and Bergen, receiving her PhD in 2012 from the University of Oslo with a thesis on Norwegian-German rightwing networks in the interwar periode ("Zwischen Nationalsozialismus und nordischer Gesinnung. Eine Studie zu den rechtsgerichteten Verbindungen norwegisch-deutscher Milieus in der Zwischenkriegszeit"). Her recent publications include "Norske Nasjonalsosialister i Tyskland 1933-1940. Politisk profil, intern struktur og nettverk", in *Utenfor det etablerte. Aspekter ved Einhart Lorenz' forsking,* eds. Øivind Kopperud, Vibeke Moe and Vibeke Kieding Banik (Oslo: HL-senteret, 2009), 97-110; "Schirmorganisation der Nordischen Bewegung. Der Nordische Ring und seine Repräsentanten in Norwegen", *NORDEUROPAforum* 1 (2009), 7-35; and "Die Nasjonal Samling während der deutschen Okkupation Norwegens 1940-1945. Nationalismus verus Pangermanismus", in *Jahrbuch für Antisemitismusforschung* 16, ed. Wolfgang Benz (Berlin: Metropol, 2007), 195-216.

Anders G. Kjøstvedt (*1979) is a Post Doctoral Researcher at the University of Oslo. He studied history, history of ideas and Russian in Oslo, receiving his PhD in 2010 from the University of Oslo with a thesis entitled "Hitler's Metropolis? The National Socialist Movement in Berlin, 1925-1933". His recent publications include "Terror eller tilslutning? Et historiografisk blikk på forskningen på nazismen og Det tredje rike", in *Ideologi og terror. Totalitære ideer og regimer,* eds. Øystein Sørensen, Bernt Hagtvet and Bjørn Arne Steine (Oslo: Dreyers Forlag, 2011), 85-115; "'Tempo? Rytme!' Nasjonalsosialismen, moderniteten og Weimarrepublikkens Berlin", in *Utenfor det etablerte. Aspekter ved Einhart Lorenz' forsking,* eds. Øyvind Kopperud, Vibeke Moe and Vibeke Kieding Banik (Oslo: HL-senteret, 2011), 133-147; and together with Tor Espen Simonsen and Katrine Randin, eds., *Høyrepopulisme i Vest-Europa* (Oslo: Unipub, 2009).

Alessandro Salvador (*1979) is a Post Doctoral Researcher at the University of Trento, funded by the *Fondazione Caritro*. He studied history in Trento, where he received his PhD in 2010 with a thesis about radical nationalism in the Weimar Republic ("Il partito nazionalsocialista e la destra radicale tedesca nella fase finale della Repubblica di Weimar"). His recent publications include his book about the Stahlhelm, to be published by the University of Trento in 2013 (Edizioni Università di Trento); and "The Paneuropa debate in Germany. Examples from the German nationalistic Press", *Zeitgeschichte* 4 (2011), 205-214.

Stefanie Schrader (*1979) works as a research assistant at the European University Viadrina Frankfurt (Oder), and is writing a thesis on the reception of Richard Wagner's compositions and writings in Britain. She studied intellectual history, history, musicology and law at the University of Sussex and the Free University Berlin. Her recent publications include *Völkische Opposition. Die parteipolitische und parlamentarische Partizipation der Deutschvölkischen Freiheitspartei/Deutschvölkischen Freiheitsbewegung in der Weimarer Republik* (Frankfurt a.M.: Peter Lang, forthcoming 2013); "Das Deutsche Tageblatt", "Der Reichswart", "Unsere Waffen. Rüstzeug der Deutschvölkischen Freiheitsbewegung", in *Handbuch des Antisemitismus. Judenfeindschaft in Geschichte und Gegenwart*, vol. 6: *Publikationen*, ed. Wolfgang Benz (Berlin: de Gruyter Saur, forthcoming 2013); "Deutscher Herold", in *Handbuch des Antisemitismus. Judenfeindschaft in Geschichte und Gegenwart*, vol. 5: *Organisationen, Institutionen, Bewegungen*, ed. Wolfgang Benz (Berlin: de Gruyter Saur, 2012).

Elisabetta Cassina Wolff (*1969) is Senior Lecturer at the University of Oslo. She holds a degree in political philosophy from the University of Turin and received her PhD from the University of Oslo in 2008, with a thesis entitled "Starting from the end. Fascist Ideology in Post-War Italy (1945-1953)". Her recent publications include "Biological Racism and Anti-Semitism as Intellectual Constructions in Italian Fascism: The Case of Telesio Interlandi and *La difesa della razza*", in *Racial Science in Hitler's 'New Europe'*, eds. Anton Weiss-Wendt and Rory Yeomans (Lincoln: University of Nebraska Press, forthcoming 2013); *L'inchiostro dei vinti. Stampa e ideologia neofascista 1945-1953* (Milan: Mursia, 2012); "The Meaning and Role of the Concepts of Democracy and Corporatism in Italian Neo-fascist Ideology 1945-1953", *Modern Italy* 16/3 (2011), 295-313.

Felix Wiedemann (*1974) is a Post Doctoral Fellow at the Berlin Excellence-Cluster TOPOI. He has studied history, political science and philosophy at the Free University Berlin, from which he received a PhD in 2006 with a thesis on images and interpretations of the European witch-trials in the 19th and 20th centuries (published as *Rassenmutter und Rebellin. Hexenbilder in Romantik, völkischer Bewegung, Neuheidentum und Feminismus*, Würzburg: Königshausen & Neumann, 2007). His recent publications include "Der doppelte Orient. Zur völkischen Orientromantik des Ludwig Ferdinand Clauß", *Zeitschrift für Religions- und Geistesgeschichte* 61 (2009), 1-24; "'Allahs Sonne' und 'Europas eigene Religion'. Die Verschränkung von Arabophilie und Neuheidentum in der rechtsextremen Ideologie Sigrid Hunkes", *Zeitschrift für Geschichtswissenschaft* 57 (2009), 891-912; "Orientalismus", in *Docupedia-Zeitgeschichte* (https://docupedia.de/zg/Orientalismus?oldid=82032).

Matthew Worley (*1970) is Professor of Modern History at the University of Reading and the co-founder and co-editor of *Twentieth Century Communism: A Journal of International History*. His PhD thesis focused on the Communist Party of Great Britain and led to a monograph entitled *Class Against Class: The Communist Party in Britain between the Wars* (London: I.B.Tauris, 2002). His recent publications include *Oswald Mosley and the New Party* (Basingstoke: Palgrave Macmillan, 2010); *Bolshevism, Stalinism and the Comintern: Perspectives on Stalinization, 1917-53* (Basingstoke: Palgrave Macmillan, 2008); *Labour Inside the Gate: A History of the British Labour Party between the Wars* (London: I.B.Tauris, 2005).

Zivilisationen & Geschichte

Herausgegeben von Ina Ulrike Paul und Uwe Puschner

Band 1 Ljiljana Heise: KZ-Aufseherinnen vor Gericht. Greta Bösel – „another of those brutal types of women"? 2009.

Band 2 Ivonne Meybohm: Erziehung zum Zionismus. Der Jüdische Wanderbund Blau-Weiß als Versuch einer praktischen Umsetzung des Programms der Jüdischen Renaissance. 2009.

Band 3 Tamara Or: Vorkämpferinnen und Mütter des Zionismus. Die deutsch-zionistischen Frauenorganisationen (1897-1938). 2009.

Band 4 Sonja Knopp: „Wir lebten mitten im Tod". Das „Sonderkommando" in Auschwitz in schriftlichen und mündlichen Häftlingserinnerungen. 2010.

Band 5 Vera Kallenberg: Von „liederlichen Land-Läuffern" zum „asiatischen Volk". Die Repräsentation der ‚Zigeuner' in deutschsprachigen Lexika und Enzyklopädien zwischen 1700 und 1850. Eine wissensgeschichtliche Untersuchung. 2010.

Band 6 Stefan Gerbing: Afrodeutscher Aktivismus. Interventionen von Kolonisierten am Wendepunkt der Dekolonisierung Deutschlands 1919. 2010.

Band 7 Karena Kalmbach: Tschernobyl und Frankreich. Die Debatte um die Auswirkungen des Reaktorunfalls im Kontext der französischen Atompolitik und Elitenkultur. 2011.

Band 8 Monika Brockhaus: „Ein Ereignis von weltgeschichtlicher Bedeutung". Die Balfour-Deklaration in der veröffentlichten Meinung. 2011.

Band 9 Klaus Geus (Hrsg.): Utopien, Zukunftsvorstellungen, Gedankenexperimente. Literarische Konzepte von einer „anderen" Welt im abendländischen Denken von der Antike bis zur Gegenwart. 2011.

Band 10 Gregor Hufenreuter: Philipp Stauff. Zur Geschichte des Deutschvölkischen Schriftstellerverbandes, des Germanen-Ordens und der Guido-von-List-Gesellschaft. Ideologe, Agitator und Organisator im völkischen Netzwerk des Wilhelminischen Kaiserreichs. 2011.

Band 11 Ghazal Ahmadi: Iran als Spielball der Mächte? Die internationalen Verflechtungen des Iran unter Reza Schah und die anglo-sowjetische Invasion 1941. 2011.

Band 12 Thomas Brünner: Public Diplomacy im Westen. Die Presseagentur *Panorama DDR* informiert das Ausland. 2011.

Band 13 Jonas Kleindienst: Die Wilden Cliquen Berlins. „Wild und frei" trotz Krieg und Krise. Geschichte einer Jugendkultur. 2011.

Band 14 Anne Katherine Kohlrausch: Literarische Selbstverortung als historische Handlung. *The Travels of Dean Mahomet*, 1794. 2011.

Band 15 Reinhard Blänkner: „Absolutismus". Eine begriffsgeschichtliche Studie zur politischen Theorie und zur Geschichtswissenschaft in Deutschland, 1830-1870. 2011.

Band 16 Jens Flemming, Klaus Saul, Peter-Christian Witt (Hrsg.), unter Mitarbeit von Simona Lavaud: Lebenswelten im Ausnahmezustand. Die Deutschen, der Alltag und der Krieg, 1914-1918. 2011.

Band 17 Philipp Küsgens: Horizonte nationaler Musik. Musiziergesellschaften in Süddeutschland und der Deutschschweiz 1847-1891. 2012.

Band 18 Anette Dietrich / Ljiljana Heise (Hrsg.): Männlichkeitskonstruktionen im Nationalsozialismus. Formen, Funktionen und Wirkungsmacht von Geschlechterkonstruktionen im Nationalsozialismus und ihre Reflexion in der pädagogischen Praxis. 2013.

Band 19 David Hamann: Gunther Ipsen in Leipzig. Die wissenschaftliche Biographie eines „Deutschen Soziologen“ 1919-1933. 2013.

Band 20 Richard Faber / Uwe Puschner (Hrsg.): Intellektuelle und Antiintellektuelle im 20. Jahrhundert. 2013.

Band 21 Nicola Kristin Karcher / Anders G. Kjøstvedt (eds.): Movements and Ideas of the Extreme Right in Europe. Positions and Continuities. 2013.

www.peterlang.de